The Second Epistle of Paul
The Apostle
to the
CORINTHIANS
and the Epistles to
TIMOTHY, TITUS and PHILEMON

CALVIN'S COMMENTARIES

CALVIN'S COMMENTARIES

The Second Epistle of Paul The Apostle

to the

CORINTHIANS

and the Epistles to

TIMOTHY, TITUS and PHILEMON

Translator
T. A. SMAIL

Editors
DAVID W. TORRANCE
THOMAS F. TORRANCE

WILLIAM B. EERDMANS PUBLISHING COMPANY
GRAND RAPIDS, MICHIGAN

THE PATERNOSTER PRESS
CARLISLE

First published 1964
Translation © 1964 Oliver and Boyd Ltd.

Published jointly in the United States
by Wm. B. Eerdmans Publishing Co.
255 Jefferson Ave. S.E., Grand Rapids, Michigan 49503
and in the U.K. by The Paternoster Press
P.O. Box 300, Carlisle, Cumbria CA3 0QS

All rights reserved

First paperback edition published 1996

Printed in the United States of America

00 99 98 97 96   7 6 5 4 3 2 1

The Second Epistle of Paul The Apostle to the Corinthians
and the Epistles to Timothy, Titus and Philemon

Eerdmans ISBN 0-8028-0810-7

British Library Cataloguing in Publication Data

A Catalogue record for this book is available from the British Library

Paternoster ISBN 0-85364-745-3

INTRODUCTION

Chief Editions of John Calvin's Commentary
on St Paul's Second Epistle to The Corinthians
and on his Epistles to Timothy, Titus and Philemon

On II CORINTHIANS

Commentaire sur la seconde épistre aux Corinthiens, Geneva, 1547.

Commentarii in secundam Pauli epistolam ad Corinthios, Geneva, 1548.

A Commentarie upon St. Paule's Epistles to the Corinthians, translated by Thomas Tymme, London, 1577.

Commentaries on the Epistles of Paul to the Corinthians,* translated by J. Pringle, Calvin Translation Society, Edinburgh, 1848.

Calvin's Auslegung der Heiligen Schrift in deutscher Übersetzung Unter Mitwirkung zahlreicher Theologen hg. von K. Müller, 12 Band, Die Briefe des Apostels Paulus an die Römer und Korinther, Neukirchen, 1901-2

On THE PASTORALS

Commentarii in utramque epistolam ad Timotheum, Geneva, 1548.

Commentaire sur les deux épistres de S. Paul à Timothee, traduites du Latin, Geneva, 1548.

Commentaire sur l'épitre de S. Paul à Tite, Geneva, 1549.

Commentarius in Epistolam ad Titum, Geneva, 1550.

Die Episteln sanct Pauli an Titum und Philemonem, ausgelegt durch H. Johannem Calvinum—Jetzt auss lateinischer und französicher Sprach in die Teutsche übergesetzt, Frankfurt, 1616.

* Pringle's translation was republished in Grand Rapids, Michigan in 1948.

INTRODUCTION

Commentary on the Epistles to Timothy, Titus and Philemon. Translated by J. Pringle, Calvin Translation Society, Edinburgh, 1856. Republished in Grand Rapids, Michigan, 1948.

THE COMMENTARY ON PHILEMON

This was included in all editions with that on Titus.

On ALL THE EPISTLES

Commentarii in omnes Pauli epistolas atque etiam in epistolam ad Hebraeos, Geneva, 1550, 1557, 1565, 1572, 1580, 1600.
Commentarii in epistolas canonicas, Geneva, 1550.
Commentaires sur les épistres canoniques, Geneva, 1556.
Commentarii in epp. Pauli atque etiam in ep. ad Hebraeos ed. A. Tholuck, 1831.
Les Commentaires à l'Ancien et au Nouveau Testament, Publication sous les auspices de la Societé Calviniste de France, Geneva, 1960 et seq.

COLLECTED WORKS

Calvini Opera, Vignon et Chovet, Geneva, 1612, 1617.
Calvini Opera Omnia, J. J. Schipper, Amsterdam, 1667, 1671.
Johannis Calvini Opera quae supersunt Omnia, ed. Bauer, Cunitz et Reuss, Brunswick, 1892 (Corpus Reformatorum).

TEXT OF SCRIPTURE

The Scripture text used in this translation is that of the Revised Version, but where Calvin's translation or his notes require a different rendering, he has usually been allowed to have his way.

Edinburgh   T. A. Smail
   December 1963

DEDICATORY EPISTLE

TO THAT MOST ILLUSTRIOUS MAN
MELCHIOR VOLMAR RUFUS, LAWYER
FROM JOHN CALVIN
GREETINGS

IF you were to accuse me not merely of carelessness but of unkindness in not having written to you for such a long time, I confess I should find it hard to excuse myself. I might indeed say that we are cut off from each other by distance and that for the last five years I have found nobody who was going in your direction, but these would be but lame excuses. And so it seemed to me that the best thing I could do would be to offer you some compensation to make up for my past neglect and clear me of all blame. Here, then, for you is my Commentary on Paul's Second Epistle to the Corinthians which I have spared no effort in preparing. I am quite sure that you will be kind enough to accept it as fair compensation and I have besides other more important reasons for deciding to dedicate it to you.

First, I remember how faithfully you have cultivated and strengthened the friendship between us which had its first beginnings so long ago, how generous you have been in putting yourself and your services at my disposal, whenever you found an opportunity of giving proof of your friendship, how assiduously you offered your help in promoting my advancement, although my calling at that time prevented me from accepting it. But the main reason has been my recollection of how, the first time my father sent me to study civil law, it was at your instigation and under your tuition that I also took up the study of Greek, of which you were at that time a most distinguished teacher. It was not your fault that I did not make greater progress. In your kindness you would have been ready to lend me a helping hand till I had completed the course, had not my father's death called me away when I was just starting. Nevertheless my indebtedness to you for this is still great for you gave me a good grounding in the rudiments of the language and that was of great help to me later on. And so I could not rest content without leaving to posterity some token of my gratitude to you, and at the same time showing you yourself that your labours with me have borne some fruit. Farewell.

GENEVA, 1st August 1546

THE THEME OF PAUL'S SECOND EPISTLE TO THE CORINTHIANS

FROM the connexion between the two epistles we may infer that the first had some good effect among the Corinthians, although not as much as it should, and, further, that some wicked men were still refusing to acknowledge Paul's authority and persisting in their obstinacy. The fact that Paul has still to dwell so much upon his own *bona fides* and the authority of his office is a sign that their confidence in him was not yet completely established. He himself expressly complains of some who have treated his first epistle with scorn rather than accepted the help it contained. And so when Paul realized that this was how matters stood in the church at Corinth and that he himself would be kept by other business from visiting them as soon as he originally intended, he wrote this epistle from Macedonia. We now understand that his purpose in writing was to complete what he had already begun, so that when he did reach Corinth, he might find everything in good order there.

Paul begins, as is his habit, with thanksgiving, praising God for marvellous deliverances from the greatest dangers. He points out in passing to the Corinthians how all his afflictions and hardships do in fact tend to their benefit and welfare and, although wicked men have been using them as a pretext to undermine his authority, he thus makes them a pledge of his solidarity with them, that should re-establish him in their favour.

Next, he apologizes for his delay in visiting them but assures them that he has not changed his plans for unimportant or frivolous reasons, nor has he meant to deceive them as to his intentions, for they will find the same consistency in his promises as they have already found in his doctrine. Here he briefly points out how sure and stable the truth he has preached to them has been, based as it is on Christ, through whom all God's promises are confirmed and ratified—a high recommendation of the Gospel.

After this he tells them that the reason why he has not come to them is that in present circumstances he could not appear in their midst in a calm and agreeable frame of mind and he thus reproaches those who have made his change of plan a further excuse for slandering his good name. He throws the blame for the delay on the Corinthians themselves because they were not at that time ready to receive him. At the same time he shows with what fatherly forbearance he has treated them in keeping away from their city, since, if he had come at that time, he might have been forced to deal with them severely.

He goes on to deal with a possible objection that in the first epistle he was far from mild in the vehemence of his rebuke to the Corinthians, by explaining that this severity was forced upon him by others against his own will. He shows them that behind this apparent harshness he has a kindly spirit by telling them to restore to favour the incestuous man, over whom he had become so heated in his first letter, but who since then has given some evidence of a change of heart. He gives further proof of his love for them by saying that he had no rest in his mind till he heard from Titus how things were going with them, for such anxiety can only spring from love.

After mentioning his journey into Macedonia, he begins to discuss the glory of his own ministry. He recalls how meticulous certain false apostles have been in detracting from it, and how easily they have won a victory over him by singing their own praises and, in order to show that he is not like them and at the same time refute their foolish boasting, he declares that he rests his reputation upon facts and is not dependent on the praises of men. In the same passage he extols in magnificent terms the efficacy of his preaching and brings out the dignity of his apostleship by comparing the Gospel with the Law. But first of all he makes it clear that he claims nothing that has been achieved as his own but acknowledges that all of it has come from God.

He recalls again with what faithfulness and integrity he has discharged the office entrusted to him and, in so doing, he reproaches those who have made malicious accusations against him and, inspired by his holy assurance, he goes so far as to declare that those who do not discern the glory of his Gospel have been blinded by the devil. Seeing that the humility of his person as one held in contempt by men is greatly detracting from the respect due to his apostleship, he takes this opportunity not only to remove the cause of offence, but even turns it to advantage, by showing that the excellence of God's grace shines all the more brightly because this precious treasure is offered in earthen vessels. Thus he turns to his praise the shameful allegations that his enemies were in the habit of making against him for, although he is pressed down by so many troubles, like a palm tree, the more he is pressed, the more he emerges victor over them all. He deals with this subject down to the middle of chapter 4.

Since, however, the Christian's true glory lies beyond this world, he reminds us that by contempt of this present world and the mortification of the outer man we must turn the whole energy of our minds to the meditation of a blessed immortality. Thus, near the beginning of chapter 5 he glories in the fact that it has been granted to him to have

THEME OF SECOND EPISTLE

no other wish than to win the Lord's approval by his obedience and his hope for himself is that he will have the Corinthians as witnesses to his sincerity. But, since he was in danger of being suspected of pride or vanity, he repeats again that it is the insolence of his ill-wishers that has compelled him to say all this and that he has not done it for his own sake out of any desire for his own reputation but only for the good of the Corinthians since it was to their advantage to know the truth about this matter and his only concern has been for their welfare. To confirm this he adds the general statement that the servants of Christ should make it their aim to forget themselves and live to their Lord; and his conclusion is that only newness of life is of any real worth so that nobody deserves to be held in esteem but the man who has denied himself. From this he passes on to expound the heart and centre of the Gospel message in order to stir up by its greatness and excellence both ministers and people to a godly fear. This he does at the beginning of chapter 6.

Having reminded them here again of how faithfully he is discharging his duty, he takes the Corinthians gently to task for having failed to take full advantage of his labours. To this rebuke he immediately adds an exhortation to flee from idolatry, which shows that they have not yet made as much progress as he would like. He has good reason to complain that this is their own fault, since they have not paid attention to such clear teaching. But in order to avoid discouraging or alienating their tender minds by too sharp a rebuke, he once again assures them of his own goodwill towards them and returns to his explanation of his past severity with them, which he broke off abruptly before, and continues with it though now in a different way. With greater confidence he says that he has no regret at having grieved them, since he did it for their own good and, by congratulating them on the successful outcome of his rebuke, he shows them how heartily he is concerned with their welfare. This brings us to the end of chapter 7.

From the beginning of chapter 8 to the end of chapter 9 he goes on to deal with cheerfulness in the giving of money, a subject he had already raised in the last chapter of the first epistle. He praises them for having made a good start but in case the ardour of their zeal should begin to cool with the passing of time, as often happens, he gives them many reasons why they should faithfully persevere as they have begun.

In the tenth chapter he begins to defend himself and his apostleship from the slanderous accusations with which wicked men have been vexing him. First he shows that he is well equipped with the weapons required in Christ's warfare. Then he declares that the sternness he showed towards them in the first epistle was based on the assurance of a good conscience and makes it clear that the sternness of his words when absent will be matched by the energy of his actions when he comes among them. Finally, by comparing himself with them, he shows them how empty all their boastings are.

In the eleventh chapter he recalls the Corinthians from the misguided enthusiasms which have been corrupting them and warns them that there is nothing more dangerous than to be led astray from the straightforward integrity (*simplicitas*) of the Gospel. The lack of regard for him and the preference for other leaders, that some of them have shown, is not due to any fault in him but to their arrogance and false sophistication. Those they have followed have brought them nothing better or superior and their only reason for despising him has been that he does not set great store by eloquence of speech or because by an act of voluntary self-denial he has shown indulgence to their weakness and not claimed what was his due. The ironical way in which he speaks implies a rebuke to their ingratitude for where was the justice in thinking less of him because he had accommodated himself to them? He makes it clear, however, that his reason for not accepting the remuneration due to him from the Corinthians was not that he loved them less than the other churches but because false apostles were using this question of remuneration as a means of discrediting him and he did not wish to give them any advantage over him.

Having thus reproved the prejudiced and malicious opinion that the Corinthians have formed of him, he bursts out into godly boasting, reminding them how much he has in which he could glory, if he were so minded. But he first makes it clear that it is for their sakes that he is making a fool of himself by singing his own praises in this way. Finally he stops his boasting in mid-course and says that his chief cause for glorying is that very humility which proud men despise, for the Lord has commanded him not to glory in anything but his infirmities.

Towards the end of the twelfth chapter he again takes them to task for forcing him to play the fool by slavishly following ambitious leaders who are estranging them from Christ. He goes on to administer a strong rebuke to those who were obstinately persisting in their wanton attacks upon him, adding to their previous faults this shameless continuation of their opposition.

In the thirteenth chapter he threatens severer punishment to such people, bids all men in general acknowledge his apostleship, pointing out that it will be to their advantage to do so, since it is dangerous for them to despise a man whom they know by experience to be the undoubted and faithful ambassador of the Lord.

CHAPTER ONE

Paul, an apostle of Jesus Christ through the will of God, and Timothy our brother unto the church of God which is at Corinth, with all the saints which are in the whole of Achaia: Grace to you and peace from God our Father and the Lord Jesus Christ. Blessed be the God and Father of our Lord Jesus Christ, the Father of mercies and God of all comfort; who comforteth us in all our affliction, that we may be able to comfort them that are in any affliction, through the comfort wherewith we ourselves are comforted of God. For as the sufferings of Christ abound unto us, even so our comfort also aboundeth through Christ. (1-5)

1. *Paul, an apostle.* His reasons for introducing himself as an apostle of Christ and for explaining that he has obtained this honour *through the will of God* are to be found in the last epistle where it has been pointed out that the only people with a right to be listened to are those whom God has sent and who speak from His mouth. Thus for any man to exercise authority two things are required, a call and the faithful discharge of his office by the man called to it, both of which Paul claims for himself. So also do the false apostles but because they lay claim to a title to which they have no right they have no success among the sons of God who can, with the greatest ease, convict them of presumptuousness. The mere name of apostle is not enough without the reality and he who claims to be an apostle must prove his claim by his actions.

Unto the church of God. It should always be noted that Paul recognizes the existence of the Church even where there was so much wrong with it. A church which has in it the true marks of religion can be recognized in spite of the faults of its individual members.

But what does he mean by saying *with all the saints*? Were these saints outside the Church? My answer is that he is referring to the believers who were scattered in the remote districts of the province. It is quite probable that in these disturbed times, when Christ's enemies were raging all around, many were scattered in places where it was scarcely possible to gather together for worship.

3. *Blessed be God.* He begins, as has been said, on this note of thanksgiving, partly to praise God's goodness, partly to inspire the Corinthians by his example to endure persecutions bravely and partly, by thus boasting of God's help, to assert himself against the malicious misrepresentations of the false apostles. For such is the world's perversity

that it disparages the martyrdoms that it ought to admire and contrives to find cause for slanders in the marvellous victories of godly men.

Blessed be God, he says. For what reason? *Because He comforteth us.* The relative pronoun *who* has here a causal sense and means *because*. He has endured his afflictions with courage and cheerfulness and he ascribes this courageous spirit to God since it is due to the support of His comfort that he has not given way.

He calls God the *Father of our Lord Jesus Christ* and that is a very suitable title when His blessings are being recalled, for, where there is no Christ, there are no blessings. But where Christ is, by whom the whole family in heaven and earth is named, there are all the mercies and consolations of God and there most of all is His fatherly love, the source from which all other blessings flow.

4. *That we may be able to comfort.* There is no doubt that, just as a little earlier Paul has been defending his afflictions from the shame and slanders that have been heaped upon them, so now he is reminding the Corinthians that the victory he has won through God's comfort has been for their sakes and to their advantage, that they may be encouraged by it to share his endurance instead of arrogantly pouring scorn upon his struggles. The apostle did not live for himself but for the Church, so that he accepted all the blessings God gave him not just for himself but as opportunities to help others more. For when the Lord blesses us, He invites us to follow His example and be generous to our neighbours. The riches of the Spirit are not to be kept to ourselves but whatever a man receives he is to pass on to others. This must have a special application to ministers of the Word but it has also a general application to every man in his own way. Thus here Paul is recognizing that he has been sustained by God's comfort in order that he may be able to comfort others.

5. *For as the sufferings of Christ abound.* This statement can be taken actively or passively. If it is taken actively the meaning will be, 'The more I am tried with various afflictions, the more opportunity I will have to comfort others.' But I prefer the passive sense, that the more his afflictions increase the greater will be the comfort God provides. David also declares that this is what happened to him, 'In the multitude of my anxieties within me, thy consolations delighted my soul' (Ps. 94.19). But this teaching is clearer in Paul's own words for he calls the afflictions of the godly *the sufferings of Christ*, just as he says in another passage that he 'fills up in his own body what is lacking in the sufferings of Christ' (Col. 1.24). It is true that both good men and bad share in the miseries and hardships of this present life, but for the ungodly they are signs of God's curse because they are the results of sin; their only message is of God's wrath and our share in Adam's doom and their

only result is to cast down the soul. But by their sufferings believers are being conformed to Christ and bear about in their body the dying of Christ, that the life of Christ may one day be made manifest in them. I am speaking of the afflictions they have to bear for the testimony of Christ for, although the punishments that the Lord imposes because of their sins are beneficial to them, they cannot rightly be said to share Christ's sufferings unless they suffer in His name, as we read in I Peter 4.13. Paul's meaning is therefore that God is always present with him in his tribulations and he is sustained in his weakness by the consolations of Christ, that he may not be overcome by the ills that befall him.

> *But whether we be afflicted for your comfort and salvation, which is effectual in the patient enduring of the same sufferings which we also suffer: or whether we be comforted for your comfort and salvation; our hope for you is stedfast; knowing that, as ye are partakers of the sufferings, so also are ye of the comfort. For we would not have you ignorant, brethren, concerning our affliction which befell us in Asia, that we were weighed down exceedingly, beyond our power, insomuch that we despaired even of life: yea, we ourselves have received the sentence of death in ourselves, that we should not trust in ourselves, but in God which raiseth the dead: who delivered us out of so great a death, and will deliver: on whom we have our hope set that he will also still deliver us; ye also helping together by your supplication on our behalf; that for the gift bestowed upon us by means of many, thanks may be given by many persons on our behalf. (6-11)*

6. *But whether we be afflicted.* The word 'and' has been inserted before the phrase 'our hope for you is steadfast' and this has led Erasmus to think that we have to understand 'it is' before 'for your comfort and salvation', thus reading 'whether we be afflicted it is for your comfort'. But it seems more probable to me that this connecting 'and' means here either 'thus also' or 'in both cases'. He has already said that he has received comfort in order to pass it on to others. Now he goes further and says that he has a steadfast hope that they will share in that comfort. Besides, some of the most ancient Greek codices add immediately after the first clause, 'and our hope of you is steadfast' and this reading removes the ambiguity. For when this comes in the middle, we have to take it with both the preceding and the following clauses. However, if anyone prefers to have a complete sentence by adding a verb in both clauses, there will be no harm done and no great difference in meaning. For if you do take it as one continuous statement, you still have to explain the two parts of it as meaning that the apostle is

afflicted and refreshed with comfort for the good of the Corinthians and his hope therefore is that they will at last share the same comfort which is in store for him. For my own part, I have followed the reading that I thought suited best.

It should be noted that the word 'afflicted' here refers not just to outward trouble but also to the inward misery of the heart, for it must correspond in meaning with the word 'comforted' (παρακαλεῖσθαι) to which it is opposed. So the meaning is that a man's heart is oppressed with anxiety because of the misery he feels. The word we translate 'comfort' is in Greek παράκλησις which also means an exhortation. But Paul uses it here to mean the kind of comfort by which a man's heart is lightened of its grief and raised above it. For example, Paul himself might almost have fallen down dead under such a load of afflictions if God had not encouraged him and raised him up by His comfort. Thus the Corinthians derive strength and courage from Paul's sufferings and take comfort from his example. To sum up briefly: Paul saw that some of the Corinthians were using his afflictions as a pretext for treating him with scorn and so he set himself to correct their error, firstly by showing them that they ought to think the more highly of him because his sufferings have been to their advantage, and secondly by leading them so to identify themselves with him that they will come to count his afflictions as their own. It is as if he had said, 'Whether I am afflicted or whether I am comforted, it is all for your benefit, and it is my sure hope that it is a benefit you will continue to enjoy.'

Paul's afflictions and consolations were of a kind that would tend to build up the Corinthians in the faith if they did not wilfully deprive themselves of the benefit of them. But Paul declares that he has such great confidence in the Corinthians that he is quite certain in his hope that he has not suffered and been comforted on their behalf in vain. The false apostles were trying to turn everything that happened to Paul into a reproach against him. If they had had their way, they would have made the afflictions Paul bore on their behalf vain and empty and they would have had no advantage from these comforts with which the Lord was refreshing him. In face of these tricks, Paul professes his confidence in the Corinthians.

His afflictions were a source of comfort to believers because they could be strengthened by seeing him suffering willingly and enduring bravely so many hardships for the Gospel's sake. For although we may readily agree that we ought to endure affliction for the Gospel's sake, our knowledge of our own weakness makes us tremble and we think we shall be unable to do what we ought. When that happens we should remember the example of the saints which should help to make us more courageous. Furthermore, Paul's personal consolation flowed out to the whole Church, because from it believers learnt that the God who had sustained Paul, and renewed him in his time of necessity, would never fail them. Thus their salvation was advanced both by his suffering and by his being comforted. That is what he brings out almost in parenthesis when he says *which is effectual in the patient enduring* etc.' He adds this clause to keep them from imagining that the sufferings he was enduring alone have nothing at all to do with them. Erasmus takes the participle ἐνεργουμένης actively but a passive meaning is better, since Paul's only intention here is to explain how everything that has happened to him is for their salvation. He says that, though it is he alone who suffers, his sufferings avail for their salvation, not because they are expiations or sacrifices for their sins, but because they strengthen them and build them up. Thus he joins together comfort and salvation to show how their salvation was to be effected.

7. *Knowing that, as ye are partakers of the sufferings.* It may be that some of the Corinthians have been temporarily alienated from Paul by the misrepresentations of the false apostles, so that his reputation has been lowered in their eyes by the way he was being shamefully treated before the world. But in spite of that Paul still associates them with himself both in the fellowship of his afflictions and in the hope of his consolation. Thus without exposing them to an open rebuke he corrects their perverse and malicious opinion of him.

8. *For we would not have you ignorant.* Paul recalls the many hard struggles he has been involved in, so that he may show more clearly the glorious victory he has won. Since he sent the last epistle, he had been exposed to great dangers and had endured violent onslaughts. Probably he is referring here to the events that Luke describes in Acts 19.23 although the greatness of the crisis is not so clearly brought out in that passage. Luke does however say that the whole city was in a tumult and it is easy to infer the rest, for we know the usual result of a popular rising, once it has broken out. Paul says that he has been oppressed by this persecution '*exceedingly, beyond our power*' so that he could not bear the burden. This metaphor is taken from people who break down under the pressure of a heavy load, or from ships that sink because they are overloaded—not that Paul himself has actually collapsed but he felt that his strength would have failed if the Lord had not given him new strength.

Insomuch that we despaired even of life. That is, 'so that I came to the point of thinking my life was already lost or, at least, that little hope was left me. I felt as though I were shut up in prison with no possibility of escape.' Was such a courageous soldier of Christ, such a brave athlete really left without strength and with nothing to hope for but death? For he has already told us that his anxiety for his life was the cause of his despair. I have already pointed out that in assessing his resources Paul is not taking God's help into account but is telling us what he felt about his own capabilities, and there is no doubt that all human strength gives way before the fear of death. Moreover even saints need to be threatened by a complete collapse of human strength, in order that they may learn from their weakness to depend entirely upon God alone. This is what he goes on to say. I prefer to take the word ἐξαπορεῖσθαι which Paul uses here as meaning simply alarming anxiety rather than follow Erasmus who renders it 'despair'. Paul only means that he was hemmed in by the greatest difficulties so that no way of saving his life seemed to be left.

9. *Yea, we ourselves have received the sentence of death*—or, as we would say, 'I thought my death fixed and decided.' He speaks of himself as a man condemned to death who has nothing to look forward to but the hour of his execution. But he goes on to say that this death sentence was self-imposed, meaning that it was only in his own judgment that his death was imminent, for he had received no revelation from God. This way of speaking goes beyond the ἐξαπορεῖσθαι of the last verse. There he said only that he was not sure of living; here he says he is certain to die. But the main thing to notice here is his explanation of why he was reduced to such straits—*that we should not trust in ourselves*. I do not agree with Chrysostom's view that Paul had no real need of such a lesson in humility but is presenting himself in this false light as an example to others. For he was a man who was in other ways subject to the same human feelings as other men, not only in relation to such things as heat and cold but in misplaced confidence, rashness and the like. I do not say that he was addicted to these faults but I do say that he could be tempted by them, and the experience he describes here was the cure that God provided at the right time to keep them from getting a grip upon him.

There are two things to be noted here. First, the fleshly confidence by which we are puffed up is so obstinate that the only way it can be destroyed is by our falling into extremities of despair. For the flesh is proud and does not yield willingly so that its pretensions cease only when it is forcibly constrained. We are not brought to real submission until we have been laid low by the crushing hand of God. Second, we should note, that the remnants of this disease of pride linger even in the saints, so that they too often need to be reduced to extremities in order to be stripped of all their self-confidence and learn humility. The roots of this evil are so deep in the human heart that even the most perfect among us are never entirely free of it, till God confronts them with death. We may gather how much our self-confidence displeases God when we see how, in order to cure it, we have to be condemned to death.

But in God which raiseth the dead. To make us give up our self-confidence and recognize our weakness and thus cease to make false claims for ourselves we must first die. But that is not enough unless we take a step further. We must begin by despairing of ourselves but only in order that we may hope in God: we must be brought low in ourselves but only in order that we may be raised up by His power. Thus Paul, as soon as the pride of the flesh has been brought to nothing, immediately puts in its place a confidence that rests in God. '*Not in ourselves*', he says, '*but in God.*'

In speaking at this point of God's power to raise the dead, Paul has an eye to the needs of his argument in the same way as in Romans 4.17 where he is dealing with Abraham. For 'to believe in God who calleth those things that are not as though they were', and 'to hope in God which raiseth the dead' is to call to mind God's power to create His elect out of nothing and to revive those that are dead. Thus Paul is saying that death has been set before his eyes in order to bring him to a greater recognition of the power of God by which he has been raised from the dead. The first step should indeed be to acknowledge God as the author of life by the strength which He gives us but our dullness is such that the light of life often dazzles our eyes so that we have to look at death before we can be brought to God.

10. *Who delivered us out of so great a death.* Here he gives his general statement a personal application, and in praise of God's grace, he declares that he has not been disappointed in his expectation for he has been rescued from death—and in a most remarkable way. This use of hyperbole is not uncommon in Scripture. It frequently occurs both in the Prophets and the Psalms and everyday speech makes use of it as well. Everyone should apply what Paul says here to his own case.

On whom we have our hope set. Paul assures himself that the kindness of God he has so often experienced in the past will continue into the future and he is right to do so for the Lord, by fulfilling in part what He has promised, bids us have good hope for what still remains. Moreover, all the favours we receive from Him are the pledges and earnests by which He confirms His promises. Although Paul had no doubt of God's willingness to be present with him, he yet exhorts the Corinthians to pray for his safety, for his assumption that they will help him by their prayers really amounts to such an exhortation. He means that they will do it not just as a duty but with real profit to him. 'Your prayers will also help me', he says. For, since God commands us to pray for each other, it is not His will that we should do so in vain. When we are told that our prayers are not only pleasing to God but profitable to ourselves as well, this should encourage us both to seek the intercessions of our brethren when we are in straits and to give them the same help in return. It is not any lack of faith that makes the apostle ask for his brethren's assistance but, although he was quite sure that God would care for his safety even if all human support were to be withdrawn, he yet recognized that it was God's will that he should have the assistance of the Church's prayers. He also took into account the promise that their support would not be in vain and since he did not wish to neglect any source of help that God meant him to have, he desired his brethren to pray for his safety.

The sum of the matter is that we are to follow God's Word by obeying its commandments and adhering to its promises. This is not done by those who have recourse to the prayers of the dead for they are not content with the means of grace God has appointed but introduce something new that has no scriptural support. For what is said here about praying for each other does not include the dead but is explicitly restricted to the living. Thus it is childish for the Papists to try to find support for their superstitious practices in this passage.

11. *That the gift bestowed by means of many.* There is some difficulty in Paul's words here and interpretations of them vary. I shall not stop to refute other renderings, for if we can agree about the true meaning, there is no need to do so. Paul has already said that the prayers of the Corinthians will be of assistance to him. He now adds a second advantage that will come from their prayers—a greater manifestation of the glory of God. 'For if the blessing that God confers upon me', he says, 'is obtained in answer to many prayers, many people will glorify God for it.' Or, we can put it like this, 'Many will give thanks to God on my behalf for in helping me He has answered the prayers not just of one man but of many.' Since it is our duty to let none of God's favours pass without praise, we are specially bound to thank Him for His mercy when He has given a favourable answer to our prayers, as He commands us in Ps. 50.15. And this applies not only when our own private interest is involved but also to matters concerning the general welfare of the Church or any of our brethren. Thus when we pray for each other and obtain what we ask, God's glory is shown forth more clearly, in that we all acknowledge with thanksgiving God's goodness both to individuals and to the whole body of the Church.

There is nothing forced in this interpretation. It is true that in the Greek the article is inserted between '*by many persons*' and 'the gift conferred upon me' and might be thought to separate them. But it does not really do so as it is often found between phrases that are closely connected. Here it is quite rightly used in place of an adversative particle for, although the gift had its source in many persons, it was conferred only upon Paul. To take διὰ πολλῶν as a neuter, as some do, does not fit the context.

It may be asked why Paul says 'from many persons' rather than 'from many men' and what the word 'person' means here. In my view it is as if he had said 'with respect to many' for the favour was conferred upon Paul in order that it might be given to many. Since, therefore, God had many in mind, Paul says that many 'persons' were involved. Some Greek codices have ὑπὲρ ὑμῶν, 'on your behalf', which seems to be far removed from Paul's meaning and from the context of the words but can in fact be explained quite suitably as meaning, 'When God has answered your prayers for my welfare and for your own also, many will give thanks on your behalf.'

> For our glorying is this, the testimony of our conscience, that in holiness and sincerity of God, not in fleshly wisdom but in the grace of God, we behaved ourselves in the world, and more abundantly to you-ward. For we write none other things unto you than what ye recognize and even acknowledge, and I hope ye will acknowledge unto the end: as also ye did acknowledge us in part, that we are your glorying, even as ye also are ours, in the day of our Lord Jesus. (12-14)

12. *For our glorying is this.* He explains why his welfare should be of general concern to all. It is because he has conducted himself with simplicity and sincerity among them all. He fully deserved their affection and it would have been ungenerous not to be anxious that such an outstanding minister of the Lord should be long preserved for the good of the Church. It is as if he had said, 'My behaviour among you has been such as to make it natural for all good men to give me their esteem and their love.' For the sake of those to whom he was writing Paul takes this opportunity to digress for a little in order to defend his integrity. But since it is not enough to have men's approval, and since Paul himself was the victim of the prejudiced and malicious judgments some people were passing against him, carried away as they were by corrupt and blind enthusiasms, he appeals to the witness of his own conscience which is just as if he had cited God Himself and appealed for the truth of his claim to His tribunal.

But how is this glorying in his own integrity consistent with what he himself says in II Cor. 10.17, 'He that glorieth, let him glory in the Lord'? And also, who is so upright that he can dare to boast before God? Firstly, Paul is not setting himself over against God as if he had anything of his own or that came from himself. Secondly, he does not make his salvation depend on the integrity he claims or put any confidence in it. Lastly, it is God's gifts of which he is boasting so that he is glorifying God as their sole author to whom they are all to be ascribed. There are three conditions under which every godly man can rightly glory in all God's blessings, whereas ungodly men cannot glory in God at all except falsely and perversely. First, we must acknowledge that everything good in us has been received from God, claiming nothing for ourselves; next, we must hold fast this foundation, that our assurance of salvation depends solely on God's mercy; finally, we must rest in God as the sole author of all good things. Then we may glory in gratitude in every kind of good thing.

That in the sincerity of God. This phrase is used here in the same sense as 'the glory of God' in Romans 3.23 and 'the glory of God and of men' in John 12.43. Those who love the glory of men seek their admiration and to stand well in their judgment. 'The glory of God' is what a man has in the sight of God. Thus Paul is not satisfied with showing that his sincerity has been seen of men but adds that he has been sincere also before God. Εἰλίκρινεια (which I have translated 'purity' or 'holiness') means much the same as sincerity, for it is an open and frank way of behaving which shows clearly what is in a man's heart. Both terms are the opposite of cunning deceitfulness and underhand schemes.

Not in fleshly wisdom. Here Paul is anticipating charges that might be levelled against him, for he readily admits, and indeed openly declares, that he lacks certain desirable qualities but he adds that he has been endowed with the grace of God, which is far better. 'I agree', he says, 'that I lack fleshly wisdom but I have been given God's power and anyone who is not satisfied with that is free to pour scorn on my apostleship. But if fleshly wisdom is of no importance, then I lack nothing that deserves real praise.' By fleshly wisdom he means everything apart from Christ that could win us a reputation for wisdom. For a fuller explanation see the first and second chapters of the first epistle. Thus we have to understand by the grace of God, which he is contrasting with this fleshly wisdom, everything that is beyond man's nature and capacity and the gifts of the Holy Spirit that by their presence openly reveal the power of God in the weakness of our flesh.

More abundantly to you-ward. He does not mean that he had been less sincere elsewhere but only that he had stayed longer in Corinth in order, among other reasons, to give them a fuller and clearer proof of his good faith. He has deliberately put it this way to show that there was no need for witnesses from a distance for they themselves were the best witnesses to all that he had said.

13. *For we write none other things.* Here he is indirectly rebuking the false apostles who were continually singing their own praises in unrestrained boasting that had little or no substance to it, and at the same time he attacks their slanders against him so that no one may think that he is claiming for himself more than he should. Thus he says that

he boasts of nothing in his words that he does not prove in his deeds and the Corinthians are his witnesses that this is so. Ἀναγινώσκειν in Greek means sometimes 'to read' and sometimes 'to recognize' and ἐπιγινώσκειν means sometimes 'to discover' and sometimes the same as the Latin verb *agnoscere*, 'to acknowledge' e.g. in the legal phrase 'to acknowledge a child', as Budaeus has also noted. Thus ἐπιγινώσκειν is stronger than ἀναγινώσκειν. A person may 'recognize' something, that is, be privately convinced of it in his own mind, and yet not 'acknowledge' it, that is, give open expression to his acceptance of it. We may now examine Paul's words. Some render them, 'We write nothing but what you read and acknowledge', but that is very dull and quite unsuitable. Ambrose changes it to read, 'You do not only read but also acknowledge', but that is clearly an impossible translation of the words. The interpretation I offer is plain and natural and the only difficulty in understanding it is the confusion caused by the different meanings of the words. In short, I take Paul's meaning to be that the Corinthians already know and can indeed bear witness to all that he is saying. The first word is *recognoscere*, which means to be convinced of a thing by experience, and the second is *agnoscere* which means to give open assent to the truth.

And I hope ye will acknowledge unto the end. The Corinthians had not yet completely regained their sound judgment so as to be able to form a just and fair opinion of Paul's good faith, but they had begun to correct the perverse and prejudiced view they had taken before. Thus Paul's meaning here is that he has better hopes of them for the future. 'Already', he says, 'you have acknowledged me in part and I hope that you will come to acknowledge more and more what I have been and how I have acted among you.' From this it becomes easier to see what he means by ἐπιγινώσκειν. This passage refers to a time when the Corinthians will come to their senses again. At first they had acknowledged Paul fully and completely, later their judgment was clouded by covert allegations but now they had begun in part to return to a sound mind.

14. *We are your glorying*. We have briefly considered how the saints can rightly glory in God's blessings, when they rest in God alone with no other aim. Thus it was right for Paul to boast that it was his ministry that had brought the Corinthians into obedience to Christ and for the Corinthians to glory in having been instructed so faithfully and honourably by such an apostle—an advantage not granted to all. This kind of glorying in men is not inconsistent with glorying in God alone. Thus he tells the Corinthians that it is greatly to their advantage to acknowledge him as a genuine, unfeigned servant of Christ, for if they break with him, they will lose their greatest glory. In these words

he accuses them of fickleness because they have given too much heed to the ill disposed and the jealous and have voluntarily deprived themselves of their chief glory.

In the day of the Lord. I take this to mean the last day which will put an end to all the fleeting glories of the world. Paul means that the glorying of which he is now speaking is not passing like the boasts that so impress men but permanent and lasting because it will stand firm in the day of Christ. For then Paul will celebrate the triumph due to the many victories he has won beneath Christ's banner and will lead in solemn procession all the peoples that have been brought under the glorious yoke of Christ by his ministry. And the church at Corinth will triumph at having been founded and instructed by such a great apostle.

> *And in this confidence I was minded to come before unto you, that ye might have a second benefit; and by you to pass into Macedonia, and again from Macedonia to come unto you, and of you to be set forward on my journey into Judaea. When I therefore was thus minded, did I shew fickleness? or the things that I purpose, do I purpose according to the flesh, that with me there should be the yea yea and the nay nay? But as God is faithful, our word toward you is not yea and nay. For the Son of God, Jesus Christ, who was preached among you by us, even by me and Silvanus and Timothy, was not yea and nay, but in him is yea. For how many soever be the promises of God, in him is the yea: wherefore also through him is the Amen, unto the glory of God through us.*
> (15–20)

15. *And in this confidence.* Paul had held out hopes that he would come to them and afterwards had changed his plan. The fact that he has now to defend himself for so doing shows that this has been made the basis of a false accusation against him. By saying that it was because of his confidence in them that he planned to visit them, he indirectly transfers the blame to the Corinthians since it is they who have hindered his coming by taking his confidence away through their ingratitude.

That ye might have a second benefit. The first benefit was that Paul had spent a whole eighteen months in winning them for the Lord; the second was that by his coming they would be confirmed in the faith they had already received and prompted to make further progress in it by his holy admonitions. The Corinthians had deprived themselves of this by not letting the apostle come to them. Thus they were punishing themselves for their own fault and had no reason for blaming Paul. If anyone prefers to follow Chrysostom and read χαράν instead of χάριν I have no great objection but my own explanation is simpler.

17 *Did I show fickleness?* There are two main reasons why men's plans are not successfully accomplished or their promises faithfully kept. The first is that they change their minds almost hourly and the second that they are too hasty in the commitments they undertake. It is a sign of instability to make plans or promises that you immediately regret. Paul says here that he is free of this failing. 'It is not', he says, 'from fickleness that I have gone back on the undertaking I gave.' He also claims to be free from rashness and unjustified self-assurance, for that is now I interpret the phrase *'to purpose according to the flesh'*. For it is, as I have said, the common habit for men to take rash and presumptuous decisions about what they will do, as though they did not depend upon God's providence and were not subject to His will. To punish their presumption God brings their plans to nothing and often exposes them to ridicule. The phrase 'according to the flesh' could be understood in a more general sense to include all evil schemes not directed to any good purpose—those, for example, dictated by ambition or avarice or any other bad motive—but in my view Paul was not concerned with these in this passage but only with the rashness which is so evident all the time in the way men make their plans. Thus 'to purpose according to the flesh' is to fail to acknowledge God's rule over us and to be carried away instead by a rash presumption which God rightly punishes and brings to scorn. To clear himself of this fault Paul puts this question into the mouth of his opponents so that it is probable, as I have already said, that malicious rumours were being circulated.

That with me there should be the yea yea. Some take this statement with what goes before and explain it thus, 'As though it were in my power to perform whatever I purpose.' So men decide to do whatever comes into their heads and order their own ways when they cannot govern even their tongues, as Solomon says (Prov. 16.1). Certainly the words do mean that an intention once affirmed should remain fixed, and what has been once rejected should never be done. So James says in his epistle (5.12), 'Let your yea be yea and your nay nay that ye fall not into dissimulation.' This interpretation would suit what has gone before very well, for to want our decisions to have without exception the force of oracles is indeed to purpose according to the flesh. It does not however suit what immediately follows—'God is faithful etc.'— for when Paul wants to assert that there has been no fickleness in his preaching he uses the same form of words and it would be absurd if in almost the same verse he counted it a fault that his yea should be yea and his nay nay and then went on to claim it as his greatest virtue. I know what reply could be made by those who have a taste for subtle distinctions but I have no liking for anything that is not solid.

I have no doubt that though these words can bear a different meaning Paul actually used them to reprove inconstancy and to free himself of the charge of habitually promising what he cannot perform. Thus the repetition of the yea and the nay does not have the same force as in Matthew 5.37 or in James but rather means 'that now yea may be yea with me and, when it seems good to me, nay nay'. At the same time it is possible that the repetition is due to a scribal error, since the Vulgate does not repeat the words. However, we need not be too anxious about the words as long as we grasp Paul's meaning which is, as I have said, made quite clear in what follows.

18. *God is faithful.* By the term 'word' (*sermo*) he means doctrine, as is shown by the reason that he adds, when he says that the Son of God who was preached by him was not variable. He wants his personal integrity to be judged on the basis of the complete consistency of his teaching and thus he rebuts the unfavourable suggestion of fickleness or bad faith that has been made against him. But it does not necessarily follow that a man who is trustworthy in his doctrine is also truthful in every word that he speaks. But Paul sets little store on what men think of him personally as long as the authority of his teaching is preserved, and his main concern is to remind the Corinthians of it. He does indeed say that he shows the same good faith in all his life as the Corinthians have seen in his ministry, but in dealing with the charge made against him it seems that he deliberately defends his doctrine rather than his person, since he would not let his apostleship be defamed even indirectly but otherwise did not care about his personal reputation.

Note how carefully he defends his teaching. He calls on God to witness how straightforward and sincere his preaching has been; it has not been ambiguous or variable or temporizing. He even swears that his teaching is as true as God Himself, as if to say, 'The truth of my preaching is as sure and certain as God Himself is faithful and true.' And this is not surprising since the Word of God, which, Isaiah says, endureth for ever (Isa. 40.8) is the very same Word that prophets and apostles have proclaimed to the world, as Peter also explains (I Pet. 1.25). This is the source of the bold confidence he shows in Galatians (1.8) when he pronounces an anathema on the angels if they dare to bring forward another gospel contrary to his own. Who would dare to make the very angels in heaven subject to his doctrine if it had not God as its author and defender? Ministers of the Word should have the same assurance of conscience when they enter the pulpit to speak in Christ's name, knowing that their doctrine can no more be overthrown than God Himself.

19. *For the Son of God.* Here we have the proof of his bold claim—his preaching had in it nothing but Christ who is the eternal and

immutable truth of God. The phrase *'preached by us'* is emphatic. It can and often does happen that Christ is disfigured by the imaginings of men and His truth adulterated by their deceits. Paul denies that he or his associates have done this and claims that with sincerity and all integrity they have held forth Christ pure and undisguised. It is not quite clear why he leaves out Apollos when he mentions Timothy and Silvanus, but probably they had been subjected more to wicked defamations and Paul takes greater care to defend them.

In these words he shows that all his teaching consisted of the simple knowledge of Christ only, for in that the whole Gospel is really included. Thus those who teach anything but Christ wander into forbidden territory, however much they may pride themselves on their show of wisdom. For Christ is the end of the Law and so the head, sum and perfection of all spiritual doctrine. Next, he shows that his teaching of Christ was not changeable or ambiguous, so as to present Christ in different shapes at different times, like Proteus. Some men do in fact treat Christ in this way, making a game of their teaching like people tossing a ball from hand to hand merely to show off their dexterity. Others, to please men, present Christ under different false disguises, and others again teach a thing one day and the next retract it out of fear. Such was not Paul's Christ nor the Christ of any true apostle. The claim of men who paint Christ in these varying colours for their own advantage to be ministers of Christ is false. For the only true Christ is He in whom can be seen this unvariable and perpetual 'yea' which Paul here declares to be characteristic of Him.

20. *For how many soever be the promises of God.* Here again he confirms how steadfast and inflexible the preaching of Christ should be since He Himself is the foundation of all the promises of God. It would be quite absurd if He, in whom all God's promises are made secure, were Himself unsteady. Although this statement is general, as we shall soon see, it is nevertheless applicable to the matter in hand in confirming the stability of Paul's teaching. Here he is not speaking only of the Gospel in general terms but is claiming this distinction for his own Gospel in particular, as if to say, 'If God's promises are sure and well founded, then my preaching must also be sure since it contains nothing but Christ in whom all these promises are established.' Since his only intention is to show that he has proclaimed a pure Gospel undistorted by any alien additions, let us consider the general doctrine that all God's promises depend upon Christ alone.

This is a notable assertion and one of the main articles of our faith. It depends in turn upon another principle—that it is only in Christ that God the Father is graciously inclined towards us. His promises are the testimonies of His fatherly goodwill towards us. Thus it follows that they are fulfilled only in Christ. The promises are testimonies of divine grace for although God does good also to the unworthy, when promises are added to these kindnesses, His special purpose is to show Himself a Father to them. Secondly, we are incapable of possessing God's promises till we have received the remission of our sins and that comes to us through Christ. Thirdly, the chief of all God's promises is that by which He adopts us as His sons and Christ is the cause and root of our adoption (*causa et radix adoptionis*). For God is Father only to those who are members and brothers of His only begotten Son. Everything comes to us from this one source. All God's promises proceed from His love for us, but apart from Christ we are more hateful than acceptable to Him. Thus it is not surprising that Paul should say here that all God's promises are ratified and established in Christ.

But the question arises whether before Christ's advent the promises were uncertain or worthless, for Paul seems to speak here of Christ as manifested in the flesh. My answer is that all the promises given to believers from the beginning of the world had their foundation in Christ. Thus, whenever Moses and the prophets are dealing with reconciliation with God or the hope of salvation or grace of any kind they mention Christ and at the same time proclaim His advent and His kingdom. I say again that the promises under the Old Testament were fulfilled to the godly, as far as was good for them, but at the same time they were in a sense suspended till Christ came for it was through Him that they obtained their true fulfilment. Believers who relied on the promises themselves deferred their true fulfilment to the appearing of the Mediator and suspended their hope until that time. In short, if anyone considers the effect of Christ's death and resurrection, he will easily understand how promises of God which would otherwise have no sure fulfilment have been sealed and confirmed in Him.

Wherefore also through him is the Amen. Here the Greek manuscripts disagree. Some have the two clauses together in one—'All the promises of God are through Him Yea and through Him Amen to the glory of God through us.' The other reading, which I have followed, is easier and gives a fuller meaning. He has already said that God has ratified all His promises in Christ and he now goes on to tell us that it is for us to give our assent to this ratification. We do this when we rest upon Christ in certain faith and thus subscribe and set our seal that God is true, as we read in John 3.33 and when we do this to the glory of God since this is the end that all things should serve (Eph. 1.13 and Rom. 3.4). I admit that the other reading is more usually adopted but it is laboured and I have no hesitation in preferring the one which contains fuller teaching and is much better suited to the context. For Paul is reminding the Corinthians that once they have been instructed in the simple truth of God it is their duty to respond with their Amen. If anyone is reluctant to depart from the common reading, there can always be drawn from it an exhortation to mutual agreement in doctrine and faith.

Now he that stablisheth us with you in Christ and anointed us is God; who also sealed us and gave us the earnest of the Spirit in our hearts.
(21-22)

God is always true and faithful in all His promises and as soon as He speaks He has always His Amen. But such is our emptiness that we respond to Him with our Amen only when He gives us a sure testimony in our hearts by His Word. This He does through His Spirit and that is what Paul is saying here. He has already told us that God's faithfulness to His call has its fitting counterpart in our acceptance in undoubting faith of the gracious adoption He offers us. It is not surprising that God should remain faithful to His offer, but for us to be equally steadfast in our faith is beyond our human power. But he tells us that God has a cure for our weakness or 'defect' (as they call it), for He corrects our unfaithfulness and strengthens us through His Spirit. So we may come to glorify Him by a firm and constant faith. Paul is here explicitly associating himself with the Corinthians in order to win their favour and create greater unity.

21. *He that anointed us is God.* He says the same thing in different words and speaks about 'anointing' and 'sealing' as well as 'stablishing' and by this double metaphor he illustrates more clearly what he has already said without any figure of speech. For when God pours out upon us the heavenly gift of His Spirit, this is His way of sealing the certainty of His Word on our hearts. Then he puts it a fourth way by saying that the Spirit has been given us as an 'earnest'—a comparison Paul often uses and which is most suitable. As the Spirit is our surety because He testifies to our adoption, and our σφραγίς and seal because He establishes the good faith of the promises, so He is well named our 'earnest' because it is His work to ratify God's covenant on both sides and without Him it would hang in suspense.

Here we should note first the relation that Paul requires between God's Gospel and our faith. Since all that God says is utterly certain, he wants us to receive it into our minds with a firm and unwavering assent. Secondly we should note that, since this degree of certainty is beyond the capacity of the human mind, it is the office of the Holy Spirit to confirm within us what God promises in His Word. That is why He is called Anointing, Earnest, Strengthener, Seal. Thirdly we should note that all who do not have the witness of the Holy Spirit, so that they answer Amen to God when He calls them to a sure hope of salvation, have no right to be called Christians.

But I call God for a witness upon my soul, that to spare you I forbare to come unto Corinth. Not that we have lordship over your faith, but are helpers of your joy: for by faith ye stand. (23-24)

CHAPTER TWO

But I determined this for myself that I would not come again to you with sorrow. For if I make you sorry, who then is he that maketh me glad, but he that is made sorry by me? (1-2)

1.23. *But I call God for a witness.* Now at last he begins to explain why he has changed his plans. Till now he has merely been repelling the false allegations of his enemies but when he says that *he spared them* he he is, by implication, throwing the blame back on them and reminding them that it would be unfair if he were to suffer because of their fault, even more unfair if they were to let him suffer and most unfair of all if they were to accept such an unjustified allegation and make an innocent man suffer for their sin. He spared them by not coming because if he had come he would have been forced to rebuke them more severely, and so he chooses rather to leave them to come to their senses before his coming that there may be no need for a more drastic remedy. This attitude shows in Paul a more than fatherly gentleness towards the Corinthians for it was a sign of great indulgence not to take an opportunity to rebuke them when he had good cause to be angry with them.

He puts this in the form of an oath to make it clear that he has not invented some excuse for not coming. For the matter was of some consequence in itself and it was of the greatest importance that he should be entirely free of all suspicion of falsehood or pretence. There are two things that make an oath legitimate and godly—the occasion and the intention. By the occasion I mean when an oath is not taken rashly in mere trifles or matters of no consequence but only in connexion with something really important. By the intention I mean that there should be regard not for private advantage but for God's glory and the good of the brethren. We should always remember that the purpose of an oath is to promote God's glory and help our neighbours in a just cause.

We should also observe the form of his oath, how first he calls on God to be his witness and then adds '*upon my soul*'. In things that are doubtful or obscure where human knowledge fails us we turn to God that He who alone is Truth may bear witness to the truth. By saying 'upon my soul' he means, 'May God punish me if I lie.' Even if this is not explicitly stated it is always to be understood in connexion with an oath because, if we are unfaithful, God remains faithful and will not deny Himself so that He will not allow the profanation of His name to go unpunished.

1.24. *Not that we have Lordship.* Here he is anticipating a possible objection for it might be said to him, 'Why are you so passionately angry that your very glance makes men tremble? This is not the earnestness of a Christian pastor but the rage of a cruel tyrant.' Paul meets this objection first indirectly by saying that it is not so, and then directly by claiming that it was his fatherly disposition towards them that made him treat them so harshly. When he says that he is not the master of their faith, he shows that such an exercise of lordship would be unjust and intolerable and would amount to tyranny over the Church. Faith should be completely free of any bondage to men. We should note well who it is that says this, for, if ever any mortal man had a right to claim such lordship, Paul was he. Thus we conclude that faith should have no master but the Word of God and is not subject to human control. Erasmus has noted that if we add the Greek particle ἕνεκα the sentence can be taken to mean 'not that we exercise lordship over you in respect of your faith', but this has almost the same meaning for he is saying that spiritual lordship belongs to none but God alone. This is always a settled principle—that pastors have no special lordship over men's consciences because they are ministers and helpers and not lords.

What then does he leave for himself and others to do? He speaks of being *'helpers of your joy'*—by which I take him to mean happiness. He contrasts this joy with the terror that is awakened by the cruelty of tyrants and by false prophets who act like tyrants in that 'they rule with rigour and with force', as Ezekiel says (34.4). He shows that his relationship to the Corinthians has been quite different for he has never claimed any rule over them but has sought to establish them in peace, free and full of gladness.

For by faith ye stand. His reason for adding this is usually passed over in silence or insufficiently explained. In my view he is still arguing from opposites. For if the nature and result of faith is to give us such support that we are able to stand on our own feet, it is absurd that it should be subject to men. Thus that unfair domination of which he says he has never been guilty is completely ruled out.

2.1. *But I had determined this.* Whoever divided the chapters made an unsuitable break here, for now at last the apostle is explaining in what way he has spared them. 'I had determined', he says, 'not to come to you any more in sorrow, i.e. to make you sorrowful by my coming.' For he had come to them once through a letter by which they had been severely mortified. And so, until they came to their senses, he was unwilling to visit them in case he should be forced to grieve them again by his presence. He preferred to allow them a longer time for repentance. The word ἔκρινα must be treated as a pluperfect; Paul is explaining a delay that has already taken place and so is referring to a decision he took some time ago.

2. *For if I make you sorry.* Here we have proof of what he has just said. No man willingly brings sorrow upon himself and Paul says that he has such a fellow-feeling with the Corinthians that he cannot be joyful unless they are happy as well. Further, he says that they are the source and the authors of his joy and they could not be that if they were sorrowful. If pastors feel like that towards their people, it will be the best way of keeping them from alarming and frightening those they ought to be encouraging with kind friendliness. For from this there springs an excessively sour severity so that we do not rejoice in the welfare of the Church as much as we ought.

> And I wrote this very thing, lest, when I came I should have sorrow from them of whom I ought to rejoice; having confidence in you all, that my joy is the joy of you all. For out of much affliction and anguish of heart I wrote unto you with many tears; not that ye should be made sorry, but that ye might know the love which I have more abundantly unto you. But if any hath caused sorrow, he hath caused sorrow, not to me, but in part (that I press not too heavily) to you all. (3-5)

3. *And I wrote this very thing.* He has just explained how he has delayed his coming so as not to come a second time in sorrow and severity, and now he also tells them that he came the first time in sadness by a letter so that they should not feel the full rigour of his severity when he was present in person among them. Thus they have no cause to complain of the sadness they felt then, for, in inflicting it, he was considering their welfare. He goes even further and tells them that when he wrote he did not want to distress them or show indignation towards them but rather give proof of his love and concern for them. In this way he removes the impression of harshness that his letter may have conveyed and shows that his intentions were kindly and full of goodwill. But when later he goes on to admit a severity that he here denies he seems to contradict himself. My answer is that there is no inconsistency because he never says that his ultimate aim was to grieve the Corinthians; it is only the method he adopts to bring them to their true joy. Here he is referring only to this ultimate aim and he does not mention till later the way of achieving it, which is not so acceptable.

Having confidence. He tells the Corinthians of his confidence in them to convince them of his goodwill towards them. Hatred begets ill-will but shared joy implies perfect love. But if the Corinthians do not live up to Paul's confidence in them, they will shamefully disappoint him.

4. *For out of much affliction.* Here he brings forward a second explanation to show that he was not as harsh as he seemed. Those who take pleasure in mocking other people's distress and thus prove their own heartlessness are unendurable but Paul declares that his own attitude has been quite different. 'It was intensity of grief', he says, 'that forced me to write as I did.' Who would not excuse and take in good part what is prompted by such grief, especially as his distress was not for himself but was caused by them and he does not give vent to that grief in order to relieve himself and burden them but rather to show them his love? That is why the Corinthians should not take offence at the severity of his rebuke.

He mentions *tears* which in a brave and courageous man are a sign of great distress. From this we see in what sort of spirit godly and holy reproofs and admonitions should be administered. For there are many noisy scolders who display an amazing fervour in denouncing and raging against other people's faults and yet are untouched at heart so that they seem to take pleasure in exercising their throat and lungs. But it belongs to a godly pastor to weep within himself before he makes others weep, to suffer in his own secret heart before he gives any open sign of his wrath and to keep to himself more grief than he causes to others. We must take note of Paul's tears which by their abundance testify to the tenderness of his heart which was more heroic than the ironhearted hardness of the Stoics. For the more tender love is, the more it is worthy of praise.

The adverb translated *more abundantly* can be taken as a comparative. Then it implies a complaint against the Corinthians that they do not return Paul's love, for their love for him is cold while his for them is warm. I interpret it more simply to mean that Paul is commending his love to them in order that this assurance may soften any severity there may be in his words.

5. *But if any hath caused sorrow.* He offers a third explanation to lessen the offence he may have caused—that he is sharing their grief with them and that the cause of it is to be sought elsewhere. 'You and I', he says, 'share the same sorrow and someone else is to blame.' But even of this other he speaks quite gently for he says 'if anyone' without pressing his accusation against any individual. Some, however, take Paul's meaning to be as follows, 'The man who caused me distress has offended against you as well. For you ought to have grieved with me but I have been left to grieve almost alone, but I do not say quite alone that I may not be too hard upon you all.' Taken this way the second clause would be a correction of the first. But Chrysostom's interpretation is much more apt, for he reads the sentence as one continuous

statement, 'That man has not grieved me only but almost all of you.' I differ from Chrysostom only over the expression 'in part'. I take it to mean 'in some measure'. I know that Ambrose renders it 'part of the saints' on the ground that the church at Corinth was divided, but that is more ingenious than sound.

> *Sufficient to such a one is this punishment which was inflicted by the many; so that contrariwise ye should rather forgive him and comfort him, lest by any means such a one should be swallowed up with his overmuch sorrow. Wherefore I beseech you to confirm your love toward him. For to this end also did I write, that I might know the proof of you, whether ye are obedient in all things. But to whom ye forgive anything, I forgive also: for what I also have forgiven, if I have forgiven anything, for your sakes have I forgiven it in the sight of Christ; that no advantage may be gained over us by Satan: for we are not ignorant of his devices.*
> (6-11)

6. *Sufficient to such a one.* He now extends his clemency even to the man who had sinned more gravely than the rest, and on whose account he had been angry with them all because they had condoned his sin. The fact that he is ready to pardon a man who had deserved a greater punishment is a clear demonstration to the Corinthians of how much Paul dislikes excessive severity. Not that he takes up this attitude just for their benefit for he was naturally of a forbearing disposition. Still the Corinthians ought to see in this proof of his great humanity. Besides he does not merely show how indulgent he is prepared to be but tells them also to receive the sinner back with the same gentleness.

But we should consider this matter in a little more detail. It concerns a man who had defiled himself by an incestuous marriage with his stepmother. This was an intolerable offence and Paul had ordered the man to be excommunicated. He had also rebuked the Corinthians severely for encouraging this sin by concealing it and tolerating it so long among them. From this passage it appears that having been warned by the Church the man repented, and so Paul now gives orders that he should be pardoned and supported by their comfort. The passage should be carefully noted, for it teaches with what impartiality and mildness the Church's discipline is to be exercised in order that it may not be unduly severe. Severity is required in order that wicked men may not be made more bold by being allowed to go unpunished —for this is rightly said to be an enticement to sin. But on the other hand there is a danger that a man who is disciplined will fall into despair so that the Church must practise moderation and be ready to pardon anyone as soon as it is sure that he has sincerely repented. In my view the bishops of the early Church lacked wisdom in this matter and no excuse can be found for them, but we should take notice of their mistake that we may learn to avoid it. For Paul it was enough that a sinner should repent and then he could be reconciled to the Church but they took no account of repentance but decreed canons demanding a period of penance lasting three years or seven years or sometimes even for life and by these they excluded poor unhappy men from the fellowship of the Church. A sinner so treated tends either to be further estranged from the Church or to be driven into hypocrisy. Even if this practice were more acceptable in itself, I could not approve of it because it departs from the method of dealing with sinners commanded by the Holy Spirit, which the apostle here lays down.

7. *Lest he should be swallowed up with overmuch sorrow.* The purpose of excommunication in relation to the person who is at fault is that he should be overcome by a sense of his sin, humbled before God and the Church and brought to ask for pardon with genuine remorse and confession of his guilt. The man who has come thus far needs comfort rather than reproof and to go on treating him harshly is not discipline but cruel abuse. We must therefore be extremely careful not to press our discipline beyond this limit. There is nothing more dangerous than to give Satan a chance of reducing a sinner to despair. Whenever we fail to comfort those that are moved to a sincere confession of their sin, we play into Satan's hands.

9. *For to this end also did I write.* He anticipates an objection that could be brought against him. For someone might say, 'What then did you mean by being so angry with us for not taking any action against this man? To change suddenly like this from severe judge to defender, is not this the sign of a man who cannot make up his own mind?' Such an impression might greatly detract from Paul's authority but his answer is that he has now got what he wanted, satisfaction has been made to him so that now his anger must give way to clemency. Now that their carelessness has been corrected there is no reason why they should not show mercy and restore the man who is prostrate and cast down.

10. *But to whom ye forgive anything.* The more easily to win their favour, he gives his approval to the pardon they have granted, as if to say, 'Do not hesitate to pardon him; I promise to confirm whatever you do and I now give my consent to your decision to forgive him.' He goes on to say that he does this for their sakes but also sincerely and from the heart. He has already proved how concerned he was for this man's salvation; he now declares that he willingly gives the Corinthians his approval.

For '*in the sight of Christ*' some prefer to read 'in the person of Christ' because in bringing about this reconciliation Paul was acting in Christ's stead and so did represent His person. But I think it more likely that he is simply declaring that his forgiveness is sincere and without pretence. He usually uses this phrase to indicate pure and unfeigned sincerity. If anyone still prefers the other reading, it should be noticed that the person of Christ is mentioned because there is nothing that should more incline us to mercy.

11. *That no advantage may be gained over us by Satan.* This could be taken to refer to what he has just said about excessive sorrow. For one of Satan's worst tricks is to deprive us of all consolation and then swallow us up in an abyss of despair. This is how Chrysostom interprets the passage. I prefer to relate it to Paul and the Corinthians. Satan was ensnaring them into a twofold danger—the danger of being too hard and severe and the danger of letting dissension arise among themselves. For it often happens that in their zeal for correction men are betrayed into a Pharisaical severity that casts the poor sinner down rather than heals him. But in my view Paul is here concerned more with the second danger, for if he had not to some extent deferred to the wishes of the Corinthians, Satan would have strengthened his position by provoking a dispute between them.

We are not ignorant of his devices. In other words: 'We know from the Lord's forewarning that his most frequent trick, when he cannot hurt us openly, is to surprise us by a secret attack when we are off our guard. Since we are aware that he is going to attack us by indirect methods and make secret attempts upon us, we must look well ahead and see that no hurt befall us. He uses the word 'devices' in the same sense as the Hebrew זִמָּה but with a bad sense, meaning the artful schemes and tricks of which believers ought to be aware, and will be if they allow the Spirit of God to rule in them. In short since God has both warned us that Satan will marshal all his forces to break in upon us and has shown us the methods he will use, it is for us to be ready to meet him so that he may find no chink in our armour.

> *Now when I came to Troas for the gospel of Christ, and when a door was opened unto me in the Lord, I had no relief for my spirit, because I found not Titus my brother: but taking my leave of them, I went forth into Macedonia. But thanks be unto God, which always leadeth us in triumph in Christ, and maketh manifest through us the savour of his knowledge in every place. For we are a sweet savour of Christ unto God, in them that are being saved, and in them that are perishing; to the one a savour from death unto death; to the other a savour from life unto life. And who is sufficient for these things? For we are not as the many, adulterating the word of God: but as of sincerity, but as of God, in the sight of God, speak we in Christ.* (12-17)

12. *When I came to Troas.* By giving this account of what he has been doing recently, the places he has visited and the route he has followed, he confirms even more strongly what he said above about his proposed visit to Corinth. He says that he came from Ephesus to Troas for the sake of the Gospel and he would not have gone that way to Achaia unless he had wished to pass through Macedonia. But when he did not find Titus, whom he had sent to Corinth, at Troas and thus did not obtain from him the information he was expecting about the state of the Corinthian church, although there was great scope and opportunity for him to do useful work there, he set all that aside and went into Macedonia eager to see Titus. It is a great proof of his very special affection for the Corinthians that his concern for them would not let him rest anywhere, not even in a place that offered great hope of success, till he had news of them. It is clear from this why he delayed his coming; it was because he did not want to come until he had spoken with Titus. Then later from what Titus told him he realized that the time for his visit had not yet arrived. Thus it is clear that Paul loved the Corinthians so much that for their sakes he was ready to modify his travelling arrangements and journey many extra miles and he came to them later than he had promised, not because he had forgotten his pledge or rashly changed his mind or been irresolute in his intentions, but because delay would be better for them.

A door was opened unto me. I have already dealt with this metaphor in the last chapter of I Corinthians; he means that an opportunity of furthering the Gospel had presented itself. Just as an open door makes an entrance possible, so the Lord's servants make progress when opportunity is given them. The door is shut when there is no hope of success. Thus when the door is shut we have to go a different way rather than wear ourselves out in vain efforts to get through it but, when an opportunity for edification presents itself, we should realize that a door has been opened for us by the hand of God in order that we may introduce Christ into that place and we should not refuse to accept the generous invitation that God thus gives us.

It may seem that Paul erred in disregarding or at any rate failing to seize this opportunity in Troas and in going on to Macedonia instead. Should he not have devoted himself to the work that lay to his hand instead of merely starting it and then hurrying away elsewhere? My answer is that Paul was never concerned only with one church but always had obligations to many others, and it would not have been right for him to neglect his duty to these others on account of the present prospects of one. Also, because his tie with the church at Corinth was so close, he had a special duty to be ready to come to its assistance. For it is obviously right that he should hold in special affection a church that his own ministry had founded. So in our day it is indeed our duty to serve the whole Church and care for the whole Body, but nevertheless everyone has a stronger and more sacred tie with his own church which he is specially bound to serve. Things in Corinth were going so badly that Paul was more than usually anxious about their outcome and, in these circumstances, it is not surprising that his anxiety should make him let pass an opportunity that otherwise he could not have neglected, since he could not be everywhere at once. In any case it is not likely that he stirred an inch from Troas till he had provided a substitute to take advantage of the 'open door' in his place.

14. *But thanks be unto God.* Here he is once again glorying in the success of his ministry and pointing out that he has not been idle in any of the places he has visited but there is no harm in this boasting since he begins it with thanksgiving and returns to it later, as we shall see. He does not celebrate his achievements out of any desire to glorify himself and he is not like the Pharisees who make a show of thanking God while within they are puffed up with pride and arrogance, but rather he sincerely desires that everything worthy of praise in his work should be acknowledged to proceed from God alone, that His power only may be extolled. Also he sings his own praises for the good of the Corinthians, that when they hear how he has served God with such success in other places, they may be ready to admit that his work among them has not been in vain and may learn to respect a ministry which God has made so glorious and so fruitful everywhere. For it is sin to despise or think lightly of something that God so greatly honours. Nothing was more harmful to the Corinthians than their mistaken views of Paul's apostleship and doctrine and nothing could be more to their advantage than to hold both in honour. Many had begun to disparage him and so he had a duty to break his silence. In addition he is contrasting this holy boasting with the maliciousness of his opponents.

Which always leadeth us in triumph. If you take the verb literally it will mean 'who triumphs over us' but Paul means something different from the common meaning of this phrase in Latin. Prisoners are said to be led in triumph when to disgrace them they are bound in chains and dragged before the chariot of the conqueror. But Paul means that he had a share in the triumph that God was celebrating because it was through his work that it was won, just as the chief lieutenants shared the general's triumph by riding on horseback beside his chariot. Thus since all ministers of the Gospel fight under God's banner and win for Him the victory and the honour of a triumph, He honours each of them with a share in His triumph according to his rank in the army and the efforts he has made. Thus they hold a triumph, but it is not their own but God's. He adds *in Christ*, since it is in His person that God Himself triumphs for on Him He has conferred all the glory of His kingdom (*imperium*). If anyone prefers to render this phrase as 'who triumphs through us', that also suits his meaning well.

The savour of his knowledge. The triumph was this, that through Paul God was powerfully and gloriously at work, filling the world with the health-giving 'savour' of His grace, as by his teaching he brought some to the knowledge of Christ. He takes the metaphor of the 'savour' further, using it to bring out both the pleasant sweetness of the Gospel and its power and efficacy in breathing life into men. Paul is also reminding them that his own preaching is so far from being savourless that by its very savour it brings souls to life. From this we may learn that the only way to make right progress in the Gospel is to be attracted by the sweet fragrance of Christ so that we desire Him enough to bid the enticements of the world farewell.

He says '*in every place*' to emphasize that he has some success and reward for his work everywhere that he goes. The Corinthians knew in how many places Paul had already sown the seeds of the Gospel, and he now tells them that from the first to the last it has been greatly blessed in them all.

15. *We are a sweet savour of Christ.* He now applies the same metaphor he has been using of the knowledge of Christ to the persons of the apostles but its meaning is still the same. As they are called the light of the world because they illuminate men by offering them the Gospel, and not because they shine with any brightness of their own, so here they are called a sweet savour not because they give forth any fragrance from themselves, but because the teaching that they bring is fragrant enough to fill the whole world with its sweet smell. It is clear that this commendation applies to all ministers of the Gospel, for wherever there is pure and unfeigned preaching of the Gospel, there this strong savour that Paul mentions here will be found. At the same time Paul is here speaking specially of himself and his associates and is making a virtue out of what his detractors alleged to be a fault. It was because many opposed and hated him that some in Corinth were beginning to despise him. But his reply to this is that faithful and sincere ministers of the Gospel have a sweet savour before God not only when they quicken souls by the fragrance of salvation but also when they bring death to unbelievers; thus the fact that the Gospel is opposed should not make us value it any less. Both savours, he says, are agreeable to God, both that by which the elect are recreated unto salvation and that by which the reprobate are tormented. This is a notable passage from which we may learn that whatever the results of

our preaching may be, it is pleasing to God provided only that the Gospel is preached and our obedience is acceptable to Him. The good name of the Gospel is in no way brought into disrepute by the fact that it does not profit all. For God is glorified when it brings about the ruin of the reprobate and so this must happen. And if anything is a sweet savour to God it ought to be so to us also, that is, we should not be offended if the preaching of the Gospel does not result in the salvation of all who hear it, but should think it quite enough if it promotes God's glory by bringing to the reprobate a just condemnation. Even if the heralds of the Gospel are in bad odour in the world, because their success is not always as great as they would wish, they have the choice consolation of knowing that they waft to God an incense of sweet fragrance and that what is offensive in the world's nostrils is a sweet savour to God and His angels.

He lays great emphasis on the word *savour*. It is as if he had said, 'The power of the Gospel is so great that it either quickens or kills not only by its taste but by its very smell. Whether the outcome be life or death, it is never preached in vain.' But the question arises how this can be consistent with the nature of the Gospel which he defines a little later as 'the ministry of life'. The answer is easy: the Gospel is preached unto salvation, for that is its real purpose, but only believers share in this salvation; for unbelievers it is an occasion of condemnation, but it is they who make it so. Thus Christ came not into the world to condemn the world—there was no need for that since we were all condemned already without Him. Yet He sends the apostles not just to loose but also to bind, not just to remit sins but also to retain them. He is the light of the world and yet He blinds unbelievers; He is the foundation stone, yet to many He is a stone of stumbling. But the proper function (*proprium officium*) of the Gospel is always to be distinguished from what we may call its accidental function (*ab accidentali*), which must be imputed to the depravity of men by which life is turned into death.

16. *And who is sufficient for these things?* Some think that this exclamation is inserted here to guard against arrogance, for he is saying that to prove himself a good apostle of Christ is a task beyond human power and is thus ascribing the praise to God. Others think he is referring to the scarcity of good ministers. I think that there is here an implied contrast which he goes on to make more explicit so that it is as if he had said, 'Profession is common and many boast of it but to have the thing itself is a very rare and distinguished excellence. I claim nothing for myself that I will not be found to possess, if I am put to the test.' Since all who exercise the office of teacher claim the honour due to it, Paul distinguishes himself from the other teachers who had little or

nothing of the Spirit's power by claiming for himself a special excellence.

17. *For we are not as the many*. Now he makes the contrast between himself and the false apostles more explicit, both in order to explain it in greater detail and to exclude them from the credit he has claimed for himself. 'I have a right', he says, 'to speak in glowing terms of my apostleship and I have no fear of being found guilty of vanity, if trial is made. But there are many who falsely make the same claims for themselves but who will be found to have nothing in common with me, for they *adulterate the word of God* which I minister in all good faith and sincerity for the upbuilding of the Church.' I do not think it likely that those who are here reproved were preaching doctrines that were openly wicked or false. More probably they were, either for gain or out of ambition, corrupting the use of right doctrine so that no power remained in it. This he calls *adulterating*. Erasmus prefers the rendering 'trading upon'. The Greek verb καπηλεύειν derives from the malpractices of traders or innkeepers in adulterating their wares to fetch a higher price. I do not know whether the verb *cauponari* had this meaning in Latin or not. But the contrast Paul is drawing here makes it quite clear that what he wants to express is a corruption of doctrine that consisted not in departing from the truth but in propounding it with a false purpose and without genuine sincerity. For the doctrine of God can be corrupted in two ways: directly, when it is mixed with falsehood and lies and so is no longer the pure and genuine doctrine of God but is given out falsely under that name; and indirectly when, though its purity is retained, it is twisted this way and that in order to please men and deformed by unworthy attempts to use it to curry favour. Thus there are some whose teaching contains nothing ungodly but who seek the world's approval by a display of cleverness or eloquence or are ambitious for some position or grasp after filthy lucre and so corrupt the doctrine itself, by wrongfully abusing it to serve their own evil ends. I therefore prefer to keep the word 'adulterate' because it explains better what usually happens when men play games with the sacred Word of God and change it to serve their own convenience. They cannot but degenerate from the truth and preach a Gospel that is to some extent spurious and adulterated.

But as of sincerity. The word 'as' is superfluous here, as in many other places. Paul is contrasting the corruption he has already mentioned with a purity that can be taken as applying both to the character of the preaching and the motives of the preacher, but in my view chiefly to the latter. Secondly, he contrasts the corruption with his own faithful and conscientious ministry, for he faithfully delivers the Gospel to the Church from hand to hand, as they say, this being the work to which he has been commissioned and with which he has been entrusted by God. Thirdly, he adds a reminder of God's presence. If a man bears these three things in mind, he is in no danger of intending to corrupt God's Word. First, we must be motivated by a true zeal for God; second, we must remember that it is His work we are doing and must introduce only what has come from Him; third, we must remember that He sees everything we do and learn to refer everything to His judgment. *In Christ* means much the same as 'according to Christ'. Erasmus' rendering, 'by Christ' is not what Paul intends.

CHAPTER THREE

Are we beginning again to commend ourselves? or need we, as do some, epistles of commendation to you or from you? Ye are our epistle, written in our hearts, known and read of all men; being made manifest that ye are an epistle of Christ, ministered by us, written not with ink, but with the Spirit of the living God; not in tables of stone, but in fleshly tables of the heart. (1-3)

1. *Are we beginning again?* Another objection against Paul seems to have been that he was too fond of rehearsing his own achievements—a charge brought by those who were annoyed that his superior excellence kept them from gaining the glory they wanted for themselves. In my view, they had already found fault with the first epistle because in it he was unrestrained in singing his own praises. To *commend* here means to indulge in vain and immoderate boasting, or at least to proclaim one's own virtues for selfish reasons. Paul's detractors had a plausible excuse for their complaint as it is indeed a disgusting thing to be for ever blowing one's own trumpet. But Paul could plead the excuse of necessity, that he was boasting only because he had to. His purpose in doing so freed him from all blame, for his sole concern was to keep the honour of his apostleship unimpaired for the edification of the Church, Had not the honour of Christ been at stake, Paul would without difficulty have allowed an attack on his own reputation to pass unanswered. But he saw that a lessening of his authority among them would do the Corinthians great harm. He starts therefore by taking notice of their accusation, thus letting them know that he is not entirely ignorant of the talk and gossip that is going the rounds among them.

Or need we. His answer is in the first place directed more to the people making the charge than to the charge itself, although he will later give a sufficient answer to it too. But now he reproves their maliciousness in taking offence because sometimes, reluctantly and under pressure, he has mentioned the grace God has conferred upon him, when at the same time they are going round everywhere begging letters stuffed entirely with flattering commendations. He says that he has no need of a verbal commendation since his deeds commend him fully. He shows that they have a hungry greed for glory, since they have pushed themselves forward by courting men's support. In this way he elegantly and appositely refutes their charge. We are not, however, to conclude from this that it is absolutely wrong to receive letters of recommendation, provided they are put to a good use. For Paul himself recommended many and he would not have done so if it had been wrong. Two things are required here, first that the commendation should not be gained by flattery but consist of an unadorned testimony, and, secondly, that it should not be given to procure any man's advancement but should serve only to advance the kingdom of Christ. That is why I said that Paul was concerned with those who had attacked him with their false charges.

2. *Ye are our epistle.* It is very astute of him to say that his claim to glory is based upon the salvation of the Corinthians, as if he had said, 'As long as you are Christians, I shall have sufficient recommendation. Your faith commends me because it is the seal of my apostleship.'

When he says *written in our hearts* he can be taken to refer to Silvanus and Timothy and then the meaning will be, 'We are content to leave the actual results of our labours to commend us; the commendations won by others flutter before men's eyes but ours has its seat in the conscience.' Or we may take it to refer in part to the Corinthians, in this sense, 'Those that seek recommendations from others have not in their consciences what they carry about on paper, and those who recommend others often do so with more indulgence than good judgment, but we have a testimonial to our apostleship inscribed on men's hearts.'

Known and read. This could also be rendered 'known and acknowledged' since the verb ἀναγινώσκεσθαι is ambiguous, and, in my view, that might be more suitable but I did not wish to depart from the received text unless I had to. The reader should consider for himself which rendering is preferable. If we accept 'acknowledged' there will be an implied antithesis between a plain letter written in obvious good faith and those that are counterfeit. And certainly the context tends to support this interpretation since the epistle of Christ is being contrasted with those that are forged and false.

3. *Ye are an epistle of Christ.* Continuing with the same metaphor, he says that the epistle was written by Christ, because the faith of the Corinthians was His work. He says that it was *ministered* by himself, likening himself, as it were, to the ink and the pen. In other words, he makes Christ the Author and himself the instrument in order that his detractors may understand that they have Christ Himself to deal with if they go on speaking maliciously against His apostle. What follows is intended to increase the authority of this epistle, but in the second clause he is already preparing the way for the comparison between Law and Gospel which is to follow. For he takes this opportunity to pass on a little later to this comparison, as we shall see. The contrasts he draws between *ink* and *Spirit* and *stones* and *hearts* are of great

assistance in making his point clear. To compare ink with the Spirit of God and stones with the heart gives us a fuller explanation than if he had simply mentioned the Spirit and the heart without any contrasting terms.

Not in tables of stone. Paul is alluding to the promises in Jeremiah 31.31 and Ezekiel 36.27 concerning the grace of the new testament. 'I shall make', He says, 'a new covenant with them, not according to the covenant that I made with their fathers, but I shall write my laws on their hearts and in their inward parts shall I write them.' And again, 'I will take away the stony heart from the midst of thee and I will give you a heart of flesh that thou mayest walk in my precepts.' Paul declares that this promise has been fulfilled in his preaching, and it is obvious from this that he is a faithful minister of the new testament—a legitimate commendation of his apostleship. The adjective *fleshly* is not used in a bad sense here but means gentle and teachable in contrast to *stony* which means hard and stubborn, the natural condition of the human heart until it has been subdued by the Spirit of God.

And such confidence have we through Christ to God-ward: not that we are capable of ourselves, to think of anything as from ourselves; but our capability is from God; who also made us capable ministers of a new covenant; not of the letter, but of the spirit: for the letter killeth, but the spirit giveth life. But if the ministration of death, written, and engraven on stones, came with glory, so that the children of Israel could not look stedfastly upon the face of Moses for the glory of his face; which glory was passing away: how shall not rather the ministration of the spirit be with glory? For if the ministration of condemnation is glory, much rather doth the ministration of righteousness exceed in glory. For verily that which hath been made glorious hath not been made glorious in this respect, by reason of the glory that surpasseth. For if that which passeth away was with glory, much more that which remaineth is in glory. (4-11)

4. *And such confidence have we.* Since he has just been commending himself and his apostleship in the highest terms, in order to avoid any appearance of arrogance, he ascribes the whole glory to God, by whom, he says, he has been given all that he has. 'By this boasting', he says, 'I extol not myself but God by whose grace I am what I am.' He adds as usual *'through Christ'* for He is, so to speak, the channel through which all God's blessings flow to us.

5. *Not that we are capable.* This disclaiming of all merit is not the abasement of a pretended modesty but he says what he really feels from the heart. We see that he leaves nothing to man, for almost the least part of any good work is the thought; in other words the thought of a good work does not have the first or even the second share of the

praise and yet he does not allow us even this. Since *to think* is less than to will, how foolish they are who claim for themselves a right will when Paul does not leave them even the power of thinking anything right! The Papists are deceived by the word 'sufficiency' which the Vulgate used in this verse. For they think they have found a way round what Paul says if they agree that man is incapable of forming good intentions, but yet attribute to him a right understanding in his mind which with just a little help from God is able to achieve something by itself. But Paul declares that man lacks not only αὐτάρκειαν but also ἱκανότητα which means competency (*idoneitas* in Latin, if there is any such word). He thus could not go further in stripping man of every good quality.

6. *Who also made us capable.* He had acknowledged himself to be completely insufficient, but now he declares that by God's grace he has been equipped for an office for which before he had been useless. From this we can infer its greatness and difficulty since it cannot be undertaken by anybody who has not been prepared and fashioned for it by God. The apostle's intention is to extol the worth of the Gospel and there is no doubt that he is by implication rebuking the poverty of those who were making magnificent boasts of their gifts when in fact they possessed not one single drop of heavenly grace.

Not of the letter, but of the spirit. He now goes into the comparison between Law and Gospel he has previously touched on. It is not clear whether he took up this discussion because he saw some perverse devotees of the Law at Corinth or for some other reason. Since I can see no evidence that the false apostles at Corinth had confounded Law and Gospel, my own view is rather that having to deal with ineffective babblers seeking favour through sheer garrulity and seeing that by this ostentatious display they were gaining the ears of the Corinthians, his purpose was to show them the chief excellence of the Gospel and the chief recommendation of its ministers, which is the efficacy of the Spirit. For this purpose a comparison between Law and Gospel is of great value and that seems to me to be why he goes into the question here.

At any rate, there is no doubt that by the *letter* he means the old testament and by the *Spirit* the Gospel. For when he has said that he is a minister of the new testament he immediately adds by way of explanation that he is a minister of the Spirit, and with the Spirit he contrasts the letter. We have now to inquire into his reasons for speaking in this way. Great authority has been given to a comment of Origen's to the effect that by the letter we should understand the grammatical and natural sense of Scripture, which he calls the literal sense, and by the Spirit the allegorical sense, which is commonly held to be spiritual. Thus for several centuries it was commonly said and accepted that here Paul is giving us a key for expounding the Scriptures allegorically, whereas in fact nothing could be further from his mind. For by the letter he means an external preaching which does not reach the heart, and by the Spirit lifegiving teaching which is, through the grace of the Spirit, given effective operation in men's souls. Thus the term 'letter' means literal preaching which is dead and ineffective and perceived only by the ear: but the Spirit is spiritual teaching that is not uttered only with the mouth but effectively makes its way with living meaning into men's minds. Paul had in mind the passage in Jeremiah 31.31 which I have already quoted where the Lord says that the Law had been promulgated in words only and was therefore of short duration, because the people had not embraced it from their heart. But He promises the Spirit of regeneration under the rule of Christ to write His Gospel, that is the new testament, on their hearts. Paul now boasts that the fulfilment of this prophecy is to be found in his preaching in order that the Corinthians may acknowledge the worthlessness of all the talk of those vain braggarts who were speaking without the Spirit's power.

But the question arises whether under the old testament God only sounded forth with an external voice and never also spoke inwardly to the hearts of the godly by His Spirit. My first answer is that Paul is here considering what belonged peculiarly to the Law, for although God was at that time working through His Spirit, that did not come about through the ministry of Moses but through the grace of Christ, as is said in John 1.17, 'The law was given by Moses but grace and truth by Jesus Christ.' Certainly God's grace was not inactive all that time, but it is sufficient for this comparison that it was not the peculiar blessing of the Law. For Moses had fulfilled his office when he had delivered the doctrine of life with its added promises and threats. That is why he calls the Law the letter because it is in itself a dead preaching, but he calls the Gospel Spirit because its ministry is living and indeed life-giving.

My second answer is that these things are not affirmed absolutely of the Law or of the Gospel, but only in so far as the one is contrasted with the other, for even the Gospel is not always Spirit. But when the two are being compared, it is true and proper to affirm that it is of the nature of the Law to teach men literally so as not to penetrate beyond their ears but it is of the nature of the Gospel to teach them spiritually because it is the instrument of Christ's grace. This depends on God's appointment for it has pleased Him to manifest the efficacy of the Spirit more in the Gospel than in the Law, for it is the work of the Spirit alone to teach men's minds effectively.

But when Paul calls himself a minister of the Spirit, he does not mean that the grace and power of the Holy Spirit are so bound to his preaching that he could, whenever he wished, breathe out the Spirit along with the words that he spoke. He simply means that Christ has blessed his ministry with His Spirit and so has fulfilled what was prophesied of the Gospel. That Christ should grant His power to a man's teaching is quite a different thing from that man's teaching prevailing in its own strength alone. And so we are ministers of the Spirit not because we hold Him bound or captive and not because at our own whim we can confer His grace upon all or upon whom we please, but because through us Christ enlightens men's minds, renews their hearts and wholly regenerates them. It is because of this bond and conjunction between Christ's grace and man's work that a minister is often given credit for what belongs to God alone. For this is done not out of regard for any mere individual but in the light of the whole dispensation of the Gospel, which consists both of the secret power of Christ and the external work of man.

For the letter killeth. This passage has been distorted and wrongly interpreted first by Origen and then by others, and they have given rise to the most disastrous error that Scripture is not only useless but actually harmful unless it is allegorized. This error has been the source of many evils. Not only did it open the way for the corruption of the natural meaning of Scripture but also set up boldness in allegorizing as the chief exegetical virtue. Thus many of the ancients without any restraint played all sorts of games with the sacred Word of God, as if they were tossing a ball to and fro. It also gave heretics a chance to throw the Church into turmoil for when it was an accepted practice for anybody to interpret any passage in any way he desired, any mad idea, however absurd or monstrous, could be introduced under the pretext of an allegory. Even good men were carried away by their mistaken fondness for allegories into formulating a great number of perverse opinions. But the meaning of this passage is that if the Word of God is offered with the mouth only, it is the cause of death, for it is life-giving only when it is received in the heart. The terms 'letter' and 'Spirit' have nothing to do with methods of expounding Scripture but with its force and fruit. Why teaching that only sounds in the ear without reaching the heart is called death-giving, we shall soon see.

7. *But if the ministration of death.* He now explains more fully the worth of the Gospel, by arguing that God gave the Law great dignity and yet that is nothing compared to the dignity of the Gospel. The Law was adorned with many miracles but here Paul mentions only one of them, the brightness that shone in the face of Moses so as to dazzle the eyes of all. That brightness was a symbol of the glory of the

Law. Arguing from the lesser to the greater, he now declares that it is fitting that the glory of the Gospel should shine with even greater brightness, since it is by far superior to the Law. First, he calls the Law the ministration of death; second, he says that its teaching was written in letters with ink; third, that it was written on tables of stone; fourth, that it was not of perpetual duration but temporary and passing, and, fifth, he calls it again the ministration of condemnation. To make the antithesis complete, Paul would have had to add as many corresponding descriptions of the Gospel, but he has only said that it is the ministration of the Spirit and of righteousness and that it endures for ever. As far as the words are concerned, the comparison is not complete, but it is sufficient to make his meaning clear. For he has already said that the Spirit is life-giving, that men's hearts served instead of stones and their wills instead of ink.

We must now examine briefly these attributes of Law and Gospel, bearing in mind that he is not speaking of the whole doctrine contained in the Law and the prophets nor of what happened to the fathers under the old testament but is taking note only of what belongs peculiarly to the ministration of Moses. The Law was engraved on stones and thus it was literal teaching. This defect had to be corrected by the Gospel, since the Law was bound to be transitory (*fragilis*) as long as it was consigned only to tablets of stone. Thus the Gospel is a holy and inviolable covenant because it was promulgated under the guarantee of the Spirit of God. From this it follows that the Law was a ministration of condemnation and death, for when men are taught of their duty and are told that all who do not satisfy God's righteousness are accursed, they are convicted and found guilty of sin and death. Thus from the Law they receive nothing but this condemnation for there God demands what is due to Him, and yet gives no power to perform it. But by the Gospel men are regenerated and reconciled to God by the free remission of their sins, so that it is the ministration of righteousness and so of life.

But this raises a question. If the Gospel is 'a savour of death unto death' (2.16) to some and Christ is 'a rock of offence' and a 'stone of stumbling set for the ruin of many' (Luke 2.34, I Peter 2.8) why does he say that only the Law brings death when the Gospel does so as well? If we reply that to be the source of death is only accidental (*per accidens*) to the Gospel so that it is the occasion (*materia*) of death rather than the cause, for in its own nature it brings salvation to all, the difficulty is not yet solved since the same can still be said of the Law. For we hear that Moses bore witness to the people that he had set before them life and death (Deut. 30.15) and Paul himself says in Romans 7.10 that the Law has turned out to our ruin not because there was anything wrong with it but because of our sin. Thus since it is accidental (*accidentale*) to both Law and Gospel to bring men condemnation the difficulty still remains.

My answer is, that in spite of this, there still remains a great difference between them. For although the Gospel is an occasion of death to many, it is still rightly called the doctrine of life because it is the means of regeneration and freely offers reconciliation with God. But because the Law only prescribes a rule for good living without reforming men's hearts into the obedience of righteousness and threatens transgressors with everlasting death, it can do nothing but condemn. Or, to put it another way, it is the function of the Law to show us the disease without offering any hope of a cure, and it is the function of the Gospel to provide a remedy for those in despair. Since the Law abandons a man to himself it consigns him to inevitable death, while the Gospel leads him to Christ and thus opens the gates of life. To kill is thus a perpetual and inevitable accident (*accidens*) of the Law for, as the apostle says elsewhere, 'All that remain under the Law are subject to its curse' (Gal. 3.10), but the Gospel does not always kill for in it 'is revealed the righteousness of God from faith to faith' and therefore it is 'the power of God unto salvation to everyone that believeth' (Rom. 1.16-17).

We have still to discuss the last contrast he makes between Law and Gospel, for he says that the Law was but for a time and had to be abolished, but the Gospel abides for ever. There are many reasons why the ministration of Moses should be said to be transient, for the shadows had to vanish at the coming of Christ and the statement that 'The law and the prophets were until John' (Matt. 11.13) applies to much more than shadows. For it means that Christ made an end of the ministration of Moses in so far as its own peculiar properties distinguished it from the Gospel. Finally the Lord declares by Jeremiah that the weakness of the old testament was that it was not written on men's hearts (Jer. 31.32-33). I, for my part, take the abolition of the Law which is in question here, to apply to the whole of the old testament in so far as it is opposed to the Gospel, so as to agree with the statement that the Law and the prophets are until John, for that is what the context requires. Paul is not concerned here merely with ceremonies but is teaching how much more powerfully God's Spirit works under the Gospel than He did formerly under the Law.

So that they could not look. Paul seems to have intended by this an indirect rebuke to those who despised the Gospel as too humble so that it was hardly worth looking directly at it. He points out that the splendour of the Law was so great that the Jews could not bear it. What then are we to think of the Gospel which has a glory that far surpasses the Law in the same way as Christ far surpasses Moses?

v. 10-12]   II CORINTHIANS 3

10. *That which hath been made glorious.* This is not a correction of what he has already said but rather a confirmation, for he means that the glory of the Law is abolished when it brings forth the Gospel. Just as the moon and the stars, though they are themselves bright and spread their light over all the earth, yet vanish before the greater brightness of the sun, so the Law, however glorious in itself, has no glory in face of the Gospel's grandeur. It follows from this that we cannot sufficiently prize or hold in reverence the glory of Christ which shines forth in the Gospel, just as the brightness of the sun shines forth in its rays, and the Gospel is absurdly abused or rather wickedly profaned when the power and majesty of the Spirit are not allowed to shine forth from it to draw up men's hearts and minds to heaven.

> *Having therefore such a hope, we use great boldness (or liberty), and are not as Moses, who put a veil upon his face, that the children of Israel should not look stedfastly on the end of that which was passing away: but their understandings were blinded: for until this very day at the reading of the old testament the same veil remaineth unlifted; which veil is done away in Christ. But unto this day, whensoever Moses is read, a veil lieth upon their heart. But whensoever it shall turn to the Lord, the veil is taken away. Now the Lord is the Spirit: and where the Spirit of the Lord is, there is liberty. But we all, with unveiled face reflecting as a mirror the glory of the Lord, are transformed into the same image from glory to glory, even as from the Lord the Spirit.* (12-18)

12. *Having therefore such a hope.* Here Paul carries his discussion a step further and deals not only with the nature of the Law or with its enduring characteristics, which we have already considered, but also with its abuse. This indeed also belonged to its nature for since it was covered with a veil it was not so clear to the eye and its brightness inspired terror—as Paul also says in Romans 8.15, where he explains how the people of Israel received from it the spirit of bondage unto fear. But here he is referring rather to an extraneous and adventitious abuse of the law. At that time the obstinate rejection of Christ by the Jews was a stumbling block for many weak consciences who were in doubt as to whether they should accept a Christ who was not acknowledged by the chosen people. The apostle removes this difficulty by showing how the blindness of God's people has been prefigured from the beginning in their refusal to look on Moses' face until it was veiled. Just as he has already shown that the brightness of Moses' countenance was a sign of the glory of the Law, so now he teaches that the veil was a sign of the future blindness of the people of Israel. Since Moses represents the Law, by their refusal to look upon him, the Jews gave

46

witness that they had no eyes to behold the Law except when it was veiled. He adds that this veil is not taken away except by Christ and concludes that only those whose minds are turned towards Christ are capable of true understanding. The chief distinction he draws between Law and Gospel is that the brightness of the Law dazzles men's eyes rather than enlightens them but in the Gospel Christ's glorious face is clearly seen. He now openly rejoices that the majesty of the Gospel is not terrifying but gentle, not hidden but intimately accessible to all. The word παρρησίαν means either the exalted greatness of spirit that should be characteristic of all ministers of the Gospel, or the open and clear manifestation of Christ. The second rendering is more likely for he contrasts this παρρησίαν with the obscurity of the Law.

13. *And are not as Moses.* Paul is not concerned with the intentions of Moses. It was his duty to proclaim the Law to his people and without doubt he intended that all of them should understand its true meaning and did not deliberately shroud his teaching in obscurity. It was obscure because the people were blind and since Moses could not renew the minds of his hearers he was content to discharge faithfully the duty laid upon him. In fact, when the Lord commanded him to put a veil between his face and the eyes of the beholders, he obeyed. Thus nothing that is said here is derogatory to Moses since it was not his duty to do more than the function assigned to him required. In addition the dullness or the weak and darkened vision of which Paul is speaking is restricted to unbelievers only for although the Law is wrapped up in figures it does not cease to impart wisdom to babes.

14. *Their understandings were blinded.* He lays the whole blame upon them since it was their blindness that kept them from gaining any advantage from the teaching of the Law. He goes on to add that that veil remains to this day meaning that the blindness did not merely last that one hour but rather prefigured what the condition of the people would be in time to come. It is as if he had said, 'That veil with which Moses covered his face when he gave the Law was a symbol of the future and abiding dullness of the people. So today when the Law is preached to them, in hearing they do not hear and in seeing they do not see. But this should not disturb us as though something new were happening. God has shown long ago under the type of the veil that it would be so.' In case any blame should be attached to the Law, he again repeats that their hearts were covered with a veil.

The veil remains unlifted but is done away in Christ. He tells us why they have remained blind so long in the midst of light. The Law is in itself full of light but we appreciate its clarity only when Christ appears to us in it. The Jews turn their eyes as far away from Christ as they can, so that it is not surprising that they should see nothing when they refuse to look at the sun. The blindness of the chosen people and especially its long continuance is a warning to us not to be puffed up with pride in our reliance on the blessings God has conferred upon us —a point he deals with in Rom. 11.20. The cause of this blindness should keep us from that contempt of Christ which God punishes so severely. And we should learn that without Christ, the sum of righteousness, there is no light even in the Law and in the whole Word of God.

16. *But whensoever it shall turn to the Lord.* This verse has been wrongly translated up till now for both the Latin and the Greek writers thought that it referred to Israel, whereas Paul is speaking of Moses. He has already said that a veil has been placed on the hearts of the Jews when Moses is read and he now adds that as soon as he turns to the Lord, that veil will be taken away. This clearly refers to Moses, that is, to the Law. Since Christ is the end of the Law, to which it ought to be referred, it was turned away in another direction when the Jews excluded Christ from it. Thus as in reading the Law they wander into byways, so the Law itself becomes twisted to them and like a labyrinth, until it is referred to its own end (*ad suum finem*), which is Christ. If therefore the Jews seek for Christ in the Law, the truth of God will appear clearly to them but, as long as they wish to be wise without Christ, they will wander in darkness and never reach the true meaning of the Law. And what is said of the Law applies to the whole of Scripture, for when it is not taken as referring to Christ, its one aim and centre (*ad unicum scopum*) it is distorted and perverted.

17. *The Lord is the Spirit.* This passage also has been badly expounded, as if Paul had intended to say that Christ is of a spiritual nature and it has been taken as equivalent to John 4.24, 'God is Spirit'. But the statement before us has nothing to do with Christ's nature but is concerned only to explain His office. It is connected with what has gone before where we have been told that the doctrine of the Law is literal, and not only dead but the cause of death to us. He now calls Christ the spirit of the Law, meaning that it will come alive and be life-giving only if it is inspired by Christ. Add the soul to the body and you have a living man endowed with understanding and perception and fitted for all the activities of life, but remove the soul from the body and there will remain a useless corpse devoid of all perception. This passage deserves special attention, for from it we can learn how to reconcile David's praises of the Law as 'converting souls', 'enlightening eyes', 'imparting wisdom to babes' (Ps. 19.8) with Paul's statements that seem to contradict them, according to which the Law is 'the ministration of sin and death', 'a letter which does nothing but kill' (II Cor. 3.7). For when the Law is animated by Christ, the things that David says

are truly applicable to it, but if Christ is removed, it is completely as Paul describes it. Thus Christ is the life of the Law.

Where the Spirit of the Lord is. Now he is telling us how Christ gives life to the Law, namely by giving us His Spirit. The word 'spirit' has a different meaning here than in the last verse. There it meant the soul and was applied metaphorically to Christ, but here it means the Holy Spirit whom Christ Himself gives to us. Christ in regenerating us gives life to the Law and shows Himself to be the source of life, just as the soul is the source from which all man's vital functions spring. Christ is therefore, so to speak, the universal soul of all men (*universalis omnium anima*) not as regards His essence, but as regards His grace. Or, to put it another way, Christ is the Spirit because he animates us with the life-giving power of His Spirit.

He mentions also the benefit that we receive from this when he says, '*There is liberty.*' By the word 'liberty' I do not understand only freedom from the slavery of sin and the flesh but also the confidence we receive from His witness to our adoption. This agrees with Rom. 8.15, 'For we have not again received the spirit of bondage to fear etc.' In that passage Paul mentions bondage and fear and the opposites of these are liberty and confidence. Thus we may properly follow Augustine in inferring from this passage that we are by nature the slaves of sin and are liberated by the grace of regeneration. For where there is the bare letter of the Law, there is the lordship of sin, but, as I have said, I interpret the term liberty in a wider sense. It would be possible to restrict the grace of the Spirit, especially to ministers, in order that this statement might correspond to the beginning of the chapter, and there ought indeed to be in ministers a different spiritual grace and a different liberty than in others. But the first interpretation pleases me better, although I have no objection to applying this to everybody according to the measure of his gift. But it is enough that we should observe that Paul is pointing out the efficacy of the Spirit which all of us who have been regenerated by His grace experience to our salvation.

18. *But we all, with unveiled face.* I do not know how it could have occured to Erasmus to apply this only to ministers when it is obviously common to all believers. It is true that the meaning of the verb κατοπτρίζεσθαι is doubtful in Greek for it means sometimes to hold out a mirror to be looked into and sometimes to look into a mirror so presented. The Vulgate has correctly noted that the second meaning is the more suitable here and I have followed its rendering. He says 'we all' so as to include the whole Body of the Church. This is a fitting conclusion to what has gone before, for he is saying that in the Gospel we have an open revelation of God. We shall hear more of this in the fourth chapter.

At the same time he points out both the force of the revelation and our daily progress in it. He uses this similitude of the image in the mirror to make three points: first, that we need not fear obscurity when we approach the Gospel for in it God shows us His unveiled face; second, that this should not be a dead and fruitless contemplation, for through it we should be transformed into God's image; third, that neither of these things happens all at once, but by continual progress we increase both in the knowledge of God and in conformity to His image. That is the meaning of *'from glory to glory'*.

When he adds, *'Even as from the Lord, the Spirit'*, he again reminds us how the whole power of the Gospel depends upon its being made life-giving to us by the grace of the Holy Spirit. The particle of comparison 'as' is not meant to suggest that the phrase is not strictly applicable but rather points to the method of our transformation. Observe that the purpose of the Gospel is the restoration in us of the image of God which had been cancelled by sin and that this restoration is progressive and goes on during our whole life, because God makes His glory to shine in us little by little.

But a question may arise here. Paul says that we behold God's glory with unveiled face and yet he has said in the first epistle (13.12) that we now know God only in a glass darkly. There seems at first sight to be a contradiction, but it is not in fact so. Our present knowledge of God is indeed obscure and feeble in comparison with the glorious vision we shall have at Christ's last appearing. At the same time He does offer Himself to us now, to be seen and openly beheld to the extent that our salvation requires and our capacity allows. Thus the apostle speaks of progress which will be perfection only when Christ appears.

CHAPTER FOUR

Therefore seeing we have this ministry, even as we obtained mercy, we faint not: but we have renounced the hidden things of shame, not walking in craftiness, nor handling the word of God deceitfully; but by the manifestation of the truth commending ourselves to every man's conscience in the sight of God. But and if our gospel is veiled, it is veiled in them that are perishing: in whom the god of this world hath blinded the minds of the unbelieving, that the light of the gospel of the glory of Christ, who is the image of the invisible God, should not dawn upon them. For we preach not ourselves but Jesus Christ as Lord, and ourselves as your servants for Jesus' sake. Seeing it is God, that said, Light shall shine out of darkness, who shined in our hearts, to give the light of the knowledge of the glory of God in the face of Jesus Christ. (1-6)

1. *Seeing we have this ministry.* He now resumes the commendation of his own person from which he digressed into the general argument about the excellence of the Gospel. Having dealt with the nature of the Gospel, he goes on to show what a faithful and sincere minister of that Gospel he himself has been. He has just explained what the true Gospel of Christ is and now he claims that it is this true Gospel that he preaches. 'Seeing', he says, 'we have this ministry'—that is, the ministry whose excellence he has just been extolling in such magnificent terms, whose power and usefulness he has so fully expounded. Thus to avoid any appearance of extolling himself too highly, he first declares that it is not by his own efforts or his own merits that he has reached such a pinnacle of honour, rather he has been advanced to it only by the mercy of God. He makes his meaning stronger by ascribing his apostleship to God's mercy rather than to His grace. *We faint not*—that is, we do not fail in our duty, but fulfil it faithfully.

2. *But we have renounced the hidden things of shame.* In commending his own sincerity he is by implication rebuking the false apostles who by their self-seeking were robbing the Gospel of the power that rightly belonged to it and whose only aim was their own advancement. Thus he indirectly imputes to them the very defects from which he himself claims to be free. By 'the hidden things' or 'the secrets of shame' some understand the shadows of the Mosaic law and Chrysostom takes him to mean the vain show in which his opponents were vaunting themselves. My own view is that the expression refers to all the pretences by which they were adulterating the pure and innate comeliness of the

Gospel. For just as chaste and honourable women are content with the gracefulness of natural beauty and do not resort to artificial adornments, whereas harlots never think themselves well adorned until they have corrupted nature, so it is Paul's boast that he has set forth the pure Gospel whereas others have offered a counterfeit Gospel decked out with unworthy additions. Since they were ashamed of the simplicity of Christ, and even more because they could not excel in the true apostolic virtues, they framed a new gospel similar in many ways to profane philosophy, swollen up with much bombast but lacking the effectual power of the Spirit. These spurious adornments that disfigure the Gospel he calls 'secrets of shame', because the nakedness of those who have recourse to such concealments and disguises must of necessity be dishonourable and disgraceful. But Paul says that he himself rejects and disdains such disguises for the more the face of Christ is seen unveiled in his preaching, the more gloriously it shines. I do not deny that there is also here an allusion to Moses' veil (Exod. 34.33) which he has already mentioned, but the veil that covers the false apostles is of a completely different kind. Moses covered his face because the surpassing splendour of the glory of the Law was too great for tender dim-sighted eyes to bear; but the false apostles put on a veil by way of adornment. If the simplicity of the Gospel were allowed to shine forth, they would be shown up as despicable and ignominious and so they hide their shame under ever so many cloaks and masks.

Not walking in craftiness. There is no doubt that the false apostles took a great delight in the very craftiness that Paul is here reproving, as though it were a great virtue, just as today we see even among those who profess the Gospel some who seem to be more subtle than sincere, more sublime than solid and whose cleverness is mere childishness. But what can be done with them? They love to win a reputation for clever ingenuity and this is a way of winning the applause of the ignorant. We are however told here what Paul thinks of this so-called virtue, for he declares that craftiness is unworthy of the servants of Christ.

Nor handling the word of God deceitfully. I am not sure if this rendering brings out Paul's meaning clearly enough. For the Greek verb δολοῦν means not so much 'to act fraudulently' but rather 'to falsify' after the manner of fraudulent dealers who try to conceal the value of their wares by giving them a false shine. In this passage at any rate the word is used to indicate the opposite of sincere preaching and this agrees with what follows.

By the manifestation of the truth. He claims for himself the commendation of having declared the pure doctrine of the Gospel simply and without pretence and says that he has *every man's conscience* to bear witness to this *in the sight of God*. He has placed the counterfeit teaching of the sophists in opposition to the manifestation of the truth and now he appeals to men's consciences and to the judgment seat of God, whereas his opponents were relying on the mistaken judgments and corrupted feelings of men and were less concerned about being really worthy of praise than about seeming worthy of it. From this we infer that he is drawing a contrast between an appeal to men's consciences and an appeal to their ears. It should be enough for the servants of Christ to have their integrity of conscience approved before God and they should pay no heed to the perverse desires of men or to their vain applause.

3. *But if our gospel is veiled.* It would have been easy to pour scorn on Paul's claim that his preaching is clear, for it had many opponents. But he meets this charge with stern authority by threatening all who do not acknowledge the power of his Gospel and warning them that this is a sign of reprobation and death. It is exactly as if he had said, 'If anyone says that he does not acknowledge that manifestation of Christ of which I boast, by that very fact he clearly proves himself a reprobate, for the sincerity of my teaching is openly and clearly discerned by all who have eyes to see.' Those to whom it is hidden must therefore be blind and lacking in every trace of rational understanding. The conclusion is that the blindness of unbelievers in no way detracts from the clarity of his Gospel; the sun is no less bright because blind men do not perceive its light.

It will be claimed that this applies equally to the Law for in itself it is 'a lamp to guide our feet' (Ps. 119.105) and 'illumines our eyes' (Ps. 19.8) and is veiled only to those who are perishing. I reply that as long as Christ is included in the Law, the sun shines through the midst of the clouds so that men have light enough for their use, but where Christ is disjoined from the Law, there is nothing left but darkness or rather a false appearance of light that dazzles instead of assisting men's eyes.

The fact that he dares to regard as reprobates all who reject his doctrine is evidence of great assurance, but it is right that all who wish to be counted ministers of God should possess a like assurance so that with a fearless conscience they may have no hesitation in citing those who oppose their teaching to appear at the judgment seat of God that they may receive there a sure condemnation.

4. *In whom the god of this world.* He means that no account should be taken of the perverse obstinacy of his opponents. 'They do not see the midday sun', he says, 'because the devil has blinded their understanding.' Nobody of sound judgment can have any doubt that here the apostle is speaking of Satan. Hilary, who had to deal with Arians

who misused this passage in support of their view that Christ was a god, though they denied His true divinity, twists the text to mean that it is God who has blinded the understanding of this world. Chrysostom later followed this rendering in order to avoid conceding to the Manichaeans their dualistic view of two first principles. Why Ambrose also accepted it is not clear but Augustine's reason was the same as Chrysostom's for he also was involved in the dispute with the Manichaeans. This is an example of what can happen in the heat of controversy for if all these men had read Paul's words with a calm mind it would never have occurred to them to twist them into a forced meaning in this way. But being hard pressed by their opponents they were more anxious to refute them than to expound Paul. But what need was there for this anxiety? It was a childish subterfuge for the Arians to argue that because the devil is called the god of this world, the word God as applied to Christ does not express true, eternal and unique divinity. Paul says elsewhere that 'many are called gods' (I Cor. 8.5) and David declares that 'the gods of the nations are demons' (Ps. 96.5). Thus when the devil is called a god because he has dominion over men and is worshipped by them instead of God, how can this detract in any way from the dignity of Christ? As for the Manichaeans this title lends no more countenance to their views than when the devil is called the prince of this world. Thus there is no reason why we should be afraid to interpret this passage as applying to the devil for that can be done without any danger. For if the Arians contend that Christ's divine essence cannot be proved from His being given the name of God any more than the divine essence of Satan can be proved from his being called a god, this quibble is easily disposed of. For Christ is called God absolutely without any qualifying phrase and He is even called 'God blessed for ever'. He is called God who was from the beginning before the creation of the world. But the devil is called the god of this world in exactly the same way as Baal is called the god of those that worship him or the dog is called the god of Egypt. To defend their perverse views the Manichaeans, as I have already said, depend upon other passages of Scripture besides this, but there is no difficulty in refuting them either. They argue not so much about the devil's name as about his power. Because there is attributed to Satan a power of blinding and a dominion over unbelievers, they infer that he by his own ability is the author of all evil so that he is not subject to God's command—as if Scripture did not in many places call the devils the ministers of God, just as much as the angels of heaven, though in a very different way. For as the angels are ministers of God's blessings to our salvation, so the devils execute His wrath. Thus good angels are called principalities and powers but only because they exercise a power God has conferred upon them. In the same way Satan is the prince of this world, not because he has conferred that princely power upon himself or obtained it by his own right or is able to exercise it as his own will, but he has it only in so far as the Lord allows it to him. Thus Scripture does not only mention the good Spirit of God and good angels but also speaks of evil spirits of God. So I Sam. 16.14, 'An evil spirit of God came upon Saul', and again in Ps. 78.49 we read of chastisements inflicted by means of 'evil angels'.

To return to the passage before us, blinding unbelievers is a work common to God and Satan, but the power they each possess is not the same nor is the manner in which it is exercised. I say nothing about the manner now, but Scripture teaches that Satan blinds men not only with God's permission but at His command to inflict His vengeance. So Ahab was deceived by Satan (I Kings 22.21), but Satan could not have done this of himself. Having offered his services to God to do harm, he was sent to be a lying spirit in the mouth of all the prophets (I Kings 22.22). God is thus said to blind men because, having deprived us of the right use of our minds, and of the light of His Spirit, He hands us over to the devil to be reduced to a reprobate mind and gives him the power of deceiving us and thus inflicts just vengeance upon us by the minister of His wrath.

Paul's meaning is therefore that all who do not acknowledge his teaching to be the certain truth of God are possessed of the devil, for it is more severe to call them the devil's slaves than to attribute their blindness to the judgment of God. A little earlier he had judged such people to be worthy of destruction and he now adds that the only reason why they are perishing is that by their own unbelief they have brought ruin upon themselves.

That the light of the gospel should not dawn upon them. This confirms what he has just said, that if anyone rejects his Gospel it is because his own blindness keeps him from accepting it. 'For nothing', he says, 'appears in it but Christ and He does not appear obscurely but shines forth clearly.' He adds that Christ is *the image of God* to make it clear that those he is describing are completely without knowledge of God, for, as John 14.7 says, 'He that knoweth not me knoweth not my Father.' This is why he pronounces such a hard sentence upon those who doubted his apostleship, because they did not behold Christ in his Gospel, though He could be seen plainly there. There is some doubt as to whether '*the gospel of the glory of Christ*' means, according to the Hebrew idiom, 'the glorious Gospel of Christ' or rather 'the Gospel in which Christ's glory shines'. I prefer the second rendering as giving a fuller meaning.

When Christ is called *the image of the invisible God* the reference is not merely to His essence, because He is, as they say, co-essential with the Father, but rather to His relationship to us because He represents the Father to us. The Father is called *invisible* because He Himself is not apprehended by the human mind but He shows Himself to us by His Son and thus makes Himself in a manner visible. I say this because the ancients, in the heat of their conflict against the Arians, over-emphasized the point that the Son is the image of the Father because of the internal secret unity of essence between them and they tended to pass over what was of more practical importance, that He is the image of God to us because He reveals to us things in His Father that would otherwise remain hidden. Thus the word 'image' has reference to us, as we shall see again soon. The adjective 'invisible' is omitted in certain Greek manuscripts but since it is not superfluous I have preferred to retain it.

5. *For we preach not ourselves*. Some take this to be an instance of zeugma[1] and render it thus, 'We do not preach ourselves as lords but the one Son of God whom the Father has set over all things.' I have no objection to this interpretation but I prefer the other rendering, 'We preach not ourselves but Christ' because it is fuller and more emphatic and has almost universal support. Men can preach themselves in other ways than by lording it over others, when, for example, they care more for ostentation than edification, when they desire to be eminent in some way or when they make money out of the Gospel. Ambition and avarice and other such faults in a minister taint the purity of his teaching so that Christ alone is not exalted in it. The man who wishes to preach only Christ must forget himself.

And ourselves your servants. In case anyone should say to him, 'But in fact you have a great deal to say about yourself', he replies that the thing he desires most of all for himself is to be their servant. It is as if he had said, 'When I speak of myself in such exalted terms and, as it seems to you, so boastingly, my aim is that I should serve you profitably in Christ.' If the Corinthians reject this explanation it can only be because they are too proud and ungrateful, and indeed the fact that they have not taken note of the holy love that Paul bore them shows the corruptness of their judgment. But here all pastors of the Church are reminded of their rank and condition for, whatever title of honour they may have to distinguish them, they are nothing more than the servants of believers, for the only way to serve Christ is by serving His Church as well. This is indeed an honourable servitude and preferable to any kind of worldly dominion but it is servitude whose only care is that Christ alone should be exalted unshadowed by any

[1] A figure of speech in which a verb or adjective is applied to two nouns although it is strictly applicable to only one of them. Tr.

rival. Thus it is the duty of a good pastor not only to restrain every desire to domineer but to regard the service of the people of God as the highest honour to which he may aspire. And it is the duty of the people on their side to esteem the servants of Christ, first for the sake of their Master's Majesty and also for the sake of the dignity and excellence of their office so that they may not despise those whom the Lord has set in so high a station.

6. *It is God that said, Light shall shine*. I see that it is possible to expound this passage in four different ways. First, God has commanded the light to shine from the darkness, that is, He has brought the light of the Gospel into the world through the ministry of men who are in their own nature children of darkness. Second, God has caused the light of the Gospel to take the place of the Law which was shrouded in dark shadows and thus has brought light out of darkness. Those who are fond of subtleties could easily accept such explanations but anyone who goes into the matter more closely will readily acknowledge that they do not express the apostle's meaning. The third explanation is that of Ambrose and is as follows: when all was shrouded in darkness, God kindled the light of His Gospel. Men were sunk in the darkness of ignorance when suddenly God shone forth upon them by His Gospel. The fourth explanation is Chrysostom's who thinks that there is an allusion here to the creation of the world. God, who by His Word created light, bringing it, so to speak, out of darkness, has now spiritually illuminated us when we were buried in darkness. This analogy (*anagoge*) between light that is visible and physical and light that is spiritual gives a more pleasing interpretation and there is nothing forced in it, although Ambrose's rendering is also quite suitable. Everyone may use his own judgment.

Shined in our hearts. We should carefully note the twofold enlightening to which he is here referring. For there is first the enlightening of the Gospel and then also that secret enlightening which takes place in our hearts. For as in His creation of the world God has poured forth upon us the brightness of the sun and has also given us eyes with which to receive it, so in our redemption He shines forth upon us in the person of His Son by His Gospel, but that would be in vain, since we are blind, unless He were also to illuminate our minds by His Spirit. Thus his meaning is that God has opened the eyes of our understanding by His Spirit to make us able to receive the light of His Gospel.

In the face of Jesus Christ. Paul has already said that Christ is the image of the Father and when he says here that in His face God's glory is revealed to us his meaning is the same. This is an important passage from which we may learn that God is not to be sought after in His inscrutable majesty (for He dwells in light inaccessible) but is to be known in so far as He reveals Himself in Christ. Thus the attempts of men to know God apart from Christ are ephemeral for they wander from the right way. It is true that at first sight God in Christ seems to be low and abject, but His glory appears to those who have the patience to pass on from the cross to the resurrection. Again we see that in the word *persona*—here rendered 'face'—there is reference to us, because it is more profitable for us to behold God as He appears in His only begotten Son than to investigate His secret essence.

But we have this treasure in earthen vessels, that the exceeding greatness of the power may be of God, and not from ourselves; while we are pressed on every side, yet not straitened; oppressed with poverty, yet not unto destitution; persecuted, yet not forsaken; smitten down, yet not destroyed; always bearing about in the body the dying of Jesus, that the life also of Jesus may be manifested in our body. For while we live we are alway delivered unto death for Jesus' sake, that the life also of Jesus may be manifested in our mortal flesh. So then death worketh in us, but life in you. (7-12)

7. *But we have this treasure.* Those who heard Paul boasting so highly of the excellence of his ministry and saw by contrast how ignoble and abject he was in the eyes of the world, would think his boasting childish and himself foolish and ridiculous, as long as they based their judgment on the meanness of his person. Wicked men especially fastened on this as a pretext that would help them to bring everything about Paul into contempt. But with the greatest skill he turns the very thing that in the eyes of the ignorant seemed most to detract from the glory of his apostleship into a means for advancing it. First he uses the metaphor of treasure which is not usually stored in a splendid and richly decorated box but rather in some cheap container worth nothing at all. He then adds that in this way the power of God is more greatly glorified and more clearly seen. It is as if he had said, 'Those who use the abasement of my person as an excuse for detracting from the honour of my ministry are unjust and unreasonable judges, for a treasure does not become less valuable through being deposited in a vessel of no value. In fact it is common practice for great treasures to be stored in earthenware pots. Thus they do not realize that things have been so ordered by the special providence of God that there should be in ministers no appearance of excellence in order that no greatness of theirs should obscure the power of God. Since therefore the abject condition of ministers and the outward abasement of their persons give God occasion for glory, it is foolish and wrong to measure the worth of the Gospel by the person of the minister.' But Paul is speaking here not only about the condition of mankind in general but about his own

personal situation, and yet it is true that all mortal men are but earthen vessels. Take the most eminent man you can find, someone wonderfully endowed with all the ornaments of birth, intellect and fortune and yet, if he is a minister of the Gospel, he will be an unworthy and earthen depository of an inestimable treasure. Paul is however thinking of himself and his associates who were often held in contempt just because they had nothing of outward show.

8. *While we are pressed on every side.* This is added by way of explanation, to show that his abject condition, so far from detracting from God's glory, rather serves to advance it. 'For', he says, 'we are reduced to straits but at length the Lord opens a way of escape; we are oppressed with poverty, but the Lord comes to our aid. Many foes are in arms against us but in God's keeping we are safe. In a word, though we are brought so low that all seems over with us, yet we do not perish.' The last possibility he mentions is the most serious of all. You see how he turns to his own advantage every charge that the wicked bring against him.

10. *The dying of Jesus.* Now he goes on to a new point, by showing that the very pretext the false apostles were pleading for holding the Gospel in contempt, far from bringing any real contempt upon it, tended rather to make it glorious. For he calls all these things that bring the world's scorn upon him the 'dying' or 'mortification' of Jesus Christ, by which he was being made ready to share in His blessed resurrection. To begin with, the sufferings of Christ, however ignominious in the eyes of men, have more honour with God than all the triumphs of generals and all the pomp of kings. But we must also look to the final outcome, that we suffer with Him in order that we may be glorified with Him. Here he is administering a fitting rebuke to those who in opposition to him were making protestations of their own fellowship with Christ. At the same time he is warning the Corinthians, in case their scorn for Paul's poor and abject appearance should lead them to insult Christ by taking offence at His sufferings which we should hold in the highest honour.

The word 'dying' or 'mortification' has a different meaning here than in many other passages of Scripture. For it often means self-denial, by which we renounce the lusts of the flesh and are renewed into obedience to God. Here it means those afflictions that make us meditate on the end of this present life. For the sake of clarity we may call the former meaning internal mortification and the latter external. By both we are conformed to Christ, directly by the one and indirectly by the other. Paul speaks of internal mortification in Col. 3.5 and in Rom. 6.6, where he teaches that 'our old man is crucified that we may walk in newness of life'. He deals with external mortification in Rom.

8.29 where he teaches that we were 'predestinated by God that we might be conformed to the image of His Son'. Suffering is called the mortification of Christ only in relation to believers for when the wicked endure the afflictions of this present life their fellowship is with Adam, whereas the elect have participation in the Son of God so that all their miseries that are in their own nature curses are made helpful for their salvation. All the sons of God have this in common that they bear about the dying of Christ but the more anyone excels others in the larger measure of his gifts, the nearer he comes to his conformity with Christ.

That the life of Jesus. The best cure for adversity is to know that just as Christ's death was the gate of new life, so we at the end of all our miseries shall come to a blessed resurrection, for Christ has joined us to Himself on condition that if we submit ourselves to die with Him in this world, we shall share His life.

The sentence which next follows can be explained in two different ways. If *delivered unto death* is taken to mean being harassed by continual persecutions and exposed to dangers, then it will refer specially to Paul and those like him who have been openly attacked by the fury of the wicked. In that case *for Jesus' sake* will mean 'for a testimony to Christ'. But since elsewhere to be delivered to death means to have death constantly before our eyes and to live in such a way that our life is really a shadow of death, I have no objection to this passage being understood in this way also so that it refers to all believers, to each in his own way. In Rom. 8.36 Paul himself interprets Ps. 44.22 in this way. In that case 'for Jesus' sake' would mean 'because this condition is imposed on all His members'. Where I have rendered '*while we live*' Erasmus has 'we who live' but my rendering gives a better sense. For Paul means that as long as we are in this world we are more like dead than living men.

12. *So then death.* This is said in irony, because it was not right that the Corinthians should live happily and freely and take their ease in security at the very time when Paul was struggling with infinite hardships. Such a distribution of lots would indeed have been quite unfair and the Corinthians have to be reproved for foolishly trying to make for themselves a Christianity without any cross, and even more for despising Christ's servants because they were not so fastidious. Just as here death means all afflictions or a life full of troubles, so also life in this verse means a prosperous and pleasant condition, as in the proverb 'Life is not merely to live but to live well.'

But having the same spirit of faith, according to that which is written, I believed, and therefore did I speak; we also believe, and therefore also we speak; knowing that he which raised up the Lord Jesus shall raise up us also with Jesus, and shall present us with you. For all things are for your sakes, that the grace, being multiplied through the many, may cause the thanksgiving to abound unto the glory of God. Wherefore we faint not; but though our outward man is perishing, yet our inward man is renewed day by day. For our light affliction, which is of marvellously short duration, worketh in us a marvellous weight of eternal glory (OR *our light affliction worketh for us more and more exceedingly an eternal weight of glory*). *While we look not at the things which are seen, but at the things which are not seen: for the things which are seen are temporal; but the things which are not seen are eternal.* (13-18)

13. *Having the same spirit of faith.* Here he corrects what he has just said in irony. He had represented the lot of the Corinthians as being quite different from his own, not because he thought it was, but because they thought so in their desire for a Gospel that was pleasant and free from every threat of the cross and in their dishonourable despising of him because his lot was too lacking in glory. But now he associates them with himself in hope of the same blessedness. It is as if he had said, 'Although God is sparing you and treating you with greater indulgence, while I am getting harder treatment, this difference between us will not prevent us both from coming at last to the glory of the same resurrection. For men who have the same faith will also have the same inheritance.' Some think that here the apostle is speaking of the holy fathers who lived under the Old Testament and is saying that they share with us in the same faith. This is quite true but is not relevant to the present subject. Here Paul is associating with himself in the fellowship of the same faith not Abraham or the other fathers but rather the Corinthians who were separating themselves from him out of a false ambition. 'However much worse my condition may now appear to be', he says, 'we shall one day have an equal share of the same glory, for we are joined to each other by one faith.' Those who examine the context carefully will agree that this is the correct interpretation. By metonymy he calls faith the spirit of faith, because it is a gift of the Holy Spirit.

According to that which is written. It is this quotation from David that has given rise to the false interpretation I have just mentioned. But the quotation should be taken to refer to the confession of faith rather than to the unity of faith, that is, to what follows rather than to what goes before. Thus, 'Because we have a sure faith in a blessed resurrection, we dare to speak and to preach what we believe, as it is written "I believed, and therefore have I spoken".' This is from Ps. 116.10[1]

---

[1] In the English versions. Calvin quotes the LXX in which it is Ps. 116.1.

where David confesses that being reduced to the last extremity he was so shattered that he almost fell, but quickly regaining his confidence, he overcame the temptation. Thus he begins his psalm, 'I have believed, therefore will I speak', for faith is the mother of confession. Paul stirs himself up to imitate the psalmist and exhorts the Corinthians to do the same. According to the Vulgate he has used the past tense instead of the future, but that is of no consequence. He simply means that believers ought to be brave and undaunted in confessing what they have believed in their hearts. Let now our false followers of Nicodemus see how they falsify the faith by wishing to keep their faith hidden within themselves and quite silent and by boasting of their wisdom because in the whole of their life they do not speak a single word of sincere confession.

15. *For all things are for your sakes.* He now associates himself with the Corinthians not only in the hope of future blessedness but in those very afflictions in which they seem to have no share, for he tells them that he is suffering affliction for their good and it therefore follows that they ought to transfer a share of it to themselves. What Paul says here depends first on the secret communion that the members of Christ have with each other and especially on the mutual relationship and close ties that there ought to be between them. This admonition was especially profitable to the Corinthians and brought with it excellent consolation. For what consolation it is to us that God should deal gently with us in our weakness and let those who are endowed with greater strength bear afflictions for the common good of us all. They were being admonished also that, since they could give Paul no other help, they should at least sustain him by their prayers and their sympathy.

That the grace, being multiplied. He now commends this unity and fellow-feeling among the members of Christ, by showing how it bears fruit in a tendency to advance the glory of God. As is usual with him, he makes 'grace' mean, by metonymy, the blessing of deliverance he has mentioned above, namely that, though he was weighed down, yet he was not in despair and, though he was in poverty, he was not left destitute, that he had, in fact, a continual deliverance from every kind of trouble. 'This grace', he says, 'is multiplied', meaning that it was not confined to himself, so that he alone enjoyed it, but extended further to the Corinthians to whom it was of great advantage. By showing that this multiplication of God's gift should bring forth gratitude to the glory of the Giver, he reminds us how by our carelessness we may lose all the blessings God confers upon us, unless we are prompt and active in giving thanks.

16. *Wherefore we faint not.* Assuming that he has won his case, he now rises to a higher confidence than before. 'There is no reason for

us to lose heart', he says, 'or grow weary under the weight of the cross, since that cross not only brings so much blessedness to me but works for the good of others also.' Thus by his example he encourages the Corinthians to be courageous if at any time they should have to endure the same affliction. Also he puts a check to their sinful insolence by which, under the influence of a false ambition, they valued a man the more highly, the further he was from Christ's cross.

Though our outward man is perishing. Some commentators quite wrongly and foolishly confuse the 'outward man' with the 'old man', but the 'old man' is really quite different, as we have explained in relation to Rom. 6.6. Chrysostom and others are also wrong to restrict the 'outward man' to the body only, for the apostle intended everything that has to do with this present life to be included. He here speaks of two men and we are to think of two kinds of life, an earthly and a heavenly. The outward man is the continuance of our earthly life and consists not only of youth and good health but also of riches, honours, friendships and other such good things. Thus when we suffer decrease or loss of these things, which are needed for the maintenance of our present life, our outward man so far perishes. Since we are too much concerned with these things, as long as everything goes according to our wishes, the Lord takes away from us bit by bit those things that engross our attention and thus calls us back to meditate on a better life. It is necessary that our present life should perish that the inner man may begin to come into his own, for the more earthly life declines, the more heavenly life advances, at least in believers. For the wicked also the outward man decays but there is nothing to make up for it. But in the sons of God this decay is the beginning and almost the cause of their regeneration. He says that this happens daily because God is continually active, stirring us up to think on the life to come. Would that it would take deep root in our minds that we might make continual progress amidst the perishing of the outward man!

17. *Our light affliction is of short duration.* Since our flesh always shrinks from its own destruction, whatever reward may be held out before us, and since we are influenced much more powerfully by our present feelings than by hope of heavenly blessings, Paul reminds us that the afflictions and miseries of the godly have little or no bitterness in comparison with the infinite blessing of eternal glory. He has already said that the corruption of the outward man ought not to grieve us because the renewal of the inward man springs from it. But the corruption is visible and the renewal invisible, and therefore, in order to free us from the fleshly influence of this present life, Paul compares present miseries with coming blessedness. This comparison alone is more than sufficient to fill the minds of the godly with patience and

moderation and keep them from giving way under the heaviness of the cross. Patience is such a difficult thing for us, only because we are stupefied by a short experience of trouble and do not raise our thoughts above. Paul here prescribes the best remedy to keep you from sinking under the pressure of affliction by contrasting with these afflictions the blessedness which is laid up for you in heaven. That comparison makes light what before seemed to be heavy, and brief and momentary what seemed to last for ever.

There is some obscurity in Paul's words here. Both the Vulgate and Erasmus take the words *'more and more exceedingly'* as describing and extolling the greatness of the heavenly glory that awaits believers or, at any rate, they take the phrase along with the verb *worketh*. I have no objection to this but, as my own interpretation is equally suitable, I leave the choice to the reader.

Worketh an eternal weight. Paul does not mean that afflictions invariably have this effect, for in many cases the evils of every kind that weigh men down are more a cause of their greater destruction than a help to their salvation. But since he is concerned here with believers, what is said here applies only to them, for this is the special blessing that God grants to them, that the troubles that all men share make them ready for a blessed resurrection.

The Papists misuse this passage to prove that affliction is the cause of our salvation but this is a very weak argument unless you take 'cause' as being equivalent to 'means', as is often done. We certainly freely grant that we must enter the kingdom of heaven through many tribulations: there is no dispute about that. But our teaching is that the momentary lightness of our afflictions works in us an eternal weight of glory, because all the sons of God are predestined to be conformed to Christ in enduring the cross, and in this way they are made ready to enjoy the heavenly inheritance which is theirs by the free and gracious adoption of God. The Papists however invent meritorious works by which the kingdom of heaven may be acquired. To repeat the same point again briefly, we do not deny that afflictions are the means by which we reach the heavenly kingdom, but we do deny that by afflictions we can merit the inheritance that comes to us only by the gracious adoption of God. The Papists, without thinking, seize hold of one little word and upon it they would build a tower of Babel—that the kingdom of heaven is not the inheritance obtained for us by Christ but a reward that can be earned by our own works. A fuller solution of this problem is to be found in my *Institutes*.

18. *While we look not at the things which are seen.* Note well what it is that will make all the miseries of this world easy to endure; it is that we should transfer our thoughts to the eternity of the kingdom of

heaven. If we look around us, a moment can seem a long time, but when we lift up our hearts heavenwards, a thousand years begin to be like a moment. The apostle's words also mean that, when we look at present things, we are deceived because everything we see is temporal and there is therefore nothing on which we can rest except confidence in a future life. Note the expression, *we look at the things which are not seen*; the eye of faith sees further than all man's natural senses and that is why faith is called 'the seeing of things which are invisible'.

CHAPTER FIVE

For we know that if the earthly house of our tabernacle be dissolved, we have a building from God, a house not made with hands, eternal, in the heavens. For verily in this we groan, longing to be clothed upon with our habitation which is from heaven: if so be that being clothed again we shall not be found naked. For indeed we that are in this tabernacle do groan, being burdened; not for that we would be unclothed, but that we would be clothed upon, that what is mortal may be swallowed up of life. Now he that wrought us for this very thing is God, who gave unto us the earnest of the Spirit. Being therefore always of good courage, and knowing that, whilst we are at home in the body, we are absent from the Lord (for we walk by faith, not by sight); we are of good courage, I say, and are willing rather to be absent from the body, and to be at home with the Lord. (1-8)

1. *For we know.* There now follows an amplification and more detailed explanation of the last point he made. Paul does this to correct our impatience, our shrinking from the cross, our weariness, our contempt for humility and all our pride and fastidiousness and this can only be done by making us despise the world and lift our minds right up to heaven. His argument is in two stages. First he points out the misery of men's lot in this life and then goes on to the supreme and perfect blessedness that awaits believers after death in heaven. Why else should men persist in a mistaken desire for this life except that they deceive themselves into thinking that they are happy in living here? Still, it is not enough to know about the miseries of this life unless we have also in view the blessedness and glory of the life to come. Both bad men and good share the desire to live. And both also are given to groaning and bewailing their condition and to wishing for a remedy for their ills, when they see that in this life they are exposed to so many great troubles—with this difference that unbelievers take into account only the ills of the body whereas the godly are more deeply concerned with spiritual distresses. But since by nature all men shrink from death, unbelievers never quit life willingly, except when they cast it away in disgust or despair. But believers depart willingly because they have a better hope held out to them beyond this world. That is the gist of the argument and we can now look at the words one by one.

'*We know*', he says; this knowledge does not come from the human intellect but by revelation of the Holy Spirit, and thus it belongs only to believers. Even the heathen had some notion of the immortality of the soul, but none of them was certain of it, none could boast that he spoke of a thing that he knew. Only believers can speak of it with assurance, for it has been made known to them by the testimony of the Word and Spirit of God. We should note that this knowledge is not merely general, as though believers had only a general assurance that they will enter a better condition after death and had no fixed assurance about themselves personally. A merely general assurance would be of little value in producing such a hard-won consolation. Rather everybody must have an individual knowledge of his own immortality, for the only thing that can bring me to face death with cheerfulness is the sure conviction that I am departing to a better life.

The body, as we now have it, he calls *the house of our tabernacle*. For just as tabernacle tents are constructed out of slight material for temporary use without solid foundation and are later taken down or fall of themselves, so a mortal body is given to men as a frail hut for them to live in for a few days. Peter uses the same metaphor in his second epistle (1.13-14) and also Job when he speaks of a 'house of clay.' With this Paul contrasts a building that will last for ever, although it is not clear whether he means by this the state of blessed immortality that awaits believers after death or the incorruptible and glorious body as it will be after the resurrection. Either meaning is quite suitable, but I prefer to take it that the blessed state of the soul after death is the beginning of this building, but its completion is the glory of the final resurrection. This explanation is better supported by the context. The adjectives that he applies to this building emphasize its perpetuity.

3. *If we are clothed*. He now restricts what he has said about the certainty of the future life to believers, since it is something that belongs only to them. The godless also are stripped of the body, but because they bring into God's sight nothing but a disgraceful nakedness, they are not clothed with a glorious body. Believers who are clothed with Christ and adorned with His righteousness receive the glorious robe of immortality. I am inclined to adopt this interpretation rather than agree with Chrysostom and others who think that nothing new is being said here, but that Paul is only repeating what he has already said about putting on an eternal habitation. The apostle is here describing how God clothes us twice, first with the righteousness of Christ and the sanctification of the Spirit in this life and then after death with immortality and glory. The first is the cause of the second since God first justifies those whom He has determined to glorify. This interpretation is suggested by the word *again* (*etiam*) which is undoubtedly meant to indicate an amplification of what has gone before, as if Paul

had said that new clothing would be provided for believers after death since even in this life they have been clothed by God.

4. *We groan, being burdened.* The ungodly also groan because they are not content with their present condition, but later a different feeling prevails, that is a desire for life so that they shrink from death and do not feel the long continuance of this mortal life to be a burden. But the groaning of believers arises from their knowledge that here they are exiles from their native land and are shut up in the body as in a work-house (*ergastulo*), and so they count this life a burden because in it they cannot obtain true and perfect happiness because they cannot escape the slavery of sin except by death and so they wish to be elsewhere. But since it is natural for all who have life to wish it to continue, how can it be that believers are glad to cease living? The apostle answers this question by saying that believers desire death, not in order to lose anything, but for the sake of a better life. But there is more in these words, for Paul admits that we have a natural aversion to leaving this life, considered by itself, just as nobody is willing to have his clothes stripped from him, but he goes on to show that this natural shrinking from death is overcome by the assurance of faith, just as a man will have no difficulty in throwing away a coarse, dirty, worn and tattered garment if he is sure that he will be arrayed in one that is comely, handsome, new and lasting.

He explains the metaphor further by saying, *that what is mortal may be swallowed up of life.* Since flesh and blood cannot inherit the kingdom of God, what is corruptible in our nature must die so that we may be thoroughly renewed and restored to a state of perfection. That is why our body is called a prison (*carcer*) in which we are held captive.

5. *Now that has wrought us.* This is added to emphasize that this preparedness for death is supernatural. Mere natural feeling will not make us willing to die, because it does not understand the hundredfold compensation that follows when a seed falls into the ground and dies; thus this readiness for death has to be wrought in us by God. He also adds here the way in which God does it—by strengthening us by His Spirit as an earnest and foretaste of what is to come. The word *also* seems to be added by way of amplification, as if he had said, 'It is God who forms that desire in us and, lest our courage should give way or waver, He gives us His Holy Spirit as an earnest, for, by His testimony, the truth of the promise is confirmed and ratified.' The Holy Spirit has two offices: first to show believers what they ought to desire, and then to remove all hesitation and influence their hearts so effectively that they may steadfastly persevere in choosing what is good. There would however be no objection to widening the meaning of the word *wrought* to include that renewal of life that God grants to His own now

in this world, for in this way He distinguishes them even now from the rest of men and shows that they have been marked out by His grace for a special destiny.

6. *Being therefore always of good courage.* That is, because we depend upon the earnest of the Spirit, for without that we always lack assurance or are brave and fearful by turns and cannot keep one uniform and even disposition of mind. That good courage of which Paul speaks has no place in us unless it is maintained by the Spirit of God. The word '*and*' that follows should be taken causally as meaning 'because'—'We are of good courage because we know that while we are at home in the body etc.' To know this is the source of our tranquillity and assurance. Unbelievers are in a constant ferment of anxiety and are for ever stubbornly murmuring against God because they think they will soon perish and they place in this life their highest and final hopes of happiness. But we live with a quiet mind and go on to meet death without hesitation because a better hope is laid up for us.

We are absent from the Lord. The whole of Scripture declares that God is present with us, but here Paul teaches that we are absent from Him, which would appear to be a contradiction, but when we recognize that there are different kinds of absence and presence the difficulty is easily solved. Thus He is present with all men in that He sustains them by His power; He dwells in them because they live and move and have their being through Him. He is present to those who believe in Him in the greater energy of His Spirit; He lives in them and dwells in their midst and even within them. Yet at the same time He is absent from us, because He does not show Himself to us face to face, because we are still exiles from His kingdom and do not yet possess that blessed immortality that the angels who are with Him enjoy. But in this passage 'to be absent' refers only to a limitation of our knowledge, as his further explanation will soon make clear.

7. *For we walk by faith.* I have translated the Greek εἶδος by the Latin *aspectum* (sight) rather than by *species* (outward appearance), which is a term that few understand. He is explaining that what he means by saying that we are absent from the Lord is that we do not yet see Him face to face. The mode of God's absence is such that we cannot openly discern Him and the reason why we do not see Him is that we walk by faith. Now faith is rightly opposed to sight because it perceives things that are hidden from men's senses and reaches forward to things still future that do not as yet appear. Believers are more like dead men than living, for they often seem to be forsaken by God and they always have the elements of death shut up within them. Thus they have to hope against hope. For now things hoped for are things hidden, as we read in Rom. 8.24, and faith is the manifestation of things which do not

yet appear. Thus it is not surprising that the apostle should say that we do not yet have sight as long as we walk by faith. We do indeed see, but in a glass darkly, which means that we rest on the Word in place of the reality.

8. *We are of good courage, I say.* He repeats what he has already said about the assurance of the godly and that, far from being broken by the hardness of the cross or being disheartened by their afflictions, they are rather made more brave by them. The greatest of evils is death and yet believers long for it, because it is the beginning of perfect blessedness. *And* here again means 'because'; 'Nothing that befalls us can shake our confidence and courage because death, which others dread so much, is to us great gain. For there is nothing better than to leave the body that we may share God's dwelling-place and enjoy His real and open presence. Thus for us the decay of the outer man brings no loss.'

Note here that, as we have already pointed out, true faith begets not merely contempt for death but desire for it and thus it is a sign of unbelief in us when the fear of death is stronger than the joy and comfort of hope. Believers desire death and yet not with such an inordinate desire as to anticipate the day their Lord has fixed for it; for they willingly battle on at their earthly post for as long as the Lord thinks fit, preferring to live to the glory of Christ rather than die for their own profit. For the desire of which Paul speaks comes of faith and is thus in no way at variance with God's will. It may also be inferred from these words that souls loosed from their bodies live with God, for if, when they are absent from the body, they have God present with them, then certainly they live with Him.

Here some raise the question as to why then some of the holy fathers so shrank from death, as, for example, David and Hezekiah and the whole Church of Israel, as is clear from Ps. 6, Isa. 38.3, and Ps. 115.17. I know the usual answer, that they dreaded death so much because the revelation of a future life was still obscure and the comfort of it therefore small. I agree that this is part of the explanation, but not the whole of it, for the holy fathers of the old Church did not always tremble before the messenger of death, but embraced it gladly and with joyful hearts. Abraham departed full of days and without regret, we nowhere have any indication that Isaac was reluctant to die and Jacob with his last breath declares that he is waiting for the Lord's salvation. The reason why David and Hezekiah on one specific occasion prayed with tears to avoid death is that they were being punished by the Lord for certain sins and thus they felt in death the Lord's anger. That was the reason for their alarm and believers could have the same experience even today under the reign of Christ. But the desire of which Paul speaks here is the disposition of a well regulated mind.

Wherefore also we make it our aim, whether at home or absent, to be well-pleasing unto him. For we must all be made manifest before the judgment-seat of Christ; that each one may recieve the things done in the body, according to what he hath done, whether it be good or bad. Knowing therefore the fear of the Lord, we persuade men, but we are made manifest unto God; and I hope that we are made manifest also in your consciences. We are not again commending ourselves unto you, but speak as giving you occasion of glorying on our behalf, that ye may have wherewith to answer them that glory in appearance and not in heart. (9-12)

9. *Wherefore we make it our aim.* He has already considered the courage that Christians need to bear afflictions and so that even in dying they may be the conquerors of death, because by afflictions and death they attain to a blessed life, and he now draws from the same premises another conclusion—that they should apply themselves and make it their chief aim to please God. For indeed the hope of resurrection and the thought of judgment are bound to make us greatly concerned to do this, just as the only reason for our negligence and remissness in our duty is that we never, or only rarely, think about what we should constantly be remembering, that we are only lodgers here for a short time and, when our course is run, we must return to Christ. Note that he says this desire is common both to the living and the dead and thus confirms again the immortality of the soul.

10. *We must all be made manifest.* Though this is something that applies to all men, all men do not have minds sufficiently exalted to remember every single moment that they must appear before the judgment-seat of Christ. Paul himself in his holy concern to act rightly was continually placing himself under Christ's judgment, and his intention here is to administer an indirect rebuke to those ambitious teachers who thought it enough to have the applause of men. For when he says that no one can escape, it is almost as if he were citing them to that heavenly assize. Although the word I have translated 'to be made manifest' could mean simply 'to appear', in my view Paul meant more—that we shall then come forth into the light, whereas now many are hidden as though in darkness. For then the books that are now shut will be opened.

That each one may receive. As this passage is concerned with rewards for our works, we must note briefly that as evil deeds are punished by God, so also good deeds are rewarded, but for a different reason. Evil deeds are given the punishment they deserve, but in rewarding good deeds God does not have regard to their merit or worth. No work of ours is so full and complete in all its parts as to deserve God's approval and, further, the only way in which a man can make his works pleasing to God is by satisfying the whole Law, and there is no one as perfect as that. Thus the only remedy is that God, of His unmerited kindness, should accept us and justify us by not imputing to us our sins. Having thus received us into His favour, He graciously accepts our works also, and it is upon this undeserved acceptance that the reward depends. There is no inconsistency in saying that He rewards good works provided we understand that that implies no denial of the fact that it is by free grace that we obtain eternal life. I have explained this point more fully in my Commentary on I Corinthians and a full discussion will be found in the *Institutes*. When Paul says *in the body* I take him to mean not just external actions but all the works that are done in this bodily life.

11. *Knowing therefore*. He now returns to himself and again gives his general teaching a personal application. 'I myself', he says, 'know well in my own experience that fear of God which ought to rule in the hearts of all the godly.' For to know *the fear of the Lord* is to share the knowledge that each of us will one day have to give an account of all his actions before the judgment-seat of Christ and if a man seriously considers that, he cannot but be moved by fear and shake off all his carelessness. Therefore he bears witness that he is discharging his apostolate faithfully and with a pure conscience remembering the account he must render and so walking in the fear of the Lord. But his enemies might object, 'You extol yourself in exalted terms but who sees the truth of what you preach?' To this he replies that he does the work of a teacher in the sight of men but it is known to God with what sincerity of heart he does it. It is as if he had said, 'My mouth speaks to men, but my heart speaks to God.'

And I hope. This is almost a correction, for he now claims that God is not the only witness who will testify to his integrity, there are also the Corinthians themselves to whom he has given full proof of it. There are two points to be noted here; first that it is not enough for a man to act honourably and with energy before men, unless his heart is right before God, and secondly, that boasting is empty without evidence of the facts to support it. For none are so bold in making claims for themselves as those who have nothing in them at all. If a man wants to be believed, he must bring forward in support of his words deeds that will prove them true. But to be *made manifest in the conscience* is more than to be made known by evidence; for conscience penetrates further than the judgment of the flesh.

12. *We are not commending ourselves*. He confirms what he has just said and at the same time anticipates a possible slander against him. The fact that he has so much to say about himself could have given the

impression that he was too concerned for his own good name. In fact it is probable that wicked men had actually been saying this about him. For when he says 'we do not commend ourselves again', he seems to be answering them. To *commend* has an unfavourable sense here and means 'to boast' or 'to brag'.

When he adds that he is *giving them an occasion of glorying*, his meaning is, first, that it is their cause rather than his own he is pleading, since he gives up everything for the sake of their glory. He is also rebuking them indirectly for their ingratitude in not seeing that it was for them to be ready to magnify his apostleship so that he would not have to do it himself and for not seeing either that it was more in their interest than in Paul's own that his apostleship should be held in honour. We are here taught that the servants of Christ ought to be concerned for their own reputations only in so far as it is for the advantage of the Church. Paul rightly claims that his concern throughout is for the Church. Let others see to it that they do not make a false excuse out of his example. We are also taught that a minister's true commendation is something he shares with the Church and is not personal to himself; in other words it is something that brings advantage to all.

That ye may have wherewith to answer. He indicates in passing the need to repress the vanity of those who make empty boasts and that this is the duty of the Church. Such ambition is a harmful pest of the first degree and it is therefore dangerous to favour it by dissimulation. Since the Corinthians had not acted in this matter in the past, Paul tells them what they should do in the future.

To glory in appearance and not in heart, means to make outward show a disguise and to regard sincerity of heart as of no importance, for those who are really wise will never boast except in God. But where there is empty show, there is no sincerity and no uprightness of heart.

For whether we are beside ourselves, it is unto God; or whether we are of sober mind, it is unto you. For the love of Christ constraineth us; because we thus judge, that one died for all, therefore all died; and he died for all, that they which live should no longer live unto themselves, but unto him who for their sakes died and rose again. Wherefore we henceforth know no man after the flesh: even though we have known Christ after the flesh, yet now we know him so no more. Wherefore if any man is in Christ, let him be a new creature: the old things are passed away; behold all things are become new. (13-17)

13. *Whether we are beside ourselves.* This is said by way of concession to his opponents. Paul's glorying was sane enough, or it was, so to say, a sober and most judicious madness but because he seemed foolish to many, he speaks from their point of view. He makes two claims: first,

that he is not concerned about himself but only to serve God and the Church, and, second, that he is not afraid of what men think of him and is ready to be thought sane or insane if only he can faithfully perform the work of God and the Church. His meaning is this, 'Men may think what they like of my frequent assertions of my good faith. But I do not do it for my own sake; my only concern is for God and His Church and I am ready both to be silent and to speak as the glory of God and the interest of the Church may require. I willingly allow the world to think me beside myself, provided that I am mad not to myself but to God.' This passage deserves not just passing notice but constant meditation, for unless we are as resolute as Paul is here, the smallest causes of offence will again and again distract us from our duty.

14. *For the love of Christ*. The word 'love' can be understood either actively or passively but I prefer the former. For unless our hearts are harder than iron, the remembrance of the great love Christ has shown us by submitting to death for our sakes is bound to make us devote ourselves entirely to Him. Paul himself makes this clear when he says that it is right that we should live unto Him and die to ourselves. He has already said that fear stirred him up to do his duty for he would one day have to render an account, and here he brings forward another motive—the measureless love of Christ towards us, of which He gave us evidence by His death. The knowledge of this love should constrain our feelings so that we cannot but love Him in return. The metaphor in the word *constrain* brings out the point that every one who truly considers and ponders the wonderful love that Christ has shown us in His death, cannot but be bound to Him by the tightest chain so as to devote Himself to His service.

One died for all. We should note the purpose of Christ's death—that He died for us that we might die to ourselves. We should also notice how he goes on to explain that to die to ourselves is to live to Christ, or to explain it more fully, it is to renounce ourselves that we may live to Christ who redeemed us that He might have us in His power as His peculiar possession. Thus it follows that we no longer belong to ourselves. There is a similar passage in Rom. 14.17-19. Two things are here brought forward separately: that we are dead in Christ, so that, we should put from us all ambition and desire for eminence without feeling it as a loss, and that we owe to Christ both life and death, so completely has He bound us to Himself.

16. *Wherefore we henceforth know no man*. Here 'to know' is equivalent to 'to judge', as if he had said, 'We do not judge according to outward appearance so as to think that the man who seems to be most outstanding is really so.' Under the term *flesh* he includes all external endowments that men usually prize and everything apart from re-

generation that is held in esteem. But he is thinking especially of deceptive outward appearances and has certainly in mind that death or mortification of the flesh he has already mentioned, as if to say, 'Since we should be dead to this present life and be nothing in ourselves, no man can be reckoned a servant of Christ on account of any excellence in the flesh.'

Even though we have known Christ. His meaning is, 'Though Christ lived for a time in this world and was known to men in these things that make up this present life, now He is to be known in a different way, that is, spiritually that we may not think of Him in any worldly way.' Some fanatics, like Servetus, have perverted this passage to try to make it prove that Christ's human nature has now been absorbed by His divinity. But it is not hard to see how far such mad thoughts are from the mind of the apostle for he is speaking here not about the substance of Christ's body but about His external appearance. He is not saying that we can no longer know Christ's flesh, but rather that we are not to judge Him after the flesh. The whole of Scripture proclaims that Christ now lives His glorious life in our flesh, just as surely as it was in our flesh that He once suffered; indeed, if this foundation is overthrown our whole faith falls in ruins, for what ground is there for our hope of immortality except the evidence that we have now in Christ? Righteousness was restored to us by Christ's fulfilling of the Law in our nature and abolishing the disobedience of Adam, and life is restored to us in the same way by Christ's opening up to our human nature the Kingdom of God from which it had been banished, and by His giving it a place in the heavenly habitation. Thus unless we still recognize Christ's humanity, all the assurance and comfort that we should have in Him perishes. But we do in fact know Christ in His flesh as true man and our brother, but we do not know Him carnally, for our trust is based only on a consideration of His spiritual gifts. He is spiritual to us, not because He has laid aside the body and been changed into a spirit, but because it is by the power of His Spirit that He regenerates and governs His own.

17. *Wherefore if any man is in Christ.* The connexion of this sentence with its context is not clear and should be brought out in this way, 'If any man desires to obtain a place in Christ, that is, in His Kingdom or His Church, let him be a new creature.' By saying this he condemns every kind of human excellence that men usually think to be great, if renewal of heart is absent from it. Learning and eloquence and other endowments are precious and honourable things, but where there is no fear of the Lord or uprightness of conscience, all their honour disappears. Let no one therefore glory in any distinction he possesses, since the chief commendation of Christians is that they deny themselves.

This is said not only to repress the vanity of the false apostles but also to correct the ostentatious and superficial standards of judgment of the Corinthians in many of whose eyes external appearances counted for more than true sincerity; and this is a fault that is common to almost every age. Where shall we find a man who does not count ostentation more important than true holiness? Let us therefore bear in mind this warning that all who have not been renewed by the Spirit of God should be nothing in the Church, whatever claims to distinction they may otherwise possess.

The old things are passed away. When the prophets speak of the kingdom of Christ they foretell that there will be 'a new heaven and a new earth' (Isa. 65.17) by which they mean that all things will be changed for the better till the happiness of the godly is complete. Since the kingdom of Christ is spiritual, this conversion must take place chiefly in the spirit and so Paul is right to begin with this. Paul is therefore making a most elegant and fitting allusion to this prophecy and adapting it to extol regeneration. He calls 'old' things that have not been reformed by the Spirit of God and so uses the word in contrast with renewing grace. The expression 'passed away' he takes to mean 'fading away', just as things of short duration decay when their season is past. Thus it is only the new man who can flower and increase in the Kingdom of God.

> *But all things are of God, who reconciled us to himself through Christ, and gave unto us the ministry of reconciliation; to wit, that God was in Christ reconciling the world unto himself, not reckoning unto them their trespasses, and having committed unto us the word of reconciliation. We are ambassadors therefore on behalf of Christ, as though God were intreating by us: we beseech you on behalf of Christ, be ye reconciled to God. Him who knew no sin he made to be sin on our behalf; that we might become the righteousness of God in him.* (18-21)

18. *All things are of God.* He means all things that belong to Christ's kingdom, as if he had said, 'If we wish to be Christ's, we must be regenerated by God, but this is no ordinary gift.' Thus he is not speaking here of creation in general, but of the grace of regeneration which God confers specially upon His own elect, and he says that this grace is of God, not in so far as He is Creator and Maker of heaven and earth, but in so far as He is the new Creator of the Church by refashioning His people into His own image. Thus all flesh is humbled and believers are admonished that now they must live to God, who has made them new creatures. This they can only do by forgetting the world since, being God's, they are no longer of the world.

Who reconciled us. There are two main points here, one concerning man's reconciliation with God and the other concerning the means by which we may obtain the benefit of it. These points have a very close connexion with what has gone before, for, having shown that a good conscience is above every other kind of distinction, the apostle now goes on to show that the whole Gospel is directed to this end. At the same time he shows the true worth of the apostolic office and admonishes the Corinthians who, because they were so impressed by mere outward appearances, could not distinguish between true and false apostles, what they ought to look for in an apostle. By this reminder he stirs them up to make greater progress in the teaching of the Gospel. For a foolish admiration for worldly men, who serve their own ambition rather than Christ, springs from ignorance of what the office of being a preacher of the Gospel includes and requires.

I return now to consider the two main points that are taken up here. The first is that *God hath reconciled us to Himself by Christ.* There follows immediately the explanation that *God was in Christ* and in His person has brought about reconciliation. The way in which He did it is next added, by *not reckoning unto men their trespasses.* And this also is explained by showing how Christ made a guilt-offering for our sins and procured righteousness for us. The second main point is that the grace of reconciliation is applied to us by the Gospel, so that we may share in it. Here, if anywhere in Paul's writings, we have a quite remarkably important passage and we must carefully examine the words one by one.

The ministry of reconciliation. This is a most remarkable description of the Gospel as a message delivered through an ambassador to reconcile men to God. It is the singular dignity of ministers of the Gospel to be sent by God to us with a mandate to be the messengers and in a manner the pledges of His good will towards us. But this is said not so much to glorify ministers as to comfort the godly so that, whenever they hear the Gospel, they may know that God is dealing with them and, as it were, negotiating an agreement with them about their return to His grace. What blessing could be more desirable than this! Thus let us remember that this is the main purpose of the Gospel, that, although we are by nature children of wrath, the quarrel between God and us can be resolved and we can be received by Him into His grace. Ministers are given authority to declare this good news to us and to increase our assurance of God's fatherly love towards us. It is true that any other person can also bear witness to us of God's grace, but Paul teaches that this duty is laid specially upon ministers. Thus when a duly ordained minister (*minister rite ordinatus*) declares from the Gospel that God has been made propitious to us (*propitiatum nobis esse Deum*) he should be heard as God's ambassador, carrying out a public duty as God's representative, and endowed with rightful authority to make this declaration to us.

19. *God was in Christ.* Some take this to mean simply 'God was reconciling the world to Himself in Christ' but the meaning is fuller and richer than that, for he is saying, first, that God was in Christ and then that by this intervention He was reconciling the world to Himself. This is said of the Father, since it would be unnatural to say that the divine nature of Christ was in Christ. Thus he is saying that the Father was in the Son, in agreement with John 10.38, 'I am in the Father and the Father in me.' Thus he who has the Son has the Father also. Paul expresses himself in this way so that we may learn to be satisfied with Christ because in Him we find God the Father also, as He communicates Himself to us by His Son. Thus what he is saying in this phrase really amounts to this, 'Whereas God had been before far distant from us, He has drawn near to us in Christ, and so Christ has been made to us the true Immanuel and His advent is the drawing near of God to men.'

The second clause deals with the work of Christ, which is to be our propitiation, since apart from Him God is displeased with us all because we have departed from righteousness. Why has God appeared to men in Christ? For reconciliation, in order that the hostility might be ended and we who were strangers might be adopted as sons. Although Christ's coming had its source in the overflowing love of God for us, yet, until men know that God has been propitiated by a mediator, there cannot but be on their side a separation which prevents them from having access to God. But of this more soon.

Not reckoning unto them. Notice how men return to God's favour— by being regarded as righteous, by obtaining remission of their sins. As long as God imputes our sins to us, He cannot but regard us with abhorrence, for He cannot look with friendship or favour upon sinners. But this may appear to contradict what is said elsewhere, that 'we were loved by Him before the foundation of the world' (Eph. 1.4), and to contradict still more John 3.16 where He says that His love for us was the reason why He expiated our sins by Christ, for the cause must always precede the effect. My answer is that we were loved from before the foundation of the world, but not apart from Christ. But I do agree that the love of God was first in time and in order also as regards God; but, as regards us, His love has its foundation in the sacrifice of Christ. For when we think of God apart from a mediator, we can only conceive of Him as being angry with us, but when a mediator is interposed between us, we know that He is pacified towards us. But since it is also needful for us to know that Christ came forth to us from the fountain of God's free mercy, Scripture explicitly teaches both; the Father's wrath has been placated by the Son's sacrifice and thus the Son was offered for the expiation of men's sins, because God has had mercy upon them and has made this sacrifice the pledge of His receiving them into His favour. To sum up: wherever there is sin there is also God's wrath for God is not propitious towards us until He has blotted out our sins by not imputing them. Since our consciences cannot grasp this blessing apart from the intervention of Christ's sacrifice, Paul is right to make it the foundation and cause of reconciliation as far as we are concerned.

Having committed unto us. He says again that a commission to offer this reconciliation to us has been given to ministers of the Gospel. For an objection could be raised. It might be asked, 'Where is Christ the peacemaker between God and men now? How far from us does He dwell?' He says that as He once suffered, so now every day He offers the fruit of His suffering to us through the Gospel which He has given to the world as a sure and certain record of His completed work of reconciliation. Thus the duty of ministers is to apply to us the fruit of Christ's death.

But in case anyone should imagine this application in some such magical manner as the Papists have invented, we should note carefully what he says next and how for him the application consists entirely of the preaching of the Gospel. For the Pope and his priests use this as a pretext to provide some shadow of warrant for the altogether ungodly and execrable traffic they conduct over the salvation of souls. 'The Lord', they say, 'has given us commission and authority to forgive sins.' I accept this, provided that they carry out the work of ambassadors as Paul here describes it. But the absolution that the Papists practise is completely magical and besides they shut up the forgiveness of sins in lead or marble statues or connect it with fictitious and frivolous superstitions. What resemblance is there between all that and Christ's commandment? The ministers of the Church restore us to God's favour in a right and orderly manner by bearing witness to us through the Gospel of how God has been reconciled to us by His grace. When this testimony is removed, all that is left is nothing but sheer imposture. Beware of placing any confidence at all in anything but the Gospel. I certainly do not deny that the grace of Christ is applied to us also in the sacraments and that in them our reconciliation with God is confirmed to our consciences, but, since the testimony of the Gospel is engraven upon the sacraments, they are not to be thought of separately by themselves, but in close connexion with the Gospel, whose appendages they are. To sum up: ministers of the Church are ambassadors for testifying and proclaiming the blessing of reconciliation only on condition that they speak from the Gospel as providing a legitimate warrant for what they say.

20. *As though God were intreating.* This is of the greatest importance and indeed absolutely necessary to give authority to our ministry. For who would allow a question that involves his eternal salvation to depend merely upon the testimony of men? The matter is too vital for us to be satisfied with the assurances of men, unless we are sure that God has appointed them and speaks to us through them. This is why Christ has Himself commended His apostles to us in such passages as Luke 10.16, 'He that heareth you, heareth me,' and Matt. 18.18, Whatsoever ye shall loose on earth shall be loosed in heaven.'

We beseech you on behalf of Christ. Here we see what good reason Isaiah had to exclaim, 'How blessed are the feet of them that preach the gospel!' (Isa. 52.7). For the one thing that is needed for our complete blessedness and without which we are most miserable is conferred upon us only through the Gospel. But if this duty is laid upon all ministers of the Church, so that he who does not discharge it cannot be counted either apostle or pastor, it is not hard to infer from this the truth about the Pope and his whole hierarchy. They certainly wish to be regarded as apostles and pastors, but since they are in fact dumb idols, how do their proud claims match up to this passage of Paul's? The word 'intreat' implies a wonderful commendation of Christ's grace in that He stoops so low as not to disdain to entreat us. Our wickedness is the less excusable, if after such kindness we do not at once show ourselves teachable and compliant.

Be ye reconciled. We should note that here Paul is dealing with believers and he declares that he has to execute his commission to them every day. Christ did not suffer just to expiate our sins once, nor was the Gospel instituted only in order that the sins we committed before baptism should be forgiven us, but rather, since we sin every day, so by a daily forgiveness God receives us into His favour. The work of the Gospel ambassadors is perpetual for the Gospel must be proclaimed ceaselessly in the Church to the end of the world and it cannot be preached without a promise of the forgiveness of sins. We have here an explicit and relevant passage to refute the ungodly teaching of the Papists which requires men to seek the forgiveness of post-baptismal sins elsewhere than in the expiation accomplished in Christ's death. The teaching common in all the schools of the Papists is that after baptism we have to merit the forgiveness of our sins by our penitence with the aid of the power of the keys. By penitence they mean satisfactions but what does Paul say here? He recalls us, as much after baptism as before it, to that one expiation made by Christ, that we may know that we always receive forgiveness by free unmerited grace.

He passes over as something quite unknown the distinction between pre-baptismal and post-baptismal sin that they have invented. Further, all their prating about the administration of the keys is to no purpose for they think of the keys apart from the Gospel, whereas in fact they are only the testimony to God's freely given reconciliation which is delivered to us in the Gospel.

21. *Him who knew no sin.* Note well how in all Paul's writings there is no other way of returning into God's favour than that which is founded exclusively upon Christ's sacrifice. Let us learn then always to look to Him, when we wish to be absolved from guilt. It is commonly taught that here 'sin' means an expiatory sacrifice for sin, so that it is rendered *piaculum* in Latin. In this and other passages Paul has borrowed this expression from the Hebrew in which אשם means both an expiatory sacrifice and a fault or a crime. But the meaning of this word and of the entire sentence will be better understood if we compare the two sides of the antithesis contained in it. Sin is opposed to righteousness for Paul teaches that we were made the righteousness of God as a result of Christ's having been made sin. Here righteousness means not a quality or habit but something imputed to us, since we are said to have received the righteousness of Christ. What then is meant by sin? It is the guilt on account of which we are accused before the judgment of God. As a man's curse used to be cast upon the sacrificial victim, so Christ's condemnation was our absolution and with His stripes we are healed.

The righteousness of God in him. First, the righteousness of God means here not the righteousness that God gives us, but rather the righteousness that makes us acceptable to Him, just as in John 12.43 the glory of God means that which God approves and the glory of men that which wins the vain approval of the world. So in Rom. 3.23 when he says that 'we have come short of the glory of God' he means that in ourselves we have nothing in which to glory before God. To appear to be righteous before men is not difficult, but that is only a false semblance of righteousness, which finally brings about our ruin, for the only true righteousness is that which God has accepted.

We may now return to the contrast drawn in this verse between righteousness and sin. How can we become righteous before God? In the same way as Christ became a sinner. For He took, as it were, our person, that He might be the offender in our name and thus might be reckoned a sinner, not because of His own offences but because of those of others, since He Himself was pure and free from every fault and bore the penalty that was our due and not His own. Now in the same way we are righteous in Him, not because we have satisfied God's judgment by our own works, but because we are judged in relation to

Christ's righteousness which we have put on by faith, that it may become our own. That is why I have chosen to retain the preposition 'in' rather than replace it by *per*, 'through', since this gives a meaning more in line with Paul's intention.

CHAPTER SIX

And working together with him we intreat also that ye receive not the grace of God in vain (for he saith, At an acceptable time I hearkened unto thee, and in a day of salvation did I succour thee: behold, now is the acceptable time; behold, now is the day of salvation): giving no occasion of stumbling in anything, that our ministration be not blamed; but in everything commending ourselves, as ministers of God, in much patience, in afflictions, in necessities, in distresses, in stripes, in imprisonments, in tumults, in labours, in watchings, in fastings; in pureness, in knowledge, in long suffering, in kindness, in the Holy Ghost, in love unfeigned, in the word of truth, in the power of God; by the armour of righteousness on the right hand and on the left, by glory and dishonour, by evil report and good report; as deceivers, and yet true; as unknown, and yet well known; as dying, and behold, we live; as chastened, and not killed; as sorrowful, yet alway rejoicing; as poor, yet making many rich; as having nothing, and yet possessing all things. (1-10)

1. *Working together.* He has referred to the command to be Christ's ambassadors which ministers of the Gospel have received from God. Having delivered their commanded message they should labour to have it prevail that their work may not be in vain. They should add to their message continual exhortations that their mission may be effective. That is what is meant by συνεργοῦντες, fellow-workers who are eager to advance the work, for it is not enough to teach if you do not also urge. Taken this way the prefix συν would refer to God or to the mission with which He entrusts His servants. For the teaching of the Gospel is assisted by exhortations that it may not lack effect and ministers bring to God's commission their own earnest zeal. But the prefix συν could also be taken to refer to the fact that ministers labour together, since, if they are in earnest with God's work, they should help each other. But I prefer the first interpretation. Chrysostom takes it to mean the hearers with whom ministers work together by rousing them from sloth and inactivity. Here ministers are taught that it is not enough merely to propound doctrine. They must labour that those who hear it should also accept it, and not once but continually. Being messengers from God to men, their first duty is to offer the grace of God, but their second is to strive with all their might to ensure that it is not offered in vain.

2. *For He saith, At an acceptable time.* He quotes a prophecy from

Isaiah (Isa. 49.8) which is very relevant to this work of exhortation with which he is dealing. There is no doubt that in this passage the prophet is speaking of Christ's kingdom, as the context makes clear. The Father in appointing the Son a leader for the gathering of the Church, addresses Him in these words, 'I have heard thee in an acceptable time.' Now we know that there is an analogy between the Head and the members. For Christ was heard in our name, for our salvation has been placed in His hands and it is His only care. Thus we are all admonished in the person of Christ not to slight the opportunity we have to obtain salvation. The Greek interpreter translates by εὐπρόσδεκτον the prophet's original רָצוֹן, which means benevolence or free favour. This quotation should be applied to the subject in hand in this way. Since God assigns a set time for the showing forth of His grace, it follows that all times are not equally suited to it, and since a particular day of salvation is named, it follows that the free offer of salvation is not open every day. This depends entirely on God's providence for the only time that is accepted is what Gal. 4.4 calls the fulness of time. We should also notice the order in which He mentions first a time of acceptance and then a day of salvation and thus indicates that the only source of our salvation is the mercy of God. Therefore we must not look into ourselves to discover why God saves us, as though we could by our works induce Him to show us His grace. Why does the day of salvation come? It is because it is the accepted time which God in His undeserved favour has ordained. In the meantime we must hold fast to Paul's purpose which is to teach the need for undelaying urgency, so that we may not miss the opportunity, for it is displeasing to God when His proffered grace is received with coolness and indifference.

Behold, now is the time. The prophet was speaking of the time in which Christ was to be manifested in the flesh for the redemption of men. Paul makes use of his prophecy by applying it to the time in which Christ is revealed through the continual teaching of the Gospel, and with good reason, for just as once, when Christ appeared, salvation was sent to the whole world, so now it is sent to us every day, when we are made partakers of the Gospel. This is a beautiful passage that has great comfort for us, since we know that as long as the Gospel is preached to us, the door into the kingdom of God is open to us, and there is raised up before us a sign of God's kindness to invite us to accept salvation, for when we are called to receive it, we may be sure that we have an opportunity of doing so. But unless we grasp this opportunity, we must fear Paul's implied threat that soon the door will be closed to all who have not entered at the right time. For retribution of this kind always follows contempt of the Word.

3. *Giving no occasion of stumbling.* We have already shown several times how Paul sometimes commends the ministry of the Gospel in general and at other times his own integrity. And so now he speaks of himself and in his own person sets before us a living picture of a good and faithful apostle, that the Corinthians may learn how unfair they have been in preferring empty braggarts to him. In thus preferring mere shams, they were holding in highest honour superficial people with no real ardour about them and holding in low estimation the ministers who were in fact the best. Without doubt the very things that Paul here mentions in his own praise are the very things in him they would have despised and they are the more worthy of blame in making reproaches out of things that justly deserved praise.

Here Paul is making three points. First he shows the excellencies that should be esteemed in preachers of the Gospel; then he shows that he himself possesses these qualities; and third he warns the Corinthians not to recognize as servants of Christ those who do not behave in the way he here by his own example lays down. His purpose is to win authority for himself and those who are like him for the sake of God's glory and the good of the Church, or rather to restore that authority where it has broken down, and also to recall the Corinthians from their foolish attachment to false apostles, which was hindering them from making progress on the Gospel to the required extent. Ministers give occasion of stumbling when by their own faults they hinder the progress of the Gospel in those who hear them. Paul claims that he is not of that company and testifies to his careful concern not to stain his apostleship with any taint of disgrace. For this is a trick of Satan—to seek for a fault in ministers which will tend to bring the Gospel into disrepute. For if he succeeds in bringing the ministry into contempt, all hope of progress is gone. Thus the man who wishes to make himself useful in Christ's service must devote all his energies to maintaining the honour of his ministry. That he can do by making sure that he is worthy of that honour for there is nothing more absurd than to struggle to maintain your reputation before others, when you are disgracing yourself by a base and wicked life. The only honourable man is he who will permit in himself nothing unworthy of the ministry of Christ.

4. *In much patience.* The aim of this list that now follows is to show that Paul has passed through all the tests by which the Lord usually tries His ministers; there is no trial he has been spared in order that the faithfulness of his ministry might be fully proved. Among the things he mentions, there are some which are always required of all Christ's servants, such as, *labours, pureness, knowledge, watchings, longsuffering, love, the word of truth, the Spirit, the power of God, the armour of righteous-*

ness. But there are others for which there is no permanent necessity; it is not necessary, in order to be Christ's servant, to have been tried by *stripes* and *imprisonments*; even the best of ministers could at times be exempt from these. But it is the duty of all to have the courage to offer themselves, if the Lord please, to trial by stripes and imprisonments like Paul.

Patience is the control of the mind in adversity and is an invariable quality in a good minister. *Afflictions* include more than *necessities* for I take the latter to mean poverty. This is shared by many ministers, since there are few who are not poor, but not by all. For why should the possession of moderate riches prevent a man from being considered Christ's servant, if in other respects he is godly, of upright mind and honourable life and otherwise excellent? A man is not considered a good minister just because he is poor, and he should not therefore be rejected just because he is rich. In fact, in another passage (Phil. 4.12) Paul glories as much in knowing how to abound as in knowing how to be in want. Thus we must note this distinction, as I have said, between temporary and permanent ministerial excellencies.

5. *In tumults*. The calmness and gentleness of Paul's character were matched by the courage he showed in standing undaunted in the face of tumults and he claims for himself the credit of meeting them with bravery, although he hated them. It is not simply that he was unmoved by tumults—for that could be said of all rioters—but that he was not thrown into alarm by tumults that other people stirred up. Both things are required of ministers of the Gospel, that they should be to the utmost of their power men of peace and yet also should pass undaunted through the midst of commotions without turning from the right course, even though the heavens should fall. Chrysostom prefers to take ἀκαταστασίας to mean the many expulsions from different places that Paul had to undergo, since he was never allowed to settle in any one place.

In fastings. He does not mean hunger due to lack of food, but the voluntary practice of abstinence. *Knowledge* may mean either the teaching itself, or skill in acting rightly and with knowledge. I think the second more probable, as he immediately adds *the word of truth*. *Spirit* means, by metonymy, spiritual gifts. Chrysostom makes a foolish comment here, inferring from the fact that the Spirit is mentioned alone and by Himself, that all the other qualities mentioned were Paul's natural endowments and had no connexion with the Spirit, as if longsuffering, knowledge, pureness, the armour of righteousness could come from any other source but the Holy Ghost. He mentions the Spirit separately as a general term among specific instances. The *power of God* showed itself in many different ways, in magnanimity, in effective defence of the truth, in spreading the Gospel, in victory over enemies and things of that kind.

7. *By the armour of righteousness.* Righteousness must be taken to mean uprightness of conscience and holiness of life. He uses the metaphor of armour because all who serve God have to fight, since the devil is always on the alert to overthrow them. And they must be armed on every side, for if the devil does not succeed in one onslaught, he at once launches another and attacks sometimes in the front, sometimes in the rear, and sometimes on one or other flank.

8. *By glory and dishonour.* This is no small trial for a man to undergo, as there is nothing harder for a man of character than to incur disgrace. From history we can see that there have been few men of heroic spirit who have not collapsed on being attacked by insults. Thus it is a sign of a mind well established in virtue, not to be diverted from its purpose, whatever disgrace it may incur. This is a rare excellence and yet a man cannot prove himself God's servant without it. We must indeed have regard to our own good name but only in so far as that is consistent with the edification of our brethren, and not to the extent of being swayed by rumours that may be circulated against us, for we should rather keep the same even course unperturbed in either glory or dishonour. For God lets us be tried even by the cursing of wicked men to prove whether we are walking uprightly and are not men-servers, for the man who is diverted from his duty by men's unkindness proves that he has not looked to God alone. Since, then, we see how Paul was exposed to infamy and insults and yet did not give up for any of them, but went straight on with unsubdued courage and broke through all hindrances to reach the goal, let us not grow weary if the same thing should happen to us.

As deceivers. Here he is not telling us merely what ungodly outsiders thought of him, but is reporting accusations made inside the Church. Here everyone may see the unworthy depths of ingratitude to which the Corinthians fell and what a brave man Paul was in struggling on against such formidable obstacles. He sharply though indirectly rebukes their mistaken judgment of him when he says that he lives and is joyful even though they despise him as one dead and overcome with grief. He reproaches them again with ingratitude when he says that when he was being despised for being poor he was making many rich. For they were among those who had been enriched by his wealth and in fact every one of them was under obligation to him in many ways. With the same irony he had previously said he was *unknown* when the fruit of his labours was in fact well known and famous everywhere. But what a cruel thing it is to despise the poverty of a man who supplies you out of his abundance! He means, of course, spiritual riches which ought to be considered much more precious than earthly.

Our mouth is open unto you, O Corinthians, our heart is enlarged. Ye are not straitened in us, but ye are straitened in your own affections. Now, for a recompense in like kind (I speak as unto my children), be ye also enlarged. Be not unequally yoked with unbelievers: for what fellowship have righteousness and iniquity? or what communion hath light with darkness? And what concord hath Christ with Belial? or what portion hath a believer with an unbeliever? And what agreement hath a temple of God with idols? for we are a temple of the living God; even as God said, I will dwell in them, and walk in them; and I will be their God, and they shall be my people. Wherefore Come ye out from among them, and be ye separate, saith the Lord, And touch no unclean thing; and I will receive you, and will be to you a Father, and ye shall be to me sons and daughters, saith the Lord Almighty. Having therefore these promises, beloved, let us cleanse ourselves from all defilement of flesh and spirit, perfecting holiness in the fear of God. (6.11–7.1)

11. *Our mouth is open.* The opening of the mouth is a sign of boldness, and if you choose to connect this with what has gone before the meaning will be, 'I have ample cause to glory and an upright conscience makes me bold to open my mouth. If you have formed an unfavourable judgment of us, that is not our fault, but because your judgment is unfair. You should have been more generous in your estimate of my ministry which God has proved honourable to you in so many ways.' But I prefer a different interpretation. For he says that his mouth is open because his heart is enlarged. But what does it mean to speak of an enlarged heart? Without doubt it means an enthusiasm that is prompted by good will. It is a common metaphor to speak of a small and contracted heart meaning grief or disgust or anger, and so an enlarged heart is used to indicate feelings of the opposite nature. Here Paul is speaking of something that we experience every day, for when we are dealing with our friends, our heart is enlarged, all our feelings are disclosed, nothing is hidden or shut, and our whole mind is eager and glad to expose itself to view. As a result the tongue also is free and unfettered, and does not stammer or produce broken syllables from the back of the throat, as happens when the mind is taken up with less happy feelings.

12. *Ye are not straitened in us.* That is, 'It is your own fault that you cannot share the eager goodwill I feel towards you. My mouth is opened to deal with you as my intimate friends, I would gladly pour out my very heart to you, but you have hardened your hearts against me.' His meaning is that because of their perverse judgment about him, they have no taste for anything he offers them.

13. *Now, for a recompense in like kind.* He softens his rebuke by addressing them gently as his sons and by appealing to them in a way that shows he still has good hopes of them. By a 'recompense in like kind' he means that the bond of duty between them is mutual, just as with fathers and sons there are duties on either side. As it is the duty of parents to nourish and instruct their children, to direct them by their good counsel and to defend them, so also justice demands that children should requite their parents. He means what the Greeks called ἀντιπελαργίαν—reciprocal affection. 'I, on my side,' he says, 'feel towards you as a father; do you on your side by your affection and your respect prove yourselves to be my sons.' There is a special point to be noted here. He tells the Corinthians that they must in turn be enlarged in their hearts, so that having found so kind a father they may repay his affection by their docility. The Vulgate has failed to understand Paul and has added the participle *habentes*, thus reading, 'having a recompense in like kind'—which is not Paul's meaning. There is, however, nothing forced in my own explanation, which follows Chrysostom.

14. *Be not unequally yoked.* Having thus regained his authority over them, he goes on to reprimand them more freely for associating with unbelievers as their partners in outward idolatry. He has exhorted them to show themselves amenable to him as to a father, and now with the right of a father he reproves the fault into which they have fallen. We have explained in the first epistle what this fault was, how they imagined that nothing was forbidden to them in outward things, and so without reserve began to defile themselves with ungodly superstitions. In frequenting the banquets of unbelievers, they were sharing in their profane and unclean rites, imagining themselves innocents when they were committing grievous sin. Thus here Paul attacks outward idolatry and commands Christians to break all connexion with it. He begins with this general statement, intending to go on to specific instances. For to be yoked with unbelievers means nothing less than to have fellowship with the unfruitful works of darkness and to hold out a hand to unbelievers to signify fellowship with them. Many think that here Paul is speaking of marriage, but the context shows clearly that they are mistaken. The word Paul uses means 'to be joined together in drawing the same yoke' and the metaphor is taken from oxen or horses which have to walk together at the same pace and share in the same work, because they are fastened under one yoke. Thus when Paul forbids us to draw the same yoke with unbelievers as our associates, he simply means that we are to have no fellowship with them in their pollutions. It is true that one sun shines on all of us, we all eat the same bread and breathe the same air, and

we cannot sever completely all connexion with them. But Paul is speaking about the yoke of ungodliness, about participation in actions which Christians cannot lawfully share. Under this prohibition marriage also falls, inasmuch as it is a snare that might implicate men and women in consent to ungodliness. But my point is that Paul's teaching here is too general to be restricted just to marriage; his subject here is the avoidance of idolatry, and to make sure that we do avoid it, we are also forbidden to marry the ungodly.

For what fellowship. He makes his exhortation stronger by showing that it is absurd and unnatural to connect things that are in themselves so opposed, for Christianity and idolatry can no more abide each other than fire and water. If they wish to avoid plunging everything into confusion, they must abstain from the pollutions of the ungodly. From this we may infer that people who disapprove of superstitious practices in their hearts are still polluted by them unless they stop dissembling and openly and without pretence take a stand against them.

15. *What concord hath Christ with Belial?* Even the Hebrews themselves cannot agree about the etymological derivation of the word Belial, but its meaning is quite clear. For Moses made a word or thought of Belial mean an ungodly and wicked thought, and in many passages criminals or men abandoned to evil are called sons or men of Belial. That is how Paul comes here to use the word meaning the devil, the chief of all evil doers. From this comparison of the two heads, he soon passes on to the members, as though to say, 'As there is an irreconcilable enmity between Christ and Satan, so we must keep ourselves free of all connexion with the ungodly.' But, of course, when Paul says that a Christian has nothing in common with an unbeliever he does not mean in such things as food or clothes or land or sun or air, as I have explained above, but he is referring to these things that are the special properties of unbelievers and from which the Lord has separated us.

16. *What agreement hath the temple of God with idols?* Till now he has been forbidding believers in general terms from associating with the ungodly. He now tells them his main reason for this prohibition, that they had ceased to consider the profession of idolatry a sin. He has already attacked this licentious attitude at Corinth in the first epistle, but it is probable that all of them have not yet been won over to accept his counsel. That is why he complains of their hardness of heart as the only thing that is holding them back. He does not however take up that subject afresh, but contents himself with a short reminder, as we often do when we are dealing with what is well known. But nevertheless, his brevity does not prevent him from hitting hard. That single phrase in which he explains that there is no agreement between idols

and the temple of God is full of vehemence. For it is sacrilegious profanation to introduce an idol or any kind of idolatrous worship into God's temple. Now we are the true temples of God, therefore it is sacrilege to defile ourselves with any contamination of idolatry. This one consideration should have as much weight as a thousand, 'If you are a Christian, what business have you with idols, for you are a temple of God.' But Paul is combatting idolatry here more by exhortation than by doctrine, as I have already said, since it would have been superfluous to deal with it at length as though the Christian attitude to it were still doubtful or obscure.

As God said, I will dwell in them. He proves that we are temples of God from the promise God once made to the people of Israel that He would dwell in their midst. We should notice first that the only way God can dwell among us is by dwelling in each one of us, and He promises this to us as a special blessing, 'I will dwell in the midst of you.' Also, this dwelling or presence cannot consist merely in the giving of earthly benefits, but must refer mainly to spiritual grace. Thus it does not mean simply that God is near us, as though He were in the air flying around us, but it means rather that He has His dwelling in our hearts. If anybody objects that the preposition 'in' simply means 'among', I agree, but I do claim that from God's promise to dwell among us we may infer that He also remains in us. The symbol of this was the ark, which Moses mentions in the passage from which Paul seems to have borrowed this text, namely Lev. 26.12. But if anybody thinks that Paul was citing rather Ezek. 37.27, the argument will be the same. For in his description of the restoration of the Church the prophet names as its chief blessing the presence of God which in the beginning He had promised through Moses. What was prefigured by the ark was manifested to us more fully in Christ, since He was made Immanuel for us. My view is that it is Ezekiel rather than Moses who is quoted here, for he not only refers to the symbol of the ark but also prophesies that this symbol will find its fulfilment under the reign of Christ. Moreover, the apostle takes it for granted that God dwells only in a holy place. If you say of a man, 'he dwells here', that does not make that place a temple, but only an ordinary house, for it is the special prerogative of God that any place that He honours with His presence He also sanctifies.

17. *Wherefore Come ye out from among them.* This exhortation is taken from Isa. 52.11, where the prophet in foretelling the people's deliverance goes on to address the priests in these terms. He addresses these words to 'ye that bear the vessels of the Lord' and that refers to the priests, for the care of the vessels used in sacrifices and other parts of divine worship was entrusted to them. There is no doubt that his

purpose is to warn them that, while they are awaiting their deliverance, they should be on their guard against being infected by the many pollutions with which the land they were in was overrun. This is as relevant to us today as it was to the ancient Levites, for if such great purity is required in the guardians of the vessels, how much more in the vessels themselves: and all our members are vessels set apart for the spiritual worship of God and we ourselves are a royal priesthood. Since therefore we have been redeemed by God's grace, it is right that we should keep ourselves undefiled by any impurity lest we pollute the sanctuary of God. But since we who remain still in this world have been redeemed and rescued from its defilements, we are not to give up our life in order to have done with all uncleanness, but rather we are to avoid all participation in it. We may sum up by saying that if with a true heart we strive for the blessing of redemption, we must beware of defiling ourselves by any involvement in the pollutions of the world.

18. *I will be to you a Father.* This promise is not made only in one passage but is often repeated. Paul has added it here in order that a knowledge of the great dignity to which God has raised us may urge us on to a greater zeal for holiness. For when God has gathered His Church from profane nations and has restored it, the result of this redemption is that believers are seen to be His sons and daughters. It is no common honour for us to be reckoned among the sons of God and it is for us, on our side, to take care that we do not become His degenerate children. For what an affront it is to God for us to call Him our Father and then to defile ourselves with the abominations of idolatry. The thought of the great nobility He has conferred upon us ought to whet our desire for holiness and purity.

CHAPTER SEVEN

1. *Having therefore these promises.* In His promises God takes the initiative and anticipates us by His pure grace, but having thus freely granted us His grace, He immediately requires of us gratitude in return. When He said to Abraham, 'I am thy God' (Gen. 17.7), that was an offer of His free undeserved kindness, but He added at the same time this demand, 'Walk before me and be thou perfect.' Since this second clause is not always explicit, Paul tells us that this condition is implied in all God's promises so that they should urge us on to promote God's glory. For where does he look for means so to stimulate us? To the fact that God confers upon us such a signal honour. It is of the very nature of God's promises that they summon us to sanctification, just as if God had inserted an implied condition. We also know what the Scriptures, in many different places, teach about the purpose of redemption and we must understand every sign of God's favour in the light of that purpose.

From all defilement of flesh and spirit. Having shown that we are called to purity, he now adds that this purity should be evident both in body and in soul, for here 'flesh' means body and 'spirit' means soul. This becomes clear when we consider that if 'spirit' meant the grace of regeneration Paul's statement about defilement of spirit would be absurd. He would have us pure from defilements, not only inwardly where God alone can discern them, but also outwardly where they come under the observation of men. It is as if he had said, 'We should not only have consciences that are pure in God's sight, but we should also consecrate to Him our whole body and all our members so that no impurity can be seen in any part of us.' If we consider the trend of his argument here, we shall easily see that it is a shameless subterfuge to try to excuse external idolatry by all sorts of excuses. For if defilement of spirit means godlessness within and any kind of superstition, what can be meant by defilement of flesh but the external profession and practice of ungodliness, whether pretended or sincere? They boast of a pure conscience, and it is a false boast, but even if we grant them their boast, they still have only half of what Paul requires from believers. And they have no reason to think that God is satisfied with that half, for if any man shows any appearance or indication of idolatry at all or takes part in wicked and superstitious rites, even if in his soul he is perfectly upright—which is impossible—he will still be guilty of having defiled his body.

Perfecting holiness. The Greek word ἐπιτελεῖν means sometimes to perfect and sometimes to perform sacred rites, but the former meaning is the more usual and that is how Paul most fittingly employs it here so as to refer to sanctification, which is his subject in this passage. For since it means perfection, it seems to have been applied deliberately to sacred functions since in divine service everything must be perfect and nothing defective. Thus rightly to consecrate yourself to God, you must dedicate both body and soul completely to Him.

In the fear of God. If the fear of God is strong in us, we shall not indulge ourselves or allow ourselves to be carried away by overweening insolence, as the Corinthians did. For how can many people take delight in external idolatry and so arrogantly defend such a gross fault, unless it is because they think that they can mock God with impunity. But if the fear of God were to rule in them, they would not need to be convinced by long arguments but would immediately give up all their worthless pretexts for their idolatry.

> *Open your hearts to us: we wronged no man, we corrupted no man, we took advantage of no man. I say it not to condemn you: for I have said before, that ye are in our hearts to die together and to live together. Great is my boldness of speech toward you, great is my glorying on your behalf: I am filled with comfort, I overflow with joy in all our affliction. For even when we were come into Macedonia, our flesh had no relief, but we were afflicted on every side; without were fightings, within were fears. Nevertheless he that comforteth the lowly, even God, comforted us by the coming of Titus; and not by his coming only, but also by the comfort wherewith he was comforted in you, while he told us your longing, your mourning, your zeal for me; so that I rejoiced yet more.* (2–7)

2. *Open your hearts to us.* He again returns from doctrine to his own personal concerns, but only to make sure that he will not be wasting his time in admonishing the Corinthians. In fact he brings this latest admonition to a close by saying the same thing as he had said by way of preface at the beginning. For the expression 'Receive us' or 'Open your hearts to us' means exactly the same as 'Be ye enlarged' (6.13), namely this, 'Do not let corrupt feelings or misguided opinions prevent my teaching from entering right into your minds and lodging itself there. For since in my fatherly earnestness I take such trouble for your welfare, it would not be right for you to turn a deaf ear.'

We wronged no man. He says that there is no reason why they should be estranged from him, since he has given them no cause of offence. He mentions three kinds of offences and claims that he is innocent of them all. The first is open hurt or injury, the second corruption brought about by false teaching and the third fraud or cheating with worldly goods. It is usually in one of these three ways that pastors estrange their people from them. Either they behave unreasonably and use their authority as a pretext for tyrannical cruelty or oppression, or they lead away into error those they should have guided aright and infect them with the corruption of false doctrine, or they give evidence of immoderate greed by coveting what belongs to another. To put it briefly, the first offence is harshness and abuse of power by over officiousness, the second is unfaithfulness in doctrine and the third avarice.

3. *I say it not to condemn you.* What he has just said was a kind of complaint and in making complaints we can hardly avoid administering a rebuke and so he softens what he has said. 'My intention', he says, 'is to clear myself in such a way that I may also avoid insulting you.' It is true that the Corinthians were unkind and, since Paul was found innocent, they deserved to be accused in his stead. For they were guilty on two counts, first, of ingratitude and, second, for bringing false charges against an innocent man. But such is the apostle's moderation that he is content simply to defend himself and refrains from recriminations.

For I have said before. We do not rail against those we love, but if they commit some fault, we cover it over and take no notice or make light of it out of kindness. A desire to reproach is a sign of hatred, and so Paul, to show that he has no desire to cause the Corinthians any distress, declares his love for them. And yet, just by saying that he does not condemn them, he does in a way do so. But as there is a great difference between gall and vinegar, so is there between the kind of condemnation with which we pursue a man out of hatred in order to flay him with infamy, and the other kind by which we seek to recall a sinner to the right way, so that along with his salvation he may regain his honour unimpaired.

Ye are in our hearts. That is, 'I carry you about with me shut up in my heart.'

To die together and to live together, that is, 'so that no change can break the bonds of love between us, for I am ready not only to live with you, but even, if need be, to die with you and to suffer anything rather than renounce your friendship.' Notice that this is how all pastors ought to feel.

4. *Great is my boldness of speech.* He now assumes that he has won from the Corinthians the openness of heart he has been asking, so that he leaves off complaining and pours out his own heart with cheerfulness, as if to say, 'Why should I spend any more labour on a task that is already accomplished? For I believe that I have already what I have been asking for; the news of you that Titus has brought me is not only enough to remove my anxiety but it gives me cause to glory with

confidence in you. In fact, his news has taken away the grief which has been caused by the many afflictions I have undergone.' He goes on here step by step working towards a climax. To glory is more than to be of a quiet mind and to be freed from the grief that afflictions bring is greater than either. Chrysostom explains this boldness in rather a different way, as follows, 'If I deal with you rather freely, it is because I rely on your great kindness towards me and think I make bold to take so much liberty with you.' My own explanation seems to me to be more likely, that Titus' report has removed the unfavourable impression that had been troubling and distressing him.

5. *For when we were come into Macedonia.* The greatness of his grief shows what powerful comfort it must have been that could remove it. 'I was being pressed', he says, 'on every side by troubles within and troubles without. But all this has not stopped the joy that you brought me from prevailing and even overflowing.' When he says that *'our flesh had no relief'* it is as though he said, 'Humanly speaking I had no relief' for he excepts the spiritual comforts by which he was all the time being sustained. Thus he was afflicted not only in body but in mind so that, as far as his human affections were concerned, he could feel nothing but great bitterness over his afflictions.

Without were fightings. By 'fightings' he means the attacks from outside being made against him by his enemies and by 'fears' the anxieties he endured over the internal ills of the Church, since it was more public than private troubles that were distressing him. His meaning is that he is not only being attacked by his avowed enemies, but is enduring as much distress from evils at home. He saw how very weak many of them, and indeed almost all of them were and he also saw how many different devices Satan was using to throw everything into confusion. He saw how few were wise, how few were sincere, how few were steadfast and how many were either hypocrites and men of no worth or ambitious or troublemakers. Amidst such difficulties it is inevitable that God's servants should tremble and be very anxious, all the more since they have to swallow many things in silence for the sake of the peace of the churches. Thus he has expressed himself well in saying that without were fightings and within were fears. Faithful pastors openly oppose the professed enemies who attack Christ's kingdom, but they are inwardly tormented and suffer secret distress when they see the Church labouring under internal troubles which they dare not speak out to cure. But although Paul was involved in these struggles almost continuously, it is probable that at the time he wrote this he was being more hardly pressed than usual. For certainly Christ's servants hardly ever have respite from fears and Paul was seldom free from outward fightings, but because he was at this time being more violently pressed, he speaks of his fightings and fears in the plural meaning that he has had to fight in many different ways against many different enemies and at the same time has had many different fears.

6. *He that comforteth the lowly.* Paul explains how he has been comforted. His meaning is that consolation was offered to him when he was cast down and almost overwhelmed with evils, because it is God's way to comfort the humble and those who are brought low. From this we may gather the most profitable lesson that the more we are afflicted, the greater is the comfort that God has prepared for us. And so this description of God contains a wonderful promise that it is specially God's concern to comfort the miserable and those bowed down to the dust.

7. *And not by his coming only.* Paul foresees a possible objection from the Corinthians who might say, 'What difference does it make to us that Titus has cheered you by his coming? Since you are very fond of him, you would no doubt be glad to see him.' Paul explains that the reason for his joy was that Titus was coming back from them and was bringing completely joyful news of them with him. Thus he declares that what has cheered him is not so much the presence of a single individual but rather the prosperous condition of the Corinthian church.

Your longing. Notice what joyful news of them Paul had. Their 'longing' sprang from their high estimate of Paul's teaching, their 'mourning' was a sign of respect since, moved by his reproof, they were bemoaning their sins, and their 'zeal' was a proof of their goodwill. From these three Paul gathered that they were repentant and this gave him complete satisfaction since his sole concern and care was for their welfare.

So that I rejoiced yet more. That is, 'so that all my griefs and distresses were overcome by joy'. From this we may see not only how great was Paul's fervour in seeking the public good of the Church but also how gentle and mild his own disposition was so that he could at once forget such grave offences that had been committed against him. This sentence could also be taken in another way as referring to what follows and it may be that such an interpretation suits Paul's intention better, but since it is a matter of small importance, I say no more.

For though I made you sorry with my espistle, I do not regret it, though I did regret; for I see that that epistle made you sorry, though but for a season. Now I rejoice, not that ye were made sorry, but that ye were made sorry unto repentance: for ye were made sorry after a godly sort, that ye might suffer loss by us in nothing. For godly sorrow worketh

v. 8] II CORINTHIANS 7

repentance unto salvation, a repentance which bringeth no regret: but the sorrow of the world worketh death. For behold, this selfsame thing, that ye were made sorry after a godly sort, what earnest care it wrought in you, yea, what clearing of yourselves, yea, what indignation, yea, what fear, yea, what longing, yea, what zeal, yea, what avenging! (8-11)

8. *For though I made you sorry.* He now begins to apologize to the Corinthians for treating them rather harshly in his first epistle. It should be noticed in how many different ways he deals with them so that he seems to be writing in several different characters. The reason is that his words were directed to the whole Church. In it some looked upon him with disfavour, some held him in the highest esteem as he deserved; some were doubtful, others sure; some were teachable, others obstinate. This diversity made Paul direct his words now to one group and now to another to accommodate himself to them all. Now he softens and indeed removes any offence that his severity may have caused them by showing that it has resulted in their good. 'Your welfare', he says, 'is of such value to me that I am delighted to see that I have done you good.' This toning down of a rebuke is in place only when a teacher has had a satisfactory response to his reproofs, for if he had found that the Corinthians still remained obstinate and no good result had come from his attempt to correct them, then he would have relaxed none of his former severity. We should notice how he rejoices at having caused sadness to those he loved, for he cared more about profiting them than pleasing them.

But what does he mean by adding '*though I did regret*'? For if we say that Paul was displeased with what he had written, we shall be driven to the absurd conclusion that the first epistle was written on a rash impulse rather than under the guidance of the Spirit. I answer that the word 'repent' is here used loosely to mean 'regret'. For when Paul inflicted grief on the Corinthians he himself shared that grief so that in a sense he inflicted it upon himself. It is as if he had said, 'Although I hurt you against my will and it grieved me to be forced to be severe with you, now I no longer grieve on that account seeing how profitable it was for you.' A father is grieved by his severity if at any time he has to chastise his son, but he approves of it nevertheless because he sees it is for his son's good. So for Paul, it was far from pleasant for him to trouble the Corinthians, but because he was convinced that there was a good reason for doing so, he did his duty rather than followed his inclination.

For I see. Here his meaning is contracted into a few words, but that does not take away from its clarity. First he says that the actual results have now shown him that his first epistle, however unwelcome at the time, has in the end been of advantage to the Corinthians, and then he adds that it is for that reason he is glad.

9. *Not that ye were made sorry.* He means that he has no delight in their sorrow, and if the choice were given, he would try to promote at the same time both their welfare and their happiness, but since there was no alternative, their welfare was of such importance to him that he was glad that they had been *made sorry unto repentance.* There are doctors who are otherwise kind and faithful and yet who have on occasion to be severe and unsparing to their patients. Paul says that he is not a man to employ harsh remedies unless he has to. But since his experiment with a harsh cure has turned out well, he congratulates himself on its success. He has already used a very similar mode of expression in chapter 5.4, 'For indeed we that are in this tabernacle do groan, being burdened, not for that we would be unclothed, but that we would be clothed upon.'

10. *Godly sorrow.* In order to understand what is meant by 'sorrow according to God' we have to note how Paul contrasts it with its opposite—'the sorrow of the world'. We should also consider the same contrast between two different kinds of joy. There is the joy of the world in which in their folly and without any reverence for God men delight in the vain things of this world and are made drunk with fleeting enjoyment so that they care for nothing higher than the things of earth. But there is also joy according to God, godly joy in which men look to God for all their happiness, take pleasure in His grace and by their contempt of the world make it clear that they enjoy earthly prosperity as though they enjoyed it not and even in adversity are light of heart. In the same way the sadness of this world is when men's hearts are cast down by earthly afflictions and are overwhelmed with grief; but sorrow according to God is when they look up to God, count it their only misery to be cut off from His grace and in fear of His judgment mourn for their sins. Paul says that this kind of sorrow is the cause and origin of repentance. This should be carefully noted for, unless a sinner is dissatisfied with himself so that he hates his own life and is in deep sorrow as he confesses his sin, he will never be converted to the Lord. But a man cannot feel this kind of sorrow without undergoing a change of heart. Thus repentance begins with grief because, as I have already said, nobody can return to the right way without first hating his sin and where there is hatred of sin there must be self-reproach and grief. He gives us a beautiful description of repentance when he says that it *'bringeth no regret'.* for however bitter it may be at the first taste, the profitable results that flow from it make it desirable. The phrase could be taken as referring to salvation rather than repentance but in my view it goes better with repentance, as if he

had said, 'The final outcome teaches us that such sorrow should not be painful or distressing to us so that, however much bitterness repentance may involve, it is called something that brings no regret because of the precious and pleasant fruit that it brings forth.'

Unto salvation. Paul seems to be making repentance the cause of salvation and if that were so, it would follow that we are justified by works. My answer is that we must take note of the precise point Paul is making here. He is not concerned with the cause of salvation, but is only recommending repentance by showing the fruit that it bears and by comparing it to a road that leads to salvation. And rightly so. Christ indeed calls us by free grace but He calls us to repentance and God forgives our sins freely but only when we renounce them. God works in us the two things at the same time, so that we are both renewed by repentance and freed from the bondage of sins and also justified by faith and freed from their curse. These are the inseparable gifts of grace and because of the invariable bond between them repentance can rightly and fittingly be called the beginning of the way that leads to salvation, but more as an accompaniment than a cause. These are not subtle evasions but a simple explanation of the difficulty for while Scripture teaches that we never obtain the forgiveness of our sins without repentance, at the same time it teaches in many places that the only ground of our forgiveness is the mercy of God.

11. *What earnest care it wrought in you.* I will not enter into any disputes about whether the things Paul enumerates here are the effects or the parts of repentance or preparations for it, since we can understand Paul's meaning without going into that. He is simply attesting the repentance of the Corinthians by the outward signs that accompany it. He makes 'sorrow according to God' the first of these from which the rest spring, and so indeed it is, for as soon as we begin to be dissatisfied with ourselves, we are stirred up to seek all the rest. What 'earnest care' means we can understand by comparing it with its opposite. While there is no acknowledgment of sin, we lie drowsy and inactive. And this drowsiness or carelessness or indifference is the opposite of this 'earnest care', so that it is an eager and active desire to correct what has been sinful and to amend our life.

Yea, what clearing of yourselves. Because Erasmus rendered this phrase 'satisfaction' unskilled commentators, deceived by the ambiguity of that word, have applied it to papistical satisfactions, while in fact the word ἀπολογίαν which Paul uses means 'defence'. That is why I have preferred to follow the Vulgate and keep the word *defensio* in the Latin, but we must notice that it is a kind of defence that has more to do with seeking for pardon than with rebutting charges. It is like a son who, desiring to clear himself with his father, does not embark on a lawyer-like pleading of his cause but acknowledges his fault and excuses himself by humble pleas rather than confident protestations. Hypocrites also excuse themselves and proudly defend themselves but more with a view to having a legal tussle with God than to returning to His favour. If the term 'excuse' is more acceptable to anybody, I have no objection since it makes no difference to the meaning, which is that the Corinthians were now prompted to clear themselves whereas before they had not cared what Paul's opinion of them might be.

Yea, what indignation. This also goes with holy sorrow so that the sinner burns hot in anger against his faults and even against himself, just as those who have a good and godly zeal are angry when they see God offended. This feeling is more intense than sorrow. The first step is that evil should displease us but the second is that we should be roused to indignation so as to deal with ourselves severely and have our consciences touched to the quick. This could however be taken to mean the indignation of the Corinthians against the faults of the man or the small group they had before been sparing, so that they repented of their consent and connivance in their sins.

Fear comes from a sense of the divine judgment when the sinner thinks, 'Remember you must render an account and what defence will you bring forward before such a judge?' Alarmed by such thoughts he will tremble with fear, but since the ungodly are sometimes affected by a similar fear, he adds *longing* which is of a more voluntary nature than fear. We are often afraid against our wills but we never desire anything except by our own inclination. Thus as by Paul's warning they had been made to dread punishment, so now they were eagerly longing for amendment. But what does *longing* mean? There is no doubt that Paul introduced it at the climax of his list so that it must mean more than just earnest concern. It can be taken to imply that they were inciting each other to mutual rivalry but it is simpler to understand by it that each was striving with great fervour of zeal to give proof of his repentance. Thus longing is the intense striving of desire.

Yea, what avenging. What has already been said about indignation may be applied to 'avenging' also, for the wickedness they had once countenanced by their connivance and indulgence they afterwards showed themselves rigorous in avenging. For a time they had tolerated incest, but after Paul's warnings they had not only ceased to favour it but had been stern judges in punishing it and this was their 'avenging'. But since we ought to punish sins wherever they are to be found and should begin first with ourselves, there is a wider application of what the apostle is saying here. He is speaking of the signs of repentance and among these there is this special sign whereby by punishing sins we in a way anticipate God's own judgment, as he teaches elsewhere, 'If we judged ourselves, we should not be judged by the Lord' (I Cor. 11.31). It must not be inferred from this that by punishing themselves men can compensate God for the penalties due to Him, so that they redeem themselves from His hand. The facts of the matter are that it is God's plan to chasten us in order to arouse us from our indifference so that having this reminder of His wrath we may be on our guard for the future. Thus when the sinner voluntarily punishes himself first, there is no need of that kind of warning from God.

It may be asked whether the Corinthians were undertaking this avenging and longing and desiring etc. for Paul's sake or for God's. My answer is that all these things are the invariable accompaniments of repentance but there is a difference between secret sin that God alone sees and open sin seen by all men. If the sin is secret, then repentance before God is enough, but if the sin is public there is also required an open manifestation of repentance. Thus the Corinthians who had sinned openly and to the great offence of good men had of necessity to show these open signs as testimony of their repentance.

> *In everything ye approved yourselves to be pure in the matter. So although I wrote unto you, I wrote not for his cause that did the wrong, nor for his cause that suffered the wrong, but that your earnest care for us might be made manifest unto you in the sight of God. Therefore we have been comforted: and in our comfort we joyed the more exceedingly for the joy of Titus, because his spirit hath been refreshed by you all. For if in anything I have gloried to him on your behalf, I was not put to shame; but as we spake all things to you in truth, so our glorying also, which I made before Titus, was found to be truth. And his inward affection is more abundantly toward you, whilst he remembereth the obedience of you all, how with fear and trembling ye received him. I rejoice that in everything I am of good courage concerning you.* (11-16)

11. *Ye approved yourselves to be pure.* The Vulgate reads, 'Ye have shown yourselves', and Erasmus, 'Ye have commended yourselves', but I have preferred this third rendering that seemed to me more suitable, that the Corinthians gave clear and genuine evidence that they were in no way involved in the crime in which their connivance seemed to implicate them. We have already seen what that evidence was. Paul does not excuse them completely but he lessens their offence. The excessive tolerance they had shown did deserve blame but he exonerates them from implication in the crime. We should also note that he does not exonerate them all individually, but merely the body of the church. We may well believe that some knew of it and con-

doned it, but although all fell into the disgrace it caused, it later became clear that only a few were at fault.

12. *So, although I wrote.* He does what people who are seeking reconciliation usually do. He wants the past to be buried, there are no more reproaches, he blames them for nothing and protests against nothing. In fact, he forgets everything because their repentance is by itself enough to satisfy him completely. And this is certainly the right way, not to press sinners any further once they have been brought to repentance. For if we still keep alive the memory of their faults it must be out of malevolent spite and not godly affection or desire for their salvation. All this Paul says by way of apology, because he had pressed hard the thing that had given him offence and wanted the man responsible to be punished, but now he suppresses what had been somewhat distasteful, as if to say, 'I would now like it to be thought that my only purpose in writing as I did was to give you a chance to show your earnest affection for me; for the rest, let us leave it be.' Others take him to mean that in what he wrote he was concerned not merely with one individual but with the common good of all of them, but the other interpretation is more natural.

Your earnest care for us. As this is the best attested reading in the Greek manuscripts I have not ventured to erase it completely, but in one old codex the reading is ἡμῶν and it would appear from Chrysostom's commentary that in his time the more generally accepted reading even among the Greeks was that of the Latin versions—'that our earnest care for you might be made manifest to you', that is, that it might appear to the Corinthians how anxious Paul was on their account. And yet the other rendering on which the majority of the Greek codices are now agreed is quite probable. For according to it Paul would be congratulating the Corinthians on having at last been taught by this test how they felt towards him, as if to say, 'You yourselves were not aware of how much affection for me you had till you were put to the test in this way.' Others take it as referring to special feelings of one individual, so as to mean 'that it might become clear among you how much respect each of you had towards me and that you might take the opportunity this matter provided for each of you to show what up till then had been hidden in your hearts'. Since it is a question of little importance, I leave my readers free to chose whatever sense they prefer, but since he immediately adds '*in the sight of God*' I rather think that he meant that each of them, having examined himself seriously as though in God's sight, knew himself better than he did before.

13. *We have been comforted.* Paul's whole purpose is to convince the Corinthians that nothing matters more to him than their welfare and

so he says that he has shared with them in their comfort. The source of this comfort was that they had acknowledged their fault and not only accepted his reproof in good part but gladly welcomed it. The bitterness of a reproof is easily sweetened as soon as we begin to taste how good for us it has been.

He now adds by way of congratulation that *we joyed the more exceedingly in the comfort* (R.V. has '*joy*') *of Titus*. Titus had been overjoyed at finding them more obedient and compliant than he could have expected, in discovering in fact a sudden change for the better. From this we may gather that Paul's gentleness has no element of flattery in it since the chief source of the joy that he shared with them was their repentance.

14. *For if in anything I have gloried to him*. Here he shows indirectly how well disposed and friendly he has always been towards the Corinthians and with what sincerity and kindness he has judged of them, for at the very time when they seemed to merit no approval, he was still looking for many virtues in them. This is a remarkable instance of how a man of upright and sincere mind will accuse to their face those he loves but will yet cherish high hopes of them and make others share these hopes. This sincerity of his should have prevented them from taking anything that came from him amiss. Paul uses this opportunity to commend to them again in passing his faithfulness in all other matters, as if to say, 'Up till now you have had a chance to prove my candour and I have proved myself to be faithful in everything and not at all fickle. I therefore rejoice that I have also now been found truthful in my boasting to others of you.'

15. *And his inward affection is more abundantly toward you*. The Latin text has *viscera*, bowels, for since the bowels are the seat of feeling mercy, love and all godly affections are known by that name. His intention was to emphasize that although Titus loved the Corinthians before, now he had been given cause to love them even better from the bottom of his heart. At the same time he is by saying this winning the affection of the Corinthians for Titus, since it is an advantage for Christ's servants to be loved, that they may have it in their power to do more good, and at the same time it encourages them to make good progress that will make them worthy of the love of all good men.

With fear and trembling. Sometimes he uses these two words just to mean respect and that would suit this passage quite well, but I have no objection to taking the trembling literally, meaning that because they had a bad conscience they were afraid to meet Titus. Even those who are obstinate in their sins begin to tremble at the sight of the judge; but voluntary trembling that springs from sincere shame is a sign of repentance. However you may choose to take it, this passage teaches how ministers of Christ should be rightly received. It is not sumptuous banquets or splendid apparel or courteous and honourable salutations or the applause of crowds that give pleasure to a faithful and upright pastor: he has his sufficient joy when the doctrine of salvation is reverently received from his lips, when he can exercise the authority that belongs to him for the upbuilding of the Church, when the people submit themselves to his direction so as to be ruled by Christ through his ministry. We see an example of this here in Titus. In closing he **again** confirms at length what he has already said, that he had never been so offended by the Corinthians as to lose his trust in them.

CHAPTER EIGHT

Moreover, brethren we make known to you the grace of God which hath been given in the churches of Macedonia; how that in much proof of affliction the abundance of their joy and their deep poverty abounded unto the riches of their liberality. For according to their power, I bear witness, yea and beyond their power, they gave of their own accord, beseeching us with much intreaty in regard of this grace and the fellowship in the ministering to the saints: and this, not as we had hoped, but first they gave their own selves to the Lord, and to us by the will of God. Insomuch that we exhorted Titus, that as he had made a beginning before, so he would also complete in you this grace also. But as ye abound in everything, in faith, and utterance, and knowledge, and in all earnestness, and in your love to us, see that ye abound in this grace also. (1–7)

If the Corinthians are still offended by Paul's severity in his first letter, it could be a hindrance to the exercise of his authority over them, and up till now, therefore, he has been trying to conciliate their affections. But now that all the offence has been removed and his ministry has regained full favour among them, he commends to them the brethren in Jerusalem that they may help them in their need. He could not have attempted this with any great success at the beginning of this epistle, and so he has wisely held it back until he had prepared their minds for it. Thus in this chapter and the next his whole concern is to encourage the Corinthians to be active and diligent in collecting money to be taken to Jerusalem to relieve the want of the brethren there, for they were afflicted with great famine, so that they could scarcely maintain life without help from the other churches. The apostles had entrusted this matter to Paul and he had promised to look after it and had already done so in part, as we saw in the first epistle. But now he presses it again.

1. *We make known to you.* He praises the Macedonians in order to rouse the Corinthians by their example, although he does not expressly say so, but the Macedonians had no need of commendation whereas the Corinthians had every need of stimulation. And to rouse the Corinthians even more to envy, he ascribes the readiness of the Macedonians to help their brethren to the *grace of God*. For although it is universally agreed that it is a praiseworthy virtue to give help to the needy, yet all men do not consider it a gain to give, nor do they ascribe it to God's grace. On the contrary they think that something of theirs

has been lost by being given. But Paul declares that when we give help to our brethren we should ascribe it to God's grace and should count it an extraordinary privilege to be eagerly sought. The grace that has been bestowed on the Macedonians is, he says, twofold; the first is that they have endured afflictions calmly and with light hearts; the second is that from their small resources they have given as much help to their brethren as might have been expected to come from abundance. Both of these are, as Paul rightly affirms, the work of the Lord, for men quickly fail when they are not sustained by the Spirit of the Lord who is the author of all comfort, and deep-rooted lack of confident faith clings to us and holds us back from all the duties of love till it is overcome by the grace of the same Spirit.

2. *In much proof of affliction.* That is to say, when they were tested by adversity, they did not cease to rejoice in the Lord but rather their joy became great enough to swallow up their sadness. For the minds of the Macedonians had to be released from their own frustrations in order that they might liberally help their brethren who would otherwise have been hard pressed. By *joy* he means that spiritual comfort by which believers sustain themselves in afflictions. The ungodly either delude themselves with empty comforts by avoiding the thought of evil and diverting their minds to vague meditations, or else they completely give way to grief and let themselves be overwhelmed by it, but believers look at their very afflictions as an occasion for rejoicing, as we may see in Rom. 8.

And their deep poverty. The metaphor is taken from empty vessels, as if to say that the Macedonians had been drained to the very bottom. He declares that even in such straits they had abounded in generosity and been rich enough not merely to have sufficient for themselves but to help others also. Notice how we can always be liberal even in the direst poverty, if we make up for the deficiencies in our purses by the generosity of our hearts.

Liberality is here the opposite of niggardliness, as in Rom. 12.8 where he requires this liberality of deacons. The thing that makes us more close-fisted than we should be with our money is that we are too careful and look too far forward at possible dangers that might come upon us and so become too cautious and anxious and work out too fretfully how much we are going to need during our whole life and how much we lose when the smallest part is taken away. But the man who depends on the Lord's blessing has his mind set free from these vexatious cares and at the same time his hand set free for beneficence. The argument is now applied from the lesser to the greater. Bad fortune and indeed poverty itself did not stop the Macedonians from doing good to their brethren: what excuse, then, could there be for the Corinthians if they in their comparative richness and affluence were to hold back?

3. *For according to their power, yea, and beyond their power.* When he says that they gave *of their own accord* he means that of themselves they were so inclined to give that no appeal from him was required. It would have been a great thing to strive according to the measure of their ability, and so to go beyond their power was proof of an excellence both admirable and rare. He speaks with reference to the common habit of men, for their usual way of doing good is as Solomon lays down, 'Drink waters out of thine own well and let the rivulets go past that they may flow onwards to others' (Prov. 5.15). The Macedonians however without thought or concern for themselves gave themselves instead to providing for others. In short those with meagre resources show themselves willing beyond their power if out of their slender means they make any gift to others.

4. *Beseeching us with much intreaty.* He enlarges further upon their readiness to give, pointing out that not only did they not wait for an appeal to be made to them but themselves approached those who would have made that appeal, if in their enthusiasm they had not anticipated every approach to them. Here again we have to apply the argument from the lesser to the greater. If the Macedonians have taken the initiative without being asked and have even been first with entreaties to be allowed to help, how disgraceful it is for the Corinthians to remain inactive especially after an appeal has been made to them. If the Macedonians lead the way in front of everybody, how disgraceful it is for the Corinthians not at least to follow their example. And what of the fact that, not satisfied with beseeching, they added to their requests *much entreaty*? From this it is clear that they asked in earnest and not merely as a matter of form.

In regard of this grace and fellowship. He uses the word 'grace' to commend almsgiving, although the word can be explained in different ways. But this interpretation seems to me to be simplest for since our heavenly Father bestows all things upon us in free grace, we must be imitators of His gracious bounty in doing good to others and, because in laying out our resources we are no more than the dispensers of the gifts of His grace. The *fellowship in ministering* refers to how Paul helped the Macedonians in this ministry. Their part was to contribute from their own resources that the money might be administered to the saints but they wanted Paul to take charge of collecting it.

5. *Not as we had hoped.* He expected from them an ordinary degree of willingness such as any Christian should show, but they surpassed his expectations for they had not only their resources in readiness but were prepared to offer themselves. *They gave their own selves first to*

God, he says, and then to us. It may be asked whether their giving of themselves to God and to Paul are two different things. It is quite usual for God, when He gives charges or commands through some minister, to associate that minister with Himself both in authority to command and in receiving obedience. 'It seemed good to the Holy Spirit and to us' say the Apostles (Acts 15.28) when they were only instruments to announce what had been revealed and enjoined by the Spirit. Again, 'The people believed the Lord and Moses, His servant' (Exod. 14.31), and yet Moses had no authority apart from God. This is also what is meant by the phrase that follows—*by the will of God.* For since they were obedient in submitting themselves to the counsel of His minister, it was consistent with this obedience that they should listen to Paul as though he spoke with the mouth of God.

6. *Insomuch that we exhorted Titus.* This appeal has greater force when they are thus expressly summoned to take their part in responding to it. His desire to have the Corinthians share in this beneficence implies no slight to the Macedonians. Titus is defended from a possible charge of pressing the Corinthians too urgently, as though he had some doubts of their good will, for he was doing it at the request of the Macedonians rather than in his own name.

7. *But as ye abound.* He has already been very careful not to give offence when he says that Titus has appealed to them, not out of his own inclination but at the bidding of the Macedonians. But he now goes further and encourages them not even to wait for the message from the Macedonian churches, at the same time praising them for their other excellent qualities, as if to say, 'You should not merely enter into partnership with the Macedonians as they request, but you should surpass them in this matter as you do in others.' He draws a distinction between *utterance* and *faith* since it is possible for a man to have faith, and even great faith, and yet not to be greatly practised in the Word of the Lord. I take *knowledge* to mean either experience or prudence. He mentions their *love* towards himself to encourage them in their regard for his person and at the same time he appeals to the private affection in which they held him for the sake of the public good of the brethren. But in all he says here he is restraining himself so that nothing in his appeal should give apparent grounds for accusations.

> *I speak not by way of commandment, but as proving through the earnestness of others the sincerity also of your love. For ye know the grace of our Lord Jesus Christ, that, though he was rich, yet for your sakes he became poor, that ye through his poverty might become rich. And herein I give my judgment: for this is expedient for you, who were the first to make a beginning a year ago, not only to do, but also to will. But now*

complete the doing also; that as there was the readiness to will, so there may be the completion also out of your ability. For if the readiness is there, it is acceptable according as a man hath, not according as he hath not. (8-12)

8. *I speak not by way of commandment.* Once again he softens his appeal by disclaiming any intention of imposing any compulsion upon them for to 'speak by way of commandment' is to enjoin some definite action and strictly require that it should be done. But if anyone asks if it would not have been right for him to require something for which he had a commandment from the Lord, the answer is easy, that God certainly always commands that we relieve our brethren's necessities, but He nowhere lays it down how much we ought to give, so that we can make a calculation and divide between ourselves and the poor. He nowhere binds us to specific times or persons or places but simply bids us be guided by the rule of love. In any case Paul is not considering here what is or is not permissible to him. He says that he does not give orders as if he thought that they needed to be compelled and would refuse to do their duty unless constrained by necessity. But he names two reasons why he nevertheless stirs them up to do their duty. Firstly, the concern he feels for the saints in Jerusalem compels him to do so and, secondly, he wants the love of the Corinthians to be shown forth to all. I do not take the meaning to be that Paul himself wished to be assured of their love, for he has already said that he is fully persuaded of it, but rather that he wished that all men should have proof of it.

Nevertheless the first clause in which he speaks of his anxiety for others admits of two meanings, either that he himself felt an anxiety about them that would not let him rest, or else that he yielded to the entreaties of others who had this matter at heart and was speaking not so much from his own volition as at their suggestion.

9. *For ye know the grace.* Having mentioned love he now refers to Christ as the perfect and unique pattern of it. 'When He was rich', he says, 'He gave up possession of all His blessings that He might enrich us by His poverty.' He does not explain why He has mentioned Christ but leaves that for them to consider for themselves, for it must be clear to everyone that by Christ's example we are incited to beneficence so that we should not spare ourselves when our brethren require our help. Christ was rich because He was God, under whose power and authority are all things, and even in our humanity, which He put on, He was, as the apostle says, 'the heir of all things', since He was placed by His Father over all creatures and all things were put in subjection under His feet. But He became poor because He gave up His possession

and for a time did not exercise His right. We see what destitution and lack of all things awaited Him right from His mother's womb and we hear what He Himself says, 'The foxes have holes and the birds of the heaven have nests; but the Son of Man hath not where to lay His head' (Luke 9.58). Thus He sanctified poverty in His own person, so that believers should no longer shrink from it, and by His poverty He has enriched us so that we should not find it hard to take from our abundance what we may expend on behalf of our brethren.

10. *And herein I give my judgment.* Here 'judgment' is contrasted with the 'command' of which he has just been speaking, as if he had said, 'I show you what is expected but only by way of advice or admonition.' Now it is not apparent to the judgment of the flesh that *it is expedient,* for where will you find a man who will agree that it is to his advantage to deprive himself of something in order to help others? There is indeed a pagan proverb which says that 'The riches you have given away are the only ones that you will always have' but the reason for that is that what is given to friends is safe from risk. But the Lord does not wish us to be influenced by the hope of a reward or any remuneration in return for our giving, but even if men are ungrateful, so that we seem to have lost what we have given them, He would have us persevere in doing good. The advantage to us comes from the fact that, as Solomon says, 'he that giveth into the poor lendeth unto the Lord' (Prov. 19.17), whose blessing, even by itself, is to be reckoned a hundred times more valuable than all the treasures of the earth. The word 'expedient' here is sometimes taken to mean 'honourable', or we may say that Paul decides what is expedient by reference to what is honourable, since it would have been disgraceful for the Corinthians to turn back or stop in midstream when they had already gone so far. And it would also have been useless, since everything they had attempted would have fallen short of God's favour.

Who had made a beginning not only to do. His way of speaking seems inappropriate since 'to do' is more than to will. But to will here does not have its simple meaning but has the added idea of a spontaneous enthusiasm that does not wait for an appeal from outside. For there are, so to speak, three ways in which we can act. First, we may sometimes act against our wills under the compulsion of shame or fear. Secondly, we may act willingly but under the impulsion of influences originating outside ourselves. Or thirdly, we may act at the promptings of our own mind when we freely set ourselves to do what we ought. Such promptitude in acting without external stimulus is better than the mere performance of the deed.

11. *Now complete the doing also.* Probably the ardour of the Corinthians had cooled quickly, for otherwise they would have carried out

their intention without any delay. But the apostle, without saying that any fault has been committed, gently appeals to them to complete what they had begun so well. When he adds 'out of your ability', he anticipates a possible objection. The flesh is always ingenious in devising excuses, and some plead that they have families it would be unkind to neglect, and some use the fact that they cannot give much as an excuse for giving nothing; 'How could I give so little?' Paul takes away all excuses of this kind by telling them that each of them should contribute according to his ability and he adds, as his reason, that God looks not at the amount but at the heart. For when he says that a willing heart is acceptable to God according to each man's ability his meaning is this, 'If you offer a small gift from your slender resources, your intention is just as valuable in God's eyes as if a rich man had made a large gift out of his abundance.' For willingness to give is not judged by what you do not have, or, in other words, God never requires that you should contribute more than your resources allow. In this way none is left with any excuse since rich men owe God a large tribute and poor men have no reason to be ashamed if what they give is small.

> *For I say not this, that others may be eased, and ye distressed: but by equality; your abundance being a supply at this present time for their want, that their abundance also may become a supply for your want; that there may be equality: as it is written, He that gathered much had nothing over; and he that gathered little had no lack. But thanks be to God, which putteth the same earnest care for you into the heart of Titus. For indeed he accepted our exhortation; but being himself very earnest, he went forth unto you of his own accord.* (13-17)

13. *Not that others may be eased.* This confirms what he has just said, that both in poverty and wealth it is a willing heart that pleases God, since God does not wish us to be reduced to straits in order that others may be at ease through our liberality. It is indeed true that we owe God not merely a part but all of what we have and are, but in His kindness He spares us to the extent of being satisfied with that measure of sharing that Paul is laying down here, so that his teaching here is to be understood as a waiving of the strict letter of the law. But at the same time it is for us to stir ourselves up from time to time to liberality, since we should not be too afraid of going to excess; the danger is rather that we shall do too little. But this teaching is needed to refute fanatics who think that you have done nothing unless you strip yourself completely and put everything in a common fund. The only thing they achieve by this madness is that nobody can give alms with a good conscience. Therefore we should carefully note Paul's ἐπιείκεια, his mildness and moderation in saying that our almsgiving pleases God,

when we relieve the need of our brethren out of our abundance in such a way that the result is not that they are at ease and we in want, but rather that we give to them something commensurate with our own resources and that we give it with a willing heart.

14. *By equality.* Equality can be taken in two ways, either as meaning mutual compensation, when each side gives an equal amount, or as a fair apportioning. I take ἰσότητα to mean that each should give a fair proportion of what he has. He uses the word with this meaning in Col. 4.1, where he exhorts masters to give to their servants what is equal. He certainly does not mean that they should be equal in condition and status, but rather the kindness and gentle forbearance that masters owe their servants. Thus the Lord commends to us this fair proportioning of our resources that we may, in so far as funds allow, help those in difficulties that there may not be some in affluence and others in want. He adds *at this present time* for at that time necessity pressed upon the Jerusalem saints. We are thus told that in exercising beneficence we should look to present need if we wish to observe the rule of equity.

And their abundance. There is some doubt as to what kind of abundance he means. Some take it to mean that, since the Gospel had come forth to the Corinthians from the church of Jerusalem, its spiritual riches had come to the aid of the Corinthians' poverty, but that is not, in my view, Paul's intention. It should rather be related to the communion of saints, which means that when a duty is laid upon one member it profits the whole body, as though he had said, 'If it is irksome to you to help your brethren with riches that are of no ultimate value, remember how many blessings of much greater value you yourselves lack, and how it is those who lack worldly goods who may be in a position to bestow them abundantly upon you. This communal sharing which Christ has instituted among the members of His body, should stir you up to greater activity and enthusiasm in doing good.' Or the meaning could possibly be this, 'You relieve them now because this is their time of need, but at some other time they will be given the opportunity to repay you.' I like the first more general interpretation better and it is supported by what he now says once again about equality. For the rule of proportional equity in the Church is that, while the members share with each other in proportion to their gifts and needs, this mutual sharing results in a fair adjustment, even although some have less and others more and the gifts are distributed unequally.

15. *As it is written.* The passage that Paul quotes here refers to manna, but we should listen to what the Lord says by Moses for He wishes this to be regarded as a perpetual warning that men do not live by bread alone but are supported by God and kept safe and preserved

by the secret power of His Will who has created all things. Elsewhere (in Deut. 8.3) Moses admonishes the people that they have been for a time fed with manna, that they might learn that men are not fed by their own industry and labour but by the blessing of God. Thus in the manna we may clearly see, as it were, in a mirror, the image of the ordinary food that we eat. Now let us come to the passage that Paul quotes. When the manna fell they were ordered to gather it into heaps, as much as each man could, but as some were more active than others, some gathered more than they needed for their daily use, and others less, yet no one took more than an omer for his own private use, for that was the amount laid down by the Lord. This being so, all had as much as they needed and none was in want. This we have in Exod. 16.18. Now let us apply the story to Paul's concern here. The Lord has not prescribed to us an omer or any other measure for the food we have each day, but He has commended to us frugality and temperance and has forbidden anyone from going to excess because of his abundance. Thus those who have riches, whether inherited or won by their own industry and labour, are to remember that what is left over is meant not for intemperance or luxury but for relieving the needs of the brethren. All that we have is manna, from whatever source it may come, provided only that it is really ours, since riches acquired by fraud or illegal tricks do not deserve the name of manna but are rather quails sent by God in His wrath. And just as manna, which was hoarded to excess out of greed or lack of faith, immediately putrified, so we should have no doubt that riches which are heaped up at the expense of our brethren are accursed and will soon perish and their owner will be ruined with them, so that we are not to imagine that the way to grow rich is to make provision for our own distant future and defraud our poor brethren of the help that is their due. I acknowledge indeed that we are not bound to such an equality as would make it wrong for the rich to live more elegantly than the poor; but there must be such an equality that nobody starves and nobody hordes his abundance at another's expense. The poor man's omer will be coarse food and a frugal diet, and the rich man's a more abundant portion according to his circumstances, and yet in such a way that they should live temperately and not fail others.

16. *But thanks be to God which putteth.* To remove all excuses from the Corinthians, he now adds that they are being given men of active enthusiasm who will attend to this matter. And first among them he names Titus, who, he says, has been stirred up by God. This was of great importance to the cause he was pleading, for Titus' impending mission would be more effective if the Corinthians recognized that he had come at the prompting of God. From this passage, as from

countless others, we infer that all godly affections proceed from the Spirit of God, and further that it is a proof of God's care for His people that He rouses ministers and guardians to try to relieve their necessities. And if the providence of God shows itself in thus providing nourishment for the body, how much greater will His care be that we should lack no spiritual food. Thus it is His special and peculiar work to raise up pastors.

17. *He accepted our exhortation* means that it was at Paul's request that Titus undertook this duty. Later he corrects this and says that Titus was not so much influenced by the advice of others but rather stirred up of his own accord and by his own interest and concern.

> And we have sent together with him the brother whose praise in the gospel is spread through all the churches; and not only so, but who was also appointed by the churches to travel with us in the matter of this grace, which is ministered by us to the glory of the Lord, and to shew our readiness: avoiding this, that any man should blame us in the matter of this bounty which is ministered by us: for we take thought for things honourable, not only in the sight of the Lord, but also in the sight of men. And we have sent with them our brother, whom we have many times proved earnest in many things, but now much more earnest, by reason of the great confidence which he hath in you. Whether any inquire about Titus, he is my partner and fellow-worker to you-ward; or our brethren, they are the messengers of the churches, they are the glory of Christ. Shew ye therefore unto them in the face of the churches the proof of your love, and of our glorying on your behalf. (18-24)

18. *We have sent with him the brother.* The fact that three messengers were sent shows what great expectations there were as to what the Corinthians might do, and thus it was for the Corinthians to attend to this duty all the more carefully so as not to disappoint the hopes of the churches. Who this second 'brother' is, is not certain but some conjecture that it was Luke and others that it was Barnabas. Chrysostom prefers Barnabas and I agree with him, especially since it was he that had been chosen by the churches to be Paul's companion. Since, however, there is nearly universal agreement that Luke was one of those through whom this letter was transmitted, I have no objection to his being considered to be the third messenger. Whoever this second person is, Paul honours him with a distinguished commendation when he says that his conduct in the Gospel deserved praise. By this he means that he had earned applause by the way he had promoted the Gospel. For although Barnabas took second place after Paul, as far as speaking was concerned, yet they were both involved in one work. He adds that this man had won praise, not just from one individual, or

even from one church but from all the churches. And to this general commendation he adds another which is specially relevant to the subject now under discussion, for he says that this brother has been chosen for this work with the consent of the churches. It is most unlikely that this honour would have been bestowed upon him unless he had been long known to be well fitted for it. We should note the method of election, by χειροτονία, a show of hands, as was customary among the Greeks. In this procedure leaders of authority and counsel took precedence and regulated the election while the common people cast their votes.

19. *Which is ministered by us.* By commending his own ministry, he gives further encouragement to the Corinthians. He says that he promotes the glory of God and their liberality; it follows that these two things are connected—God's glory and their generosity—so that the generosity cannot cease without the glory being so far diminished. There is besides the efforts of these notable men which it would be absurd to reject or to allow to pass without result.

20. *Avoiding this, that any man should blame us.* In case anyone should imagine that the churches did not trust Paul's honesty, and had associated others with him as partners in the way that guards are often assigned to people under suspicion, he says that he himself is the instigator of this arrangement in order to provide against trouble. Here someone will ask if there could have been anyone shameless enough to dare to insult by the slightest breath of suspicion a man whose trustworthiness must have been beyond all question everywhere. I answer by asking if anyone can be immune from Satan's slanderous attacks, when even Christ Himself was not spared, for if He was exposed to the reproaches of the ungodly, how can His servants expect to remain in safety? On the contrary, it is when a man is completely upright that Satan launches all his devices against him in an attempt to find some means or other of injuring his reputation, for his fall could be a much greater cause of offence. Thus the higher the position we occupy, the greater is our need to imitate carefully Paul's circumspection and modesty. He was not so exalted as to refuse to be put under surveillance just like an ordinary member of the flock: he was not so complacent as to think it below his dignity to avoid false accusations. He wisely avoided dangers and showed great caution so that no ill-disposed person should be given an opportunity to accuse him. And certainly there is nothing that so leaves a man open to sinister insinuations as the mangement of public funds.

21. *We take thought for things honourable.* My view is that even among the Corinthians there were some who would not have hesitated to speak ill of Paul, if a chance had been given them. Thus he

wanted them to know how matters stood so that all accusations might be stilled. Thus he declares that he takes care not only to have a good conscience before God but also to have a good reputation before men. There can be no doubt that by his example here he wishes to teach the Corinthians and everyone else that in judging how to act rightly the opinion of men is not to be ignored. The first concern is certainly to be a good man, and this is secured not only by outward deeds but by an upright conscience; but the second concern is that the people among whom you live should acknowledge you to be the good man that you are. But we must remember to what end this approval of men is to be sought, for nothing is worse than selfish ambition which vitiates all the best things, deforms the most honourable and makes the sweetest sacrifices offensive to the Lord. This passage is rather dangerous as it might encourage somebody to pretend to be like Paul and care for a good reputation, and yet be of a very different mind than Paul who looked to things that were honourable in the eyes of men, only so that nobody should be made to stumble by his example but rather that all should be edified by it. So, if we want to be like him, we must take care not to want a good name for our own sakes; 'the man who neglects his reputation', says Augustine, 'is cruel, because it is as necessary before our neighbour as a good conscience is before God.' That is true, provided that you are ready to glorify God by consulting the welfare of your brethren and are prepared to bear reproaches and disgrace instead of praise, if it seems good to the Lord. Yet a Christian man should always take care to lead a life that tends to the edification of his neighbours and should take careful precautions that the ministers of Satan can find no excuse for slandering him, to the dishonour of God and the offending of good men.

22. *By reason of the great confidence.* The meaning is, 'I have no fear that their coming to you may be fruitless and in vain, for I have had from the start great confidence that their mission would have a happy issue, so clear to me are their faithfulness and zeal.' He says that the brother whose name he does not mention was even more eager, partly because he saw what a good opinion he, Paul, had of the Corinthians, partly because Titus had roused his enthusiasm, and partly because he saw many eminent men apply their united efforts to the same task. Thus only one thing remained, that the Corinthians themselves should not fail in their duty.

When he speaks of *the messengers of the churches,* there are two possible explanations of what he means, either that God has set them apart as messengers to the churches, or that they had been appointed by the churches to undertake this work. The second interpretation is better. They are also called *the glory of Christ* because, since He alone is the glory of believers, He must in turn be glorified by them. All those who excel in godliness and holiness are the glory of Christ, since all that they have is Christ's gift to them.

In conclusion he makes two points. 'See that our brethren behold your love' and 'See to it that I have not boasted of you in vain.' The Greek phrase εἰς αὐτούς seems to mean 'before them', for it refers not to the poor but to the messengers who have just been mentioned, for he immediately adds that these messengers would not be the only witnesses but that through their report the word would go out even to churches far away.

CHAPTER NINE

For as touching the ministering to the saints, it is superfluous for me to write to you: for I know your readiness, of which I glory on your behalf to them of Macedonia, that Achaia hath been prepared for a year past; and your zeal hath stirred up very many of them. But I have sent the brethren, that our glorying on your behalf may not be made void in this respect; that, even as I said, ye may be prepared: lest by any means, if there come with me any of Macedonia, and find you unprepared, we (that we say not, ye) should be put to shame in this confidence. I thought it necessary therefore to intreat the brethren, that they would go before unto you, and make up beforehand your aforepromised bounty, that the same might be ready, as a matter of bounty, and not of niggardliness. (1-5)

At first sight this statement does not seem to fit, or at least not well, what goes before. He seems to be speaking about a new subject he has just introduced, when in fact he is continuing the same subject. Readers should, however, note that Paul is dealing here with exactly the same matters as before; he is still explaining that it was not out of any lack of confidence that he was appealing to the Corinthians, nor was his admonition accompanied by any kind of reproach for their past record, but he has other reasons that prompt him. Thus the meaning of what he now says is this, 'I am not teaching you the duty of ministering to the saints, for what need is there of that? It is well enough known to you and your deeds have given evidence that you have no intention of failing them, but the reason why I cannot keep silent is that I have been boasting everywhere of your generosity and my reputation is at stake as well as yours.' Such anxious pleading might have been rather offensive to the Corinthians, if it had had some other motive behind it, since they might have thought either that they were being accused of negligence or that Paul suspected them. But by this most apt explanation he secures for himself the freedom not only to exhort them without offence but to urge them repeatedly.

Some may suspect that here Paul is professing a confidence that he does not feel. But that would be quite absurd, for if he thinks that they are sufficiently inclined to do their duty, why does he show so much restraint in his admonitions, and if he is doubtful of their willingness why does he say that admonition is superfluous? Love involves both good hope and anxious concern and Paul would never have commended the Corinthians so highly if he had not been convinced of the truth of what he said. He had seen the promising start they had made, he hoped that their further progress would be equally satisfactory, but because he was so well aware of the fickleness of men's minds, he could not take too much care to ensure that they did not turn aside from their sworn intention.

1. *Ministering.* This word does not seem very suitable for application to those who give their money to the poor since liberality deserves a more splendid description, but Paul had in mind what believers owe to their fellow-members in the same body. The members of Christ have a duty to minister to each other, so that when we come to the help of our brethren we only discharge the ministry that is their due. On the other hand, to neglect the saints when they need our help is more than just unkindness; it is to defraud them of their due.

2. *Of which I glory.* He now gives proof of his good opinion of them, since he has, so to speak, gone surety for them by boasting of their readiness to give. But what if he has recklessly said more than the facts will bear out? It already looks as if this might be the case, for he was boasting that they had had prepared for a year money that he was at that very time urging them to get ready. My answer is that what Paul says is not to be taken as meaning that their givings were already stored in a chest; he is simply saying what they have decided among themselves. There is no blame for irresponsibility or mistake involved; he is simply speaking of this promise they have made.

3. *But I have sent the brethren.* He now tells them why he has been so much at pains to exhort and encourage them to give, even though he is quite certain of their good intentions to do so. 'I am concerned', he says, 'for my own good name and for yours, for since I made a promise on your behalf, we should both be disgraced if deeds and words did not agree. Thus you should take my apprehension in good part.'

4. *In this confidence.* The Greek word is ὑπόστασις and the Vulgate has therefore rendered it by the Latin *substantia*, substance, and Erasmus by *argumentum* meaning here subject-matter, but neither is really suitable. Budaeus observes that the word is sometimes used to mean boldness or confidence as in Polybius when he says: οὐχ οὕτω τὴν δύναμιν ὡς τὴν ὑπόστασιν καὶ τόλμαν αὐτοῦ καταπεπληγμένων τῶν ἐναντίων, 'It was not so much his strength as his boldness and daring that confounded the enemy.' Thus ὑποστατικός sometimes indicates one who is bold and confident. Now everyone must recognize that this rendering is well suited to Paul's context here and it becomes obvious that by not noticing it other interpreters have fallen into error.

5. *As a matter of bounty and not of niggardliness.* Some put 'collection' instead of 'bounty' in this passage but I have preferred to keep the

literal rendering as the Greeks used the word εὐλογίας to render the Hebrew ברכה which means a blessing, that is a prayer for good fortune, as well as beneficence. I take the explanation of these two meanings to be that the term is first used of God, for we know that God effectively bestows a blessing upon us by the mere exercise of His will. Thus when the word is transferred to men, it keeps the same meaning, improperly indeed, because man's blessing does not have the same efficacy as God's, and yet not unsuitably by transference from the one to the other. With this blessing Paul contrasts πλεονεξίαν, a word that in Greek means both excessive greed and niggardliness. In the antithesis being drawn here niggardliness gives the best meaning, for Paul wants them to give not grudgingly but in a liberal spirit, as will be seen more clearly from what follows.

> But this I say, He that soweth sparingly shall reap also sparingly; and he that soweth with blessings shall reap also with blessings. Let each man do according as he hath purposed in his own heart; not grudgingly or of necessity: for God loveth a cheerful giver. And God is able to make all grace abound unto you; that ye, having always all sufficiency in everything, may abound unto every good work: as it is written, He hath scattered abroad, he hath given to the poor; His righteousness abideth for ever. (6-9)

6. *But this I say.* He now commends almsgiving in a fine comparison in which he likens it to sowing. In sowing the seed is thrown from the hand, scattered here and there over the ground, is harrowed and finally wastes away so that it almost seems to have been lost. It is the same with almsgiving; what goes from you to somebody else seems to lessen what you have, but harvest time will come when the fruits will be gathered. For the Lord counts whatever is given to the poor as given to Himself and so repays it later with large interest. But to come now to Paul's comparison, he says that the man who is sparing in his sowing will have a harvest as sparse as his sowing, but the man who sows generously and with an open hand will likewise reap a bountiful harvest. This teaching should be firmly fixed in our minds, so that whenever fleshly prudence holds us back from doing good out of fear for what we shall lose, we may immediately resist its promptings by remembering how the Lord declares that in doing good we are sowing seed. This harvest should be understood both in terms of the spiritual reward of eternal life and also as referring to the earthly blessings with which God honours the beneficent. Not only in heaven does God reward the well-doing of the godly, but in this world as well. It is as if he had said, 'The more liberal you are to your neighbours, the more liberal you will find the blessing that God pours forth on you.'

Here again he uses the word 'blessing' as the opposite of 'sparing' just as a little ago he had contrasted it with niggardliness. The word seems to be used to mean a large and bountiful liberality.

7. *Each according as he hath purposed in his heart.* Having enjoined them to give liberally, he has now to make it clear that God judges liberality not by the amount given but from the motive. Certainly he wanted them to give a large amount so that the brethren might be helped the more abundantly, but he had no desire to extort anything from them against their wills. Thus he tells them to give liberally as much as they feel they ought. He contrasts *purpose of heart* with *grudgingly* and *of necessity*. When we act under necessary compulsion we do not act according to the purpose of our heart but with reluctance. The necessity here referred to is what is known as extrinsic necessity, that is necessity imposed from without. Certainly we obey God because that is necessary and yet we do it from the heart. For in this case we impose the necessity upon ourselves of our own free will, and since our flesh is reluctant we often go so far as to force ourselves to perform a necessary duty. But when we are compelled from outside to do something that we would fain avoid if we could, then we do that thing not eagerly or cheerfully but reluctantly and with a forced consent.

For God loveth a cheerful giver. He brings us back to God, for, as I said at the outset, alms are a sacrifice and only a willing sacrifice can please God. For when he says that God loves a cheerful giver he implies the contrary, that He rejects the mean and the coerced. It is not His will to lord it over us like a tyrant; He shows Himself to be a Father towards us and so He requires from us the free obedience of sons.

8. *And God is able.* Once again he meets the unworthy suggestion that our lack of faith is always whispering in our ears, 'What, will you not rather think about your own interests? Do you not see that when you have given this away, there will be less left for you?' To refute this suggestion Paul arms us with the wonderful promise that whatever we give away will turn out to our own advantage. I have already said that we are by nature extremely niggardly because we are prone to the lack of faith which tempts everyone to hold on eagerly to his own. To correct this fault we must lay hold on this promise, that those who do good to the poor in fact look to their own interests as much as if they were watering their fields. For by their almsgiving they make so many water channels along which God's blessing will flow to enrich them. Paul's meaning is this, 'Such liberality will be no loss to you, but will ensure that what you give away will return to you in much greater abundance.' He speaks of God's power not like the poets but in the usual manner of Scripture which ascribes to Him a power that shows itself in action, so that we ourselves may experience its present effect,

II CORINTHIANS 9 [v. 8-10

and not an inactive potentiality which we have merely to imagine.

All sufficiency in everything. He describes the twofold result of the grace he had promised to the Corinthians—that they should have enough for themselves and something over with which to do good to others. By the word *sufficiency* he means the amount that the Lord knows to be profitable to us, for it is not always to our good to be filled to satiety. The Lord administers to us as much as is profitable for us, sometimes more and sometimes less, but always so that we are satisfied and that is worth much more than having the whole world with which to gorge ourselves. In this sufficiency we must abound to the good of others. For God does not do good to us so that each should keep for himself what he receives, but in order that there should be a mutual sharing among us, as necessity requires.

9. *As it is written, He hath scattered abroad.* As proof of what he has been saying, he cites Ps. 112.9 where, among the other virtues of a godly man, the prophet mentions that he will not be found wanting in beneficence, but just as water always flows from an unfailing fountain, so the flow of his liberality will never cease. Paul's purpose is that we should not grow weary in well-doing and that is what the prophet's words also mean.

> *And may he that supplieth seed to the sower and bread for food, supply and multiply your seed for sowing, and increase the fruits of your righteousness: ye being enriched in everything unto all liberality, which worketh through us thanksgiving to God. For the ministration of this service not only filleth up the measure of the wants of the saints, but aboundeth also through many thanksgivings unto God; seeing that through the proving of you by this ministration they glorify God for the obedience of your confession unto the gospel of Christ, and for the liberality of your contribution unto them and unto all; while they themselves also, with supplication on your behalf, long after you by reason of the exceeding grace of God in you. Thanks be to God for his unspeakable gift.*
> (10-15)

10. *He that supplieth.* This is a beautiful description of God and full of excellent consolation. For the man who sows at the right season appears in reaping to gather in the fruit of his own toil and labour, so that the sowing seems to be the source from which our food comes to us. But Paul denies this and maintains that the seed is provided and the food supplied by God's grace to the farmers who sow it and imagine that it is by their labour that others are nourished. The same thing is expressed in Deut. 8.16-18, 'God fed thee with manna, which thy fathers knew not, lest perhaps when you come into the land that I shall give thee, thou shalt say, "My hand and my strength hath gotten

v. 10–11] II CORINTHIANS 9

me this wealth", because it is the Lord that giveth thee power to get wealth' etc.

Supplieth. Here there are two variant readings even in the Greek. Some versions have the three verbs in the future, *will supply, will multiply, will increase.* This would make this sentence a confirmation of the one immediately preceding it, and it is not unusual for Paul to repeat the same promise in other words in order to impress it upon the mind. In other versions the verbs are in the infinitive and it is well known that the infinitive is sometimes used instead of the optative. I prefer this latter rendering both because it is more generally accepted and because Paul usually follows his exhortations with prayers in which he entreats from God the thing that has been the subject of his exhortation, and yet there is nothing wrong with the first reading either.

Bread for food. He mentions the twofold result of God's blessing upon us—first, that we have sufficient for the support of life and then that we have something to give to relieve other people's necessities. For as we are not born for ourselves alone, so a Christian man ought not to live for himself or use what he has only for private purposes. By the words *seed* and *fruits of righteousness* he means alms. The fruits of righteousness he indirectly contrasts with the profits of their labours that men store up in vaults, barns and storehouses, so that they may all gorge themselves with whatever they can collect or scrape together for their enrichment. By speaking of seed he refers to the means of doing good, and by the fruit he means the work itself or the assistance that is given: for here righteousness is used by synecdoche for beneficence as if he had said, 'May God not only supply you with what is sufficient for your own use, but in such measure that the springs of your liberality may ever flow and never be exhausted.' Since it is a part of righteousness—and by no means the least part—to assist the wants of our neighbours, those who neglect this part of their duty must be counted unrighteous.

11. *Being enriched unto all liberality.* Here again he uses the word liberality to explain the nature of real well-doing, when, with all our care cast on God, we gladly lay out our possessions for whatever purpose He may direct. He teaches that believers enjoy true richness when they rely on God's providence to support them in sufficiency and are not held back from doing good by lack of faith. It is with good reason that he uses the word affluence to describe the sufficiency of a generous heart content with its own moderate supply. For none are more frustrated or starving than men of no faith whose anxiety over their possessions takes all their peace away.

Which worketh through us. He commends the alms they are about to give for another good effect they will have—they will tend to promote the glory of God. He goes on to amplify the point and explain it more clearly as follows, 'As well as the usual fruits of love they will also produce thanksgiving.' He expands this by saying that thanks will be given to God by many, not only for the liberality which has come to their aid but for the whole godly state of the Corinthians.

By *ministration* he means that which he himself had undertaken at the request of the churches. The word that we render '*service*' is in Greek λειτουργία, which sometimes means a sacrifice and sometimes a publicly assigned office. Either meaning suits the present passage well, for we are familiar with the fact that almsgiving is called a sacrifice and, when offices are distributed among the citizens of a country, no one grudges to undertake the duty conferred upon him, so that in the Church sharing of resources must be counted a necessary duty. By helping the brethren in Jerusalem, the Corinthians and the rest were offering God a sacrifice or discharging a rightful service that was binding upon them. Paul was the minister of that sacrifice. The word 'ministry' or 'service' could also be taken as referring to the Corinthians, but it is a matter of little importance.

13. *Through the proving by this ministration.* Proving here, as in many other passages, means proof or trial. This was a suitable occasion for proving the love of the Corinthians, that they were so generous to brethren so far from them. But Paul means more than that; he is thinking of their harmonious obedience to the Gospel, for it is by such proofs that we make it clear that we are obedient to the Gospel's teaching. Their harmony in this is made clear by the fact that the alms are conferred with the common consent of them all.

14. *With supplication.* He leaves out no advantage resulting from their beneficence that might have some weight in moving the Corinthians. First he mentioned the comfort believers would experience, next the thanksgiving by which God would be glorified and that this would be also a confession by which proof would be given of their unanimous consent in faith and godly obedience: now he adds the reward the Corinthians would receive from the saints, namely benevolence finding expression in gratitude and earnest prayers. 'They will have', he says, 'the means of repaying you, for they will regard you with the love that is your due, and they will take care in their prayers to commend you to God.' In conclusion, as though he has gained his object, he is carried away to sing God's praises for he wants to show them his confidence in them by treating the matter as already settled.

CHAPTER TEN

Now I Paul myself intreat you by the meekness and gentleness of Christ, I who in your presence am lowly among you, but being absent am of good courage toward you: yea, I beseech you, that I may not when present shew courage with the confidence wherewith I count to be bold against some, which count of us as if we walked according to the flesh. For though we walk in the flesh, we do not war according to the flesh (for the weapons of our warfare are not of the flesh, but mighty before God to the casting down of strong holds); casting down reasonings and every high thing that is exalted against the knowledge of God, and bringing every thought into captivity to the obedience of Christ; and being in readiness to avenge all disobedience, when your obedience shall be fulfilled. (1-6)

Having completed his exhortation, he now goes on partly to refute the false charges levelled against him by the false apostles and partly to curb the insolence of certain ungodly men who could not endure to be held in check. In order to undermine Paul's authority both of these groups were making out that the vehemence with which he thundered in his letters was mere θρασοδειλίαν, the bravado of a cowardly braggart, since, when he was present, his countenance and speech did not match up to the tone of his letters but was quite unostentatious and contemptible. 'See,' they were saying, 'here is a man who, well aware of his inferiority, is in our presence so very modest and timid, but now when he is far away, he bursts out into fierce attacks upon us. Why is his speech less bold than his letters? And if we despise him in his presence, shall we be afraid of him when he is far away? Whence comes this confidence that makes him think he can treat us in whatever way he will?' Notions of that kind were being put into circulation to bring his severity into ridicule and make it offensive. Paul's answer is that he is bold only when there is some need for it, and that the unpretentiousness of his physical presence, for which they held him in contempt, in no way lessened his authority, which was marked by its spiritual excellence and not for its fleshly show. Thus those who derided his exhortations or reproaches or threatenings would not escape with impunity. The words *I myself* are very emphatic as if to say that however much the ill-intentioned might blame him for inconsistency, he himself was not variable but remained always the same.

1. *I intreat you.* He speaks abruptly, as often happens when strong feelings are roused. The meaning is: I ask and earnestly intreat you by the gentleness of Christ not to be so obstinate as to compel me to be more severe than I want to be, or than I am going to be against those who despise me, because I have nothing notable in my external appearance, and do not recognize the spiritual excellence with which God has endowed me and by which I should rather be judged.

The form of entreaty which he uses is suggested by the matter under discussion, for he appeals to them *by the meekness and gentleness of Christ.* His detractors were finding fault with him because his bodily appearance lacked dignity and also because he thundered at them through letters from afar. Both charges he satisfactorily refutes, as has been said, but he also points out that nothing lies nearer to his heart than gentleness, which becomes a minister of Christ and of which the Lord Himself gave an example, 'Learn of me,' He said, 'for I am meek and lowly in heart. For my yoke is easy and my burden is light' (Matt. 11.29, 30). Again the prophet, speaking of Him, says, 'His voice shall not be heard in the streets, a bruised reed shall he not break' etc. (Isa. 42.2, 3). The gentleness that Christ Himself showed He also requires from His servants. In making mention of it here Paul shows that he is no stranger to it, as if he had said, 'I entreat you not to despise that gentleness which Christ showed us in His own person and daily shows us through His servants and which you see in me.'

Who in your presence. He repeats the charge being made against him by his enemies. Verbally he seems to admit the truth of their accusation but in fact he concedes nothing to them, as we shall see.

2. *Yea I beseech you.* Some think that this sentence is incomplete and that he does not explain what it is he is beseeching. My own view is that he is completing here what was lacking in the previous clause so that the exhortation becomes quite general; 'Show yourselves gentle and compliant towards me lest I am compelled to be more severe.' It is the duty of a good pastor to entice his sheep to follow in a peaceful and kindly manner so that they allow themselves to be guided, rather than to force them violently. I agree that severity is sometimes needed, but he should always begin in gentleness and persevere in it as long as his hearer shows himself to be tractable. Severity is a last resource and all other methods are, I say again, to be tried before we become rigorous; in fact, we should never be rigorous except under compulsion. He goes on to say that they were mistaken in thinking him weak-minded and timid when he was present with them, and threatens to resist the obstinate boldly face to face. 'They despise me', he says, 'as a man of weak spirit but they will find me braver and more spirited than they wish, when the real battle begins.' This makes it clear that

we ought to act with severity after we have found by trial that allurements and mildness have no effect. 'I shall do it with reluctance', says Paul, 'but yet I have decided to do it.' This is a most praiseworthy moderation for, although we must to the utmost of our ability draw men rather than drive them, yet when gentleness proves useless in dealing with those who are hard and obstinate, then rigour must needs be exercised. To do anything else would not be meekness or serenity but lax cowardice.

Which count of us. Erasmus translates, 'those that think that we walk according to the flesh', but the Vulgate in my view comes nearer Paul's original meaning, 'those who judge of us as if we walked according to the flesh'. At the same time, that rendering is not good Latin and does not bring out the apostle's meaning fully. For here λογίζεσθαι means to reckon or to esteem, 'they think of us', says Paul, 'or they esteem us as though we walked according to the flesh'.

To walk according to the flesh. Chrysostom says that it means to act unfaithfully or to behave badly in one's office and Paul does often use the expression in this sense. But I prefer to explain flesh as referring here to the external pomp or show, the only standards by which the false apostles usually commend themselves. Paul is complaining of the unreasonableness of those who looked only at his flesh, that is his visible external appearance after the usual habit of men all of whose energies are devoted to selfish ends. Since Paul excelled in none of those endowments which ordinarily win praise or reputation among the children of this world, he was despised as one of the common herd. But by whom? By the selfishly ambitious, who were judging him only by his appearance and had no concern for what lay hidden within.

3. *For though we walk in the flesh.* Here 'to walk in the flesh' means to live in the world or, as he expresses it elsewhere, to be at home in the body (5.6 above). He was indeed shut up in the work-house (*ergastulo*) of his body, but that did not prevent the power of the Holy Spirit from marvellously asserting itself in his weakness. Here again there is the kind of concession that is really of no assistance to his adversaries.

Those who *war according to the flesh* are men who in everything they do rely on the worldly resources of which alone they boast. Their assurance is not founded on the government and guidance of the Holy Spirit. Paul says that he is not such a man, since he is equipped with different weapons than those of the world and the flesh. What he says about himself applies also to all ministers of Christ. For, as I have said before, they bear an inestimable treasure in their earthen vessels and however much they may be encompassed by the weaknesses of the flesh, nevertheless that spiritual power of God shines forth brightly in them.

4. *For the weapons of our warfare.* The kind of weapons correspond to the kind of war. Paul glories in being equipped with spiritual weapons, thus his warfare is also spiritual, and so the contrary follows, that it is not according to the flesh. The comparison between the ministry of the Gospel and warfare is most apt for the whole life of a Christian man is a perpetual warfare, for the man who devotes himself to God's service will never have any peace from Satan but will be troubled by a continual disquietude. But it is for ministers of the Word and pastors to be standard-bearers marching before the rest. And certainly there are none whom Satan harasses more, who are more severely set upon, or who sustain greater and more grievous wounds. The man who girds himself to fulfil this office is mistaken unless he is endued with courage and fortitude for the struggle. For all his work is to fight. He must learn to think of the Gospel as a fire at which the wrath of Satan is enkindled, and so he cannot but arm himself to the fight whenever he sees an opportunity for advancing the Gospel. But with what sort of weapons is Satan to be repelled? He can be repelled only with spiritual weapons, and a man who is not armed with the power of the Holy Spirit, though he may boast that he is a minister of Christ, will soon prove that he is not. But if we look for a complete definition of spiritual weapons, then doctrine must be joined to zeal, a good conscience to the effectual working of the Spirit, and other necessary graces. Let the Pope, if he will, claim for himself titles of apostolic dignity, but what could be more ridiculous if this rule of Paul is to be the standard of our judgment?

Mighty before God. The meaning is either 'mighty according to God' or 'mighty from God'. My view is that there is here an implied antithesis by which this mightiness is contrasted with the weakness that appears outwardly in him before the world, so that he counts all the judgments of men as worth nothing and seeks approval of his courage from God. The antithesis holds good at the same time in another sense, since the power of his arms depends on God and not on the world.

To the casting down of strong holds. By *strongholds* he means counsels and every high thing erected against God and he will speak more of them later, but the word is suitable and significant. For his intention is to boast that there is nothing in the world so strongly fortified as to be beyond his power to overthrow. It is as if he had said, 'I know what pride carnal men take in their boastings and with what disdain and unconcern they hold me in contempt; as though there were nothing in me but what was mean and base, while they were exalted to lofty eminence. But their assurance is foolish; for the armour of the Lord in which I fight will prevail against all the defences on which they rely and think themselves invincible.' Since there are two ways in which the world usually arms itself to wage war on Christ, on the one hand by cunning, wicked artifices, subtlety and other secret machinations, and on the other by cruelty and oppression, he deals with them both. By *reasonings* he means everything connected with carnal wisdom. A *high thing* is any kind of worldly glory and power. There is no reason therefore for Christ's servant to tremble before any opposition to his teaching, however formidable. Let him persevere in spite of it and he will put all sorts of machinations to flight. In fact the only way in which Christ's kingdom can be set up and established is by bringing low everything in the world that is exalted. For nothing is more opposed to the spiritual wisdom of God than the wisdom of the flesh, and nothing more opposed to His grace than man's natural ability, and it is the same with everything the world thinks exalted. Thus the abasement of man is the only foundation of the Kingdom of Christ. The prophets say the same thing, 'The moon shall be ashamed and the sun shall be confounded when the Lord shall begin to reign in that day.' And again, 'The loftiness of man shall be bowed down and the high looks of mortals shall be humbled, and the Lord alone shall be exalted in that day' (Isa. 5.15 and 2.17), since in order that God alone may shine forth, the whole world's glory must pass away.

5. *Bring into captivity.* In my view, having just spoken of the conflict of spiritual arms with the hindrances that oppose Christ's Gospel, he now deals with the ordinary process of preparation by which men are to be brought into obedience to Him. For as long as we rest content with our own experiences and are wise in our own eyes, we are far away from any approach to the doctrine of Christ. Thus we have first to accept that he who would be wise must first become a fool, that is, we must give up our understanding and renounce the wisdom of the flesh and offer to Christ empty minds that He may fill them. We should notice the expression he uses, 'bringing every thought into captivity', which is to say that the liberty of the human mind is to be restrained and bridled so that it will seek no wisdom outside the doctrine of Christ, and the only way for its boldness to be restrained is for it to be made captive. But this comes when, by the leading of the Spirit, it allows itself to be brought into order and remains in voluntary captivity.

6. *And being in readiness to avenge.* He adds this in case insolent men should range themselves in opposition to his ministry under the impression that they may do so with impunity. Thus he says that power has been given to him not only to bring willing disciples into obedience to Christ, but also to take vengeance on the rebellious, and

his threats are not empty attempts to frighten them, but he is ready to put them into execution. Further, this vengeance has its warrant in Christ's word 'Whatsoever ye shall bind on earth shall be bound also in heaven' (Matt. 18.18). For although God does not immediately thunder forth at the very moment when the minister pronounces the sentence, nevertheless the judgment is ratified and will in time be fulfilled—on condition that the minister is fighting with spiritual arms. Some think that this refers to corporal punishments by which the apostle took vengeance on the obstinate or the ungodly, just as Peter struck Ananias and Sapphira dead, and Paul inflicted Elymas the sorcerer with blindness (Acts 5.1-10 and 13.6-11). But the first meaning suits better since the apostles did not make universal and indiscriminate use of that power to punish. Paul is speaking here in general terms and saying that he has vengeance ready at hand against all the disobedient.

When your obedience shall be fulfilled. How prudently he guards against alienating any of them by too great severity! Having threatened punishment to the rebellious, in case he should seem to provoke them he says that his duty towards them is different; it is simply to make them obedient to Christ. And this is indeed the aim and end proper to the Gospel, as he teaches at the beginning and end of the Epistle to the Romans (Rom. 1.5 and 16 26). Therefore all Christian teachers should make this their invariable method, first to strive with gentleness to bring their hearers to obedience and to appeal to them kindly, before they go on to visit punishment on rebelliousness. That is why Christ gave His command to loose before His command to bind

> *Ye look at the things that are before your face. If any man trusteth in himself that he is Christ's, let him consider this again with himself, that, even as he is Christ's, so also are we. For though I should glory somewhat abundantly concerning our authority (which the Lord gave for building you up, and not for casting you down), I shall not be put to shame: that I may not seem as if I would terrify you by my letters. For, His letters, they say, are weighty and strong; but his bodily presence is weak, and his speech of no account. Let such a one reckon this, that, what we are in word by letters when we are absent, such are we also in deed when we are present.* (7-11)

7. *The things that are before your face.* The phrase 'before your face' can be taken in two ways, either as meaning the things that they saw visibly and openly before them, or as meaning an outward mask put before their faces in order to deceive. Also the sentence can be taken either as a statement or a question and the verb βλέπετε can be either indicative or imperative. In my view the sentence conveys a reproach; Paul is chiding the Corinthians for letting their eyes be dazzled by an

empty show, as if he had said, 'You make much of other men who are swollen with their own importance and you despise me because I have no show or boasting.' For Christ Himself contrasts with 'righteous judgment' 'the judgment that is according to appearance' (John 7.24 and 8.15). He is reproving the Corinthians for being content with outward show and not considering carefully who ought to be recognized as servants of Christ.

If any man trusteth in himself. He speaks here with great confidence, taking it for granted that he is so assuredly a minister of Christ that it is impossible to deny him the distinction. 'Whoever wishes to be considered a minister of Christ', he says, 'must recognize that I am also such.' Why so? '*Let him*', he says, '*consider this with himself*, for all the qualifications that he may find in himself making him worthy of this office, all these he will also find in me.' This was his way of hinting to them that those who slandered him, whoever they were, should not be reckoned among Christ's servants. It is not for all men to speak with such assurance, for it can and does easily happen every day that the same claim is made presumptuously by men of no standing, who are nothing but a disgrace to Christ. But all that Paul said about himself he had proved to the Corinthians by plain and sure evidence. But if anyone vaunts himself in the same kind of way, but without any proof of the reality of what he says, he can do nothing but make himself ridiculous. To *trust in oneself* means to take to oneself power or authority under the pretext of serving Christ, when in fact one wishes only to be thought important.

8. *For though I should glory somewhat abundantly.* It was a mark of his modesty that he included himself in the number of Christ's servants, when in fact he greatly excelled the rest, but he was not ready to be modest to the point of having his authority impaired. Thus he adds that he has said less than he had a right to say, for he was not one of the common order of ministers (*ex vulgari ordine ministrorum*) but was outstanding even among the apostles. And so he says, 'Though I should glory somewhat abundantly, *I shall not be put to shame*, for there are good grounds for it.' Here he is anticipating an objection that he also is quite ready to speak to his own glory, but he does not mention it any more so that the Corinthians may understand that he boasts only reluctantly, for, unless the false apostles had forced him to it by their wicked charges, he would not have done it at all. By *authority* he means the apostolic authority that he had among the Corinthians, for although all ministers of the Word have the same office (*commune idemque officium*) in common, yet there are degrees of honour among them (*honoris gradus*). God had placed Paul above the others by using his labour to found that church and by adorning his apostleship in

many other ways. In case ill-intentioned persons should stir up ill-will against him because he speaks of having authority, he explains the purpose for which this authority has been given him—for the well-being of the Corinthians. From this it follows that his power should not be offensive or unendurable to them, for it is easy to endure and even to love something that we know to be profitable to us. Here also there is a contrast between his authority and that in which the false apostles gloried, for from it the Corinthians received no advantage and found no edification. However, there is no doubt that all ministers of the Word are endowed with authority for what would the preaching of doctrine be without it? Thus Christ's saying is of universal application, 'He that heareth you heareth me and he that rejecteth you rejecteth me' (Luke 10.16). But since many make false claims to an authority they do not possess, we should carefully note that Paul sees that his authority has its sole purpose in the edification of believers. Thus those who exercise their authority in destroying the Church prove themselves not pastors but tyrants and robbers. Secondly we should note that he claims that his authority has been given to him by God. This means that the man who seeks authority to do something must be given that authority by God. There are those who make false claims here also, like the Pope when he puffs out his cheeks and thunders that he is the vicar of Christ. But what proof of this can he offer? For Christ did not confer this kind of authority on dummies but on apostles and other ministers of His, so that the teaching of His Gospel might not go undefended. Thus the whole authority of ministers is based upon the Word, and in such a way that Christ always remains Lord and Master. Let us remember therefore that there are two requirements for rightful authority, that it should be conferred by God and that it should be exercised for the welfare of the Church. It is well known on whom God has conferred this authority and what limits He has imposed upon its exercise. Those who faithfully obey His command exercise rightful authority.

Here however a question may arise. God's words to Jeremiah are, 'Behold I set thee over the nations and over the kingdoms to plant and to pluck up, to build and to destroy' (Jer. 1.10) and we have just learnt in verse 5 that apostles are set apart on the same basis, that they should destroy everything that is exalted against Christ, and in any case the only way in which teachers of the Gospel can build up is by destroying the old man and they preach the Gospel to the death and condemnation of the ungodly. My answer is that what Paul is saying here has no reference to the ungodly. He is speaking to the Corinthians to whom he wished his apostleship to be beneficial and everything that he did among them was for their upbuilding. We have already seen that

Paul expressly states this fact in order that they may know that it was Satan, the enemy of their salvation, who was attacking his authority, and the purpose of that authority was their upbuilding. It is also in general true that by its own nature the teaching of the Gospel tends to upbuild and not destroy. When it destroys, it is not because of anything intrinsic to itself but because of the sin of men, who stumble on the stone on which they were meant to build as a foundation. Though it is true that it is by the destruction of the old man that we are restored into the image of God, this in no way contradicts what Paul says here. For the destruction of the old man is a good thing but here he speaks of something that is bad, the ruin of what is God's or the death of the soul. He is saying here that his authority is not harmful to them but clearly useful in promoting their welfare.

9. *That I may not seem as if I would terrify.* He mentions again the charge brought against him that he has already refuted, that in his letters he was bold but in their presence his courage failed. They were making this an excuse for disparaging his writings. 'What!', said they, 'is he going to terrify us with letters from a distance, when, if he were present, he would hardly dare to open his mouth?' To prevent his letters from losing their authority he replies that this objection cannot in any way destroy or detract from the good name either of himself or his teaching, for deeds count for at least as much as words, and his actions when he was with them were every bit as strong as the words sent in his absence, so that it is not right that his bodily presence should be held in scorn. By *deed* I take him to mean the effectiveness and success of his preaching as well as all his courageous deeds that befitted an apostle and the whole manner of his life. By *speech* he means not the substance of his teaching but simply its form and outward shell, for he would have been much more vehement in defending his doctrine. The cause of their contempt was his lack of that polished and splendid eloquence that is sure to win favour.

> *For we are not bold to number or compare ourselves with certain of them that commend themselves: but they themselves, measuring themselves by themselves, and comparing themselves with themselves, are without understanding. But we will not glory beyond our measure, but according to the measure of the limit which God apportioned to us—a measure to reach even unto you. For we stretch not ourselves overmuch, as though we reached not unto you: for we came even as far as unto you in the gospel of Christ: not glorying beyond our measure in other men's labours; but having hope that, as your faith groweth, we shall be magnified in you according to our limit unto further abundance, so as to preach the gospel even unto the parts beyond you, and not to glory in*

another's limit in regard of things ready to our hand. But he that glorieth, let him glory in the Lord. For not he that commendeth himself is approved, but whom the Lord commendeth. (12-17)

12. *For we are not bold.* He says this ironically for he goes on not only to compare himself boldly with the others but to pour scorn on the vanity of their claims and to leave them far behind him. By this irony he hits not only at the foolish boasters themselves but at the Corinthians who were encouraging their folly by their misplaced approval. 'I for my part', he says, 'am content with my own moderation and I would not dare to involve myself with your apostles who are the heralds of their own excellence.' He goes on to point out that their glorying has nothing to it but words and boasting, and thus shows how foolish and worthless they are and at the same time claims for himself the reality instead of the words, that is, he has real and solid grounds for glorying. But it may seem that he himself falls into the very folly that he has been blaming in others, for he at once goes on to commend himself. My answer is that we must remember his reason for so doing. For those who are entirely free from selfish ambition desire only to serve the Lord profitably and do not make their own commendation their aim. As far as this passage goes we need only direct attention to the words themselves: for the people who are said to *commend themselves* are men who are poor and starving for true praise and who exalt themselves by vain glorying and falsely give themselves out to be what they are not. This becomes clear from what follows.

But they themselves, measuring themselves by themselves. Here he lays his finger on their folly. A one-eyed man sees clearly enough among the totally blind, a half deaf man hears plainly enough among the totally deaf. Such were those men who were so pleased with themselves and were showing off before the others simply because they deliberately disregarded anybody who was superior to them, for if they had compared themselves with Paul or somebody like him, they would soon have been forced to give up their foolish idea of their own superiority and been turned from boasting to shame. To find an application for this passage we need look no further than the monks, for though they are all completely unlearned asses, yet solely on account of their long robes and hoods they have the reputation of being learned men. If one of them has even a slight smattering of cultured literature, he spreads out his feathers proudly like a peacock, his fame spreads far and wide and he is almost worshipped by his fellows. If the disguise of the cowl were to be removed and a fair examination made, their vanity would at once be discovered. Why so? The old proverb is true,

'Ignorance is bold', but the excessively insolent pride of the monks comes chiefly from the fact that they measure themselves by themselves, and since in their cloisters there is nothing but barbarism, it is no wonder if the one-eyed man is king in the country of the blind. Such were Paul's rivals for they flattered each other among themselves and did not pause to consider what qualities would win them true praise and how far they were from the excellence of Paul and those like him. To take nothing more than that into account would have reduced them to blushes but it is the just punishment of the ambitious that their folly makes them ridiculous—the very thing above all others they wish to avoid—and instead of the glory they so immoderately desire they get only shame.

13. *But we will not glory beyond our measure.* He now contrasts his own moderation with the folly of the false apostles and shows that our glorying is real and genuine when we confine ourselves within the limits set by God. 'The Lord has given me this and I will be satisfied with this measure and will not desire or make claims to be anything more.' That is what he means by *the measure of the limit.* For the limit beyond which a man ought not to try to stretch the gift and the vocation God has given him. Not that it is right for us to glory on our own behalf even in the gift and the calling of God, but only in so far as it may be necessary to advance His glory, who is so liberal to us in order that we may acknowledge that we have received everything at His hand.

A measure to reach. By this he means that he had no need of wordy phrases among the Corinthians for they were a part of his glory or, as he puts it elsewhere, 'Ye are my crown' (Phil. 4.1), but he carries on with the same figure of speech he has already used. 'I have', he says, 'a most ample field for boasting without going beyond my limits and one portion of this field is you.' He is gently reproving their ingratitude in almost overlooking his apostleship which ought to have been held in specially high esteem among them since it had the stamp of God's approval upon it. Throughout we have also an implied contrast with the false apostles who had no such stamp of approval to show.

14. *For we stretch not.* He is thinking of people stretching out their arms or standing on tiptoe to reach something that is not immediately at hand. A greedy desire for glory is like this but is often more shameful. For ambitious people do not merely stretch out their hands and stand on tiptoe but are rushed off their feet by any pretext for obtaining glory. He infers that his rivals were like that. Next he declares how he had come to the Corinthians, namely, to found their church by his ministry. So he says that he came *in the gospel of Christ* for he had not come to them with empty hands but had been the first to bring them

the Gospel. Some understand the preposition *in* differently as being equivalent to 'by'—'by the Gospel of Christ'—and there is nothing wrong with this rendering. Paul appears nevertheless to be pointing out what an advantage his coming to Corinth was, since he had brought with him so precious a gift.

15. *In other men's labours.* He now reproves the false apostles more freely as men who stretch out their hands to reap another man's harvest and who yet dare to revile those whose sweat and labour had prepared the place for them. Paul had built up the church in Corinth with a great struggle and against innumerable difficulties: they appeared later and found the road made and the door open. In order to appear people of importance, they shamelessly lay claim to what they have no right to and ridicule Paul's labours.

But having hope. He once again administers an indirect reproof to the Corinthians for being a hindrance to his progress in spreading the Gospel. For when he says that he hopes that *when their faith groweth* the bounds of his glory will be increased, he implies that the weakness of their faith was the reason for that progress being in some measure retarded. As if he had said, 'If you had progressed as far as you ought, I should by now be occupied in gaining new churches and I should have your assistance in doing so. But, as things are, you are delaying me by your weakness. Yet I hope that the Lord will grant you to make greater progress in the future, so that the glory of my ministry may be increased according to the measure of the calling of God'. *To glory in things ready to hand* means the same as to glory in another's labours; Paul had fought the battle but they were holding the triumph.

17. *But he that glorieth.* He says this to correct any wrong impression that his own glorying is itself very much like empty boasting. Thus he recalls himself and others to God's judgment, pointing out that the only people who have a right to glory are those who are approved of God. To glory in the Lord has a different meaning here than in the first chapter of the first epistle (v. 31) or in Jer. 9.24. There it means to acknowledge that God is the Author of all good things, so that everything good should be ascribed to His grace and men should not extol themselves but glorify Him only. Here it means to submit our glorying to the judgment of God alone and to count everything else as worth nothing, for whereas some depend on the opinions of men and weigh themselves in the false balance of public opinion and others are deceived by their own arrogance, Paul bids us care for only one kind of glory, namely that we should please the Lord by whose judgment we stand or fall. Even pagans recognize that true glory consists of a pure conscience and that is so far right but not the whole truth. For since nearly everybody is blinded by an excess of self-love,

we ought not to rest secure in our own estimate of ourselves. For we must remember what he says elsewhere (I Cor. 4.4), that he is not conscious of any wrong in himself and yet is not thereby justified. For we should remember that the right of pronouncing judgment upon us is reserved to God alone for we are not competent judges in our own cause. What follows next confirms this interpretation, *For not he that commendeth himself is approved.* For men are easily deceived by a false impression and this happens every day. Thus, forgetting everything else, let us make it our one aim to win God's approval and let us be content with His approbation alone, since by right it should be regarded as worth more than all the applauses of the whole world. There was a man who said that to him the approval of Plato alone was worth the applause of a thousand, but here we are not dealing with human judgments or deciding who is superior to whom, but with the judgment of God Himself whose prerogative it is to overthrow all the judgments of men.

CHAPTER ELEVEN

Would that ye could bear with me in a little foolishness: nay indeed bear with me. For I am jealous over you with a godly jealousy: for I espoused you to one husband, that I might present you as a pure virgin to Christ. But I fear, lest by any means, as the serpent beguiled Eve in his craftiness, your minds should be corrupted from the simplicity and the purity that is in Christ. For if he that cometh preacheth another Jesus, whom we did not preach, or if ye receive a different spirit, which ye did not receive, or a different gospel, which ye did not accept, ye do well to bear with him. For I reckon that I am not a whit behind the very chiefest apostles. But though I be rude in speech, yet am I not in knowledge; nay in everything we have made it manifest among all men to you-ward. (1-6)

1. *Would that ye would bear with me.* Seeing that the ears of the Corinthians are still partly tuned to his rivals, he uses another device by which to win them by going on to express a wish, as people do when they do not dare to make an open request. But immediately afterwards, as though his confidence has returned, he does ask that the Corinthians should bear with his foolishness. He calls the splendid heralding of his praises that follows *foolishness,* not because he was a fool to glory, for he did it under the compulsion of necessity and restrained himself to such a degree that nobody could rightly say that he had passed the bounds of moderation; but he calls it foolishness because it is an unseemly thing to sing one's own praises and quite alien to a man of modesty, and he does it only because he has to.

I have taken *bear with me* to be an imperative whereas Chrysostom makes it an affirmative statement, for the Greek word is ambiguous and either rendering will suit well enough. But since the reasons that he adds are designed to induce the Corinthians to bear with him and later he will again take them to task for conceding him nothing, I have followed the Vulgate. By saying 'Would that' etc. he had seemed to lose confidence but now, as if correcting his hesitation, he openly and freely commands.

2. *For I am jealous.* This is why he plays the fool, for jealousy sweeps a man off his feet. It is as if he had said, 'Do not expect me to show the calmness of a man at ease and unexcited by any strong feeling: for the strength of the jealousy I feel for you will not let me rest.' But since there are two kinds of jealousy—one that springs from our self-love which is evil and perverse, and another that we endure on behalf

of God, he tells us which this is. There are many who are jealous on their own account and not on God's, but the only right and godly jealously is that which looks to God's interest to see that He is not defrauded of the honour that is His due.

For I espoused you to one husband. He brings forward the motive behind his preaching to prove that his jealousy was of the second kind, for its aim was to join them in marriage to Christ and to keep them in their union with Him. Here in his own person he shows us a picture of a good minister; for there is one sole Bridegroom of the Church— the Son of God. All ministers are 'friends of the bridegroom', as the Baptist says of himself (John 3.29), and so they should all be concerned that the fidelity of the holy marriage remains entire and inviolate. This they can only do if they share the love of the Bridegroom for the Church, so that each is as concerned for her purity as a husband is for the chastity of his wife. Away with all coldness and indifference in this matter, for he who is cold cannot be suited for this office, but at the same time let ministers beware of pursuing their own interests rather than Christ's and of intruding themselves in His place, lest, while they pretend to be the bridegroom's friends, they are in fact adulterers who seduce the bride's love to themselves.

As a pure virgin. We can be married to Christ only if we bring virginity as our dowry and keep it inviolate from every corruption. Thus it is the duty of ministers of the Gospel to purify our souls that they may be chaste spouses to Christ, for otherwise all their labour is in vain. We may take the meaning here to be either that they should present themselves individually as chaste virgins, or that a minister should present the whole people and bring them forward into Christ's presence. I prefer the second interpretation and so I have rendered it differently from Erasmus.

3. *But I fear.* He begins to explain what this virginity is, namely that we should with our whole mind cleave in purity to Christ alone. God everywhere requires of us that we should be joined to Him in body and spirit, and declares Himself to be a jealous God who avenges with the utmost severity the wrong done to Him, if any man turns away from Him. But this joining of us to God is brought about in Christ, as Paul teaches in Eph. 5. In the present passage he tells us of the method by which it is accomplished, when we remain in the pure simplicity of the Gospel, for just as when marriages are arranged among men a contract (*tabulae*) is drawn up, so the spiritual marriage between us and God's Son is confirmed by the Gospel as a kind of contract (*tanquam tabulis*). Let us maintain the fidelity, love and obedience that we have there promised and He on His side will keep faith with us.

II CORINTHIANS 11 [v. 3–4]

Paul now says that he is concerned that the minds of the Corinthians should not be *corrupted from the simplicity that is in Christ*. The Greek has εἰς Χριστόν and Erasmus renders it 'towards Christ', but the Vulgate in my view comes nearer to Paul's meaning. By the simplicity that is in Christ he means that which keeps us in the original and pure doctrine of the Gospel and admits no extraneous corruptions. He is telling us here that our minds are debauched as soon as they deviate even a very little from the pure doctrine of Christ. And his warning is right, for who would not condemn a married woman as guilty of unchastity from the moment she first begins to listen to a seducer? Thus we also, when we pay attention to ungodly and false teachers who are Satan's seducers, give clear evidence that we are not maintaining conjugal fidelity towards Christ. We should also note the word *simplicity*. Paul's fear was not that the Corinthians would make an immediate, open and complete break with Christ, but that they would turn aside little by little from the simplicity and purity they had learnt to profane and alien inventions and would at length fall away.

He next institutes a comparison. *As the serpent beguiled Eve in his craftiness*. If false teachers have a show of wisdom to persuade us, if they are strong in their eloquence, if they can plausibly insinuate themselves into the minds of their hearers and instil their poison by quiet craftiness, then they work by the same methods that Satan employed to deceive Eve, for he did not openly declare himself her enemy, but crept in secretly under plausible excuses.

4. *For if he that cometh*. Now he takes the Corinthians to task for their over-readiness to receive false apostles. For although towards Paul himself they were excessively peevish and extremely irritable, so that they were offended on the slightest pretext if he reproved them even in a moderate way, there was nothing they did not allow to the false apostles, whose pride, haughtiness and unreasonable demands they willingly endured. He condemns this unreasonable veneration which only proved their lack of discrimination and judgment. It is as if he had said, 'How can you allow these people to take so many liberties with you and you yet patiently endure their domineering? If they had brought you another Christ or another Gospel or another Spirit than those you have received from me, I would certainly approve of your deference towards them, for then they would deserve such high honour. But since they have given you nothing I did not give you first, what sort of gratitude is it almost to worship them to whom you owe nothing, and to despise me through whom God has showered upon you so many great blessings?' The Papists show the very same kind of gratitude today to their false bishops. For while they are most sorely oppressed by their tyranny, yet they endure it without difficulty, but

they do not hesitate to despise Christ Himself. *Another Christ* and *another gospel* mean something different here than in Gal. 1.8. For in that passage 'another' means false and fictitious as opposed to what is true and genuine, but here he means a Gospel that has come to them by some other ministry than his own.

5. *For I reckon that I am.* He now shows up their ingratitude by removing the one valid excuse they might have for it, for he shows that he is the equal even of the chief of the apostles. Thus the Corinthians were failing in gratitude in not esteeming him more highly, when they knew well by experience what kind of a man he was, and they were transferring the authority which by right belonged to him to people of no worth. For modesty's sake he says that he *reckons* this to be his position, but the fact that it was so was clear and well known to all. His meaning is that God has honoured his apostleship with no lesser marks of His favour than that of John or Peter. Moreover if a man despises God's gifts after he has clearly recognized them, he cannot defend himself from being adjudged malicious and ungrateful. Wherever we discern God's gifts, we must reverence God Himself. I mean that every man is worthy of honour in so far as he excels in God's gifts of grace and especially if these gifts have been of some advantage to us.

6. *But though I be rude in speech.* This was the one thing in which at first sight he could be thought inferior—his lack of eloquence. He anticipates and corrects this criticism here by agreeing that in speech he is rude and unpolished, but he claims for himself knowledge. By *speech* he means in this context elegance of expression and by *knowledge* the substance of his teaching. Just as a man is made up of both soul and body, so in our doctrine there is the thing that is being taught and there is the verbal adornment in which it is clothed. Thus Paul is maintaining that he knows what must be taught and what must be known, even if he is not an eloquent orator who knows how to set off his doctrine by the polish and choiceness of his speech.

And yet the question arises whether eloquence is not a necessity for apostles, for without it how can they be qualified to teach? For other men perhaps knowledge is enough, but how can a teacher be dumb? My answer is that Paul does not say that he is so rude in speech as to be entirely incapable of saying anything like an infant, but since he cannot rival others in the splendour of their eloquence, he admits their superiority in this, but claims for himself the thing that mattered most, a grasp of the substance of the teaching, leaving to them the possession of garrulity without gravity. But if anyone asks why the Lord, who has formed the tongues of men, has not endowed so great an apostle with eloquence, so that he should have no deficiency, my answer is that he was given in abundance qualities which could amply compensate his want of eloquence. For we see and feel what majesty there is in his writings, what heights he reaches, what sublimities he reveals, what power he possesses. In fact they are not words at all but thunderbolts. And is it not true that the efficacy of the Holy Spirit appears more clearly in bare unpolished words than under a guise of eloquence and ornament? But there is a fuller treatment of this subject in the last epistle and we may sum it up by saying that he gives verbal assent to the objection of his opponents but at the same time denies its substance. We should learn from his example to prefer the reality to the word and, in the words of a rough but common Latin proverb, 'Let others have the word but give us the reality.' If eloquence is added let it be regarded as something extra and let it not be used to twist or adulterate doctrine but to explain it in its native simplicity.

Nay in everything. Since it was a very sweeping claim to make himself equal to the chief apostles, in order that no one may put it down to arrogance, he calls on the Corinthians to judge whether or not it is true, on condition that they judge from what they have themselves experienced. For they had much evidence to show them that his glorying was not in vain or without cause. His meaning is therefore that he has no need of words since fact and experience clearly prove what he says.

> *Or did I commit a sin in abasing myself that ye might be exalted, because I preached to you the gospel of God for nought? I robbed other churches, taking wages of them that I might minister unto you; and when I was present with you and was in want, I was not a burden on any man; for the brethren, when they came from Macedonia, supplied the measure of my want; and in everything I kept myself from being burdensome unto you, and so will I keep myself. As the truth of Christ is in me, no man shall stop me in this glorying in the regions of Achaia. Wherefore? because I love you not? God knoweth. But what I do, that will I do, that I may cut off an occasion for them which desire an occasion; that wherein they glory, they may be found even as we.* (7-12)

7. *Did I commit a sin.* He was being reproached because of his humble abasement, when in fact it was an excellence deserving more than ordinary praise. Abasement here means voluntary abasement, for he had behaved modestly as though he had no special worth, so that many regarded him as one of the common people and this he had done for the good of the Corinthians. His zeal and care for their well-being burned so strong within him that he cared more for them than for himself. So he says that he has freely surrendered his greatness that

they might become great through his abasement. For his aim was to promote their salvation. And now he indirectly charges them with ingratitude for turning such a godly intention into a fault—not that he wants to reproach them, but in order to recall them to a right mind. Although, in fact, his irony would wound them more than a straight unadorned reproof. He might have said, 'What is this, do you despise me because I have abased myself for your sakes?', but this method of asking pointed questions which he uses was more effective in putting them to shame.

Because I preached to you for nought. This is part of his abasement for he has waived his rights as though his condition were inferior to that of others: but their unreasonableness was such that they thought the less of him on this account, as though he were not worth any wage. His reason for giving the Corinthians his labour for nothing is at once added—for this was not his universal practice, but in Corinth, as we saw in the last epistle, there was a danger of providing the false apostles with a pretext for misrepresenting his motives.

8. *I robbed other churches.* In my view he has deliberately used an objectionable word to bring out more clearly how unworthy the Corinthians' contempt for him was. 'I have', he says, 'procured pay for myself from the spoils of other churches in order to serve you. Since I have spared you in this way, how unworthy of you it is to make me so poor a return.' This is a metaphor drawn from military usage, for just as conquerors take spoils from defeated peoples, so all that Paul took from the churches he had won for Christ was, so to speak, the spoils of his victory. Although he would never have taken anything from them against their will, what they freely contributed was so to speak due by right of spiritual warfare. Note however how he says that he *was in want,* for unless he had been forced to it by need, he would never have been a burden to them. All this time he was engaged in manual labour, as we have already learnt, but since the work of his hands was not enough to support life, an additional contribution was made by the Macedonians. Thus he does not say that the Macedonians had provided him with a living but only that they had supplied what he lacked. We have spoken elsewhere of the apostle's godly prudence and carefulness in providing against dangers: here we should note the godly zeal of the Macedonians, who had no hesitation in contributing of their substance to his support so that the Gospel might be proclaimed to others, and even to those who were richer than themselves. How few Macedonians there are today, but how many Corinthians everywhere!

10. *As the truth of Christ is in me.* In case anyone should imagine that Paul's words had behind them an intention to make the Corinth-

ians more liberal towards him in future, in an attempt to make amends for their past deficiencies, he declares with an oath that he will take nothing either from them or from the other churches in Achaia, even if it should be offered. The expression 'as the truth of Christ is in me' is in the form of an oath and is equivalent to saying, 'Let no one believe that the truth of Christ is in me if I do not retain this glorying among the men of Achaia.' Corinth was in Achaia.

11. *Is it because I love you not?* We treat those whom we love with a greater degree of familiarity. In case the Corinthians should be offended at his refusal of their liberality, while he was accepting help from the Macedonians, and at his declaration on oath that he would go on refusing, he deals with this suspicion also. In order to reply to their possible objection he first asks, as it were, in their name whether this is an indication that he has little goodwill towards them. He gives no direct answer to this question but an indirect reply is more effective, and this he gives by calling on God to witness his goodwill towards them. Notice how three verses contain two oaths, but they are legitimate and holy oaths, because they have a good end in view and are employed in a legitimate cause. To condemn all oaths without distinction is to act like a fanatic who cannot distinguish between black and white.

12. *But what I do.* He explains again why he is acting in this way. The false apostles took no pay in order to attract ignorant men to them for their serving for nothing was a show of apparently unusual zeal. If Paul had exercised his rights, they would have been able to triumph over him, as though they were by far superior. Thus Paul, to deny them such an opportunity for harming him, also preached the Gospel for nothing. This is what he means by saying that he wishes *to cut off an occasion from them that desire an occasion.* The false apostles were trying to use this trick to insinuate themselves and so far to detract from Paul's reputation, as if they were in some ways his superiors. But he refuses to give them this opportunity. 'We shall be found', he says, 'to be their equals in that glorying which they wish to have for themselves alone.' This passage is useful in reminding us not to give wicked men opportunities they can use against us as often as they desire them. One way of overcoming them is just to refuse to give them weapons by our imprudence.

> For such men are false apostles, deceitful workers, fashioning themselves into apostles of Christ. And no marvel; for even Satan fashioneth himself into an angel of light. It is no great thing therefore if his ministers also fashion themselves as ministers of righteousness; whose end shall be according to their works. (13-15)

13. *For such men are false apostles.* Although he has already refuted the chief claim of his opponents, he is not content with showing that he is their equal where they claimed to surpass him, but he leaves them no credit at all. To despise money seemed highly praiseworthy but he says that with them it is a deceptive trick, just as if a harlot were to borrow the clothes of an honourable married woman. It was necessary to strip off the disguise that was obscuring the glory of God. He calls them *deceitful workers*, that is, they do not show their wickedness to a first glance but cleverly insinuate themselves under some fair pretext. Thus they must be carefully and thoroughly examined to prevent us from accepting them as true servants of Christ, because at first sight they have a superficial show of excellence. Paul is not putting an unfavourable construction on real virtue out of motives of malice and jealousy, but he is rather forced by their dishonesty to expose the underlying evil, for there was a dangerous desecration of virtue in their false claims to be aflame with a greater zeal than all the servants of Christ.

14. *And no marvel.* This is an argument from the greater to the lesser. If Satan, the most depraved of all beings and so the head and chief of evil men, can transform himself, what will his ministers do? We have experience of both these things every day, for when Satan tempts us to evil, he does not profess to be what he really is. He would achieve nothing if we were aware that he was our mortal enemy and the destroyer of our salvation. Thus he always covers himself with some disguise in order to trick us and does not immediately show us his horns, as the common saying goes, but rather takes pains to appear to be an *angel of light*. Even when he drives us to gross crimes, he still uses some plausible pretext to get us off our guard and draw us into his nets. He attacks us under the appearance of good, and even in the very name of God. And his satellites, as I have said, follow the same methods as their master. These are golden preambles, Vicar of Christ, successor of Peter, servant of the servants of God, but, when the masks are removed, who and what will the Pope be discovered to be? Satan himself, his master, can scarcely outdo his most accomplished pupil in any kind of abomination. There is a well-known saying about Babylon, that she gives him poison to drink in a golden cup. Thus we must be on our guard against false appearances. But it may be asked if this means that we should regard everybody with suspicion. That was certainly not Paul's intention. But there are ways of discriminating between people which it is unwise and foolish to overlook. Paul wished only to draw our attention to this, so that we should not immediately judge a lion by his skin, for if we are not overhasty in our judgment, the Lord will see to it that soon the ears will appear. In

the same way he wished to warn us, so that in our estimates of the servants of Christ we should not be swayed by outward appearances but look for things of greater importance. *Ministers of righteousness* is a Hebrew form of expression meaning faithful and upright ministers.

15. *Whose end shall be.* He adds this for the comfort of the godly. It is the statement of a man of courage who despises the foolish judgments of men and awaits with patience the day of the Lord. Meanwhile he shows that he has a singular boldness of conscience which has no dread of God's judgment.

> *I say again, Let no man think me foolish; but if ye do, yet as foolish receive me, that I also may glory for a little. That which I speak, I speak not after the Lord, but as in foolishness, in this confidence of glorying. Seeing that many glory after the flesh, I will glory also. For ye bear with the foolish gladly, being wise yourselves. For ye bear with a man if he bringeth you into bondage, if he devoureth you, if he taketh you captive, if he exalteth himself, if he smiteth you on the face. I speak by way of disparagement, as though we had been weak. Yet whereinsoever any is bold (I speak in foolishness), I am bold also.* (16-21)

16. *I say again.* The apostle's purpose is twofold; partly he wants to expose the disgusting vanity of the false apostles, who are such tireless trumpeters of their own praise: and then he wishes also to expostulate with the Corinthians for having made him boast against his will. 'I say again', he says, for he had abundantly shown before that there was no reason why he should be despised, and at the same time he had shown that he was quite different from the others and should not have his boasting measured by the same yardstick as theirs. He once again tells them what his purpose in boasting has been, namely, to clear his apostleship of contempt, for, if the Corinthians had behaved as they ought, no word of this boasting would ever have passed his lips.

But if ye do, yet as foolish receive me. 'If you think me a fool, at least allow me the right to speak foolishly like a fool.' This is a reproof for the false apostles who, though they were extremely foolish in this matter, were not merely tolerated by the Corinthians but received with great applause. He goes on to explain what kind of folly he means—that of singing his own praise. This was something his opponents did without end or limit but he shows that for him it is quite unusual by saying—*for a little*. I understand this phrase in a temporal sense as meaning that Paul is not prepared to go on boasting for long but assumes for the moment a character strange to him and then immediately lays it aside, just as we usually pass over lightly matters irrelevant to the purpose in hand whereas fools are constantly over-concerned ἐν παρέργοις, with matters of merely secondary importance.

17. *What I speak, I speak not after the Lord.* His heart was indeed centred upon God, but his outward appearance might seem unsuitable for a servant of God. At the same time the things Paul says about himself are things he condemns in the false apostles, for his purpose was not to praise himself but only to contrast himself with them in order to humble them. Thus he transfers to himself things that were characteristic of them in order to open the Corinthians' eyes.

The word I have rendered *confidence* is in the Greek ὑπόστασις and its meaning has already been dealt with in chapter 9. The renderings 'subject matter' or 'substance' are quite inappropriate here.

18. *Seeing that many glory.* The meaning is, 'If anyone brings against me the objection that what I do is wrong, then what about the others who do the same? Am I not following their example? Am I the only person or the first to glory according to the flesh? If it is praised when they do it, why is it criticized when I do it?' So far is Paul from having any selfish motives in singing his own praises, that he is quite prepared to be blamed for it, provided he can expose the vanity of the false apostles. *To glory after the flesh* is to boast in outward show rather than in a good conscience. For the word 'flesh' stands here for the world, as when we seek praise from outward appearances which are always considered worthy of note and of great value by the world. A little earlier he made use of the term 'in appearance' which means the same.

19. *For ye bear with the foolish gladly.* In my view Paul is being ironical when he calls the Corinthians wise. They were despising him, a thing they would never have done, had they not been inflated with the most overweening pride. Thus he says, 'Since you are so very wise, act the part of wise men in bearing with me to whom you are showing the contempt due to a fool.' I infer from this that what Paul says here is not directed at all the Corinthians, but rather he is rebuking a certain group of them who were behaving very unkindly towards him.

20. *For ye bear with a man.* Three meanings are possible here. He might be rebuking the Corinthians in irony for being so refined that they could bear nothing; he might be charging them with carelessness in giving themselves over to such a shameless bondage to the false apostles, or he might be repeating charges being made against himself without any justification, as though he claimed to have the right of tyrannical domination over them. The second interpretation has the support of Chrysostom, Ambrose and Augustine and is commonly

accepted, and it does suit the context best, although the third interpretation is in my view just as good. For we see how again and again he was slandered by ill-intentioned opponents as though he were a domineering tyrant—which he certainly was not. As the other interpretation is more generally received, however, I have no objection to its being adopted as correct. What he says here is connected with what goes immediately before as follows, 'You endure everything from others, even if they oppress you or make demands upon you or treat you with contempt. Why are you less tolerant towards me, when these others are in no way superior to me?' For when he says that he is not *weak*, his meaning is that God has bestowed upon him such outstanding graces that he should not be thought of as an ordinary man. The word 'weak' has hidden implications, as we shall soon see again. It always has been and always will be the custom of the world to resist God's servants, to burst out in rage against them at the slightest pretext, to grumble and murmur without respite, to complain of a moderately strict discipline, and in fact to hold all discipline in abhorrence, while at the same time they put themselves into servile subjection to false apostles, imposters and worthless pretenders, give them liberty to do whatever they like and patiently submit to endure any burden they choose to impose. So in our day you will hardly find one man in thirty who will bow beneath the yoke of Christ, whereas all men have endured without complaint the harsh tyranny of the Pope. The very people who fly into a passion against the fatherly and wholesome rebukes of their pastors are those who once calmly swallowed the most atrocious insults of the monks. Can it be that those whose ears are so tender and backward in hearing the truth deserve Antichrist's racks and tortures rather than Christ's gentle sway? But so it has been from the beginning.

21. *Yet whereinsoever any is bold.* Paul has been asking why the Corinthians were showing more respect to others than to him, since he had not been by any means weak, that is, contemptible. He now confirms this by saying that if a comparison is made, he will not be found inferior to anybody in those things that give a man a right to glory.

Are they Hebrews? so am I. Are they Israelites? so am I. Are they the seed of Abraham? so am I. Are they ministers of Christ? (I speak as one beside himself) I more; in labours more abundantly, in prisons more abundantly, in stripes above measure, in deaths oj:. Of the Jews five times received I forty stripes save one. Thrice was I beaten with rods, once was I stoned, thrice I suffered shipwreck, a night and a day have I been in the deep; in journeyings often, in perils of rivers, in perils of robbers, in perils from my countrymen, in perils from the Gentiles, in perils in the city, in perils in the wilderness, in perils in the sea, in perils among false brethren; in labour and travail, in watchings often, in hunger and thirst, in fastings often, in cold and nakedness. Beside those things that are without, there is that which presseth upon me daily, anxiety for all the churches. Who is weak, and I am not weak? Who is made to stumble, and I burn not? (22-29)

22. *Are they Hebrews?* By enumerating examples he now shows them more clearly that if it came to a comparison, he would certainly not be found inferior. First of all he mentions the glory of his race of which his rivals were boasting most strongly. 'If', he says, 'they boast of their noble birth, then I am their equal, for I am also an Israelite of the seed of Abraham.' This is a foolish and empty boast and yet Paul uses three phrases in order to express it and in fact specifies by them three different marks of superiority. By this repetition he is in my view indirectly rebuking their folly, since they were trusting for the sum and substance of their claim to excellence to a thing so trivial, and this boast was so continually upon their lips that it became quite revolting, just as empty-headed men usually pour forth torrents of verbal bombast about nothing at all.

As far as the name 'Hebrews' is concerned, it appears from Gen. 11.14 that it denotes descent and is derived from Heber, and also in Gen. 14.13 it is probable that Abraham is called a Hebrew with no other meaning in mind but that he is descended from Heber. Those who explain the word as meaning 'those who dwell beyond the river' can produce no substantial evidence in support of their conjecture. It is true that we do not read of anyone being called a Hebrew before Abraham, who had indeed crossed the river when he left his native land, and afterwards the name did become familiar in his family, as is obvious from the story of Joseph. But the termination shows that the word refers to descent and this is sufficiently confirmed by the passage to which I have referred.

23. *Are they ministers of Christ?* When he comes now to deal with things that really do give grounds for praise, he is not content with being acknowledged their equal but claims to be their superior. Up till now he has scattered their fleshly glories like smoke before the wind by comparing with them similar glories of his own; but since they had no solid worth, he rightly makes a clear distinction between himself and them, when it comes to serious glorying in things that matter. For to be a servant of Christ is a far greater honour and dignity than to be the firstborn of all the firstborn of the house of Abraham. But once again to prevent misrepresentations he prefaces his claims by

saying that he speaks as *one beside himself.* 'Granted that this boasting is foolish,' he says, 'it is still nevertheless true.'

In labours. This is his way of proving that he is a more outstanding servant of Christ than they, and surely the proof is reliable when the argument consists not of words but of deeds. He speaks here of 'labours' in the plural and later on of 'labour' in the singular. I see no difference between them except perhaps that in the second case he is speaking more generally, combining together the things he goes on to enumerate one by one. In the same way we can take *deaths* to mean any kind of danger that threatens imminent death and he then goes on to name these dangers. It is as if he had said, 'I have proved myself in "deaths often" and in "labours" even more often.' He spoke of deaths in the same sense in chapter 1.

24. *Of the Jews.* It is certain that at the time the Jews had no powers of jurisdiction, but as this was one of the group of so-called moderate punishments, they were probably still allowed to inflict it. The Law of God was that those who did not deserve capital punishment should be beaten in the presence of the judge, but that not more than forty strokes should be inflicted, so that the body might not be disfigured or mutilated by cruelty. It is probable that in the process of time the custom grew up of stopping at the thirty-ninth lash in case in the heat of the moment they should exceed the number laid down by God. Many such precautions of rabbinic origin are found among the Jews, making some restriction on what the Lord had allowed. Thus perhaps, as time passed and things degenerated, they came to think that all criminals should receive that number of strokes, although what the Lord laid down was not how far severity was to go but at what point it was to stop. Some prefer to take this as meaning that they exercised greater cruelty upon Paul than upon others, and that is by no means improbable, for if it had been their practice to deal so severely with all criminals, he might have said that he was beaten in the usual way. His mentioning of the number implies the extreme severity of the flogging he received.

25. *Thrice was I beaten with rods.* This makes it clear that the apostle suffered many things of which Luke makes no mention. For Luke recounts only one stoning and one shipwreck. But Luke's account is not complete, for he does not mention everything that happened but only outstanding events.

By *perils from my countrymen* he means the things that befell him at the hands of his own people as a result of hatred for him felt by all Jews. He also had the *Gentiles* as his enemies, and from a third direction snares set by *false brethren* threatened him. So it happened that for the name of Christ he was hated by all. *Fasting* I understand to mean voluntary fasting, as he has already spoken of hunger and starvation. These were the arguments he used to give good grounds to his claim to be an eminent servant of Christ. For what better way can there be to recognize Christ's servants than by proofs so many, so great and so dire. By contrast the untried boasters who had neither done nor suffered anything for Christ were shamelessly thrusting themselves forward. But it may be asked whether anyone can be Christ's servant without undergoing so many evils, dangers and vexations. My answer is that all these things are not necessarily required of everyone but, where they are seen, a greater and more illustrious testimony is given. The man who is singled out by so many marks of distinction will not despise others who are less noble or less tried, nor will he be puffed up with pride; and yet, whenever the need arises, he will be able, following Paul's example, to exalt over false pretenders and men of no worth with a holy triumph, provided he does it for Christ's sake and not his own—for nothing but pride or selfishness could corrupt or deform all these excellencies. And yet when all is said and done, the chief thing is that we should serve Christ with a pure conscience; everything else is merely additional.

28. *Besides those things that are without.* 'Besides those things', he says, 'that fall upon me from all sides and are, so to speak, extraordinary, what conception can anyone form of the ordinary burden that presses upon me continually, the *anxiety* I have *for all the churches.*' It is appropriate that he should call this anxiety his ordinary burden, and so I have taken the liberty of translating ἐπισύστασιν in this way, since it sometimes means whatever presses upon us. Any man who is seriously concerned for the Church of God harasses himself and bears a heavy burden on his shoulders. What a picture we have here of a complete minister, whose care and zeal embrace not only one church or ten or thirty, but all the churches at once, so that he teaches some, strengthens others, exhorts some and counsels others, and for yet others cures their diseases. From Paul's words here we may infer that nobody can have a heartfelt concern for the churches without being burdened by many difficulties: for the government of the Church is not a pleasant occupation which we can undertake with joy and delight; it is, as has already been said, a hard and bitter warfare, in which Satan again and again stirs up for us as much trouble as he can and leaves no stone unturned to annoy us.

29. *Who is weak?* How many there are who allow all offences to pass unheeded or who despise the weakness and infirmities of their brethren or trample them underfoot. This is because they are not moved by any concern for the Church. For it is certain that concern produces συμπάθειαν, fellow-feeling, which makes the minister of

Christ take upon himself the feelings of all and put himself in the place of all, that he may adapt himself to all needs.

If I must needs glory, I will glory of the things that concern my weakness. The God and Father of the Lord Jesus, he who is blessed forever more, knoweth that I lie not. In Damascus the governor under Aretas the king guarded the city of the Damascenes, in order to take me: and through a window was I let down in a basket by the wall, and escaped his hands.
(30-33)

30. *If I must needs glory.* This is the conclusion of all that has gone before, that Paul would rather boast of all those things that are concerned with his *weakness*, that is, things that might bring him contempt rather than glory in the world's eyes, like hunger, thirst, imprisonments, stonings, stripes and so on—things of which indeed we are usually ashamed as through them we incur great disgrace.

31. *The God and Father.* As he is about to give an account of a strange and little-known exploit, he confirms it with an oath. Notice however the form of a godly oath by which, for the sake of establishing the truth, we reverently call upon God to be our witness. This adventure was, as it were, Paul's first apprenticeship to persecution, as Luke clearly shows. And if the raw recruit underwent such trials at the beginning, what shall we say of him when he is a veteran! Since however a story about his flight is hardly evidence of a brave heart, it may be asked why he mentions it here. My answer is that the closing of the gates of the royal city shows with what great fury the ungodly were incensed against him, and they did not feel like that for nothing. If Paul had not been fighting for Christ with a fresh and unusual zealousness, the wicked would never have been thrown into such a passion. But his remarkable perseverance became specially clear in the fact that after escaping from such hard persecution he did not cease to provoke the whole world against him by carrying on fearlessly with the Lord's work. It may be that here Paul's intention is to mock at those self-seeking opponents of his who wanted to be thought very distinguished when in fact they had never experienced anything but applause, favours, honourable salutations and agreeable lodgings. Against all that he tells us how he was trapped, so that it was only with the greatest difficulty that he was able to save his life by a miserable and ignominious flight.

Some raise the question as to whether it was right for Paul to climb over the town walls since this was a capital crime. My answer is first, that it is not certain if that punishment was in fact sanctioned by law in the east and, secondly, even if it was, Paul committed no crime since he climbed the wall not as an enemy or for sport but from necessity.

v. 31] II CORINTHIANS 11

For the law would not punish a man who threw himself from the walls to save his life from fire, and what difference is there between a fire and a fierce attack by rascals? In thinking of the law, we must always have regard to equity and fairness. That consideration will absolve Paul from all blame.

CHAPTER TWELVE

I must needs glory, though it is not expedient; but I will come to visions and revelations of the Lord. I knew a man in Christ fourteen years ago (whether in the body, I know not; or whether out of the body, I know not; God knoweth), such a one caught up even to the third heaven. And I know such a man (whether in the body or apart from the body, I know not; God knoweth), how that he was caught up into Paradise, and heard unspeakable words, which it is not lawful for a man to utter. On behalf of such a one will I glory: but on mine own behalf I will not glory, save in my weaknesses. (1-5)

1. *It is not expedient to glory.* He now restrains himself, so to speak, in mid course and administers a most timely rebuke to the impudence of his rivals and shows with what great reluctance he is taking part in this boasting contest with them. How shameful it was for them to go about everywhere begging for testimonials to put them on the same level with such a man as Paul. And by his example of reluctance in boasting, he reminds us that the greater and the more excellent are the graces in which each of us abounds, the less he ought to think of them. Such dwelling on our own excellence is always dangerous for, like a man entering a labyrinth, we are soon hemmed in by it and become too aware of our gifts and too ignorant of ourselves. Paul is afraid that that might happen to him. The graces God gives us are certainly to be acknowledged, so that we may both be roused to gratitude for them and then be led to use them rightly, but to make them a pretext for boasting is full of very great danger.

But I will come to visions. 'I shall not creep on the ground but rather be constrained to mount aloft, although I am afraid that the height of the gifts may carry me away so that I forget myself.' Certainly if Paul had boasted out of self-regard he would have plunged headlong from these heights, for the only thing that can secure our greatness in God's eyes is humility. There is a distinction between *visions* and *revelations*. Revelation often takes place either by a dream or in an oracle in which nothing appears to the eyes, whereas a vision is hardly ever granted without a revelation, that is, without the Lord making plain what He means by it.

2. *I know a man in Christ.* Desiring to keep himself within bounds, he chooses only one example and treats it in such a way as to make it clear that it is not by his own desire that he is mentioning it at all; for

why else should he speak of himself in the third person? It is as though he had said, 'I should prefer to be silent and keep this whole matter to myself, but my opponents will not let me. Therefore I shall mention it hesitantly so as to make it clear that I speak against my will. Some think that the phrase *in Christ* is introduced as an oath to confirm what he says. In my view Paul's intention is rather to make it clear that here he has no concern with himself but looks to Christ alone. What he says about not knowing whether he was *in the body* or *out of the body* brings out more clearly the greatness of the revelation. He means that God acted upon him in a way that he himself did not understand. We should not find that hard to believe, since sometimes God shows Himself to us also in such a way that we do not know how He does it. But this in no way detracts from the certainty of our faith, which depends entirely on our awareness that it is God who is speaking to us. Moreover we should learn from this, that we should seek to know only what we need to know and leave the rest to God. Thus he says that he does not know whether he was taken up into heaven entire, soul and body, or whether only his soul was caught up.

Fourteen years ago. Some would like to know about the place where this happened, but it is not our business to satisfy their curiosity. At the beginning the Lord showed Himself to Paul in a vision when He wished to convert him from Judaism to the faith of the Gospel, but that was not the time when he was admitted into these secrets, for then he still needed Ananias to instruct him in the first rudiments of the Gospel (Acts 9.12). The vision was only a preparation to make him ready to be taught. It is possible that he is referring here to the vision mentioned by Luke in Acts 22.17. But there is no need to take much trouble over guesses of that kind, since we are told that Paul himself kept silent for fourteen years, and would never have said a word if he had not been forced to by the unreasonableness of wicked men.

Even to the third heaven. He is not here drawing fine philosophical distinctions between the different heavens so that each planet is assigned a heaven of its own. The number three is used as a perfect number to indicate what is highest and most complete. Also the word heaven by itself means here God's blessed and glorious kingdom above all spheres and the firmament itself and all the framework of the world. But not content with using the simple word heaven, Paul adds that he had reached its utmost height and its innermost chambers. Our faith climbs up and enters heaven and those who excel in knowledge penetrate higher and further, but to reach the third heaven has been given to very few.

4. *Into Paradise.* In Scripture every place that is specially agreeable and blessed is called 'the garden of God' and thus the habit grew up

among the Greeks of using the word 'Paradise' for the heavenly glory. It was thus used even before Christ, as is clear from Eccles. 40.17 and 27. It is also used in this sense by Christ in His answer to the thief in Luke 23.43, 'Today thou shalt be with me in Paradise', that is, 'You will enjoy the presence of God in the condition and life of the blessed.'

Heard unspeakable words. I do not take 'words' to mean 'things' here, as the word often can in Hebrew, for the verb 'heard' would not suit that interpretation. If anyone asks what these words were, the answer can be brief, that it was with good reason they were called 'unspeakable' and such as it is 'not lawful to utter'. If anyone retorts that in that case what Paul heard was superfluous and useless, for what good was there in hearing something that had to be held back in perpetual silence, my answer is that this thing happened for Paul's own sake, for a man who had awaiting him troubles hard enough to break a thousand hearts needed to be strengthened in a special way to keep him from giving way and to help him to persevere undaunted. If we consider for a moment how many great adversaries his teaching had to contend with and in how many ways it was subjected to attack, we shall not wonder why he heard more than it was lawful to utter. From this passage we should allow ourselves to be reminded of the bounds we must set to our knowledge. We are naturally given to curiosity so that we tend to pass over carelessly, or, at least, taste only slightly teaching that tends to edification while we become involved in frivolous questions. To this curiosity we add boldness and rashness, so that we are ready without hesitation to pronounce on things about which we know nothing and which are hidden from us. From these two sources there has sprung up a great deal of scholastic theology and everything that that trifler Dionysius has had the audacity to invent about the hierarchies of heaven. It is all the more incumbent upon us to seek to know nothing but what the Lord has been willing to reveal to His Church. Let that be the limit of our knowledge.

5. *On behalf of such a one.* It is as if he had said, 'I have good reason to glory but I do so most unwillingly, for it is more to my purpose to *glory in my infirmities.* Should however these malicious people meddle with me any more and make me boast more than I wish, they will discover that they have to do with a man whom God has greatly honoured and exalted on high in order to confute their follies.'

> *For if I should desire to glory, I shall not be foolish; for I shall speak the truth: but I forbear, lest any man should account of me above that which he seeth me to be, or heareth from me. And by reason of the exceeding greatness of the revelations—wherefore, that I should not be exalted*

overmuch, there was given to me a thorn in the flesh, a messenger of Satan to buffet me, that I should not be exalted overmuch. Concerning this thing I besought the Lord thrice, that it might depart from me. And he hath said unto me, My grace is sufficient for thee: for my power is made perfect in weakness. Most gladly therefore will I glory in my weaknesses, that the power of Christ may rest upon me. Wherefore I take pleasure in weaknesses, in injuries, in necessities, in persecutions, in distresses, for Christ's sake: for when I am weak, then am I strong.
(6–10)

6. *For if I should desire to glory.* In order that what he has said about having no desire to glory should not be used as a pretext for false accusations, and in order that malevolent opponents might not be able to retort, 'You do not wish to, because you cannot', he anticipates such a retort by saying, 'I could glory with good reason and without any fear of being rightly accused of vanity, for I have something to boast of, but I abstain.' 'Folly' as used here has a different meaning than before, for even those who have good grounds for their glorying are foolish and affected if they give way to empty bragging and self seeking. But the folly is more offensive and intolerable if someone boasts without good grounds, that is, pretends to be what he is not. For then there is impudence as well as stupidity. But the apostle here takes it as settled that his glorying as well as being justified is also done in humility. Erasmus has translated, 'I spare you', but I prefer, 'I refrain', or, as I have actually rendered it, 'I forbear'.

Lest any man should account of me. He now adds his reason for this forbearing—that he is content to fill the place that God has assigned him. 'My appearance and my speech', he says, 'give no promise of anything outstanding in me, and I do not object to being held in low esteem as far as they are concerned.' Here we see how very modest he was, for he was in no way put out by the poorness of appearance and speech that he recognized in himself, although he was otherwise endowed with many excellent gifts. There would be no absurdity in taking the verse to mean that he is content with the fact of his superiority, and therefore says nothing about himself at all as an implied rebuke to the false apostles who were making many boasts about themselves that had no evidence to support them. I prefer the interpretation mentioned first.

7. *In order that I should not be exalted by the excellence of revelations.* This is a second reason for his forbearance, that God, wishing to restrain every sign of insubordination in him, subdued him with a rod. This rod he calls a *thorn* or a goad, using a metaphor drawn from the driving of oxen. The word *flesh* is in the dative case in Greek and

Erasmus has translated it 'by the flesh', but I prefer to understand it as meaning that the prickings of this goad were in his flesh.

Now the question arises as to what this goad was. Those who think that Paul was tempted to lust are quite ridiculous and we must put their ideas aside. Others have thought that he was troubled with frequent headaches. Chrysostom's view is that the reference is to Hymenaeus and Alexander and people of that kind, who, at the devil's bidding, caused Paul great annoyance. I for my part think that this phrase is meant to sum up all the different kinds of trial with which Paul was exercised. For here in my view flesh does not mean body, but rather the part of the soul which is not regenerate, so that the meaning would be, 'To me there has been given a goad to jab at my flesh for I am not yet so spiritual as to be exempt from temptations according to the flesh.' He also goes on to call it the *messenger of Satan*, for since all temptations are instigated by Satan, as soon as they come upon us, they warn us that Satan is at hand. Thus at every touch of temptation we should rouse ourselves and quickly put on our armour to drive back Satan's attacks. It was most profitable that this should come into Paul's mind, for knowing this he could not sit at ease like a man who was in no danger. For a man who is still surrounded with perils and is in fear of the enemy can sing no song of triumph. 'The Lord', he says, 'has provided me with the best remedy against undue elation, for while I am taken up with seeing that Satan does not take advantage of me, I am kept safe from pride.'

And yet this is not the only means God employs to cure him, for he is also humbled. For he adds, *to buffet me* and this is a most eloquent way of indicating that he was brought back into order. To be buffeted is a severe indignity. If anyone's face is beaten black and blue, shame prevents him from showing himself to others, and so when we labour under any kind of infirmity we should remember that we are, as it were, being buffeted by the Lord to make us ashamed, so that we may learn humility. This should be borne in mind especially by those who are outstanding for their distinguished excellencies, for if they have defects mixed with their virtues, if they are persecuted out of hatred, if they are attacked with curses, these are not merely the rods of their heavenly instructor but the buffetings which are designed to restrain all haughtiness and fill them with modesty. Therefore let all godly men take note 'What a dreadful poison pride is, so that the only antidote to it is another poison', as Augustine says in his third sermon 'On the Sayings of the Apostle'. As it was the first cause of man's ruin, so it is the last fault against which we have to struggle, for other vices are connected with evil deeds, but pride is to be feared because of its connexion with the best deeds that we perform, and also because it naturally clings to us with such obstinacy and is so firmly rooted that it is only with the greatest difficulty that it can be removed. And let us note carefully who it is that is saying this. He had overcome so many torments and perils and other evils, he had won a triumph over all Christ's enemies, he had driven out the fear of death and renounced the world, and yet he had not completely subdued his pride, so that there still went on in him a conflict so doubtful that he could not conquer without being buffeted. Taught by his example, as we wage war against our other faults, let us devote our main efforts to combating pride. But what is the meaning of the fact that Satan, who was a murderer from the beginning, played the part of physician to Paul, not merely in curing his body but in the greater task of bringing health to his soul? My answer is that Satan's only intention, in accordance with his character and custom, was to kill and destroy, and the goad of which Paul speaks was dipped in deadly poison, so that it was a special act of mercy for the Lord to turn into a means of healing what was by nature the means of death.

8. *Concerning this thing I besought the Lord thrice.* Here *thrice* stands for frequent repetition. His meaning is that this annoyance had so distressed him that he had often prayed for it to be taken away. If it had been slight or easy to bear, he would not have been so eager to be free of it, and yet he says that he has not been granted his request, and that makes it clear how great his need of being humbled was. This confirms what he has already said, that this thing was a bridle that held him back from haughtiness. If it had been to his advantage to be free of it, he would not have been refused. But this would appear to imply that Paul had not prayed in faith, if all God's promises are not to be made out to be vain. In many places in Scripture we are told that whatsoever we ask in faith, we shall obtain. But Paul prays and he does not obtain. My answer is that just as there are many kinds of asking, so there are two kinds of obtaining. We ask without qualification for those things about which we have a sure promise, such as the perfecting of God's kingdom and the hallowing of His name, the forgiveness of sins and everything profitable to us. But when we imagine that God's kingdom can and indeed must be furthered in such and such a way, or that this or that is necessary for the hallowing of His name, we are often mistaken, just as, in the same way, we are often deluded as to what in fact tends to our own welfare. Thus we ask for these things that are certainly promised with full confidence and without reserve, but it is not for us to prescribe the means, and if we do specify them, our prayer always has an unexpressed qualification included in it. Now Paul was well aware of this, and as far as the intention and purpose of his prayer was concerned, he was without doubt answered,

even if the form in which he made his request was refused. From this we should be warned not to be despondent, when God does not meet or satisfy our requests, as though our prayer were wasted effort. For His grace ought to be sufficient for us, that is, it should be enough that He has not forsaken us. This is why He sometimes withholds from the godly in His mercy things that He grants to the ungodly in His wrath, because He Himself can foresee better than our minds what is good for us.

9. *He hath said unto me.* It is not clear whether or not this answer came to him by a special oracle, but it is a point of little importance. For God answers us when He strengthens us inwardly by His Spirit and sustains us by His comfort, so that our hope and patience do not fail. He tells Paul to be satisfied with His grace and not to refuse chastisement. So we must endure under affliction, however long it may continue, knowing that we are excellently well treated as long as God's grace is with us to support us. Here the word *grace* does not mean as elsewhere God's favour but is used by metonymy for the help of the Holy Spirit which comes to us from God's undeserved favour. This grace should be sufficient for godly men, for it is a sure and unconquerable support that should keep us from ever giving way.

For my power. Our weakness appears to be an obstacle against God's perfecting His power within us, but Paul not only denies that that is so, but asserts the opposite, that it is only when our weakness becomes apparent that God's strength can be perfected. To understand this clearly we must distinguish between God's strength and ours, for here the word *my* is emphatic. 'MY power', says the Lord (that is, the power that helps men in their need, that raises them up when they have fallen and that recreates them when they faint), 'is made perfect in men's weakness; it has an opportunity to exert itself when human weakness becomes evident, and in such circumstances, moreover, it is more clearly acknowledged as it deserves to be.' The verb 'to be made perfect' refers to the perception and acknowledgment of men, since God's strength is made perfect only when it shines out clearly enough to win the praise that is its due. For men have no taste for it till they are convinced of their need of it and they immediately forget its value unless they are continually reminded by awareness of their own weakness.

Most gladly therefore. This confirms the explanation I have given. *I will glory*, he says, *in my weaknesses, that the power of Christ may rest upon me.* The man who is too ashamed to glory in this way shuts the door against Christ's grace and in a way drives it from him, for we make room for Christ's grace when with a resigned mind we feel and confess our own weakness. The valleys are watered with rain to make them fruitful while the summits of lofty mountains remain dry. A man must become a valley if he wants to receive the heavenly rain of God's spiritual grace. He adds *most gladly* to show that he burns with such a desire for Christ's grace that he will refuse nothing for the sake of obtaining it. We see very many people yielding to God because they are afraid of sacrilege in coveting His glory, and yet their yielding is reluctant or, at any rate, less spontaneous than it should be.

10. *I take pleasure in weaknesses.* He is clearly using the word 'weakness' in different senses. Above he was referring to the prickings of his thorn in the flesh, but now he uses it to mean external accidents that earn the world's scorn. Having spoken of every kind of weakness in a general way, he now returns to the special kind of weakness from which this whole discussion started. We should notice therefore that weakness is a general term which covers both the infirmity of our nature and all the outward signs of humiliation. The discussion started with Paul's outward abasement, but from that he went on to show how the Lord humbled him in every way, in order that His glory might shine out the more clearly in his defects, since human glory often hides and conceals divine glory. At the same time he speaks again about his own excellencies, which in the common view of men won him more scorn than praise.

For when I am weak. That is, 'The more I fail, the more liberally does the Lord provide of His strength all that He sees that I need.' The strong-mindedness praised by philosophers is only stubborn insolence or mad frenzy typical of fanatics. But the man who really desires to be strong must not refuse also to be weak; he must be weak in himself in order that he may be strong in the Lord. If anyone objects that here Paul is not speaking of lack of strength but about poverty and other afflictions, my answer is that all these are the means of making our own weakness clear to us, for if the Lord had not inflicted such trials upon Paul, he would never have been so clearly aware of his own weakness. Thus his reference is not just to poverty and all kinds of hardship, but also to the effects that these things have in making us aware of our own weakness and in bringing us to distrust ourselves and be humble.

> *I am become foolish: ye compelled me; for I ought to have been commended of you: for in nothing was I behind the very chiefest apostles, though I am nothing. Truly the signs of an apostle were wrought among you in all patience, by signs and wonders and mighty works. For what is there wherein ye were made inferior to the rest of the churches, except it be that I myself was not a burden to you? forgive me this wrong. Behold, this is the third time I am ready to come to you; and I will not be a burden to*

you; for I seek not yours, but you: for the children ought not to lay up for the parents, but the parents for the children. And I will most gladly spend and be spent for your souls. If I love you more abundantly, am I loved the less? (11-15)

11. *I am become foolish.* Up till now he has been bringing forward many excuses to explain why he is singing his own praise, a thing so contrary to his own habits and so unsuited to his apostolic office. Now instead of apologizing he accuses, and lays the blame upon the Corinthians who ought themselves to have been praising him. Since the false apostles were belittling Paul, they should vigorously have opposed them and borne faithful witness to his excellencies, as he deserved. In this way he administers a timely rebuke so that those who are ill-disposed towards him should not put a discreditable interpretation upon this self-defence which their ingratitude has forced him to make, and should not continue with their false accusations against him.

For in nothing. We are lacking in gratitude to God if we allow His gifts, which are evident in ourselves, to be disparaged or despised. This is the fault with which Paul here charges the Corinthians, for they had recognized that he was the equal of the very chiefest apostles and yet they had listened to the slanders of his accusers. Some take *the very chiefest apostles* to refer to those of his rivals who claimed the highest rank for themselves, but I take him to mean the chief among the twelve, as if he had said, 'If I am compared with any of the apostles, I have no fear of being found inferior.' For although Paul enjoyed the friendliest relationships with all the apostles and was ready to extol them high above himself, he did dispute claims that were falsely attached to their names. The false apostles were founding their false pretensions on the fact that they had been in the company of the twelve, and so understood all their intentions and knew all their institutions and so on. Thus Paul, seeing their bogus pride in these outward appearances and counterfeit titles and the impression that they were making on simple men, was compelled to make this comparison. The added correction, *though I am nothing* means that Paul's intention was not to claim anything as his own merit but only to glory in the Lord. Or it may seem preferable to some to take this as an expression of what his adversaries and slanderers were saying against him.

12. *The signs of an apostle.* By the signs of an apostle he means the seals that attest the genuineness of his apostleship or, in other words, the proofs and witnesses of it. It is as if he had said, 'God has confirmed my apostleship among you so abundantly that it requires no proof.'

The first sign he mentions is *patience*, either because he has stood unconquered in brave opposition to all the assaults of Satan and his enemies and has never yielded, or because without thought of his own distinguished position he has endured with an untroubled mind all injuries, infinite grievances and by patience overcome indignities. Such heroic virtue is like a heavenly seal by which the Lord marks out his apostles.

The second thing he mentions is miracles for when he speaks of *signs and wonders and mighty works*, he uses three terms (as in II Thess. 2.9) with the same meaning. He calls them *signs* because they are not merely meaningless spectacles but are designed to instruct men. He calls them *wonders* because by their novelty they should rouse and astonish, and he calls them powers or *mighty works* because they are more evidently examples of divine power than those which we discover in the ordinary course of nature. Now we know that at the first coming of the Gospel the chief function of miracles was to give its doctrine greater authority. Thus the more power a man was given to work miracles, the more confirmation his ministry was given—as I have said in my comments on Rom. 15.

13. *For what is there.* Their ingratitude appears in even blacker colours when we see how his excellency has been to their advantage, for they have benefited from the proofs of his apostleship he has given, and yet they were now approving the slanders of the false apostles. In irony he adds that his only inferiority was that he was not a burden to them, for in reality this was the climax of the many blessings he had bestowed upon them, that he had served them for nothing. After all that, to pour contempt upon him, as they were doing, was an insult to his moderation. He has therefore good reason for this sharp rebuke of their foolish pride.

Forgive me this wrong, he says. They were being doubly ungrateful, for not only were they despising the man to whom they were under such obligation for all the blessings he had given them, but they were even turning his generosity into a reproach. Chrysostom thinks that there is no irony here, but that this is a genuine apology. But if the whole context is carefully examined, it will not be hard to see that this view is quite contrary to Paul's meaning.

14. *Behold, this is the third time.* He now commends the very action for which the Corinthians had been most ungrateful. He says that he refrained from taking their money for two reasons, first, because he sought them and not their wealth and, second, because he wanted to treat them like a father. It is clear from this what praise his moderation deserved, although in fact it won him only contempt among the Corinthians.

For I seek not yours. It is the duty of a true and upright pastor not to seek for gain from his sheep, but rather to seek for their salvation, although it should also be noted that we are not to seek for men with a view to making them our own disciples. It is a bad thing to be devoted to gain or to undertake the office of pastor for the sake of making profit from it, but it is much worse to divert the loyalty of disciples to oneself for reasons of personal ambition. Paul's meaning here is that he has no desire for payment, but is concerned only with the welfare of souls. But there is more elegance in what he says, which amounts to this, 'I seek larger wages than you think, for I am not content with your riches but I seek the whole of you in order to present you to the Lord as a sacrifice from the fruits of my ministry.' But what if a man should keep himself by his own labour? Is he then seeking the substance of his people? Certainly if a man is a faithful pastor, he will always seek the welfare of his flock and nothing else. His stipend will be an appendage but his only aim ought to be as I have said. Woe to those who set their heart on anything else.

Parents for their children. Was not Paul a father to the Philippians also, who supported him even when he was absent from them? And were none of the other apostles fathers, seeing that the churches ministered to their support? This is certainly not his meaning, for it is no new thing for parents to be supported by their children in their old age. Thus those who live at the expense of the Church are not necessarily unworthy of the honour due to fathers, but Paul only wished to show that what he had done proceeded from his fatherly affection. The argument should not therefore be pressed so as to draw negative implications from it. What he did, he did as a father, but if he had done otherwise, he would not have ceased to be a father.

15. *And I will most gladly spend.* This is proof of an affection that is more than fatherly, since he was ready to expend in their service not only his work and whatever substance he might possess, but his life as well. And even although he has had from them but scant affection, he still continues in this mind towards them. What stony heart would not soften or even break at such warmth of love, especially when it is joined to such faithfulness! But here Paul is not speaking of himself merely to make us admire him, but that we may also imitate him. Let all pastors learn from what he says what they owe to their churches.

But be it so, I did not myself burden you; but being crafty, I caught you with guile. Did I take advantage of you by any one of them whom I have sent unto you? I exhorted Titus, and I sent the brother with him. Did Titus take any advantage of you? walked we not by the same Spirit? walked we not in the same steps? Ye think that we are again excusing ourselves unto you. In the sight of God speak we in Christ. But all things, beloved, are for your edifying. For I fear, lest by any means, when I come, I should find you not such as I would, and should myself be found of you such as ye would not; lest by any means there should be strife, jealousy, wraths, factions, backbitings, whisperings, swellings, tumults; lest, when I come again, my God should humble me before you, and I should mourn for many of them that have sinned heretofore, and repented not of the uncleanness and fornication and lasciviousness which they committed. (16-21)

16. *But be it so.* These words mean that Paul had been accused by malevolent enemies of procuring secretly, through people he had bribed, the payment he refused to accept into his own hands. Not that he had done any such thing, but they were measuring others, as the saying goes, by their own ell. For wicked men usually and shamelessly impute to the servants of God the very things they themselves would do if they had the chance. Thus to clear himself of this shamelessly trumped up charge, Paul is obliged to defend the integrity of those who have been his messengers. For if they had sinned in any way, it would have been imputed to him. Who could be surprised at his great caution in accepting gifts of money, since after all his care he was still troubled by such unfair charges. But let his case be a warning to us that it will be no new or unbearable fate that befalls us if at some time we have to answer false charges of the same kind. And most of all let it be a warning to us to observe the strictest caution so as to give no pretext to those who are ill-disposed towards us. For we see that it is not enough to give proof of our own integrity, unless those whose assistance we employ are also found to be upright. Thus our choice of such assistants should not be lightly made or as a matter of form but with the most minute care.

19. *Think ye again.* Since those who have a bad conscience are sometimes more than usually anxious to defend themselves, Paul's defence of his own ministry in the first epistle was probably being used as the basis of a charge against him. Once again it is a fault in the servants of Christ to be too anxious about their reputations. To rebut these two false charges, he first declares that he speaks in the sight of God, whom evil consciences always dread. Next he maintains that he is thinking less of himself than of them. He was ready to face good report or bad report and even to be reduced to nothing, but it was to the good of the Corinthians that he should retain the reputation he deserved so that his ministry might not be brought into contempt.

20. *For I fear.* He explains how the vindication of his integrity tends to their edification, for, thinking that he had fallen into contempt, many were already growing wanton, as though the restraining reins had been loosened. Respect for him would have been a means of

bringing them to repentance, for they would have attended to his admonitions. This fear of which he speaks sprang from love, for if their welfare had not been of great concern to him, he would easily have overlooked all this. He had nothing to gain for himself from it and usually we are afraid to give offence when we see that it will be hurtful to us.

And I shall be found by you. His second fear is of being forced to act more severely. To shrink from severity and to seek gentler remedies is a sign of love and even of indulgence. It is as if he had said, 'I struggle now to assert my authority and I strive to bring you back to obedience so that I may not have occasion to punish your obstinacy more severely, if I come and find in you no amendment.' Thus he teaches us by his example that pastors should always seek moderate remedies for correcting faults before they have recourse to extreme severity; by advising and reproving final rigour can be avoided.

Lest by any means there should be strife. He enumerates the chief faults of the Corinthians which almost all spring from one source. If everyone had not been devoted to himself, there would never have been strife among them, they would never have been jealous of each other and there would have been no slander among them. The sum and substance of this first list of their faults is lack of love because φιλαυτία and self-love have prevailed.

21. *Lest, when I come again, my God should humble me.* His humility had been considered a fault, but he throws the blame for it back upon the Corinthians who should have honoured his apostleship, but have instead loaded it with disgrace. Their progress in holiness would have been the honour and glory of Paul's apostleship, but being in the grip of so many faults, they had instead brought disgrace upon him, as much as in them lay. He does not bring this charge against all of them, but only against a few who had irresponsibly scorned all his advice. The meaning is, 'They think contemptuously of me because I seem to be despicable. Let them then avoid giving me any more cause for humiliation, but let them rather give up their frowardness and begin to feel shame and embarrassment over their faults; let them bow themselves down to the ground instead of looking down haughtily on others.' Paul reveals to us the mind of a true and sincere pastor when he says that he will look on the sins of others with grief. It is right that every pastor should bear the concerns of the Church on his heart, should feel its ills as if they were his own, sympathize with its sorrows and grieve for its sins. We see how Jeremiah begs for a 'fountain of tears' (9.1) that he may bewail the disaster of his people. We see how godly kings and prophets, to whom the government of the people was entrusted, felt in the same way. This is something common to all

v. 21]　　　II CORINTHIANS 12

godly men, to be grieved whenever God is offended, to lament the downfall of their brethren and to come before God as if they were themselves guilty in their stead, and this is required of pastors in even greater degree. Here also Paul introduces a list of faults that all come under the one head of unchastity.

CHAPTER THIRTEEN

This is the third time I am coming to you. At the mouth of two witnesses or three shall every word be established. I have said beforehand, and I do say beforehand, as when I was present the second time, so now, being absent, to them that have sinned hertofore, and to all the rest, that, if I come again, I will not spare; seeing that ye seek a proof of Christ that speaketh in me; who to you-ward is not weak but is powerful in you: for he was crucified through weakness, yet he liveth through the power of God. For we also are weak in him, but we shall live with him through the power of God toward you. (1-4)

1. *This is the third time.* He goes on further with his reproof of the insolence of those of whom he has been speaking, some of whom are living dissolute and licentious lives, others carrying on contentions and disputes among themselves and who care nothing for his rebuke. His words do not apply to the entire body of the Church but only to certain diseased and half-rotten members in it. He now allows himself to speak much more sharply, seeing that he is dealing with private individuals and not with the whole people, and with such individuals as will not yield to kindness or gentle remedies. Having first spent a year and a half among them, he had visited them a second time. Now he warns them that he will come a third time and he says that his three comings will be like three witnesses to convict them of obstinacy. He quotes the law about the authority of witnesses, using it not in its natural and literal meaning but metaphorically adapting it to his present purpose. 'The law declares', he says, 'that in settling disputes we have to rely on the testimony of two or three witnesses.' The word *established* means that a decision is given in a case so that strife may cease. 'I indeed am but one, but by coming three times I shall have the authority of three witnesses' or 'my three comings will take the place of three testimonies'. For his threefold effort for their welfare and his constancy proved on three different occasions might well be considered the equivalent of three different men.

2. *I have said beforehand.* His frequent friendly and quiet remonstrations have had no effect, and so he betakes himself to a severer remedy with which he had already threatened them verbally when he was with them. When we see him acting so strictly we may be sure that they were unusually ungovernable and obstinate, for his writings make it plain how much mildness and unwearied patience he was

capable of showing elsewhere. It is characteristic of a good father to overlook and tolerate many things, and yet it is the mark of a stupid father who has no regard for the welfare of his children to be unwilling, on occasion, to use severity and to mingle strictness with mildness. We are well aware that nothing is more harmful than excessive indulgence. Let us therefore be mild when it is safe to be so and in our mildness earnest and moderate, but let us act more severely should necessity arise.

But the question is raised why the apostle allowed himself to expose the private faults of individuals so openly as to almost point his finger at the people concerned. My answer is that he never would have done it if the sins had been hidden, but, since they were well known to all and were published openly as a most harmful example, it was necessary that he should not spare those who had committed a public offence. The second question is about what kind of correction he was threatening to inflict upon them, since he could hardly castigate them more severely with words. I have no doubt that he means that he will punish them with excommunication. For there is nothing more to be dreaded than to be cut off from the Body of Christ, expelled from God's kingdom and handed over to Satan for destruction, unless you repent.

3. *Seeing that ye seek a proof.* There are two possible interpretations of these words. The first is, 'Since you wish proof of whether I speak of myself or whether Christ speaks through me . . .' and Chrysostom and Ambrose expound it in this way. I would rather take him to mean that, when his authority is weakened, Christ is more concerned than he is himself, and when they spurn his warning they try Christ's patience. It is as if he had said, 'It is Christ who speaks through me, and so, when you bring my teaching under your criticism, you harm Him more than you harm me.'

But someone will object, 'Is a man's teaching to be exempt from all examination just because he boasts that Christ is its Author? Every false prophet will claim this for his teaching, and how then shall we distinguish between true and false? And what are we to make of the word, 'Try the spirits, whether they are of God' (I John 4.1)? Paul anticipates all objections of this kind by saying that Christ has worked in power among them through his ministry. For the two phrases *Christ speaking in me* and *who to you-ward is powerful and not weak* are to be taken closely together and understood in this way, 'Christ, by exercising His power toward you in my teaching, has proved that He speaks through my mouth so that there is no excuse for your ignorance.' We see that he does not boast in words alone, but proves that in reality Christ is speaking in him, and he convinces the Corinthians of this before he demands that they should accept his claim. Thus it is right to make examination of the doctrine of any man who speaks in the Church, whatever title he may claim, until Christ has manifested Himself in his teaching, for then it is not Christ that is being judged but the man. But when it is clear that it is God's Word that is being proclaimed, then what Paul says holds good, that it is God Himself who is being disbelieved. Moses spoke with the same kind of assurance, 'What are we, I and Aaron? You are tempting God' (Num. 16.11). So also Isa. (7.13), 'Is it too small a thing that ye grieve men, unless you grieve my God also?' There is no room for evasion when it is clear that it is a minister of God who is speaking and that he is discharging his office faithfully. To return to Paul, since his ministry had had such effective proof among the Corinthians and the Lord had shown Himself openly in it, it is not surprising that he takes the opposition to it so hardly. He had good grounds for reproaching them with being rebels against Christ.

4. *For he was crucified*. He has a special reason for speaking of Christ's humiliation, for he wished to point out indirectly that, what they despised in him, they would also have been ready to despise in Christ Himself when He was abased even to death upon the cross (Phil. 2.8). At the same time he shows how absurd it is to despise in Christ the humiliation of the cross, since it is joined to the incomparable glory of His resurrection. It is as if he had said, 'Will you esteem Christ less because He showed His weakness in His death, as though the heavenly life that He lived after His resurrection were not a clear token of His divine power?' Just as the word 'flesh' stands for Christ's human nature, so here the word 'God' denotes His divinity.

This passage raises the question whether Christ laboured under such infirmity because He was subjected to it by necessity and against His will, for when we suffer because of our weakness, we suffer under compulsion and not of our own choice. In ancient times the Arians misused this argument to oppose the divinity of Christ, and the orthodox fathers gave this explanation, that it happened by Christ's appointment, because He so willed it, and not because any necessity compelled Him. This answer is correct, provided that it is rightly understood. There are however some who mistakenly extend this appointing of weakness to Christ's human will, as though weakness were not the condition of His nature but only something contrary to His nature that He permitted. For example, they say that He died not because His humanity was of itself subject to death, but because by His own appointment He chose to die. I certainly agree that He died by His own choice, but what was this choice but a decision to clothe Himself with our mortal nature? For if we make Christ's human nature so unlike our own, the chief foundation of our faith is overthrown. Let us therefore understand it thus, that Christ suffered by His appointment and not by necessity because, being 'in the form of God' He could have escaped this necessity, but nevertheless He suffered 'through weakness' because He 'emptied Himself'.

For we are weak in Him. To be weak in Christ means here to share Christ's weakness. Thus Paul makes his own weakness glorious, because in it he is conformed to Christ, and he no longer shrinks from the disgrace of it, for it is something he has in common with the Son of God. He says that he will live towards them after Christ's example. 'I also', he says, 'will share in Christ's life, after my weakness is taken away.' He opposes 'life' to 'weakness' and by life he means a condition in which a man flourishes and is full of honour. The phrase *towards you* can be taken along with *the power of God*, but it is of no importance, since the meaning remains the same; that the Corinthians, when they began to have a right judgment, would think reverently and honourably about God's power in Paul and would no longer despise his outer weakness.

> *Try your own selves, whether ye be in the faith; prove your own selves. Or know ye not as to your own selves that Jesus Christ is in you? unless indeed ye be reprobate. But I hope that ye shall know that we are not reprobate. Now we pray to God that ye do no evil; not that we may appear approved, but that ye may do that which is honourable, though we be as reprobate. For we can do nothing against the truth, but for the truth. For we rejoice, when we are weak and ye are strong: this we also pray for, even your perfecting.* (5.-9)

5. *Try your own selves.* He confirms what he has just said, that Christ's power has appeared openly in his ministry. He calls them to judge of this by looking into themselves and acknowledging what they have received from Him. Firstly, since there is but one Christ, it is necessary that He should dwell both in minister and people, and if He dwell in the people, how shall He deny Himself in the minister? Further, He had shown His power in Paul's preaching so clearly and unambiguously that the Corinthians could not doubt it, unless they were completely foolish. For how had faith come to them, and Christ and everything else besides? It is with good reason that they are called to look into themselves, that they may discover there what they despise as a thing unknown. The only true and well founded confidence a minister has is that he should be able to appeal to the consciences of those he has taught for approval of his teaching, so that if they have anything of Christ and of sincere godliness, they may be obliged to acknowledge his faithfulness. This, as we can now see, is Paul's purpose

here. But there are two reasons that make this passage worthy of special attention. First, it shows the relationship between the people's faith and the minister's preaching: for the preaching is the mother who conceives and brings forth, and faith is the daughter who ought to be mindful of her origin. Second, this passage serves to prove the assurance of faith, a doctrine which the sophists of the Sorbonne have so corrupted for us that it is now almost uprooted from the minds of men. They hold that it is rash temerity to be persuaded that we are members of Christ and have Him dwelling in us, and they bid us rest content with a moral conjecture, which is a mere opinion, so that our consciences remain perpetually undecided and perplexed. But what does Paul say here? He declares that those who doubt their possession of Christ and their membership in His Body are reprobates. Let us therefore understand that the only true faith is that which allows us to rest in God's grace, not with a dubious opinion but with firm and steadfast assurance.

Unless indeed ye be reprobate. He gives them a choice, so to speak, between being considered reprobates, and giving their due testimony to his ministry, for he leaves them no middle course between recognizing his apostleship and admitting themselves to be reprobate. For there was no doubt that their faith was based on his teaching, and the only Christ they had, they had received from him, and they had no other Gospel than the one he had brought them, so that there was no way in which they could separate any part of their salvation from the acceptance of his good faith.

6. *But I hope that ye shall know.* He presses them still more urgently but he is still confident that they will not reject him. They must do one of two things, either pay Paul the honour due to an apostle or condemn themselves for unbelief and confess that they have no Church. He softens the severity of what he says by using the word 'hope', but nevertheless still reminding them of their duty, for to disappoint the hopes of those who are expecting us to do the right thing is very cruel. 'I hope', he says, 'that when you have been restored to a right mind you will know.' At this point he wisely says nothing about himself, but calls them to think of God's blessings with which they have been endowed, placing the emphasis on their salvation rather than on his own authority.

7. *Now we pray to God.* Once again he declares that he cares nothing for his own honour but is concerned only with their welfare. For nothing could do them more harm than to be deprived of the benefits of his teaching and this was already beginning to happen because of their pride and contempt. 'I have no anxiety', he says, 'for myself or for my reputation; my only fear is that you should offend God, and I

am ready to be as a reprobate myself, if only you are free from all blame'—a reprobate, that is, in the judgment of men, who very often reject those who are worthy of the highest honour. The particle *as* is by no means superfluous here, for it corresponds with what he says elsewhere—'as deceivers, yet true' (6.8). It is indeed a sound rule that is here laid down, that a pastor should have no regard for himself, but should be devoted exclusively to the building up of the Church. Let him be concerned for his own reputation in so far as he sees that it affects the public advantage, but let him also be ready to neglect it, whenever he can do so without public disadvantage.

8. *For we can do nothing*. That is, 'I do not seek or desire any other power than that which God has conferred upon me in order that I may serve the truth. False apostles care only for power for its own sake, and have no concern about putting it to good use.' In other words, he maintains and defends the honour of his ministry in so far as it is connected with the truth of God. It is as if he had said, 'What does it matter to me? For unless I am concerned with promoting the truth, all my claims will be false and unjustified. But if I devote whatever authority I have to promoting the truth, then I am not consulting my own interests, and when the authority of my doctrine is unimpaired and the truth is unharmed, I have what I desire. Thus in fighting so keenly I am not motivated by any personal regard for myself.' That is why he says that the man who fights and labours solely for the sake of the truth will not take it amiss, should the need arise, to be considered a reprobate in the eyes of men, provided that no harm is done to the glory of God, the upbuilding of the Church and the authority of sound teaching. This passage should be carefully noted, for it sets limits to the power that pastors of the Church ought to have, no more than is needed to carry out their function as ministers of the truth. The papists quote to us in loud voices, 'He that heareth you heareth me; he that despiseth you despiseth me' (Luke 10.16), and 'Obey them that are set over you' (Heb. 13.17), and they use these texts as excuses for claiming the utmost freedom to make infinite claims of domination, while at the same time they are the professed and sworn enemies of the truth and aim at its destruction with all their strength. This one statement of Paul is enough to rebuke such immoderation, since it declares that they themselves ought to be in subjection to the truth.

9. *For we rejoice*. The causal particle γάρ should either be taken as meaning 'therefore' or as introducing a second reason why he does not refuse to be considered a reprobate for their sakes and to their advantage. The reader may decide how he prefers to take it, for it is of little importance. When he says, 'I shall willingly allow myself to be thought weak, provided you are strong', there is an antithesis in the words but

not in the meaning. Here weakness means contempt as before, but he means that the Corinthians will be strong, if they are full of God's power and grace.

This also. As often before, so now again he repeats that it was from necessity and not from his own inclination that he has been more severe with them than they would wish, and he points out that by speaking in this way he spared them from the need of an even more severe remedy when he came. The *perfecting* of which he speaks consists of a right co-ordination and sound condition of all the members. His allusion is to good doctors who care for particular diseases in a way that avoids injury to any part of the body, and, since he is concerned to secure a perfect condition of this kind among them, he provides against the necessity of resorting to sterner remedies. For we see how those who at first shrink from the slight pain or uneasiness of a plaster are at length driven to endure the torture of burning or amputation, even when the result is very dubious.

> *For this cause I write these things while absent, that I may not when present deal sharply, according to the authority which the Lord gave me for building up and not for casting down. Finally, brethren, farewell. Be perfected; be comforted; be of the same mind; live in peace: and the God of love and peace shall be with you. Salute one another with a holy kiss. All the saints salute you. The grace of the Lord Jesus Christ, and the love of God, and the communion of the Holy Ghost, be with you all. The second epistle to the Corinthians was sent from Philippi in Macedonia by Titus and Luke.* (10-14)

10. *According to the power.* In the first place he shows that the strictness with which he speaks has behind it God's commandment, so that it should not be considered thunder without lightning or the feeling of a man excited without a cause. Now he lets them know that he would rather use his power for a different purpose, and the one for which it was properly intended—to build them up. It is as if he had said, 'I shall not have hasty recourse to cruel remedies nor shall I give sway to my anger, but I shall simply carry out the command which the Lord has given me.' When he speaks of power given him for upbuilding rather than for destroying he uses these words in a rather different sense than in chapter 10. In that passage he was commending the Gospel by pointing out the advantage that it brings us, since what is to our advantage is usually agreeable and gladly acceptable to us. Here his purpose is only to show that, though he might with justice punish the Corinthians severely, he is much more inclined to use his power for their good rather than for their ruin, for that is its proper purpose. Since the Gospel is by its own nature 'the power of God

unto salvation' (Rom. 1.16) and 'the savour of life unto life' (II Cor. 2.15, 16) and is only contingently 'a savour of death', the authority conferred upon ministers of the Gospel ought to be used for the salvation of those who hear them, for if it turns out to their destruction, that is against its nature. The meaning is therefore, 'Do not by your own fault turn what God has ordained for your salvation into your condemnation.' At the same time Paul admonishes all pastors by his example as to how they should limit the exercise of their power.

11 *Finally, brethren.* He moderates whatever sharpness there may have been in the whole epistle, as he wanted to leave their minds not exasperated but calmed. Reproofs are only beneficial when they are, as it were, seasoned with honey, so that the hearer may calmly accept them, if that is possible. At the same time he seems to turn from a few diseased members back to the whole Church. Thus he declares that his concern is for their *perfecting* and his desire for their *comforting*. *To be of one mind* and *to live in peace* are different, in that the second is the result of the first; the first has to do with a consensus of opinions, and the second with benevolence and a union of hearts.

And the God of peace. He said this in order to strengthen his exhortation and at the same time he declares that God will be with us if we cultivate peace among ourselves, for those who are at variance with one another are cut off from Him. Wherever there are disputes and contentions, there it is certain that the devil reigns. For what agreement is there between light and darkness (cf. 6.14 above)? He calls Him the God of peace and love, because He has recommended to us peace and love, for He loves them and is their Author. We have spoken of the *kiss* in the two preceding epistles.

14. *The grace of the Lord Jesus.* He closes the epistle with a prayer which has three parts in which the whole of our salvation in contained. He desires for them, first, the grace of Christ, second, the love of God and third, the communion of the Spirit. The word 'grace' does not mean here free favour, but stands by metonymy for the whole blessing of redemption. The order may appear to be inverted, since the love of God is mentioned second, although it is the source of His grace and so is first in priority. My answer is that there is not always in Scripture such exact care for the arrangement of terms, but it can also be said that the order here agrees with the common form of doctrine, as contained in Scripture, according to which *we, while we were enemies to God, were reconciled by the death of his Son* (Rom. 5.10), though the Scripture usually speaks of this in two different ways. Sometimes it speaks in the way I have just quoted from Paul, and says that there was enmity between us and God, until we were reconciled by Christ. On the other hand, we are told in John 3.16 that 'God so loved the world

that he gave his only begotten Son.' These two statements seem to contradict each other, but it is easy to reconcile them, for in the second we are viewing the thing from God's side, and in the first from our own. For God, as far as He Himself is concerned, loved us from before the foundation of the world and redeemed us solely because He loved us, but we, when we look at ourselves, see nothing but sin which provokes wrath, and we cannot grasp God's love for us without a Mediator. Thus, as far as we are concerned, Christ's grace is the beginning of God's love. Looking at the matter in the first way, Paul would not be right to put the grace of Christ before the love of God, because that would be to put the effect before the cause, but from the second point of view, it is right to start with the grace of God by which God adopted us as His sons, and honoured with His love those whom He had before held in hate and abomination because of sin.

The communion of the Holy Ghost. This is added because it is only under the guidance of the Spirit that we come into possession of Christ and all His benefits. He seems also to be alluding to the variety of the Spirit's gifts which he mentions elsewhere, since God does not give the Spirit to a man as an isolated individual but distributes to each according to the measure of grace, so that the members of the Church may share their gifts with one another and so cherish their unity.

The First and Second Epistles of Paul
The Apostle to
TIMOTHY

THE DEDICATORY EPISTLE

TO THE MOST ILLUSTRIOUS
AND TRULY CHRISTIAN PRINCE,
THE LORD EDWARD, DUKE OF SOMERSET,
EARL OF HERTFORD,
PROTECTOR OF ENGLAND & IRELAND,
TUTOR TO THE KING
GREETINGS

MOST noble Prince, the brilliant reports that have reached us, not only of all your heroic virtues, but especially of your outstanding godliness, produce such a universal and warm affection towards you in the hearts of all good men, even among those who have never seen you, that you must surely be regarded with extraordinary feelings of love and reverence by all right minded people in England. For to them it is given not only to see the good things which others must admire from afar, but also to reap all the advantages which a most excellent governor can confer both on the whole body of the people and on every one of its members. Nor can the praises bestowed upon you by constant report be thought to be false or to have their origin in flattery, for the deeds you have done clearly prove them to be true.

A tutor's work is difficult enough even with a private pupil of moderate fortune: but you are appointed tutor not only to a king but to a very large kingdom, and you discharge your office with such skill and wisdom that your success is universally admired. And to prove that your excellence is not confined to matters of law and to a commonwealth at peace, God has given it opportunity to be seen in war also, which under your auspices has been waged with both good success and great courage.

Nevertheless, the many great difficulties with which everyone knows you have had to contend, have not prevented you from making the restoration of religion your chief care. This consideration for the Gospel is as profitable to the public welfare of a kingdom as it is befitting for a prince. The prosperity of kingdoms can be assured, and those who guard them found faithful, only when He on whom they were founded and by whom they are preserved—the Son of God Himself—rules over them. Thus there is no way that you could more firmly establish the kingdom of England than by banishing idols and setting up there the true worship of God. For it was necessary to restore the genuine doctrine of godliness, which had been so long crushed and oppressed by the sacrilegious tyranny of the Roman antichrist—and to restore it is indeed to place Christ on His throne. And this act which in itself is excellent becomes all the more worthy of praise when we remember how few present-day rulers there are who are ready to bring their high dignity under the sceptre of Christ.

It has therefore been of the greatest advantage to the most illustrious king to have a man like you among his family to be the guide of his boyhood. For although all men speak of his most noble nature, such an instructor was yet very much required both to train him in habits of manly firmness and to regulate the Church of England for as long as his age should prevent him from doing so himself. I have no doubt that even now he is well aware that you were given him by God's providence in order that he might a little later take over his affairs in excellent condition from your hand.

For my own part, neither great distance nor the humility of my station could keep me from congratulating you upon your most outstanding achievement in promoting Christ's glory. And since it has pleased God to make me one of those by whose toil and labour He is today restoring to the world the purer doctrine of the Gospel, why should not I, however widely separated from you, express, as strongly as I can, my reverence for you, whom God by His singular kindness has also made a guardian and defender of the same teaching? And since I had no other proof to give in token of my regard, I thought I should offer you these Commentaries of mine on two of Paul's epistles. And I have not chosen my gift at random, but have selected the one that seemed most suitable. For here Paul advises his beloved Timothy with what kind of teaching he is to build up God's Church, what vices and enemies he is to resist, and how many annoyances he must endure. He exhorts him not to yield in face of any difficulty, to overcome all crises by his courage, to restrain by his authority the licentiousness of wicked men and not to bestow gifts out of a selfish desire for men's favour. In short, in these two epistles we are shown a living picture of the true government of the Church.

Now since in the name of your king you are making strenuous efforts to restore the Church of England, which, like almost every other part of the Christian world, has been miserably corrupted by the shocking wickedness of Popery, and since you have many Timothys engaged in that work, you and they could not direct your efforts better than by following the pattern here laid down by Paul. For everything in these letters is highly relevant to our own times, and there is hardly anything needful for the building up of the Church that cannot be drawn from them. I trust that my work will afford at least some help, but I prefer to leave that to emerge by trial of it,

DEDICATION

rather than to boast of it in words. If you, most noble Prince, should approve of it, I shall have abundant reason to be satisfied and your well-known kindness leaves me in no doubt that you will take in good part the service I now perform.

May the Lord, in whose hands are the ends of the earth, long uphold the safety and prosperity of England, adorn its excellent king with the royal spirit, bestow on him an ample share of every blessing and grant you good progress in your noble career, that through you His name may be more and more widely glorified.

Geneva, 20th July 1556

THEME OF PAUL'S
FIRST EPISTLE TO TIMOTHY

In my view this epistle was written more for the sake of others than for Timothy himself, and those who carefully consider the whole matter will agree with me. I do not of course deny that Paul intended to teach and advise Timothy also, but my contention is that the epistle contains many things that there would have been no need to include, had Timothy alone been in view. He was a young man not yet possessed of sufficient authority to restrain the headstrong men that rose up against him. It is clear from Paul's words that there were at that time some who made a great show of themselves and would not submit to anybody, and were so aflame with selfish ambition that there was no limit to the havoc they might have caused in the Church, if someone stronger than Timothy had not intervened. It is also clear that there were many things at Ephesus that required to be set in order and that needed Paul's sanction and the authority of his name. His intention was to give Timothy advice about many things but also to use what he said to Timothy to give advice to many others as well.

In the *first* chapter, he attacks certain self-seeking persons who were drawing attention to themselves by discussing profitless questions. It can be inferred that they were Jews who, out of a pretended zeal for the law, forgot about edification and cared only for frivolous disputations. It is intolerable profanation of God's law to derive from it nothing useful but merely to make use of it as material for empty chatter and to make it a false pretext for burdening the Church with frivolous trifles. Corruptions of this kind have prevailed for many centuries too long in the Papacy. For what was scholastic theology but an immense chaos of empty and useless speculations? Even in our own day there are many who, in order to show how acute they are in handling God's Word, allow themselves to play with it as though it were profane philosophy. Paul promises to support Timothy in correcting this fault and points out the chief lessons to be learnt from the law, making it clear that those who use the law for different ends are in fact corrupting it. Next, to prevent his own authority from being brought into contempt, having confessed his own unworthiness, he declares in lofty terms what kind of man he has by God's grace begun to be. Finally, he closes the chapter with a solemn threat designed to strengthen Timothy both in sound teaching and in a good conscience

THEME OF PAUL'S FIRST EPISTLE TO TIMOTHY

and also to terrify others by reminding them of the example of Hymenaeus and Alexander.

In the *second* chapter he enjoins that public prayers should be offered to God for all men and especially for princes and magistrates, and this leads him into a digression in which he discusses the advantages derived from civil government. The reason he gives why prayers should be offered for all men is that God, in offering the Gospel and Christ as Mediator to all men, shows that He wishes all men to be saved. This Paul confirms, from his own apostleship which was directed specially to the Gentiles. Thus he invites all men of all places and races to pray to God, and he also makes an opportunity for pointing out how much modesty and subjection women ought to show in the sacred gatherings of the Church.

In the *third* chapter he declares the excellency of the office of bishop and goes on to paint a picture of a true bishop, enumerating the qualities required of him. Next he describes the qualities needed in deacons and in the wives of bishops and deacons. In order that Timothy may be the more diligent and conscientious in observing all these instructions, he reminds him of what is involved in governing the Church, which is the house of God and the pillar of truth. Finally he mentions the chief of the principles of all revealed doctrine and as it were their hinge (*totius coelestis doctrinae praecipuum caput et quasi cardinem*), God's Son manifest in the flesh. In comparison with this all other things, to which he saw that men eaten up with ambition were so entirely devoted, were to be reckoned of no importance whatever.

In what follows at the beginning of the *fourth* chapter he severely condemns false teaching about marriage and the prohibition of certain foods and absurd fables that are at variance with his teaching. Next he adds that the only enemies of himself and godly men who hold to the doctrine of the Gospel, are those who cannot endure that men should place their hope in the living God. At the end of the chapter he once again strengthens Timothy with an exhortation.

In the *fifth* chapter, after recommending modesty and gentleness in administering reproofs, he enters into the subject of widows who at that time were admitted into the service of the Church. He forbids them to accept all widows indiscriminately, but only those who have earned approval by their whole way of life, who have reached the age of sixty and have no domestic ties. From this he passes on to speak of presbyters and how they ought to conduct themselves, both in their manner of life and in the exercise of discipline. This teaching he confirms by a solemn oath and once again forbids Timothy to accept anybody into the presbyterate (*in ordinem presbyterii*) rashly. He exhorts him for his health's sake to drink wine instead of water and at the end of the chapter he tells him to suspend judgment on hidden sins.

In the *sixth* chapter he gives instructions about the duties of servants, and goes on to a strenuous attack upon false teachers who dispute about useless speculations and show themselves more concerned with gain than edification, and he shows that covetousness is a most deadly disease. As before he concludes with a solemn oath to ensure that his instructions to Timothy may not be in vain. Having made passing reference to riches, he once again forbids Timothy to become involved in vain doctrines.

I do not agree with the common Greek inscription at the end of this epistle which holds that it was written from Laodicea. Since Paul in his epistles to the Colossians says that he has never seen the Laodiceans, those who support the view of the inscription have to invent another Laodicea in Asia Minor, of which there is no mention in any ancient writer. Besides, when he went into Macedonia, Paul left Timothy at Ephesus, as his own words declare. He wrote this epistle either on the road or on returning from his journey. Now Laodicea is further from Macedonia than Ephesus and it is not likely that Paul on his return went to Laodicea and passed Ephesus by, especially since there were so many reasons why he should visit it. Thus I am inclined to think that he wrote from some other place. But the matter is not of sufficient importance for me to wish to argue it out with those who think differently. I only point out what is in my opinion the more probable explanation.

CHAPTER ONE

Paul, an apostle of Christ Jesus according to the commandment of God, our Saviour, and Christ Jesus our hope; unto Timothy, my true child in faith: Grace, mercy, peace from God the Father and Christ Jesus our Lord. As I exhorted thee to tarry at Ephesus, when I was going into Macedonia, that thou mightest charge certain men not to teach a different doctrine, neither to give heed to fables and endless genealogies, the which minister questionings rather than a dispensation of God which is in faith; so do I now. (1-4)

1. *Paul an apostle.* If he had been writing to Timothy alone, there would have been no need to set forth his titles and reassert his claims to apostleship, as he does here, for the name alone would certainly have been enough for Timothy. He knew that Paul was Christ's apostle and needed no proof to convince him, for he was perfectly willing and long used to acknowledge it. Thus Paul is here aiming at others who were not so willing to give him a hearing or so ready to accept what he said. It is for their sake that he asserts his apostleship, to keep them from treating what he says as of no importance. And he claims also that his apostleship is by the commandment or appointment of God, since no man can make himself an apostle. But the man whom God has appointed is a true apostle and worthy of honour. But he does not make God the Father the sole source of his apostleship but adds also the name of Christ. For in the government of the Church the Father does nothing except through the Son, so that all His actions are taken together with the Son. He calls God *the Saviour*, a title more usually assigned to the Son. And yet it is a title well befitting the Father Himself, for it was He who gave us His Son, so that it is right to assign the glory of our salvation to Him. For we are saved only because the Father so loved us that it was His will to redeem us and save us through the Son. Christ he calls *our hope*, a title that belongs specially to Him, in that it is when we look to Christ that we begin to have good hope, for in Him alone all our salvation is found.

2. *Unto Timothy, my true child.* This commendation gives great praise to Timothy, for Paul acknowledges him to be his true son, not unworthy of his father, and he wants others to acknowledge him as such; in fact, he commends Timothy as if he were another Paul. But how is this consistent with Christ's commandment 'Call no man your father on the earth' (Matt. 23.9) and with the apostle's own statement

'Though ye have many fathers according to the flesh, yet there is but one who is the Father of spirits' (1 Cor. 4.15, Heb. 12.9). My answer is that Paul's claim to be called a father in no way abrogates or diminishes the honour due to God. It is often said that if one thing is subordinated to another, there will be no conflict between them. That is true of Paul's claim to the name of father in relation to God. God is the only Father of all in faith, for He regenerates all believers by His Word and the power of His Spirit and He alone confers faith. Those whom He is graciously pleased to employ as His ministers in doing this He allows to share in His honour and yet without surrendering any of His own. Thus, God was the spiritual Father of Timothy and, strictly speaking, He alone; but Paul, who was God's minister in begetting Timothy, claims a subordinate right to the title for himself.

Grace, mercy and peace. By introducing the word mercy here in second place he departs from his usual custom, perhaps out of his special love for Timothy. But he is not observing the exact order of the words for he has put first 'grace' which ought to come second, since it is from mercy that grace flows. It is because He is merciful that God first receives us into His grace, and then goes on loving us. But it is quite usual to mention the cause after the effect by way of explanation. I have spoken of *grace* and *peace* elsewhere.

3. *As I exhorted thee.* Either the statement is left incomplete or the particle ἵνα is redundant, but in either case the meaning is obvious. First he reminds Timothy why he has been asked to stay in Ephesus. It was with great reluctance and only under the compulsion of necessity that Paul parted with such a well beloved and faithful assistant as Timothy, that, as his deputy, he might carry out duties so demanding that there was no other competent to fulfil them. This must have had a great influence upon Timothy and not only have kept him from wasting his time, but helped him to rise to an excellence of behaviour beyond the ordinary. Here also he encourages Timothy to oppose false teachers who were adulterating pure doctrine. In this injunction to Timothy to do his duty at Ephesus, we should note the apostle's godly concern. For though he had his hands full in gathering many new churches, he did not leave the earlier ones without a pastor. And certainly, as the writer says, 'To keep safe what you have gained needs as much ability as to gain it.' The word *charge* implies authority, for it was Paul's purpose to equip Timothy with authority to restrain others.

To teach a different doctrine. The Greek word ἑτεροδιδασκαλεῖν which Paul uses here is a compound and may be translated to mean either 'To teach in a different way, i.e. by a new method' or 'to teach a new doctrine'. Erasmus' rendering, 'to follow a new doctrine', does not satisfy me since it could apply as well to hearers and not just teachers.

If we read 'to teach in a different way', the meaning will be wider, for Paul will be forbidding Timothy to allow the introduction of new methods of teaching, which are inconsistent with the true and genuine method he had given them. Thus in the second epistle he does not merely advise Timothy to keep to the substance of his teaching but uses the word ὑποτύπωσιν which means a living likeness of his teaching. As God's truth is one, so there is but one way of teaching it, that is free from false pretence and savours more of the majesty of the Spirit than of the outward show of human eloquence. If anyone departs from this, he deforms and vitiates the doctrine itself, and thus 'to teach differently', must refer to the form.

If we read 'to teach something different' it will refer to the substance of the teaching itself. It is worth noting that by new doctrine is meant not only teaching that is in open conflict with the pure doctrine of the Gospel, but anything that either corrupts the pure Gospel by new and adventitious inventions or obscures it by unholy speculations. All the imaginings of men are so many corruptions of the Gospel, and those who put the Scriptures to frivolous uses in an ungodly way, so as to make Christianity a clever display, darken the Gospel. All teaching of that kind is opposed to God's Word and to that purity of doctrine in which Paul enjoins the Ephesians to remain.

4. *Neither to give heed to fables.* In my view he means by fables not so much contrived falsehoods but rather trifles and foolish tales that have nothing solid in them. A thing which is not false may yet be fabulous. In this sense Suetonius spoke of 'fabulous history' and Livy uses the verb 'to fable' to mean foolish and irrational chatter. There is no doubt that μῦθος, the word Paul uses here, means in Greek φλυαρία, trifles, and when he mentions one kind of fables as an example of what he means, no doubt remains. For he includes disputes about genealogies among the fables, not because everything that can be said about them is fictitious, but because it is foolish and unprofitable. The passage may therefore be taken as meaning that they are not to heed fables of the same character and description as genealogies. This is in fact just what Suetonius means by fabulous history and it is something that, even among men of letters, has rightly been always held in derision by people of good sense. For it was impossible not to regard as ridiculous curiosity that which neglected useful knowledge in order to spend a lifetime examining the family tree of Achilles or Ajax and exhausted its ingenuity in reckoning up the sons of Priam. If this is intolerable in the learning of the schoolroom, where there is a place for pleasant diversions, how much more so in our knowledge of God. He speaks of *endless genealogies* because empty curiosity knows no limits but continually sinks from labyrinth to labyrinth.

Which minister questionings. He judges doctrine by its fruit. All that is unedifying is to be rejected, even if there is nothing else wrong with it, and all that serves only to stir up controversy should be doubly condemned. Such are all these subtle questions on which self-seeking men exercise their abilities. We should remember that this is the rule by which all doctrines are to be tried; those which tend to edification may be approved but those that prove themselves material for fruitless controversies are to be rejected as unworthy of the Church of God. If this test had been applied over several centuries, then, although religion might have been corrupted by many errors, at least there would have been less of that devilish art of disputation which goes by the name of scholastic theology. For that theology is nothing but contentions and idle speculations with nothing of value in them. The more learned in it a man is, the more wretched he should be thought to be. I am aware of the plausible arguments with which it is defended, but they will never succeed in proving false what Paul says here by way of condemnation of all this sort of thing.

A dispensation of God (aedificationem Dei). Subtleties of this kind build up men in pride and vanity but not in God. He speaks of edification that is godly, either because God approves of it, or because it is obedient to God, and in this he includes love of one another, the fear of God and repentance, for all these are the fruits of faith, which always leads to godliness. Knowing that the whole worship of God is founded on faith alone, he thought it sufficient to mention the faith on which all the rest depend.

> *But the end of the charge is love out of a pure heart and a good conscience and faith unfeigned: from which things some having swerved have turned aside unto vain talking; desiring to be teachers of the law, though they understand neither what they say, nor whereof they confidently affirm. But we know that the law is good, if a man use it lawfully, as knowing this that the law is not made for a righteous man, but for the lawless and unruly, for the ungodly and sinners, for the unholy and profane, for murderers of fathers and murderers of mothers, for manslayers, for fornicators, for abusers of themselves with men, for men-stealers, for liars, for false swearers, and if there be any other thing contrary to the sound doctrine; according to the gospel of the glory of the blessed God, which was committed to my trust.* (5-11)

These unprincipled men with whom Timothy had to deal were boasting that they had the support of the law, and here Paul is anticipating their objection and showing that the law not only gives them no support but, on the contrary, is in complete agreement with the Gospel he has himself taught them. Their defence was not unlike that brought forward against us today by those who love the subtle questions of the schools. They tell us that our only intention is to destroy sacred theology, as if they alone nourished it in their bosoms. In the same way Paul's opponents spoke of the law in a way calculated to stir up ill feeling against him. And what is his reply? To make an end of their illusions, he anticipates their attack and shows plainly that his doctrine agrees perfectly with the law and it is they, who try to use the law for some other purpose, who utterly abuse it. So today, when we define true theology, it is quite clear that it is we who desire to restore something which has been wretchedly mangled and disfigured by those triflers who are puffed up by the empty title of theologian, but offer nothing but emasculated and meaningless trifles. By *charge* here he means the law, using the part to stand for the whole.

5. *Love out of a pure heart.* If the object and end of the law is that we should be instructed in the love that is born of faith and a good conscience, the contrary follows, that those who turn its teaching into curious questions are bad interpreters of the law. In this passage it is of no great importance whether love is taken to refer to both tables of the law or only to the second. We are commanded to love God with all our heart and our neighbours as ourselves, although when love is mentioned in Scripture, it is more usually confined to love of neighbours. In this passage, I would not hesitate to understand love as being for both God and neighbour, if Paul had mentioned love by itself. But since he adds faith and a good conscience, the interpretation I am going to give will suit very well the context in which he is writing. The sum of the law is that we should worship God with true faith and a pure conscience and also that we should love each other, and all who turn aside from this corrupt God's law by twisting it to serve some other purpose alien to it.

But here a doubt may arise, in that Paul seems to place love before faith. My answer is that those who think so are being childish, for the fact that love is mentioned first does not mean that it has the first grade of honour, since Paul also makes it clear that it springs from faith. Now the cause has an undoubted priority over the effect and if the whole context is taken into account what Paul is saying amounts to this, 'The law has been given to us in order to instruct us in faith, which is the mother of a good conscience and of love.' Thus we have to begin with faith and not with love.

There is little distinction between *a pure heart* and *a good conscience*. Both are the fruits of faith. Acts 15.9 speaks of a pure heart when it says that 'God purifieth hearts by faith' and Peter says that a good conscience is founded on Christ's resurrection (I Peter 3.21). From this passage it is clear that there can be no genuine love without fear of God and integrity of conscience. We should notice the terms Paul uses to describe each of these virtues. There is nothing commoner or easier than to boast of faith and a good conscience, but there are very few who prove by their deeds that they are free from every trace of hypocrisy. Especially we should notice how he speaks of faith as *unfeigned*, meaning that any profession of faith which does not prove itself by a good conscience and manifest itself in love is insincere. Since man's salvation depends on faith, and the complete worship of God consists of faith and a good conscience and love, we need not wonder that Paul says that these are the sum of the law.

6. *From which things some have turned aside.* He continues to speak in terms of a goal or an object to be attained, for the verb ἀστοχεῖν, the participle of which is used here, means to turn aside or err from a mark. This is a noteworthy passage in which he condemns as *vain talking* all teaching which does not aim at this single end, and declares at the same time that the talents and ideas of all who aim at some other object vanish away. It is indeed possible that many will admire useless trifles, and yet Paul's statement stands that everything which does not build up men in godliness is ματαιολογίαν. We should therefore take the greatest possible care not to seek in God's holy Word for anything but solid edification, lest otherwise He punish us severely for abusing it.

7. *Desiring to be teachers of the law.* Here he is not reproving directly those who openly attack the teaching of the law, but rather those who boast that they are teachers of it. He says that such people have no understanding, since they weary their brains uselessly over curious questions. At the same time he rebukes their arrogance by adding *whereof they confidently affirm.* For none are more forward than the teachers of such trifles in making rash pronouncements on things of which they know nothing. We see today with what pride and haughtiness the schools of the Sorbonne prate about their decisions. But on what subjects? Those that are completely hidden from the minds of men and that have never been clarified by any word of Scripture or any revelation. They have greater confidence in their imagined purgatory than in the resurrection of the dead, and as for their fabrications about the intercession of the saints, unless we accept them as Gospel, they cry out that the whole of religion is being overthrown. And what is there to say about the huge labyrinths they have constructed about the hierarchies of heaven, the doctrine of relations and other such fictions? The list is endless. The apostle declares that in all these the old proverb is fulfilled, 'Ignorance is bold', just as he says in Col. 2.18 'Puffed up by their fleshly mind they intrude into the things that they know not.'

8. *But we know that the law is good.* He once again anticipates a false

accusation being brought against him, for whenever he resisted these men's empty show, they would try to shield themselves as follows, 'What, do you wish to have the law buried and blotted out from the remembrance of men?' In order to repel this false charge, Paul agrees that the law is good, but adds that it needs to be used lawfully. Here he is using terms related to each other to help his argument for the word lawful (*legitimus*) is derived from the word law (*lex*). But he takes the matter further by showing that the law is in full agreement with his teaching and thus turns the same accusation back on them.

9. *The law is not made for a righteous man.* It was not the apostle's intention to set out all the functions that the law fulfils; his argument is rather directed *ad homines*, to those with whom he was dealing. It often happens that those who wish to be thought to have the greatest zeal for the law prove by their whole way of life that they are its greatest despisers. The clearest example of this in our own day is those who maintain justification by works and defend free will. They are for ever talking about perfect holiness of life, merits and satisfaction, but their whole life cries out that they are outrageously wicked and ungodly, that they provoke God's wrath in every possible way and boldly scorn His judgment. They extol in lofty terms the free choice of good and evil, but their deeds prove them slaves of Satan, for they are held by him in chains of the strictest captivity. In order to restrain the haughty insolence of such enemies, Paul warns them that the law is, as it were, God's sword to slay them, while he and those like him have no reason to fear or hate the law, since the law is no enemy to just men, that is, to those who are godly and who freely worship God.

I am well aware that certain learned men draw a more subtle meaning from these words, as if Paul were writing a theological treatise on the nature of the law. They argue that the law has nothing to do with the sons of God who have been regenerated by His Spirit, since it was not for righteous men that it was given. But the context of the passage makes me adopt a simpler explanation. Paul is taking for granted the common saying that good laws spring from bad morals and holds that God's law was given to restrain the licentiousness of the ungodly, for those who are good of their own accord do not need the law to control them. The question arises whether there is any mortal man who does not belong to the category of those who are restrained by the law. My answer is that Paul here calls righteous not those who are absolutely perfect—since no such men will be found—but those who aim at what is good as the chief desire of their hearts, so that their godly desire is like a voluntary law that needs no external pressure or restraint. His intention was to repress the impudence of adversaries who armed themselves with a profession of the law against godly men whose whole life was exhibiting the genuine rule of the law, since those very adversaries stood themselves in greatest need of the law and yet did not greatly care for it. This is made clearer in the next clause. If anyone does not agree that in Paul's list of wicked deeds there is implied an indirect accusation of his adversaries, it can still be taken as a simple rebuttal of the false charge made against him. If their zeal for the law was not feigned but sincere, they should have been using it to arm themselves against all these offences and crimes rather than making it a pretext for their own self-seeking and silly talk.

For the lawless and unruly. Some interpreters render 'lawless' instead of 'unrighteous' for the Greek has ἀνόμους, lawless, which has much the same meaning as the second word, unruly. By *sinners* he means profligates who live a base and immoral life.

For the unholy and profane. These words might fittingly have been rendered 'profane and impure', but I have no wish to be fastidious in matters of small importance.

9-10. *For men-stealers.* The Latin word *plagium* was used by classical writers to mean the abduction or enticement of another man's slave or the false sale of a free man. Those who wish fuller information should consult the legal authorities on the Flavian law.

Here Paul mentions different kinds of sin and touches briefly on all kinds of transgressions. The root of them all is obstinacy and rebellion, as described by his first phrase, 'lawless and unruly'. 'The unholy and profane' seems to indicate transgressors of the first and second tables of the law respectively. To those he adds the impure who lead a base and dissolute life and, since there are three main ways in which men can injure their neighbours, violence, dishonesty and lust, he reproves these three in order, as we can easily see. First he speaks of violence in the form of murder and patricide, next he mentions shameful lusts and thirdly he goes on to robberies and other crimes.

If there be any other thing. Here he declares that his Gospel, far from contradicting the law, is its best confirmation. He says that in his preaching he supports the sentence which the Lord has pronounced in His law against all those things that are contrary to sound doctrine. From this it follows that those who draw back from the Gospel do not hold to the heart of the law but merely pursue its shadow.

Sound doctrine is contrasted with frivolous questions which, as he says elsewhere, bring foolish teachers to grief and, from the results they produce, are rightly judged to be harmful.

The gospel of the glory. By using the word 'glory' of the Gospel in which God displays His glory, he sharply rebukes those who were threatening to bring it into disrepute. He expressly adds that it has been *committed to his trust* that all may understand that the Gospel which he preaches is the only Gospel of God, so that all the fables he has been rebuking are at variance with both law and Gospel.

> *I thank him that enabled me, even Christ Jesus our Lord, for that he counted me faithful, appointing me to his service; though I was before a blasphemer and a persecutor, and injurious: howbeit I obtained mercy, because I did it ignorantly in unbelief;* (12-13)

12. *I thank him.* The dignity of the apostleship Paul has claimed for himself is great and, remembering his former way of life, he could not think himself in any way worthy of so great an honour. Therefore, to avoid being condemned for presumption, he has to refer to himself, and he at once confesses his unworthiness and yet affirms that he is an apostle by the grace of God. In fact he goes further and turns the circumstances that seemed to detract from his authority to his advantage, by showing that because of them the grace of God shines in him the more brightly. By giving thanks to Christ he removes the objection that might have been brought against him and leaves no occasion to raise the question whether or not he is unworthy of so honourable an office, for though in himself he has no excellence of any kind, it is enough that he has been chosen by Christ. There are many who use the same form of words to make a show of humility, but who have none of Paul's sincerity, for his intention was not only to boast glowingly in the Lord, but really to give up all boasting of his own. But what is it he is giving thanks for? It is because he has been given a place in the ministry, and from this he infers that he has been *counted faithful.* Christ does not receive men indiscriminately, but rather makes choice of those who are suitable and so we acknowledge as worthy all those on whom He bestows honour. It is not inconsistent with this that Judas, according to the prophecy of Ps. 109.8, was raised up for a short time that he might quickly fall. It was otherwise with Paul who obtained his office for a different purpose and under different conditions, for Christ declared (Acts 9.15) that he was to be 'a chosen vessel unto Him'.

By saying this Paul seems to be making the faithfulness that he showed beforehand the cause of his being called. If that were so, then his thanksgiving would be feigned and absurd, for he would owe his apostleship not so much to God as to his own merit. I do not agree that his meaning was that he was chosen for apostolic work because his faith was foreknown to God, for Christ could foresee in him nothing good except what the Father had conferred upon him. Thus it always remains true that 'it is not you who have chosen me, but I who have chosen you' (John 15.16). But Paul's meaning is quite different: for him the fact that Christ had made him an apostle provided proof of his faithfulness. He says that those Christ makes apostles must be held to be pronounced faithful by Christ's decree. This verdict does not rest upon foreknowledge but is rather a testimony directed to men, as though he had said, 'I give thanks to Christ who called me into this ministry, and thus openly declared that He approved of my faithfulness.'

He now turns to another of Christ's blessings and says that He has strengthened or *enabled* him. By this he does not only mean that at the beginning he was formed by God's hand in such a way as to be well qualified for his office, but he includes also the continued bestowal of grace. To have been declared faithful once would not have been enough if Christ had not strengthened him by His continual help. Thus he says that it is by Christ's grace that he was first raised to the apostleship and that he now continues in it.

13. *A blasphemer and a persecutor*—a blasphemer against God and a persecutor and oppressor of the Church. We see how candidly he confesses to what could have been turned into a reproach against him, how he does not try to extenuate his sins and how, by thus willingly acknowledging his own unworthiness, he magnifies the greatness of God's grace. Not satisfied with calling himself a persecutor, he expresses his fury and rage more fully by recalling how *injurious* he was to the Church.

Because I did it ignorantly in unbelief. 'I obtained pardon for my unbelief', he says, 'because it stemmed from ignorance' for persecution and violence were the fruits of unbelief. But he seems to suggest that there can be pardon only when there is an extenuating plea of ignorance, and that leads us to ask whether, if a man sins knowingly, God will never forgive him. My answer is that we should note the word unbelief for that restricts Paul's statement to the first tables of the law. Transgressions of the second table, even though deliberate, are forgiven; but he who knowingly and willingly violates the first table sins against the Holy Spirit, for he is in direct opposition to God. Such a man does not err through weakness, but by rising up in rebellion against God gives a sure sign of his reprobation. From this there can be gathered a definition of the sin against the Holy Spirit. First, it is direct rebellion against God in transgression of the first table; second, it is a malicious rejection of the truth, for when God's truth is rejected without deliberate malice, then the Holy Spirit is not resisted. Lastly, in this statement unbelief is the general term and malicious intent, which is the opposite of ignorance, is the qualifying condition. Thus those who hold that the sin against the Holy Ghost consists in transgression of the second table are wrong, and those who make so great a crime out of blind and thoughtless violence are also mistaken. The sin against the Holy Spirit is committed only when mortal men wage wilful war against God so that the light of the Spirit offered to them is extinguished. This is horrifying wickedness and monstrous temerity. There is no doubt that here there is an implied threat intended to frighten all who had once been enlightened, so that they would not attack the truth they had acknowledged, for to fall would be fatal. If it was because of his ignorance that God forgave Paul his blasphemies, those who blaspheme knowingly and deliberately should expect no pardon.

But it may be thought that what Paul says is beside the point, since there can be no unbelief that does not involve ignorance, for unbelief is always blind. My answer is that among unbelievers there are some so blind that they are led astray by their false conceptions of what is right, whereas with others, though they too are blind, malice is the decisive factor. Although Paul also had an evil disposition in some measure, with him it was thoughtless zeal that carried him away, so that he thought he was doing what was right. Thus he was not a deliberate enemy of Christ, but only so by error and ignorance. On the other hand, the Pharisees who accused Christ falsely and with a bad conscience were not altogether free of error and ignorance, but their motives were self-seeking and a perverse disinclination for sound teaching, in short, a furious rebelliousness against God, so that out of malice and quite deliberately they set themselves against Christ.

And the grace of our Lord abounded exceedingly with faith and love which is in Christ Jesus. Faithful is the saying, and worthy of all acceptation, that Christ Jesus came into the world to save sinners; of whom I am chief: howbeit for this cause I obtained mercy, that in me as chief might Jesus Christ shew forth all his long-suffering, for an ensample of them which should hereafter believe on him unto eternal life. Now unto the King eternal, incorruptible, invisible, the only God, be honour and glory for ever and ever. Amen. (14-17)

14. *And the grace abounded.* Once again he magnifies God's grace towards him, not only to remove ill will and testify to his own gratitude, but also to defend himself against the slanders of his malicious enemies whose whole aim was to denigrate his apostleship. For when he says that grace 'abounded', and indeed 'abounded exceedingly', he implies that the memory of the past was effaced and so completely swallowed up that it did not disadvantage him in any way that the other men to whom grace was shown had been good men.

With faith and love. It is possible to take both words as referring to God, so that the meaning would be that God has shown Himself faithful and given an example of His love in Christ by bestowing this grace upon Paul. But I prefer a simpler interpretation whereby faith and love are signs or testimonies of the grace he has just mentioned, so that he might not be thought to boast needlessly or without good reason. Faith is the opposite of the unbelief he had formerly lived in, and love in Christ is the opposite of the cruelty he had once shown towards believers; as if he had said that God had so completely changed him that now he was a different and a new man. Thus by its signs and effects he extols the excellence of the grace bestowed on him, which must obliterate all remembrance of his former life.

15. *Faithful is the saying.* Not content with having defended his ministry from infamy and unjust accusations, he now turns to his own advantage what his enemies might have brought as a reproach against him. He shows that it was profitable for the Church that he had been the kind of man he was before he was called to the apostleship, for by giving in Paul a pledge of His grace, Christ has called all sinners to a sure expectation of obtaining forgiveness. When he was changed from a fierce and savage beast into a shepherd and pastor, Christ gave a remarkable example of His grace, which might bring all men to a sure confidence that access to salvation is closed to no man, however serious and outrageous his sins.

First he makes the general statement that *Christ came to save sinners*, introducing it with a preface, as is his custom when dealing with matters of supreme importance. In the doctrine of our religion, this is indeed the chief point, that we who are lost in ourselves should come to Christ to gain our salvation from Him. For although God the Father a thousand times offers us salvation in Christ, and Christ Himself proclaims to us His own saving work, yet we do not cease to be afraid or, at any rate, to wonder within ourselves whether it be so. Thus, whenever any doubt about the forgiveness of sins comes into our mind, we should learn to drive it out, using as our shield the fact that it is truth sure and certain and should be received without any controversy or demur.

To save sinners. The word 'sinners' is emphatic. Even those who recognise that Christ's work is to save admit that it is more difficult to believe that this salvation belongs to sinners. Our mind is always prone to dwell on our own worthiness and, as soon as our unworthiness becomes apparent, our confidence fails. Thus the more a man feels the burden of his sins, he ought with greater courage to betake himself to Christ, relying on what is here taught, that He came to bring salvation not to the righteous but to sinners. We should notice how in this verse Paul bases what he has said about himself on this general truth about the work of Christ, so that what he has just said about himself might not by its novelty seem to be absurd.

I TIMOTHY 1 [v. 15-17

Of whom I am the chief. We are not to think that the apostle was speaking here out of any false modesty. He wished to make a confession that was not only humble but also true and that came from the bottom of his heart. But someone may ask why he considers himself the chief (*primum*) of sinners, if he fell only out of ignorance of sound doctrine and in other ways lived a life that was blameless in the eyes of men. But in these words we are warned of how grave and serious a sin unbelief is in God's eyes, especially when accompanied by obstinacy and raging cruelty. It is easy for men to pass off all that Paul has confessed about himself as the result of heedless zeal; but God values the obedience of faith too highly to allow Him to reckon unbelief, obstinately persisted in, a little sin. We should note carefully the teaching of this passage, that a man who is not only harmless in the world's eyes but of outstandingly excellent virtues and with a life worthy of all praise, can yet be reckoned one of the greatest sinners because of his opposition to the doctrine of the Gospel and the obstinacy of his unbelief. From this we can easily understand how much all the pomp of hypocrites is worth in God's eyes, as long as they obstinately resist Christ.

16. *That in me as chief might Jesus Christ show.* When he says 'chief' (*primo*) here he is again saying that he is the chief of sinners, so that the word means the same as chiefly or above all. His meaning is that right from the very beginning God showed this example of His grace that could be seen clearly and widely, so that no one should doubt that if only he comes to Christ in faith, he may obtain pardon. All our distrust is removed when we see in Paul a visible type of that grace which we seek.

17. *Now to the King eternal.* His enthusiasm breaks out into this exclamation, since he could find no words to express his gratitude. These sudden outbursts of Paul's come mainly when the vastness of the subject overpowers him and makes him break off what he is saying. For what could be more wonderful than Paul's conversion? At the same time he admonishes us all by his example, that we should never think of the grace shown in God's calling without being lost in wondering admiration. This sublime praise of God's grace swallows up all the memory of his former life. How great a deep is the glory of God! The attributes here ascribed to God, though they are His always, nevertheless suit the present context well. He calls him the King eternal, or King of the ages who never changes. He calls Him *invisible* because He dwells in light inaccessible, as he puts it later on. He calls him *only wise* because He makes foolish and condemns as vanity all the wisdom of men. All this agrees with his conclusion in Rom. 11.33, 'O the depth of the riches etc. How incomprehensible

are His designs! How unsearchable His ways!' He wants us to behold the immense and incomprehensible wisdom of God with such reverence that, if His works overwhelm our minds, still wonder may hold us fast. There is some doubt whether by 'only' he means to claim all glory for God alone or to call him alone wise, or the only God. The second meaning seems best to me, for it suits his present subject well to point out how the understanding of men must bend to the secret counsel of God. Not that I deny that he is saying that God alone is worthy of all glory, for, while He scatters on His creatures the sparks of His glory, still it remains His in its wholeness and entirety. But either interpretation makes it quite clear that there is no glory but in God alone.

> *This charge I commit unto thee, my child Timothy, according to the prophecies which went before on thee, that by them thou mayest war the good warfare; holding faith and a good conscience; which some having thrust from them made shipwreck concerning the faith: of whom is Hymenaeus and Alexander; whom I delivered unto Satan that they might be taught not to blaspheme.* (18-20)

18. *This charge I commit unto thee.* All that he has said about his own person and position has really been a digression from the main subject. Since it was his intention to invest Timothy with authority (*instruere auctoritate*), he had first to establish his own supreme authority and refute the views of those who were opposed to it. Having now proved that his apostleship should not be held in any less repute because he had once fought against Christ's kingdom and so disposed of this objection, he turns again to the main subject of his exhortation. The *charge* here is the one he mentioned at the beginning.

By calling Timothy his *son* he not only shows his own affection for him but recommends him to others. To encourage him still more he reminds him what kind of testimony he had received from the Spirit of God. For it was a great source of assurance to him to know that his ministry had divine approval, that he had been called by the revelation of God before he was chosen by the votes of men. 'If it is shameful not to live up to human expectations, how much more to annul, in so far as it is possible for you to do so, the judgment of God.'

But we must first understand what *prophecies* he is referring to here. Some think that Paul was instructed by special revelation to confer office on Timothy (*ut Timotheo munus iniungeret*). I agree with this but add that others had shared in these revelations, for that must be Paul's reason for using the plural. Thus we may gather from these words that several prophecies were given concerning Timothy in order to recommend him to the Church. Since he was so young, his age might have brought scorn upon him, and Paul might have been open to criticism for promoting young men prematurely to the office of presbyter. Moreover, God had appointed him for great and difficult work; for he was not an ordinary minister but one second only to the apostles, who often represented Paul in his absence. Thus he needed a special testimony to prove that his office was not conferred on him rashly by men, but that he was chosen for it by God Himself. To be honoured by the praises of prophets was not at that time an ordinary occurrence but, since Timothy's was a special case, God did not wish to have him admitted to office by men without being first approved by His own voice; it was not God's will that he should enter into the exercise of his ministry until he had been called by the revelations of prophets. The same thing happened to Paul and Barnabas when they were ordained as teachers to the Gentiles. This was a new and extraordinary departure and this was the only way in which it could escape a charge of innovating rashness.

Some will now object, 'If God had pronounced by His prophets what kind of minister Timothy was to be, what purpose was served by admonishing him to show himself to be such? Could he make false prophecies uttered by God?' My answer is that the outcome could only be what God had promised, but in the meantime it was Timothy's duty not to give himself up to laziness and inactivity, but to show himself by his obedience a lively and willing instrument of God's providence. Thus Paul, wishing to spur him on to greater zeal, has good reason to recall the prophecies by which God had sponsored him and given pledges to the Church concerning him; in this way he was reminded of why he had been called.

Thus he adds *that thou mayest war the good warfare*, meaning by this that Timothy, relying on this approval that God has given him, ought to fight more bravely. For what can and should put heart into us more than to know that we are doing what we are doing by God's express appointment. This is our armour and our defence and, with its aid, we shall never fail. By the word 'warfare' he implies that there must be a contest, and this applies universally to all believers, but especially to Christian teachers, who may be said to be the leaders and standard-bearers in Christ's army. It is as if he had said, 'Even if you cannot exercise your ministry without a struggle, remember that you are equipped with the oracles of God and so have a sure hope of victory, and let that renew your courage.' A *good* warfare is one that is glorious and serviceable and in which we fight under the auspices of God Himself.

19. *Holding faith and a good conscience.* I take the word 'faith' in a general sense to mean sound teaching. This is how he uses the word

later when he speaks of 'the mystery of faith' (3.9). These are indeed the chief things required of a teacher, that he should hold to the pure truth of the Gospel, and that he should minister it with a good conscience and honest zeal. Where these two things are present, the rest will follow of themselves.

Which some having thrust from them. He shows how necessary it is that a good conscience should accompany faith, for the penalty of a bad conscience is to turn aside from the right way. Those who do not serve God with a pure and honest mind, but give way to evil dispositions, though they may start with a sound understanding, in the end lose it completely. This passage should be carefully noted. We know that the treasure of sound doctrine is invaluable and there is nothing more to be dreaded than to lose it. But here Paul tells us that the only way to keep it is to hold fast to it with a good conscience. Why is it that so many reject the Gospel and rush to join ungodly sects or become involved in monstrous errors? It is because God punishes hypocrisy with this kind of blindness, just as, on the other hand, a sincere fear of God gives us strength to persevere. From this we may learn two lessons. Firstly, teachers and ministers of the Gospel, and through them the whole Church, are warned how much they ought to abhor a false and feigned profession of true doctrine, since it is punished so severely. Secondly, this passage removes the difficulty which disturbs so many when they see some who once professed Christ and His Gospel not only falling back into their former superstitions, but much worse, becoming fascinated by more monstrous errors. By such examples God is openly vindicating the honour of the Gospel and openly declaring that He cannot endure that it should be profaned. This is something that can be learnt from the experience of every age; all the errors that have arisen in the Christian Church from the beginning have sprung from this source; sometimes covetousness and sometimes self-seeking have extinguished genuine fear of God. Thus a bad conscience is the mother of all heresies, and today we see a vast number of men, who had never embraced the faith with honesty and sincerity, stampeded like brute beasts into the madness of the Epicureans, so that their hypocrisy is exposed. And not only so, but contempt for God is spreading everywhere and the licentious and depraved lives of almost all classes of men show that there is but the smallest portion of integrity left in the world, so that there is good reason to fear that the light which has been kindled may soon be put out, and God may leave a pure understanding of the Gospel to very few.

The metaphor of a shipwreck is very apt, for it suggests that if we wish to reach port with our faith intact, we should make a good conscience the pilot of our course, or otherwise there is danger of shipwreck; faith may be sunk by a bad conscience as by a whirlpool in a stormy sea.

20. *Hymenaeus and Alexander.* Paul will mention the first of these two men again in the second epistle and there the kind of shipwreck that has befallen him is made clear, for he said that the resurrection of the dead was past. It is possible that Alexander also was crazed by this absurd error. When we see how even one of Paul's companions could perish in such a dreadful fall, we shall not be surprised if today Satan with his various enchantments is able to delude men. He mentions both these men to Timothy as people he would know well. I have no doubt that this is the same Alexander who is mentioned by Luke in Acts 19.33 as the man who tried without success to quell the commotion at Ephesus. He belonged to Ephesus and, as we have already said, this letter was written chiefly for the benefit of the Ephesians. We now learn what end Alexander came to and we should learn from it to keep possession of our faith by a good conscience that we may hold it safe to the end.

Whom I delivered unto Satan. As we pointed out in connexion with I Cor. 5.5 some take this to mean the infliction of some extraordinary chastisement and they connect it with the δύναμις, powers, that Paul mentions in 12.28 of the same epistle. As the apostles were endowed with the gift of healing as a testimony of God's grace and favour towards the godly, so they were armed against the ungodly and rebellious with power either to deliver them to the devil to be tormented or to inflict some other punishment upon them. Peter has given us an instance of the exercise of this power in his dealings with Ananias and Sapphira (Acts 5.1) and Paul in his dealing with the magician Bar-Jesus (Acts 13.6).

But I prefer to interpret this phrase to mean excommunication, for the view that the incestuous man in Corinth received any other punishment is not supported by any probable argument. And if Paul handed him over to Satan by excommunicating him, why should not the same expression have the same meaning here? Since it is in the Church that Christ holds the seat of His kingdom, outside the Church there is nothing but the dominion of Satan. Thus he who is cut off from the Church must necessarily fall for a time under Satan's tyranny, till he is reconciled to the Church and returns to Christ. I make one qualification, that because of the enormity of the offence, Paul may have pronounced perpetual excommunication against these two men, but I would not venture to make any definite assertion about that.

But what is the meaning of the last clause, *that they might be taught not to blaspheme*? The man who has been cast out from the Church acquires greater freedom of action for himself, since he is no longer under the restraint of ordinary discipline and can break out into greater insolence. My answer is that to whatever heights their wickedness may soar, the door will remain shut against them, so that their example may not harm the flock. For the greatest harm evil men do is when they worm their way in on the pretext of holding the same faith. Thus the power of doing harm is taken from them when they are marked out for public disgrace, so that no simple man may remain ignorant of the fact that they are irreligious and detestable, so that everyone should shun their society. It sometimes happens that, smitten by this mark of disgrace inflicted upon them, they themselves turn from their evil ways. Thus, although excommunication sometimes makes men worse, it is not always without effect in taming their fierceness.

CHAPTER TWO

I exhort therefore, first of all, that supplications, prayers, intercessions, thanksgivings, be made for all men; for kings and all that are in high place; that we may lead a tranquil and quiet life in all godliness and gravity. This is good and acceptable in the sight of God our Saviour; who willeth that all men should be saved, and come to the knowledge of the truth. (1-4)

1. *I exhort therefore.* The religious exercises he enjoins here maintain and strengthen in us the sincere worship and fear of God and cherish the good conscience of which he has already spoken. The word *therefore* is thus quite appropriate, since these exhortations follow naturally from his charge to Timothy given above.

First he deals with public prayer and orders that it should be made not only for believers but for all mankind. Some might argue, 'Why should we care for the welfare of unbelievers, since they have no connexion with us? Is it not enough if we who are brethren pray for one another and commend His whole Church to God? Strangers are nothing to us.' Paul sets himself against this perverse outlook and tells the Ephesians to include all men in their prayers and not to restrict them to the body of the Church.

I admit that I do not completely understand the difference between three of the four kinds of prayer Paul mentions. Augustine's view which twists Paul's words to fit the ceremonial usage of his own time is childish. The simpler view is better, that *supplications* are requests to be delivered from evil, *prayers* requests for something profitable to ourselves, and *intercessions* our lamenting before God injuries we have endured. But I myself do not go in for subtle distinctions of that kind, or rather I draw a different kind of distinction. $Προσευχή$ is the general Greek term for every kind of prayer and $δεήσεις$ denotes these forms of prayer in which some specific request is made. Thus these two words are related as genus and species. $Ἐντεύξεις$ is Paul's usual word for the prayers we offer for each other, and the word used in Latin is *intercessiones*, intercessions. Yet Plato in the second Alcibiades dialogue uses the word differently to mean a definite petition made by a person for himself, and in the inscription of that book as well as in many passages in it he shows plainly that $προσευχή$ is, as I have said, a general term.

But not to dwell disproportionately long on a matter of no great importance, Paul is in my view simply saying that whenever public prayers are offered, petitions and supplications should be made for all men, even those who at present have no connexion with us. The heaping up of terms is not superfluous; Paul seems to me to use three words with the same meaning on purpose, the better to commend and the more urgently to press upon us earnestness and constancy in our praying. We know how sluggish we are apt to be in this religious duty, so that it is not surprising that the Holy Spirit through the mouth of Paul should use many ways to arouse us and stir us up.

About the meaning of *thanksgivings* there is no obscurity, for he not only bids us pray to God for the salvation of unbelievers, but also to give thanks for their prosperity and well being. The wonderful goodness which God shows us every day in making 'His sun to rise on the good and the bad' is worthy of all our praise, and our love of our neighbour ought to extend to those who are unworthy of it.

2. *For kings.* He mentions kings and other magistrates expressly because the Christians might have had cause to hate them more than all others. All the magistrates of that time were sworn enemies of Christ, so that they might have concluded that they ought not to pray for people who were devoting all their power and wealth to opposing Christ's reign, whereas for Christians the extension of that reign is of all things most desirable. The apostle meets this difficulty and expressly commands that prayers should be offered for them. Human depravity is no reason for not cherishing something instituted by God. Therefore, since God has appointed magistrates and princes for the preservation of mankind, however much they may fall short of the divine appointment, we must not on that account cease to cherish what belongs to God and to desire its preservation. That is why believers, in whatever country they live, should not only obey the laws and the behests of the magistrates, but should also in their prayers commend their welfare to God. Jeremiah said to the Israelites, 'pray for the peace of Babylon, for in their peace, ye shall have peace' (29.7). This is the universal teaching of Scripture, that we should desire the continuance and peaceful state of the powers of this world which have been ordained by God.

That we may lead a tranquil and quiet life. He adds a further inducement, by showing how this will profit us ourselves and by enumerating the advantages which a well ordered government provides. The first is a quiet life, for magistrates are armed with the sword to keep the peace. Unless they restrained the boldness of wicked men, the whole world would be full of robberies and murders. Thus the right way of keeping peace is that every man should be given what is his own and the violence of the powerful should be curbed. The second advantage is the preservation of *godliness*, that is, when magistrates undertake to promote religion, to maintain the worship of God and to require reverence for sacred things. The third advantage is the care of public *gravity*: for the benefit of magistrates is that they prevent men from abandoning themselves to bestial impurity or shameful wantonness, and preserve modesty and moderation. If these three things were taken away, what kind of life would be left to men? If therefore we have any concern for public tranquillity or godliness or decency, let us remember our duty to care for those through whom such important benefits are obtained.

From this we conclude that fanatics who wish magistrates to be abolished are devoid of all humanity and promote only cruel barbarism. What a difference between Paul who says that for the sake of preserving justice and decency and of promoting religion we ought to pray for kings, and those men who say that not only kingly power but all government is opposed to religion. What Paul says has the Holy Spirit as its Author, so that the view of the fanatics must be of the devil.

If the question is raised whether we ought to pray for kings from whom we do not receive these advantages, my answer is that we ought to pray that, under the guidance of the Holy Spirit, they may begin to grant us these blessings they have up till now failed to provide. Thus we should not only pray for those who are already worthy, but we should ask God to make wicked rulers good. We must always hold to the principle that magistrates are appointed by God for the protection of religion and of the public peace and decency, just as the earth has been ordained to produce food. Thus just as when we pray for our daily bread we ask God to make the earth fertile by His blessing, so we ought to consider magistrates as the ordinary means which He has ordained in His providence for bestowing those other blessings. To this it must be added, that, if we are deprived of those blessings which Paul makes it the duty of magistrates to give us, it is our own fault. It is the wrath of God that makes magistrates unprofitable to us, just as it makes the earth barren. Thus we should pray for deliverance from punishments brought upon us by our own sins.

On the other hand, magistrates and all who hold office in the magistracy are here reminded of their duty. It is not enough for them to restrain injustice by giving to each his own, and maintaining peace if they are not also zealous to promote religion and regulate morals by wholesome discipline. The exhortation of David that they should 'kiss the Son' (Ps. 2.12), and Isaiah's word that they sould be nursing fathers to the Church are very relevant. Thus they have no cause to congratulate themselves if they neglect to give their assistance in maintaining the worship of God.

3. *For this is good and acceptable.* Having shown that the command he has given is expedient, he now appeals to the stronger argument that it is pleasing to God; for when we know that this is God's will, that should be the best of all reasons for doing it. By 'good' he means what is right and lawful, and, since the will of God is the rule by which we must regulate all our duties, he proves that it is right because it is acceptable to God.

This passage deserves close attention, for from it we may derive the general principle that the only genuine rule for right and proper action is to look to God's good pleasure and to undertake only what He approves. And this is also the rule of godly prayer, that we should make God our Leader, so that all our prayers are regulated by His will and command. If this rule had held sway, the prayers of the Papists today would not be so full of corruptions. For how can they prove that they have God's authority to rely on the intercessions of dead saints, or themselves to make intercessions for the dead? In short, in all their way of praying, what can they point to that is pleasing to God?

There now follows as confirmation of this last argument the fact that *God willeth that all men should be saved.* For what could be more reasonable than that all our prayers should be conformed to this decree of God? In conclusion, he is showing that God has at heart the salvation of all men, for He calls all men to acknowledge His truth. This is an argument from an observed effect back to its cause. For if 'the Gospel is the power of God unto salvation for every one that believeth' (Rom. 1.16) it is certain that all those to whom the Gospel is preached are invited to a hope of eternal life. In short, since calling is proof of secret election, so God admits into possession of salvation those to whom He gives a share in His Gospel, for the Gospel reveals to us God's righteousness which guarantees an entrance into life.

From this the childish illusion of those who think that this passage contradicts predestination becomes apparent. They argue, 'If God wills all men without distinction to be saved, then it is not true that by His eternal counsel some have been predestinated to salvation and others to perdition.' There might be some grounds for holding this if in this passage Paul were concerned with individuals, although even then there would still be a good answer. For although it is true that we must not try to decide what is God's will by prying into His secret counsel, when He has made it plain to us by external signs, yet that does not mean that God has not determined secretly with Himself what He wishes to do with every single man.

But I pass from that point which is not relevant to the present context, for the apostle's meaning here is simply that no nation of the earth and no rank of society is excluded from salvation, since God wills to offer the Gospel to all without exception. Since the preaching of the Gospel brings life, he rightly concludes that God regards all men as being equally worthy to share in salvation. But he is speaking of classes and not of individuals and his only concern is to include princes and foreign nations in this number. God's will that they also should share the teaching of the Gospel is clear from the passages already quoted and from others like them. Not for nothing was it said 'Now, kings, understand' (Ps. 2.10) and again in the same psalm, 'I will give thee the Gentiles for an inheritance and the ends of the earth for a possession' (Ps. 2.8). Paul's intention was to show that we should consider not what kind of men princes are, but rather what God willed them to be. There is a duty of love to care a great deal for the salvation of all those to whom God extends His call and to testify to this by godly prayers.

It is in the same connexion that He calls God *our Saviour*, for from what source do we obtain salvation but from God's undeserved kindness? The same God, who has already brought us into His salvation, may at some time extend the same grace to them also. He who has already drawn us to Himself may add them also to us. He takes it for granted that God will do so among all ranks and all nations, for so it has been foretold by the prophets.

For there is one God, one mediator also between God and men, himself man, Christ Jesus, who gave himself a ransom for all; the testimony to be borne in its own times; whereunto I was appointed a preacher and an apostle (I speak the truth in Christ, I lie not), a teacher of the Gentiles in faith and truth. (5-7)

5. *There is one God.* At first sight this argument looks rather weak, that, because God is one, He wishes all men to be saved, but there is in fact a way of passing from God to men that makes the argument valid. Chrysostom and many others take his meaning to be that there are not many gods, as idolaters imagine. But I think Paul's intention was different, that there is here an implied comparison between the one God and the one world with its various nations, and this comparison makes him look at them both in relation to each other. As he says in Rom. 3.29 'Is he the God of the Jews only? Is he not the God of the Gentiles also? Yes it is one God who justifies the circumcision by faith and the uncircumcision through faith.' Thus, whatever diversity there was among men at that time, in that many ranks and nations were strangers to faith, Paul reminds believers of the oneness of God, that they may know that there is a bond between them and all men, because there is one God over all, that they may know that those who are

under the power of the same God are not excluded forever from hope of salvation.

His meaning is the same in what he goes on to say about the *one mediator*. For as there is one God, the Creator and Father of all, so, he declares, there is one Mediator, through whom access to God is opened to us, and this Mediator is not given only to one nation, or to a few men of a particular class, but to all, for the benefit of the sacrifice, by which He has expiated for our sins, applies to all. Since at that time a great part of the world had alienated itself from God, he explicitly mentions the Mediator through whom those who were far off now draw nigh. The universal term 'all' must always be referred to classes of men but never to individuals. It is as if he had said, 'Not only Jews, but also Greeks, not only people of humble rank but also princes have been redeemed by the death of Christ.' Since therefore He intends the benefit of His death to be common to all, those who hold a view that would exclude any from the hope of salvation do Him an injury.

The man Jesus. In calling Him man, he does not deny that He is also God, but since his purpose here is to draw attention to the bond that unites us with God, he mentions Christ's human nature rather than His divine, and this should be carefully noted. For the reason why from the beginning men have departed further and further from God by inventing for themselves one mediator after another was that they were possessed by the erroneous notion that God was at a great distance from them, and so they did not know where to turn for help. Paul remedies this evil by showing that God is present with us, for He has come down to us so that we do not have to seek Him above the clouds. Here he is saying the same thing as in Hebrews 4.15, 'We have not an high priest who cannot sympathize with our infirmities, for in all points He was tempted.' And if it were deeply impressed on the hearts of all men that the Son of God holds out to us the hand of a brother and is joined to us by sharing our nature, who would not choose to walk in this straight highway rather than wander in uncertain and rough byways? Thus, whenever we pray to God, if the thought of His sublime and inaccessible majesty fills our minds with dread, let us also remember the man Christ who gently invites us and takes us by the hand, so that the Father whom we had dreaded and feared becomes favourable and friendly to us. This is the only key able to reopen to us the door of the kingdom of heaven, so that we may appear with confidence in God's presence.

Thus, in every century Satan has tried to overturn this confidence in order to lead men astray. I say nothing of how before Christ's advent he distracted men in many different ways into devising other means for reaching God. But even from the very beginning of the

Christian Church, at the time when Christ had only just appeared with such a sure pledge of God's favour, and when His delightfully gentle word, 'Come unto me all ye that labour' etc. (Matt. 11.28), was still resounding throughout the earth, there were some wily deceivers who were bringing forward in His stead angel mediators, as can easily be gathered from Col. 2.1-18. And this corruption that Satan was at that time contriving in secret, he later carried to such lengths that scarcely one man in a thousand acknowledged Christ as Mediator even in name—and if the name was unrecognized, still more was the reality unknown.

And now, when God has raised up sound and godly teachers whose care it has been to restore and recall to men's minds what should have been one of the best known and chief articles of our faith, the Roman sophists are busy contriving all manner of ways in which to obscure something so plain. First, the name is so hateful to them that if anyone so much as mentions Christ's mediatorship without bringing in the saints, he at once falls under suspicion of heresy. And since they do not dare totally to reject what Paul says here, they evade it by the foolish comment that He is called 'one mediator' and not 'the only mediator', as though Paul had mentioned God as one of a great multitude of gods, for the two statements that there is one God and one Mediator are closely connected. Thus those who make Christ one among many must apply the same interpretation to God as well. Would they rise to such a high pitch of impudence if they were not impelled by blind rage to attack Christ's glory?

There are others who think themselves more acute and make Christ the only Mediator of redemption, calling the saints mediators of intercession. The context of this passage shows the foolishness of such an interpretation, since Paul is here explicitly dealing with prayer. The Holy Spirit bids us pray for all, because our one Mediator bids all to come to Him, since by His death He has reconciled all to the Father. And those men still claim to be counted Christians, who with such outrageous sacrilege strip Christ of His honour!

It will be objected that there seems to be a contradiction here, for in this very passage Paul bids us intercede for others, whereas in Rom. 8.34 he says that the work of intercession belongs to Christ alone. My answer is that the intercessions by which the saints help one another do not conflict with the fact that they all have one sole Intercessor, for no man is heard either on his own behalf or on another's unless he trusts to Christ's advocacy. Our intercessions for one another, far from detracting from Christ's unique intercession, actually depend upon it completely. It may perhaps be thought that it is therefore easy to reach agreement between us and the Papists, if they will subordinate all that they attribute to the saints to the unique intercession of Christ. That is not so, for their reason for transferring the office of intercession to the saints is that they imagine that otherwise we would have no advocate. It is commonly held among them that we need an intercessor, because, of ourselves, we are unworthy to appear before God's face. In so saying they deprive Christ of the honour that belongs to Him. It is shocking blasphemy to assign to the saints a worthiness that could procure us God's favour; all the prophets, apostles and martyrs and the very angels themselves are so far from being able to do so that they need the same advocate as ourselves.

It is a mere figment of their imaginations that the dead intercede for the living and to base our prayers upon it is to withdraw completely our trust from God and our prayers to Him. Paul lays down as the right way to call upon God faith grounded on God's Word (Rom. 10.17). We are therefore right to reject the imaginary things that men's minds fabricate apart from God's Word.

Not to dwell on the matter further than the exposition of the passage requires, we may sum it up by saying that those who have learnt of the work of Christ will be satisfied with Him alone, whereas those who know neither God nor Christ fashion mediators at their own pleasure. From this I conclude that the teaching of the Papists, which obscures and almost buries Christ's mediatorship, and introduces fictitious mediators without any scriptural authority, is full of godless distrust and wicked temerity.

6. *Who gave himself.* The mention of redemption in this passage is not superfluous, for there is a necessary connexion between Christ's sacrificial death and His continual intercession (Rom. 8.34). They are the two parts of His priestly office, for when Christ is called Priest (Heb. 7.17) the meaning is that once by His death He made expiation for our sins to reconcile us to God, and now, having entered the heavenly sanctuary, He appears in the presence of the Father for our sakes that we may be heard in His name. This is a further exposure of the sacrilegious wickedness of the Papists in making dead saints the associates of Christ in this office, and thus transferring to them the glory of His priesthood. Read the last part of Hebrews 4 and the beginning of Hebrews 5 and you will find the confirmation of my assertion that the intercession by which God's favour is won for us is founded on sacrifice—a thing made clear also by the whole system of the ancient priesthood. It therefore follows that no part of His work of intercession can be transferred from Christ to others without stripping Him of His title as Priest.

Moreover by calling Christ $\dot{\alpha}\nu\tau\dot{\iota}\lambda\upsilon\tau\rho o\nu$ he rules out all other satisfactions. I am not unaware of the subtle argument brought forward by the Papists whereby they falsely claim that the price of our redemption, paid by Christ in His death, is applied to us in baptism, so that original sin is destroyed, but thereafter we are reconciled to God by satisfactions. In this way they restrict to a short period of time and to one class of people a benefit that is universal and perpetual. But a full treatment of this subject may be found in the *Institute*.

7. *The testimony to be borne*—that is, that this grace might be published at the appointed time. The phrase 'to all' might raise the question why God chose one special people, if it was His purpose to reveal Himself as a reconciled Father to all without distinction, and if there was one redemption in Christ in which all were to share? He answers such a question by showing that the right time for such a revelation of grace was appointed by the counsel of God. In winter we are not surprised that the trees are bare, the fields covered with snow and the meadows frozen hard, or that by the gentle warmth of spring what seemed to be dead revives again, because God has ordained the succession of the seasons. Why then should we not allow His providence to have the same authority in other things? Are we to accuse God of being fickle and changeable just because at the appointed time He introduces what He always had fixed and settled in His own counsel? Although in the eyes of the world the revelation of Christ as Redeemer of Jews and Gentiles without distinction was sudden and unexpected, we are not to think that God decreed it suddenly, but are rather to subordinate all our thoughts to the ordering of His wonderful providence. When we do that we shall see that all that He sends us comes at the right time. The admonition to do this occurs frequently in Paul's writings, especially in connexion with the calling of the Gentiles, which was at that time astounding and confusing many by its unheard of novelty. Those who are not content with the answer that God has ordered the succession of times by His own secret wisdom, will one day discover that He was using the time they think wasted in getting hell ready for the over curious!

7. *Whereunto I was appointed*. So as not to seem to make rash assertions on a subject he did not fully understand, as many people do, he declares that God has appointed him to bring the Gentiles, who were formerly strangers to God's kingdom, into participation in the Gospel. His apostleship to the Gentiles was a sure proof that God was calling them, and that is why he takes such trouble to defend and assert it, since many had great difficulty in accepting it. He adds an oath or protestation to mark this as a matter of great importance—saying that he is *in faith and truth* a teacher of the Gentiles. These two words denote a good conscience, but must also rest upon a certain assurance of God's will. His meaning is that he preaches the Gospel to the Gentiles not

only with a sincere heart, but also with an upright and fearless conscience, because all that he does, he does at God's command.

I desire therefore that the men pray in every place, lifting up holy hands, without wrath and disputing. In like manner, that women adorn themselves in modest apparel, with shamefastness and sobriety; not with braided hair, and gold or pearls or costly raiment; but (which becometh women professing godliness) through good works. (8-10)

8. *I desire therefore.* This follows from what he has just been saying. As we saw in Gal. 4.5, in order to call upon God rightly, we have to be endowed with the Spirit of adoption. Thus, having expounded Christ's grace for all men, and mentioned his own appointment as apostle to the Gentiles, that they equally with the Jews might enjoy the same blessings of redemption, he invites all men to pray in the same way. For faith leads to calling upon God. In Rom. 15.9 also he proves the calling of the Gentiles by citing these scriptural texts: 'Let the Gentiles rejoice with his people' (Ps. 67.5). 'All ye Gentiles, praise the Lord' (Ps. 117.1). 'I will confess thee among the Gentiles' (Ps. 18.49. II Sam. 22.50). The argument holds good both ways, from faith to prayer and from prayer to faith, from cause to effect and from effect to cause. This should be noted, because it reminds us that God reveals Himself to us by His Word in order that we may call upon Him, and this is the chief exercise of faith.

In every place. The phrase means the same as in I Cor. 1.2, that there should now be no difference between Gentile and Jew, between Greek and barbarian, because God is the common Father of them all and the prophecy of Malachi is fulfilled in Christ, that pure sacrifices should be offered to God not only in Judaea but in all the earth.

Lifting up holy hands. It is as if he had said, 'Provided that they have a good conscience there is nothing to prevent all nations everywhere from calling upon God.' But he has used the outward sign for the inward reality, for our hands indicate a pure heart. In the same way Isaiah in attacking the cruelty of the Jews rebukes them for lifting up to God hands stained with blood (Isa. 1.15). Moreover this custom has been practised in worship in all ages, for it is natural for us to look upwards when we seek God, and the habit has been so strong that even idolaters, though they fashion gods in images of wood and stone, yet keep this custom and lift up their hands to heaven; we should learn therefore that this practice is in keeping with true godliness, provided that the truth it represents also accompanies it; firstly, knowing that God is to be sought in heaven, we should form no earthly or carnal conception of Him, also that we should lay aside fleshly affections so that nothing may prevent our hearts from rising above this world.

Idolaters and hypocrites, when they lift up their hands in prayer, are like asses, for, though by the external sign they make a profession that their minds are raised upwards, the idolaters are in fact fixed on wood or stone, as though God were shut up in them, and the hypocrites are ravelled up in their vain concerns or wicked thoughts and so fall back to earth. Thus by showing a sign that is untrue to what is in their hearts, they bear testimony against themselves.

Without wrath. Some take this to mean an outburst of indignation as when conscience fights with itself and, as it were, makes complaints to God, a thing that usually happens when adversity presses hard upon us. Then we are displeased that God does not immediately come to our aid and we are distressed with impatience. Faith is shaken by many different attacks upon it for, since God's help is not apparent, we are seized by doubts about whether He cares for us and wishes us to be saved and so on. Those who take this view think that the word *disputing* here means the confusion of a doubting mind. So, according to them the meaning would be that we should pray with a quietened conscience and an unshaken confidence. Others, such as Chrysostom, think that Paul means here that our minds should be at peace both with God and with men and thus be free from every upsetting influence, for nothing hinders sincere prayer more than quarrels and strife. That is why Christ also commands (Matt. 5.24) that if anyone has a quarrel with his brother he should be reconciled before he brings his gift to the altar.

In my view both these interpretations are quite true, but when I consider the context of the present passage, I have no doubt that Paul had in mind the quarrels that broke out because the Jews were angry at having the Gentiles made equal with them, and were therefore raising a controversy about the reality of their calling, were in fact rejecting them and excluding them from a share in grace. Thus Paul desires that dissensions of this kind should be stilled and that all the sons of God, of whatever race and land, should pray together with one heart. However, there is no reason why we should not derive general teaching from this special situation.

9. *In like manner women.* As he commanded men to lift up pure hands, so now he gives instructions as to how women should prepare themselves for praying aright. There seems to be an implied contrast between the virtues he here commends and the external sanctificatory rites of Judaism; for he holds that no place is profane and that in all places both men and women may have access to God, provided their vices do not hinder them.

Further, since opportunity offered, it was his intention to correct a fault to which women are almost always prone. It is possible that at

Ephesus, a city of great wealth and with a famous market, this fault was specially prevalent. The fault is excessive concern and eagerness about dress. Paul's wish is that their dressing should be regulated by modesty and moderation, for luxury and extravagance come from a desire to make a display, which can spring only from vanity or wantonness. So we have to look for a rule of moderation, for, since dress is a matter of no great importance (like other external things), it is difficult to lay down a certain permissible limit. Magistrates may indeed make laws by which extravagant desires may be to a certain extent restrained, but godly teachers, whose task is to regulate men's consciences, should always have in mind the purpose of such legal control. This at least is beyond all controversy, that any fashion in clothes which is inconsistent with modesty and moderation should be disapproved. But we must always start from the inner disposition, since there will be no chastity when wantonness reigns within, and when self-seeking reigns within, there will be no modesty in outer dress. But since hypocrites usually conceal their wicked intentions with whatever pretexts they can find, we are compelled to bring their secret dispositions to light. It would be very wrong to deny the suitability of modesty to honourable and chaste women as their special and perpetual mark of distinction, or that in the same way all men should keep within the limits of moderation; whatever is opposed to that cannot be defended. Paul attacks by name certain kinds of immoderation, such as curled hair, jewels and golden rings—not that jewels of gold are completely forbidden but, whenever there is a shining display of them, they tend to bring with them all the evils I have mentioned and which spring from self-concern or unchastity.

10. *Which becometh women.* Without doubt the dress of an honourable and godly woman ought to be different from that of a harlot. These are marks of distinction that Paul here lays down, since if godliness should prove itself by good works, it should also be visible in chaste and becoming clothes.

Let a woman learn in quietness with all subjection. But I permit not a woman to teach, nor to have authority over a man, but to be in quietness. For Adam was formed first, then Eve; and Adam was not beguiled, but the woman being beguiled hath fallen into transgression; but she shall be saved through the child-bearing, if they continue in faith and love and sanctification with sobriety. (11-15)

11. *Let a woman learn in quietness.* Having dealt with dress, he now goes on to speak of the modesty women ought to show in the sacred assembly. And first he bids them learn quietly: for quietness means silence, that they should not presume to speak in public, a point he

at once goes on to make more explicit by forbidding them to teach.

12. *But I permit not a woman to teach.* Paul is not taking from women their duty to instruct their family, but is only excluding them from the office of teaching (*a munere docendi*), which God has committed exclusively to men. This is a subject we have already gone into in relation to I Corinthians. If anyone challenges this ruling by citing the case of Deborah and other women of whom we are told that God at one time appointed them to govern the people, the obvious answer is that God's extraordinary acts do not annul the ordinary rules by which He wishes us to be bound. Thus, if at some time women held the office of prophets and teachers and were led to do so by God's Spirit, He who is above all law might do this, but being an extraordinary case, it does not conflict with the constant and accustomed rule. He goes on to mention something closely connected with the office of teaching—*nor to have authority over a man.* The reason that women are prevented from teaching is that it is not compatible with their status, which is to be subject to men, whereas to teach implies superior authority and status. This argument may not seem to be very strong, since, it may be said, even prophets and teachers are subject to kings and other magistrates. My answer is that there is no absurdity in a man's commanding and obeying at the same time in different relationships. But this does not apply to women who by nature, (that is, by the ordinary law of God) are born to obey, for all wise men have always rejected γυναικοκρατίαν, the government of women, as an unnatural monstrosity. Thus for a woman to usurp the right to teach would be a sort of mingling of earth and heaven. Thus he bids them be silent and abide within the limits of their sex.

13. *For Adam was formed first.* He gives two reasons why women should be subject to men, that God imposed this as a law from the beginning, and also that He inflicted it upon women by way of punishment. Thus he teaches that, even if the human race had remained in its original integrity, the true order of nature prescribed by God lays it down that woman should be subject to man. And it is no objection to this to argue that Adam by his fall from his first dignity deprived himself of his authority, for in the ruins that result from sin there remain some remnants of the divine blessing, for it would not be right that woman should improve her position by her sin. Still, Paul's argument, that woman is subject because she was created second, does not seem to be very strong, for John the Baptist went before Christ in time and yet was far inferior to Him. But Paul, although he does not explain all the circumstances related by Moses in Genesis, nevertheless intended that his readers should take them into account. The teaching of Moses is that woman was created later to be a kind of appendage to

the man on the express condition that she should be ready to obey him. Thus, since God did not create two 'heads' of equal standing, but added to the man a lesser helpmeet, the apostle is right to remind us of the order of their creating in which God's eternal and inviolable appointment is clearly displayed.

14. *And Adam was not beguiled.* He is referring to the punishment inflicted upon the woman, 'Because thou hast obeyed the voice of the serpent, thou shalt be under the authority of thy husband and thy desire shall be to him' (Gen. 3.16). Since the counsel she had given had been fatal, it was fitting that she should learn to depend upon the power and will of another. Since she had seduced the man from God's commandment, it was fitting that she should be deprived of all her freedom and placed under the yoke. Moreover the apostle does not base his argument simply or merely on the cause of the transgression, but on the sentence pronounced upon it by God. Nevertheless, there may seem to be a contradiction involved in saying both that the subjection of woman was the punishment for her transgression, and also that it was imposed upon her from the creation, for it would seem to follow that she was doomed to servitude before she sinned. My answer is that there is no reason why obedience should not have been her natural condition from the beginning, while servitude was a later consequence resulting from her sin, so that the subjection became less voluntary than it had been before.

Further, some have found in this passage justification for the view that Adam did not fall by his own error, but was only overcome by the allurements of his wife. They think that only the woman was deceived by the craftiness of the serpent into believing that she and her husband would be as gods. But Adam was not so persuaded, and tasted the fruit only to satisfy his wife's whim. But it is easy to refute this view, for, if Adam had not believed Satan's lie, God would not have reproached him by saying 'Behold, Adam is like one of us' (Gen. 3.22). There are other arguments which I do not mention, since the error is not worth a long refutation and has no probability to support it. By these words Paul does not mean that Adam was not involved in the same diabolical deception but only that the cause and source of his transgression came from Eve.

15. *But she shall be saved.* The weakness of her sex makes woman more timorous and timid, and what Paul has just said is calculated to perturb and confuse even the most manly minds, and so he modifies what he has just said by adding a consolation: for the Spirit of God does not accuse or reproach us in order to cover us with shame and then triumph over us, but when we are cast down, He soon raises us up again. It could, as I have said, reduce women to despair to hear the

whole ruin of the human race imputed to them. For what will the judgment of God upon them be?—a question that becomes all the more unnerving from their constant awareness of their subjection as a present token of God's wrath. Thus Paul, seeking to comfort them and make their condition bearable to them, reminds them that, although they suffer temporal punishment, the hope of salvation remains to them. The good effect of this consolation is twofold and should be noted. First, with the hope of salvation offered them, they are kept from despair and fear at the remembrance of their guilt, and second they become accustomed to bearing with equanimity and calmness the necessity of being in servitude to their husbands, so that they willingly submit to them, when they are reminded that obedience of this kind is both good for them and pleasing to God. If this passage is twisted to support justification by works, as the Papists do, the solution is easy. Since the apostle is not dealing here with the cause of salvation, his words cannot and should not be used to infer the merit of works. All he is concerned to do is to point out the way by which God leads us to the salvation He has by His grace appointed for us.

Through bearing children. Acute critics may find it ridiculous that an apostle of Christ should not only exhort women to give their attention to bearing children, but should urge this upon them as a godly and holy work, and even go so far as to say that by it they may obtain salvation. In fact we see with what reproaches hypocrites who wanted to appear holier than other men have defamed the marriage bed. But it is easy to reply to these ungodly sneers. For, in the first place, the apostle is dealing here not merely with bearing children, but with the many severe troubles that have to be borne both in bearing children and in bringing them up. Secondly, whatever hypocrites or wise men of the world may think, God is better pleased with a woman who considers the condition God has assigned to her as a calling and submits to it, not refusing to bear the distaste of food, the illness, the difficulty, or rather the fearful anguish associated with childbirth or anything else that is her duty—God is better pleased with her than if she were to make some great display of heroic virtues and refuse to accept the vocation given her by God. To this we should add that no apter or more effective comfort could be provided than to show that in the punishment itself are the means (so to speak) of securing salvation.

If she continue in faith. The Vulgate translates 'in bearing children, if *they* continue in faith' and this clause was usually taken to refer to the children. But Paul uses only one Greek word for 'bearing children' —τεκνογονία. Thus the faith must apply to the woman. The fact that the noun is singular and the verb plural need give no difficulty, for, when an indefinite noun refers to a whole class, it has the same force as a collective noun, so that the change of number in the verb is easily admissible. Further, to avoid suggesting that all female virtue is embraced by the duties of marriage, he immediately after adds a list of greater virtues in which godly women ought to excel and which should mark them off from the irreligious. Even child-bearing is an act of obedience pleasing to God only when it proceeds from *faith* and *love*. To these he adds *sanctification*, which describes all that purity of life which befits Christian women. Last follows *sobriety*, which he mentioned a little earlier when dealing with dress, but which is now extended in meaning to cover other parts of life.

CHAPTER THREE

Faithful is the saying, If a man seeketh the office of a bishop, he desireth a good work. The bishop therefore must be without reproach, the husband of one wife, temperate, soberminded, orderly, given to hospitality, apt to teach; no brawler, no striker, but gentle, not contentious, no lover of money; one that ruleth well his own house, having his children in subjection with all gravity (but if a man knoweth not how to rule his own house, how shall he take care of the church of God?), not a novice, lest being puffed up he fall into the condemnation of the devil. Moreover he must have good testimony from them that are without, lest he fall into reproach and the snare of the devil. (1-7)

1. *Faithful is the saying.* Chrysostom thinks that this phrase belongs to the previous section but I do not agree. Paul usually uses this expression as a preface to a statement of some importance and the previous subject had no need of such strong expression. What he is going to say now is much more weighty, so let us take the phrase as a preface intended to indicate the importance of what follows, for Paul is now beginning a new discussion about the appointing of pastors and how the government of the Church should be ordered.

If a man seeketh the office of a bishop. Having just forbidden the teaching office to women, he now takes the opportunity to speak of that office itself. His reason is first to make it clear that he had good reasons for excluding women from the exercise of such a demanding duty, second, to avoid the appearance of excluding only women and of being ready to admit all men indiscriminately, and thirdly because it was right that he should warn Timothy and others how much care they should take in choosing bishops. Thus the connexion with the previous passage is, in my view, as if Paul had said that, so far from women being fit to obtain that office, not even men should be admitted to it without discrimination.

Thus he affirms that this is no common work, such as any man might dare to undertake. When he describes it by the word καλόν I have no doubt that he is alluding to the ancient proverb often quoted by Plato δύσκολα τὰ καλά, which means that things that are excellent are also arduous and difficult. Thus he connects difficulty with excellence, or rather argues that the office of bishop does not belong to every man, since it is a valuable thing. I think that Paul's meaning is now sufficiently clear, although none of the commentators, as far as I can see, has understood it. The general meaning is that discrimination must be exercised in admitting bishops, since the office is laborious and difficult, and those who aspire to it should be careful to consider whether they are capable of bearing such a heavy burden. Ignorance is always rash and a discreet knowledge of things makes a man modest. The reason why men who have neither ability nor wisdom often desire so confidently to hold the reins of government is that they rush into it with closed eyes. Thus Quintilian remarked that the ignorant speak boldly while the greatest orators tremble.

To restrain such boldness in seeking episcopal office, Paul first affirms that it is not a dignified sinecure but a *work*, and, next, that it is not any kind of work but an excellent work and therefore hard and full of difficulty, as indeed it is. For it is no light matter to represent God's Son (*sustinere personam Filii Dei*) in such a great task as erecting and extending God's Kingdom, in caring for the salvation of souls whom the Lord Himself has deigned to purchase with His own blood, and in ruling the Church which is God's inheritance. But it is not my present intention to preach a sermon, and Paul will return to this subject in the next chapter. Here the question arises as to whether it is in any circumstances legitimate to seek episcopal office. For it seems absurd that the desires of men should anticipate the call of God. But, although Paul censures rash desire, he does seem to admit of a restrained and modest aspiration for this office. My own view is that if self-seeking ambition is to be condemned in general, it is even more reprehensible in relation to the episcopate. But the apostle is speaking here of a godly desire, which consecrated men have, to apply their knowledge of doctrine to the edification of the Church. For if it were completely wrong to seek the teaching office (*docendi munus*), what point would there be in men spending their youth in the study of the Holy Scriptures in order to prepare themselves for it? And what are the theological schools if not nurseries for pastors? Thus those who have been so instructed not only may, but ought to make a freewill offering of themselves and their work to God, even before they are admitted to office, provided, that is, that they do not thrust themselves forward and do not, at their own desire, set themselves up as bishops, but are merely ready to accept the office, if their labour is required. And if it should turn out that they are not called in the way the order of the Church prescribes (*legitimo ordine*), then let them know that God willed it so, and not take it ill that others have been preferred to them. Those whose desire was only to serve God and who had no thought of themselves will take it in this way and will have enough modesty not to be envious if others are counted more worthy.

If the objection is raised that the government of the Church is so difficult that it ought to terrify men of sound judgment rather than entice them, I reply that godly men desire it, not because they have any confidence in their own industry and virtue, but because they rely on God's help, who is our sufficiency, as Paul says elsewhere (II Cor. 3.5).

We should also note what Paul means here by the office of bishop, especially in view of the fact that the early generations were led away from the true meaning by the custom of their times. Paul includes in the designation 'bishop' all pastors, while they mean one who was elected out of each presbyteral college to preside over his brethren. Let us therefore bear in mind that this word means the same as minister, pastor or presbyter.

2. *The bishop therefore must be without reproach.* The particle 'therefore' confirms the explanation I have given, for from the dignity of the office he infers that it requires no ordinary man, but one endowed with rare gifts. If the right rendering had been 'a good work', as the common translation has it, or 'an honourable work', following Erasmus, the inference to this next statement would not be so suitable.

He wants a bishop to be *without reproach*, or, as he puts it in Tit. 1.7, ἀνέγκλητον. The meaning of both terms is that he ought not to be marked by any disgrace that would detract from his authority. There will certainly not be found a man who is free from every fault, but it is one thing to be burdened with ordinary faults that do not hurt a man's reputation, because the most excellent men share them, but quite another to have a name that is held in infamy and besmirched by some scandalous disgrace. Thus, in order that the bishops may not lack authority, he gives charge that those who are chosen should be of good and honourable reputation, and free of any extraordinary fault. Also, he is not merely directing Timothy as to the sort of men he should choose but he is reminding all who aspire to the office that they should carefully examine their own life.

The husband of one wife. It is childish nonsense to take this as meaning that he is to be the pastor of a single church. Another interpretation more generally accepted is that the bishop must not have been married more than once, and therefore, since his wife is dead, he is not now a married man. But both here and in the first chapter of Titus Paul's words are 'who *is* the husband', not 'who has been the husband' and later in chapter five, when he is expressly dealing with widows, he does use the participle that is here present in the past tense. Besides, if this were his meaning, he would be contradicting what he himself has said in I Cor. 7.35 where he says that he has no wish to lay a snare of this kind for their consciences. The only right exegesis is that of Chrysostom, who takes this to be an express prohibition of polygamy in a bishop at a time when it was almost legal among the Jews. This sprung partly from a perverse imitation of the fathers—for they read that Abraham, Jacob, David and the like were married to more than one wife at the same time, and they thought that it was permissible for them to do the same—and partly it was a corruption learnt from the peoples around them, for the men of the East never observed marriage with proper conscientiousness and fidelity. But however that may be, polygamy was certainly very prevalent among the Jews and it was very much to the point for Paul to insist that a bishop must be free of this stain.

And yet I do not entirely disagree with those who think that here the Holy Spirit was taking advance measures against the devilish superstition about this subject that arose later; as if he had said, 'bishops must not be compelled to celibacy, because marriage is a highly proper state for all believers'. This would not demand that they must be married, but simply commend marriage as in no way inconsistent with the dignity of their office.

But my own interpretation is simpler and better founded, that Paul is forbidding polygamy to bishops, as it is the sign of an unchaste man who does not observe conjugal fidelity. Here the objection could be raised, that what is sinful for all men should not have been condemned in the case of bishops only. The answer is easy. The fact that it is expressly forbidden to bishops does not mean that it is freely allowed to others, for there can be no doubt that in every case Paul would condemn something that was contrary to God's everlasting law. For God's decree is fixed, 'They shall be one flesh' (Gen. 2.24). But he might have to some extent tolerated in others something that in bishops was quite intolerably disgraceful. It is not just that this is a law for the future, that a bishop who has one wife shall not marry a second or third, but Paul is rejecting from the episcopate those who have in the past been guilty of such an offence. Thus, what had been already done and could not be corrected must be endured, but only among the common people. For what remedy was there? That those who had fallen into polygamy under Judaism should divorce their second or third wives? But such a divorce would not have been free of wrongdoing. Thus he left untouched something that was wrong, with this exception, that no one blemished by such a stain should be a bishop.

Soberminded. Erasmus renders the word as 'watchful'. The Greek word νηφάλιος has both meanings and readers may take their choice. Σώφρονα I have chosen to render *temperate* rather than sober, for temperance has a wider reference than sobriety. An *orderly* man is one who behaves decently and honestly.

Given to hospitality. This hospitality is towards strangers and was a more common practice in the Early Church, for it would have been disgraceful for honest men, and especially for well-known ones, to lodge in inns. In our day things are different and yet for many reasons this will always be a highly necessary virtue in a bishop. Besides, in that time of cruel persecution of believers, it was necessary for many to change their dwelling suddenly, and the homes of bishops had to be retreats for exiles. In these times necessity compelled the members of the Church to give each other mutual aid and that involved hospitality. If the bishops had not shown the way to others in this duty of hospitality, most would have followed their example and neglected to do this kindness, so that the poor exiles would have been left in despair.

Apt to teach. Teaching is mentioned with greater emphasis in the letter to Titus, and here skill in teaching is only touched upon. It is not enough for a man to be eminent in profound learning if it is not accompanied by a talent for teaching. There are many who, either because of defective utterance or insufficient mental ability, or because they are not sufficiently in touch with ordinary people, keep their knowledge shut up within themselves. Such people ought, as the saying goes, to sing to themselves and the muses—and go and do something else. Those who are charged with governing the people should be qualified to teach. And what is required here is not merely a voluble tongue, for we see many whose easy fluency contains nothing that can edify. Paul is rather commending wisdom in knowing how to apply God's Word to the profit of His people.

It is worthwhile noticing that the Papists hold that on this point Paul's rules do not apply to them. I shall not go through all the details, but what sort of concern do they show on this one point for what Paul says? To them this gift of teaching is something quite superfluous, which they reject as low and common and yet for Paul it was a bishop's special concern and chief care. Everyone knows how far it is from Paul's intention to assume the title of bishop and to boast of being a dummy that never speaks, but only appears dressed up in theatrical clothes. As if a horned mitre, a richly jewelled ring, a silver cross and such trifles and all the idle display that goes with them made up the spiritual government of the Church, which in fact can no more be separated from teaching than a man can from his soul.

3. *No brawler.* By this word the Greeks described not just drunkenness but any kind of intemperate drinking of wine. Excessive drinking is not only unseemly in a pastor, but usually results in many things still worse, such as quarrels, foolish attitudes, unchastity and others there is no need to mention. But the antithesis that follows shows that Paul goes further than this, for, just as he contrasts with a striker one who does not fight, and with a man who desires filthy lucre one

who is not covetous, so he contrasts with ὁ πάροινυς, the wine drinker, one who is gentle and kind. Chrysostom's interpretation is correct, that men of drunken and violent dispositions should be rejected from episcopal office. But as for his view that a *striker* means someone who wounds with his tongue, that is, who indulges in slander or outrageous accusations, I do not accept it. I am not convinced by his argument that it is of no great importance whether a bishop strikes a man with his hand or not, for I think that here Paul is rebuking in a general way that military fierceness common among soldiers, but quite unbecoming in the servants of Christ. It is common knowledge how ridiculous it is to be more ready to strike a blow or draw the sword than to settle other people's quarrels by the exercise of responsible authority. Thus by 'strikers' he means men who deal in threats and warlike deeds.

Those *desirous of filthy lucre* [cf. A.V.] are all covetous persons. For all avarice has about it this baseness of which the apostle is speaking. 'The man who wants to be rich also wants to be rich soon', says Juvenal. The result is that all greedy men devote themselves to acquiring dishonest and unlawful gains, even if there is no open evidence of it. With this vice he contrasts contempt for money, since that is the only way to correct it. I repeat that the man who will not bear poverty patiently and willingly will inevitably become the victim of mean and sordid covetousness.

With the striker he contrasts the man who is *gentle and not contentious*. Gentle is the opposite of being addicted to wine and is a word used of a man who knows how to bear injuries peacefully and with moderation, who excuses much, who swallows insults, who does not make himself dreaded for his harsh severity, nor rigorously exact all that is due to him. The man who is not contentious is he who avoids disputes and quarrels, for, as he writes, elsewhere (II Tim. 2.24), 'The Lord's servants must not be quarrelsome.'

4. *One that ruleth well his own house*. Paul does not require of a bishop that he should be without experience in the ordinary life of men, but rather that he should be a good and well-tested family man. However much we may admire celibacy and a philosophical life remote from ordinary living, wise and thoughtful men have learnt from their own experience that those who know ordinary life and are well practised in the duties that human relationships impose, are far better trained and fitted to rule in the Church. In the next verse he explains this by saying that a man who does not know how to rule his own family is unsuited to govern in the Church of God. But this is in fact the case with very many bishops, and indeed with almost all who are dragged out from an idle and solitary life as though from dens and caverns; for they are like savages and lack all humanity.

But the man who here wins the apostle's approval is not the one who is clever and cunning in domestic matters, but he who has learnt to rule his family with wholesome discipline. He refers especially to *children* who may be expected to reflect the disposition of their father. Thus it would be a great disgrace for a bishop to have sons who lead a dissolute and scandalous life. He deals with wives later but here, as I have said, he touches on the chief part of family life.

In the first chapter of Titus he shows what he means by the word *gravity*. For having said that a bishop's children should not be unruly and disobedient, he immediately adds that they should not be liable to the reproach of dissoluteness or intemperance. His meaning is, in short, that their behaviour should be regulated in all chastity, modesty and gravity. The argument is from the lesser to the greater, and it is quite clear that a man who is not fit to rule his own family will be quite incapable of governing a whole people. Besides the fact that he obviously lacks the necessary qualities, what authority could a man have among a people when his own family life brings him into contempt?

6. *Not a novice.* At that time many men of outstanding ability and learning were being brought to faith, but Paul forbids that they be made bishops immediately they have professed Christ. And he shows how dangerous that would be; for it is clear that such converts are usually vain and full of ostentation, so that arrogance and ambition can very easily run away with them. What Paul says here we can confirm from our own experience; for novices are not only bold and impetuous, but are puffed up with foolish self-confidence, as though they could fly beyond the clouds. There is good reason to debar them from episcopal office till, with the passing of time, their highflown notions have been subdued.

The condemnation of the devil can be interpreted in three ways. For some take διαβόλος to mean Satan and some to mean slanderers. I am inclined to the former view, for it is rare for the Latin word *iudicium* to mean slander. But, as well as that, it is possible to understand the condemnation of Satan either actively or passively. Chrysostom takes it passively and I agree with him. For it makes an elegant antithesis which heightens the danger to take it to mean, 'lest he who is set over God's Church fall by his pride into the same condemnation as the devil'. Nevertheless I do not reject the active meaning, that he will give the devil occasion to condemn him, but Chrysostom's rendering is nearer the truth.

7. *Good testimony from them that are without.* It seems difficult to think that a godly man should have unbelievers who are most eager to tell lies about us as witnesses to his integrity. The apostle's meaning is that,

as far as external behaviour is concerned, even unbelievers should be forced to acknowledge that he is a good man. For though they slander all God's children without cause, yet they cannot make a rascal out of a man who behaves honourably and innocently among them. This is the sort of acknowledgment of uprightness that Paul is referring to here. The reason is added, *lest he fall into reproach and the judgment of the devil*, which I explain as follows: lest, being open to infamy, he begin to harden his heart and abandon himself more freely to all kinds of wickedness, which is indeed to entangle himself in the devil's snares. For what hope remains for a man who sins without shame?

> *Deacons in like manner must be grave, not double tongued, not given to much wine, not greedy of filthy lucre; holding the mystery of the faith in a pure conscience. And let these also first be proved; then let them serve as deacons, if they be blameless. Women in like manner must be grave, not slanderers, temperate, faithful in all things. Let deacons be husbands of one wife, ruling their children and their own houses well. For they that have served well as deacons gain to themselves a good standing, and great boldness in the faith which is in Christ Jesus.* (8-13)

8. *The deacons in like manner.* The different interpretations need not occasion us any doubt. It is certain that the apostle is referring to men who hold public office in the Church and this refutes the view of those who think that by deacons he means domestic servants. There is no foundation either for the other view that he is referring to presbyters inferior to the bishop, for it is clear from other passages that the title of bishop was held in common by all the presbyters. This is something that is bound to be universally acknowledged and is proved especially clearly by a passage in Titus 1. The conclusion is that by deacons we are to understand those mentioned by Luke in Acts 6.3, officers, that is, who are entrusted with the care of the poor. But anyone who wishes to know more of this office is referred to the *Institute*.

The four chief qualities Paul requires them to possess are well enough known, but it should be carefully noted that he admonishes them not to be *double-tongued*, for this is a fault that is hard to avoid in that kind of work, and yet which more than any other should be completely absent from it.

9. *Holding the mystery of the faith.* It is as if he had said, 'Holding the pure doctrine of our religion from the heart with a sincere fear of God, men who are rightly instructed in the faith, ignorant of nothing that it is needful for a Christian man to know'. He gives to the sum of Christian teaching the dignified title of 'the mystery of the faith', since through the Gospel God reveals to mortal men a wisdom that makes the angels in heaven wonder, so that it is not surprising if it is too great

for human capacity. Let us therefore remember that it should be embraced with the greatest reverence and, since by our own strength we could never aspire to such heights, let us humbly ask God to make it possible for us by the Spirit of revelation. And when we see the ungodly either ridiculing the faith or treating it with indifference, let us acknowledge that it is due to God's grace that things that are hidden from others are in our hearts and before our eyes, as Moses says (Deut. 30.14). Thus he wants deacons to be well instructed in the 'mystery of faith', for, although they do not hold a teaching office, it would be quite absurd for them to hold public office in the Church (*publicam in Ecclesia personam sustinere*) and be quite unskilled in the Christian faith, especially since they will often have to give advice and comfort, if they are not going to neglect their duties. He adds *in a pure conscience* which extends to their whole life, but has especial reference to their knowledge of how to serve God.

10. *And let these also be proved.* He wants those who are chosen deacons to be men of experience whose integrity has been proved, just as with the bishops. From this it is clear that to be *blameless* means to be free from any notorious fault. And this proving process is not for a single hour but consists of a long period of trial. In a word, the appointment of deacons should not be a rash and random choice of any who come to hand, but men who have commended themselves by their past manner of life should be selected, so that as a result of full inquiry they are found to be suitable.

11. *Women in like manner.* He refers here to the wives of both bishops and deacons, for they must help their husbands in their office and they can do that only if their behaviour is better than other people's. Having mentioned women, he once again lays down for deacons what he has already required of bishops, that each should be content with one wife, should set an example of chaste and honourable family life and should keep their children and their whole household in a holy discipline. This passage clearly refutes the views of those who take this section to be dealing with domestic servants.

13. *They that have served well as deacons.* In view of the practice of choosing presbyters from among the deacons that was introduced in the first or second century after the apostles, this passage has been taken to refer to a translation to a higher status, as if the apostle were calling those who had been faithful deacons into office as presbyters. I for my part, without denying that the diaconate may sometimes be the nursery from which presbyters are chosen, yet prefer a simpler explanation of Paul's words, that those who have discharged this ministry well are worthy of no small honour, for it is not a menial task but a highly honourable office. By so speaking he makes it clear now profitable it

is for the Church to have this work done by carefully chosen men, for the holy performance of its duties procures esteem and reverence.

It is, however, more than absurd for the Papists to maintain that in their appointment of deacons they carry out Paul's instructions. For, first, why do they appoint deacons only to carry the chalice in a procession and to impress the ignorant with all sorts of ridiculous exhibitions? And they do not even keep to that, for not a single man has been made deacon for the last five hundred years except with the intention that he should be promoted to the priesthood almost immediately. What shameless hypocrisy it is to boast of advancing to the higher rank men who have ministered well as deacons, when in fact they have never fulfilled one single duty of the diaconate.

And liberty in the faith. He has good reason to add this; for nothing so tends to produce liberty as much as a good conscience and a life free from evil and reproach, just as, on the contrary, a bad conscience inevitably brings timidity with it. For though such men sometimes exult in their freedom, it is not a complete or lasting freedom and has no firm foundation. Thus he describes the kind of freedom he means. *In the faith which in Christ,* he says, meaning a liberty which lets them serve Christ with greater boldness. In the same way those who have failed in their duty have a closed mouth and tied hands and are incapable of doing anything well, so that no trust can be placed in them and no authority given to them.

> *These things write I unto thee, hoping to come unto thee shortly; but if I tarry long, that thou mayest know how men ought to behave themselves in the house of God, which is the church of the living God, the pillar and ground of the truth. And without controversy, great is the mystery of godliness; he who was manifested in the flesh, justified in the spirit, seen of angels, preached among the nations, believed on in the world, received up in glory.* (14-16)

14. *These things write I unto thee.* He gives Timothy hope of his coming, partly to encourage him and partly to repress the stubbornness of those who were becoming too indolent in his absence. But this is not a fictitious promise nor does he frighten them under false pretences, for he fully expected that he would come, and, if he wrote this Epistle when travelling through Phrygia, as Luke relates in Acts 18.23, then the probability is that he did in fact come. But this should prove to us with what anxious care he looked after the churches, since he could not endure even a short delay in remedying a present evil. And yet he at once goes on to add that his letter was written to give instructions to Timothy, if he should happen to be delayed longer than he thought.

15. *How men ought to behave in the house of God.* In these words he is

commending the importance and worth of the pastoral office, for pastors are like stewards to whom God has committed the charge of ruling His house. If a man is responsible for a large household, he must be busy day and night in anxious care that nothing go amiss through his carelessness, inexperience or negligence. If such care is taken for mere men, how much more for God. There are good reasons why God should call the Church His House, for not only has He received us as His sons by the grace of adoption, but He Himself dwells in the midst of us.

It is no ordinary dignity that is ascribed to the Church when it is called *the pillar and ground of the truth*. For what higher terms could he have used to describe it? For there is nothing more venerable and holy than that truth which embraces both God's glory and man's salvation. Were all the praises which its admirers have lavished on heathen philosophy gathered together into one, it could not compare with the worth of this heavenly wisdom which alone has a title to be called light and truth and instruction for living, the way and the kingdom of God. But this truth is preserved in the world only through the Church's ministry. Thus what a weight of responsibility rests upon pastors to whom has been entrusted the charge of such an inestimable treasure. How shameless are the triflings of the Papists who infer from Paul's words that all their absurdities should be considered the oracles of God, because they are the pillars of the truth and so infallible.

But first we have to see why Paul bestows such a high title on the Church. Clearly he wishes, by expounding to pastors the greatness of their office, to remind them with what faithfulness, diligence and reverence they ought to discharge it, and at the same time how dreadful is the retribution that awaits them if by their fault harm comes to the truth which is the image of God's glory, the light of the world and the salvation of men. This thought should certainly bring to pastors an awareness of the awesomeness of their task, not to discourage them but to spur them on to greater vigilance. Thus it is easy to infer in what sense Paul means these words. The Church is the pillar of the truth because by its ministry the truth is preserved and spread. God does not Himself come down from heaven to us, nor does He daily send angelic messengers to publish His truth, but He uses the labours of pastors whom He has ordained for this purpose. Or, to put it in a more homely way: is not the Church the mother of all believers, because she brings them to new birth by the Word of God, educates and nourishes them all their life, strengthens them and finally leads them to complete perfection? The Church is called the pillar of truth for the same reason, for the office of administering doctrine which God has put in her hands is the only means for preserving the truth, that it may not pass from the memory of men. In consequence, this commendation applies to the ministry of the Word, for if it is removed God's truth will fall. Not that it becomes in itself any less certain, if men do not lend it their support, as some Papists idly claim. It is shocking blasphemy to say that God's Word is uncertain until it obtains a certainty borrowed from men. Paul's meaning is the same as in Rom. 10.17; since faith comes from hearing, without preaching there can be no faith. Thus in regard to men the Church maintains the truth, because in her preaching she proclaims it and preserves it pure and complete and transmits it to posterity. If there be no public teaching of the Gospel, and no godly ministers who by their preaching rescue the truth from darkness and oblivion, falsehoods, errors, impostures, superstitions and corruption of every kind will immediately seize control. In short, silence in the Church means the departure and suppression of the truth. There is nothing at all forced in this exposition of this passage.

Now that we have grasped Paul's meaning, let us return to the Papists. Their first fault is to transfer this commendation of the Church to themselves, for they deck themselves out in borrowed plumes. Supposing that the Church were exalted above the third heaven, that would have nothing to do with them. In fact I turn the whole of this passage against them. For if the Church is the pillar of the truth, it follows that the Church is not among them, where the truth not only lies buried, but is shockingly destroyed and trampled under foot. Paul will not acknowledge the Church except where God's truth is exalted and plain. In Popery there is no evidence of anything like that, but only desolation and ruin. Among them the true mark of the Church is not found. The source of their illusion is that they do not think that the essential thing is that God's truths should be maintained by the pure preaching of the Gospel, and its support does not depend on human faculties or feelings, but on something far more exalted, that it should not depart from the simple Word of God.

16. *Great is the mystery of godliness.* Here is a further amplification of his praise. To prevent God's truth from being esteemed at less than its true worth because of human ingratitude, he declares its true value by saying that the secret of godliness is great, because, that is, it does not deal with common themes but with the revelation of God's Son, in whom are hidden all the treasures of wisdom (Col. 2,3). From the greatness of these things pastors ought to understand the importance of their office and devote themselves to it with the greater conscientiousness and reverence.

God manifest. The Vulgate leaves out the word 'God' and relates what follows to the mystery, but this lacks skill and suitability, as will be clear even from a first reading, and although it has the support of

Erasmus, he destroys the authority of his own rendering, so that there is no need for any refutation from me. All the Greek manuscripts undoubtedly agree on the reading 'God manifested in the flesh'. But, even supposing Paul had not expressly written the name of God, anyone who considers the whole matter with care will agree that the name of Christ should be supplied. I for my part have no difficulty in following the accepted Greek text. His reason for calling the manifestation of Christ which he now goes on to describe, a great mystery is easy, for this is the height, depth and breadth of wisdom which he mentions in Eph. 3.18, and by which our faculties are inevitably overwhelmed.

Let us now examine the different clauses of this verse in order. The most fitting description of Christ's person is contained in the words, 'God manifested in the flesh.' First, we have here a distinct affirmation of both natures, for he declares Him to be at once true God and true man. Secondly, he takes note of the distinction between the two natures, for he first calls Him God and then declares His manifestation in the flesh. And, thirdly, he asserts the unity of His Person by declaring that it was one and the same Person who was God and who was manifested in the flesh. In this single phrase the true and orthodox faith is powerfully armed against Arius, Marcion, Nestorius and Eutyches. There is great emphasis laid on the contrast between the two terms, God and the flesh. The difference between God and man is very great, and yet in Christ we see God's infinite glory joined to our polluted flesh so that the two become one (*videmus in Christo coniunctam cum hac nostra carnis putredine, ut unum efficiant*).

Justified in the spirit. As the Son of God emptied Himself by taking upon Him our flesh, so also there appeared in Him a spiritual power that testified that He was God. This passage has been interpreted in different ways but I am satisfied with explaining the apostle's meaning as I understand it and shall add no more. First, justification here means an acknowledgment of divine power, as in Ps. 19.9 where it is said that God's judgments are justified, that is, wonderfully and completely perfect. Note also Ps. 51.4, where God is said to be justified, meaning that the praise of His righteousness is clearly displayed. So also in Matt. 11.19 and Luke 7.35 where Christ says that wisdom is justified of her children, meaning that in them wisdom's worth is made clear. Again, in Luke 7.29 it is said that the publicans justified God, meaning that in due reverence and gratitude they acknowledged God's grace which they discerned in Christ. Thus what we read here means the same as if Paul had said that He who appeared clad in human flesh was at the same time declared to be the Son of God, so that the weakness of the flesh in no way detracted from His glory.

By the word 'Spirit' he includes everything in Christ that was divine and superior to man, and this he does for two reasons. First, since Christ had been humbled in the flesh, Paul now contrasts the Spirit with the flesh by making clear His glory. Secondly, the glory worthy of God's only begotten Son, which John teaches us was seen in Christ (John 1.14) did not consist of outward show or earthly grandeur but was almost completely spiritual. The same form of expression is used in the first chapter of Romans (1.3) 'who was born of the seed of David according to the flesh, who was declared to be the Son of God in the power of the Spirit' but with this difference that in that passage he mentions one special manifestation of His glory, the resurrection.

Seen of angels, preached to the nations. All these statements are wonderful and astonishing: that God should honour the Gentiles who, till then, had erred in their blindness with the revelation of His Son which had been hidden from the very angels in heaven! For to say that He was seen of angels means that this was a sight that by its novelty and excellence drew the attention of the angels. How new and extraordinary the calling of the Gentiles was we have explained in discussing Eph. 2. Nor is it strange that it was a new sight for the angels, for although they knew of the redemption of humanity, they did not at first know how it was to be accomplished, and it must have been concealed from them in order that the greatness of God's kindness might make them admire the more.

Believed on in the world. It was above all things wonderful that God should have given an equal share in His revelation to profane Gentiles and to the angels who were the everlasting inheritance of His Kingdom. But this great efficacy of the preached Gospel whereby Christ overcame all obstacles and brought into the obedience of faith those who seemed quite incapable of being subdued—this was no ordinary miracle. So completely closed and shut was every way of approach that nothing appeared to be less probable. And yet by an almost incredible victory, faith conquered.

Finally he says that He was *received into glory*, that is, after this mortal and miserable life. Thus both in the world through the obedience of faith and in the Person of Christ a wonderful change was wrought, for He was exalted from the mean state of a servant to the Father's right hand that to Him every knee might bow.

CHAPTER FOUR

But the Spirit saith expressly, that in later times some shall fall away from the faith, giving heed to seducing spirits and doctrines of devils, through the hypocrisy of men that speak lies, branded in their own conscience as with a hot iron; forbidding to marry, and commanding to abstain from meats, which God created to be received with thanksgiving by them that believe and know the truth. For every creature of God is good, and nothing is to be rejected, if it be received with thanksgiving: for it is sanctified through the word of God and prayer. (1-5)

1. *But the Spirit saith.* He has been giving Timothy careful advice on many subjects and now he shows why such care was necessary, since it was right to take measures against a danger declared by the Holy Spirit to be fast approaching, that false teachers would come and offer their own trifling inventions as the teaching of the faith, and who by making holiness a matter of external observances would obscure that spiritual worship of God which alone is lawful. And there has indeed been a constant struggle between God's servants and men such as Paul here describes. For since men are naturally inclined to hypocrisy, Satan easily persuades them that God can be worshipped rightly by ceremonies and by discipline in outward things. In fact even without a teacher, this is a conviction that nearly everyone has, deep rooted in his heart. Later the craftiness of Satan is added to complete the error and the result has been that in every age there have been impostors to recommend false worship by which true godliness has been brought to ruin. This plague brings another in its train, by which compulsion is brought to bear on men in connexion with matters that are indifferent. For the world easily allows itself to be forbidden things that God had allowed it, in order to be allowed to transgress God's laws with impunity. Here therefore Paul is warning not only the church at Ephesus through Timothy, but all churches everywhere against false teachers, who, by introducing false worship and ensnaring consciences with new laws, adulterate God's true worship and corrupt the pure doctrine of the faith. This is the real purpose of this passage which we must specially keep in mind.

Further, that all may receive what he is going to say with greater attention, he first declares that this is a sure and quite unobscure prophecy of the Holy Spirit. There is of course no reason to doubt that everything else he says is also inspired by the Spirit, but, although we should at all times listen to him as the very instrument of Christ, yet here in a matter of great importance he particularly wished to have it stated explicitly that he said nothing except by the Spirit of prophecy. Thus by this solemn assurance he commends this prophecy to us, and not satisfied with that, he adds that it is plain and free from all ambiguity.

In later times. At that time nobody could have expected that with the clear light of the Gospel any would fall. But this is exactly what Peter says (II Pet. 3.3), that just as false teachers once troubled the people of Israel, so they will always disturb the Church of Christ. It is as if he had said, 'Now the teaching of the Gospel flourishes, but Satan will not be long inactive in trying to choke the good seed with tares.' This warning was useful in Paul's own time in making pastors and others give careful attention to pure doctrine and in keeping them from being deceived. It is no less useful to us today when we see that everything has fallen out according to the express prophecy of the Spirit. We should specially notice God's great care for His Church in giving such early warning of coming dangers. Satan has many wiles by which to lead us into error and he attacks us by many strange tricks, but God gives us sufficient armour, as long as we ourselves do not want to be deceived. We have therefore no reason to complain that the darkness is stronger than the light or that truth is conquered by falsehood, but rather when we are led astray from the right way of salvation, we are paying the penalty of our own carelessness and indolence.

But those who indulge themselves in their errors object that it is hardly possible to decide what kind of people Paul is describing here. As though it were to no purpose that the Spirit issued this prophecy and declared it so long before. For if there were no certain indication of who were intended by it, the present warning would be both superfluous and ridiculous. But we dare not think that God's Spirit alarms us without cause or that, when He foretells danger, He does not also show us how to guard against it. Paul's own words are quite sufficient by themselves to refute this false complaint, for he lays his finger on the evil he is warning us to avoid. He does not merely speak generally about false prophets, but clearly gives an express example of false teaching, a teaching which by making godliness consist of outward exercises perverts and profanes the spiritual worship of God, as I have already said.

Some will fall away from the faith. It is not clear whether he is speaking of the teachers or the hearers, but I prefer to take it as applying to the latter since he goes on to deal with the teachers when he calls them *seducing spirits.* And it makes the meaning more emphatic to say that not only will there be those who spread ungodly teachings and pollute the purity of the faith, but they will not lack pupils to make up their sect. When a lie thus increases its influence, it causes greater trouble. But this is no trifling fault of which he is speaking, but a most dreadful evil, apostasy *from the faith*, although at first sight there would not seem to be so much evil in the teaching he mentions. For how can faith be completely overturned by a prohibition of certain foods or of marriage? But we must take a wider consideration into account, that here men are inventing a perverted worship of God at their own pleasure, and by daring to forbid the use of good things God has permitted, are claiming to be masters of their own consciences. And as soon as purity of worship is perverted nothing remains whole or healthy any longer and faith is completely destroyed. Thus, although the Papists laugh at our criticisms of their tyrannical laws about external observances, we know that we are dealing with a most serious and important matter, for, as soon as the worship of God is infected with such corruptions, the doctrine of faith is destroyed. The controversy is not about flesh or fish, or about black or ashen colours, or about Wednesday or Friday, but about the mad superstitions of men who wish to obtain God's favour by such trifles and by contriving a carnal worship, invent for themselves an idol in God's place. Who would deny that this is apostasy from the faith?

Seducing spirits. He means prophets or teachers and he gives them this name because they were boasting of their possession of the Spirit and were thus making an impression on the people. It is indeed generally true that all sorts of men speak at the prompting of a spirit, but it is not the same spirit that prompts them all. For sometimes Satan is a lying spirit in the mouth of false prophets to deceive unbelievers who deserve to be deceived (I Kings 22.21-23). But everyone who pays Christ His due honour speaks by the Spirit of God, as Paul says (I Cor. 12.3). This way of speaking had its origin in the claim made by God's servants that all their public utterances came to them by a revelation of the Spirit, and, since they were the Spirit's instruments, they were given the Spirit's name. But later the ministers of Satan by a false imitation like apes began to make the same claim for themselves and likewise falsely assumed the same name. That is why John says, 'Try the spirits whether they are of God.'

Paul explains his meaning further by adding *and doctrines of devils*, which is equivalent to saying, 'giving heed to false prophets and their devilish teachings'. Once again that is not a small error and not something to be glossed over, when men's consciences are bound by human inventions and at the same time God's worship is perverted.

2. *In hypocrisy speaking lies.* If this phrase is taken with demons, then speaking lies will refer to men who speak falsely at the devil's prompt-

ing. But is it possible to supply 'through the hypocrisy of men that speak lies'. Taking up a particular instance, he says that they speak lies in hypocrisy and are *branded in their own conscience as with a hot iron*. And we should note that these two things belong together and that the first springs from the second. Bad consciences that are branded by the hot iron of their evil deeds always resort to hypocrisy as an easy refuge, that is, they contrive hypocritical pretences to deceive the eyes of God. This is indeed the very thing that is done by those who try to please God by unreal external observances. Thus the word *hypocrisy* must be understood in relation to the present context. It should be taken first in relation to doctrine, and as meaning that kind of doctrine which substitutes bodily gestures for God's spiritual worship and thus adulterates its genuine purity, and so it includes all methods of appeasing God or of obtaining His favour contrived and invented by man. His meaning may be summed up thus: first, that all who introduce a contrived holiness are acting at the instigation of the devil, for God is never worshipped aright merely by external rites. True worshippers 'worship Him in spirit and in truth' (John 4.24). And secondly, that this external worship is a useless medicine by which hypocrites try to relieve their pains, or rather a dressing under which bad consciences conceal their wounds to no purpose and to their own great ruin.

3. *Forbidding to marry*. Having described the false teaching in general terms, he now takes note of two specified examples of it—the prohibition of marriage and of certain foods. These have their origin in the hypocrisy that abandons true holiness and then seeks for something else as a disguise. For those who do not abstain from self-seeking, hatred, avarice, cruelty and such like, try to acquire righteousness for themselves by abstaining from those things which God has left free. The only reason why consciences are burdened by such laws is that perfection is being sought apart from the law of God. This is done only by hypocrites who, in order to transgress with impunity against that inner righteousness which the law requires, try to hide their inner wickedness by those outward observances, with which they cover themselves as with veils.

This was a clear prophecy of danger which it would not have been difficult to observe, if men had attended to the Holy Spirit when He gave so distinct a warning. Yet we see that Satan's darkness generally prevailed, so that the clear light of this plain and memorable prediction was of no avail. For not long after the apostles' death there arose Encratites—who took their name from the Greek word for continence —Tatianists, Catharists, Montanus with his sect, and at length the Manichaeans, who had an aversion to the eating of flesh and to marriage and condemned them as profane. Although they were repudiated by the Church because of their arrogance in wishing to make others comply with their views, yet it is plain that even those who resisted them yielded to their errors more than they should. Those of whom I now speak had no intention of imposing a law on Christians, but yet they attached overmuch importance to superstititious observances like avoiding marriage and not eating flesh. Such is the characteristic of the world, always imagining that God could be worshipped in a carnal way, as if He Himself were carnal. Matters became gradually worse till a condition of tyranny became established in which it was not lawful for priests or monks to marry or for anyone on certain days to dare to eat flesh. Thus we have good reason for holding today that this prophecy applies to the Papists, since they enjoin celibacy and abstention from foods more strictly than they do any of God's commandments. They think that they can escape this accusation by twisting Paul's words to apply to the Tatianists or Manichaeans or suchlike, as if the Tatianists could not have avoided them in the very same way by turning Paul's censures on to the Cataphrygians and Montanus, their founder; or as if the Cataphrygians could not easily have brought forward the Encratites as the guilty parties in their place. But here Paul is not concerned with people, but with the views that they held, and even if a hundred different sects be brought forward, all of them labouring under the same hypocrisy in forbidding foods, they will all incur the same condemnation. Thus it is in vain for the Papists to bring forward ancient heretics, as though they alone were the object of Paul's condemnation. We must still see whether they themselves are not guilty in the same way. They claim that they are different from the Encratites and Manichaeans in that they do not absolutely forbid marriage and foods, but compel abstention from flesh only on certain days and require a vow of celibacy only from monks, priests and nuns. But this is a completely frivolous excuse, for they do make holiness to consist of these things, and they do set up a false and spurious worship of God, and they do bind the consciences of men by a compulsion from which they should be free. In the fifth book of Eusebius there is a fragment from the writings of Apollonius, in which among other things he reproaches Montanus with being the first to dissolve marriages and to lay down rules for fasting. He does not say that he forbade marriage or foods universally. It is enough to lay on men's consciences an obligation to do these things and to worship God by observing them. To forbid things that are free, whether universally or in special cases, is always a devillish tyranny. But this will become clearer as far as food is concerned from the next phrase.

Which God created. We should note the reason given why we should be content with the liberty God has granted us in the use of foods. It is because He created them for this purpose. It gives the greatest joy to all godly men to know that all the kinds of food they eat are put into their hands by the Lord, so that to enjoy them is blameless and quite legitimate. How do men dare to take away what God has freely bestowed? Can they create food, or can they make God's creation of it void? Let us always remember that He who created it also gave us free enjoyment of it, and it is vain for men to try to prohibit it.

God created food *to be received*, that is, in order that we should enjoy it. But he adds *with thanksgiving*, for the only recompense we can make to God for His liberality is a testimony of our thanks. Thus he exposes to even greater detestation those wicked legalists, who by novel and hasty enactments hinder the sacrifice of praise which God specially requires us to offer Him. Moreover, there cannot be thanksgiving without sobriety and moderation, and there can be no true acknowledgment of God's kindness by a man who wickedly abuses it.

By them that believe and know. But how so? Is it not true that God makes His sun to rise daily on the good and the evil (Matt. 5.45), and if the earth at His command brings forth bread for the godly, are not the very worst of men also fed by His beneficence? There is indeed that general blessing which David describes in Ps. 104.14, but here Paul's subject is lawful enjoyment and of how we are assured of it in God's sight. This is something that wicked men cannot share because of their impure conscience which contaminates everything, as Titus 1.15 says. And indeed strictly speaking God has destined the whole world and all that is in it only for His sons and that is why they are also called the heirs of the world. For at the beginning Adam was appointed lord of all things on condition that he should remain in obedience to God. Thus his rebellion against God deprived himself and his posterity of this right which has been bestowed upon him. But since all things are subject to Christ, we are through His goodness fully restored to our rights, but only through faith. Thus all that unbelievers enjoy may be regarded as the property of another which they rob and steal. In the last clause he defines believers as those who have a knowledge of sound teaching, for there is no faith except from God's Word, so that we must not falsely imagine that faith is a confused opinion, as the Papists do.

4. *For every creature of God is good*. How food should be used depends partly on what food it is and partly on the character of the man who eats it. The apostle refers to both factors. Of the food he declares that it is pure, because God created it and its use is consecrated to us by faith and prayer. The goodness of the creatures he mentions relates to men, and not to their body or their health but to their consciences. I make this remark to discourage curious speculations that have no reference

to the purpose of this passage, for Paul's meaning is, in a word, that all that comes to us from God's hand is not unclean or polluted in His sight and is meant for our use, so that we can eat freely with a good conscience. If it be objected that under the law many animals were once declared unclean, and that the fruit of the tree of knowledge of good and evil brought death to men, the answer is that creatures are called pure not just because they are God's works, but because they are given to us with His blessing. We must always have regard to God's appointment, both what He commands and what He forbids.

5. *For it is sanctified.* This is a reinforcement of the previous phrase—'to be received with thanksgiving'. It is an argument based on opposites, for holy and profane are such opposites. We must now ask what kind of sanctification of all the good things that sustain our present life he has in mind. He declares that it consists of God's Word and of prayer, but we should also note that faith is needed to understand the Word in order that it may do us good. For although God Himself sanctifies all things by the Spirit of His mouth, we receive the blessing of it only by faith. To this prayer is added, for we not only ask for our daily bread according to Christ's commandment, but we also offer thanksgiving for His Goodness. Paul's teaching is based on the principle that there is no legitimate possession of any good thing unless our conscience witnesses that it is rightly ours. Which of us would dare to claim for himself one grain of wheat, were we not convinced by God's Word that the earth was our inheritance? Commonsense does indeed hold that the riches of the earth are naturally intended for our use, but, since our dominion over the world was taken from us in Adam, every gift of God that we touch is defiled by our stains and it on its side is unclean to us, till God graciously helps us and, by incorporating us into the Body of His Son, makes us anew lords of the earth, so that we may legitimately enjoy as our own all the wealth He supplies.

Paul therefore has good reason to connect rightful enjoyment with the Word by which alone we regain what was lost to us in Adam. For we must acknowledge God as our Father before we can be His heirs, and Christ as our Head before the things that are His can become ours. From this it may be inferred that the use of all God's gifts is unclean unless it is accompanied by true knowledge and supplication of God's name, and to sit down at table without any prayer and, when satisfied, to go off without any remembrance of God is a way of eating fit only for brute beasts. And if such sanctification is required for ordinary food, which like ourselves, is subject to corruption, what shall we think about spiritual sacraments? Here we must note the distinction between the blessing of the sacramental table and that of the ordinary table. We bless the food that we eat to nourish our body in order to receive it legitimately and without uncleanness, but we consecrate the bread and the wine in the sacrament supper in a more solemn manner that they may be to us pledges of Christ's body and blood.

> *If thou put the brethren in mind of these things, thou shalt be a good minister of Christ Jesus, nourished in the words of the faith, and of the good doctrine which thou hast followed until now: but refuse profane and old wives' fables. And exercise thyself with godliness: for bodily exercise is profitable for a little; but godliness is profitable for all things, having promise of the life which now is, and of that which is to come. Faithful is the saying and worthy of all acceptation. For to this end we labour and strive, because we have our hope set on the living God, who is the Saviour of all men, especially of them that believe.* (6-10)

6. *If thou put the brethren in mind.* He thus exhorts Timothy to remind them frequently of these things and he later repeats this a second and a third time, for they are things that should be frequently remembered. We should note the contrast implied by the way he opposes the teaching he recommends not to false or ungodly doctrines, but to useless and unedifying trifles. He tells Timothy to maintain his teaching but wants these other things to be completely forgotten.

Thou shalt be a good minister. Men often set before them some other aim than to approve themselves to Christ; many seek applause for their cleverness, eloquence or profound knowledge, and that is why they pay less attention to the basic necessities which are apt to produce less popular admiration. But Paul tells Timothy to be content with this one thing, that he should be a faithful minister of Christ. And we should certainly regard this as a far more honourable title than being called a thousand times over seraphic and subtle doctors. Let us remember therefore that it is the greatest honour than can befall a godly pastor to be accounted a good servant of Christ, so that during his whole ministry this should be his only aim. For those who have some other ambition may well succeed in winning men's approval, but they will not please God. Thus not to be deprived of so great a blessing, let us learn to seek nothing else, to think nothing else so important, and indeed to think everything else relatively worthless.

Nourished. Since the verb is in the middle in Greek, it could also be translated actively as 'nourishing', but since there is no object following the verb, this construction seems to me to be rather forced. I prefer to take the participle as a passive as confirming what he has just said about Timothy's education. It is as if he had said, 'Having been rightly instructed in the faith from your infancy, and having, so to speak, sucked in sound doctrine with your mother's milk, and having made till now continual progress in it, take pains by a faithful ministry to prove that you are still the same.' This interpretation also brings out the root meaning of the verb.

Faith means here the sum of Christian teaching and the phrase about *good doctrine* is added to explain more clearly what faith is. He means that however plausible other doctrines may be, they are not at all profitable. The phrase *which thou hast followed* indicates his perseverance. Many who have purely learned Christ from their boyhood afterwards fall away with the passing of time, but Paul says that Timothy was not one of them.

7. *Exercise thyself.* Having instructed him in what sort of doctrine he should teach, he now advises him as to what sort of example he should give to others, and he says that he should be employed in godliness. For when he says 'exercise thyself' he means that this is Timothy's proper occupation, his main concern and his chief care. It is as if he had said, 'There is no reason why you should weary yourself with other matters to no purpose. You will do the thing of greatest value, if with all your zeal and ability you devote yourself to godliness alone.' By the word 'godliness' he means the spiritual worship of God which is found only in a pure conscience, and this becomes even clearer in what follows when godliness is contrasted with bodily exercise.

By the exercise of the body he does not mean hunting or racing or digging or wrestling or manual labour, but rather all outward actions undertaken for the sake of religion, such as vigils, long fasts, lying on the ground and such like. Here he is not censuring the superstitious observance of these things, for then he would condemn them totally as he does in Col. 2.21. But here he only disparages them and says they are of little profit. Thus even though the heart be pure and the motive upright, Paul finds nothing in outward actions he can value highly. This is a needed warning, for the world always has a strong tendency towards worshipping God by external observances, which can be fatal. Even leaving out the perverse notion that there is merit in it, our nature always disposes us strongly to think that the ascetic life is of great value, as though it were a notable part of Christian sanctification. There is no clearer proof of this than the fact that very soon after Paul had laid down this commandment, an empty type of bodily exercise won the immoderate admiration of the whole earth. From this monasticism sprang and all the much admired discipline of the Early Church, at least that part of it which rates highest in popular opinion. If the ancient monks had not believed that there was some divine or angelic perfection in their austere rule of life, they would never have practised it with such ardour. In the same way if pastors had not unduly overvalued the practices then observed as a means of mortifying the flesh, they would never have been so strict in requiring them. And yet Paul says the opposite, that even if a man has worn himself out much and long in these exercises, the profit will be small and meagre, for they are nothing but the rudiments of a childish discipline.

8. *But godliness is profitable for all things.* This means that the man who has godliness lacks nothing, even though he does not have the small assistance these ascetic practices can afford. Godliness is the beginning, middle and end of Christian living and where it is complete, there is nothing lacking. Christ did not follow as ascetic a way of life as John the Baptist, and yet He was not for that reason any whit inferior. Thus the conclusion is that we should concentrate exclusively on godliness, for when once we have attained to it, God requires no more of us, and we ought to give heed to bodily exercises only to the extent that they may hinder or retard the practice of godliness.

Having promise. It is a very great comfort to know that God does not wish the godly to lack anything. Having decreed that our perfection should be in godliness, He now makes provision that godliness should find its fulfilment in true happiness. And since it is the source of happiness in this life, he extends to this life also the promises of divine grace, which can alone make us happy, and without which we shall be the most miserable of men. For God declares that even in this life He will be a Father to us. But we must remember to distinguish between the blessings of the present and those of the future. For in this world God blesses us in such a way as to give us a mere foretaste of His kindness, and by that taste to entice us to desire heavenly blessings with which we may be satisfied. That is why the blessings of this present life are not only mixed but almost destroyed by very many afflictions, for it is not good for us to have abundance here lest we should begin to luxuriate in it. Further, in case anyone should attempt to draw from this passage a doctrine of merit, we should note that godliness includes not only a good conscience towards men and reverence for God, but also faith and prayer.

9. *Faithful is the saying.* He now lays down at the conclusion of his argument something that he has already said twice at the start of it, and he seems to do this on purpose, for he immediately goes on to deal with arguments that could be brought against it. He has good reason for asserting this point so strongly, for it is a paradox strongly opposed to our experience in the flesh to hold that God in this world supplies to His people what is required for a blessed and happy life, since so often they lack all good things and indeed count themselves forsaken of God. Thus not satisfied with simply enunciating this teaching, he repels all attacks upon it and admonishes believers to open the door to the grace of God which our unbelief shuts out. For without doubt, if we were

more ready to receive God's blessings, He would treat us more liberally.

10. *For to this end we labour.* Here he anticipates an objection by considering the question whether believers, pressed hard as they are by every kind of affliction, are not the most miserable of all men. Thus, in order to show that their real condition is not to be judged by outward appearances, he distinguishes them from others in relation both to the cause and the result of their sufferings. From this it follows that in being troubled with adversity, they lose none of the promises he has mentioned. The conclusion is that believers are not miserable in their afflictions, because a good conscience sustains them and a blessed and joyful end awaits them.

Now since the happiness of this present life consists of two main parts, honour and comforts, he contrasts with them *labours and reproach*, meaning by the former all kinds of discomforts and troubles, such as poverty, cold, nakedness, hunger, exile, plundering, imprisonment, flogging and other persecutions.

We have our hope set on the living God. This comfort refers to the reason why we suffer, for when we suffer for the sake of righteousness, so far from making us miserable, our sufferings are rather good reasons for thanksgiving. Besides in our afflictions our hope is set on the living God—in fact hope is our foundation, and hope never maketh ashamed (Rom. 5.5). From this it follows that all that happens to the godly should be counted gain.

Who is the Saviour. The second comfort depends on the first, for the deliverance of which he speaks is, so to speak, the fruit of hope. The reasoning here is from lesser to greater. For here σωτήρ is a general term, meaning one who guards and preserves. His argument is that God's kindness extends to all men. And if there is no one without the experience of sharing in God's kindness, how much more of that kindness shall the godly know, who hope in Him. Will He not take special care of them? Will He not pour out of His bounty much more freely upon them? In short, will He not keep them in all things safe to the end?

These things command and teach. Let no man despise thy youth; but be thou an ensample to them that believe, in word, in manner of life, in love,[1] *in faith, in purity. Till I come, give heed to reading, to exhortation, to preaching. Neglect not the gift that is in thee, which was given thee by prophecy, with the laying on of the hands of the presbytery. Be diligent in these things; give thyself wholly to them; that thy progress may be manifest unto all. Take heed to thyself and to thy teaching. Continue*

[1] Calvin's text read, as in A.V., 'in love, in spirit, in faith'.

in these things; for in doing this thou shalt save both thyself and them that hear thee. (11-16)

11. *These things command.* He means that his teaching is of such a kind that nobody ought ever to grow weary of it, even though he were to hear it every day. There are indeed other things that have to be taught, but he lays the emphasis on 'these things', because he believes them to be of great importance, so that it is not enough to take brief and passing notice of them. They are rather worthy of daily repetition for they cannot be too much inculcated. It is the duty therefore of a wise pastor to consider what things are most essential and to dwell on them. There is no reason to fear that this will become wearisome for those who belong to God will gladly hear again and again things that need to be said so often.

12. *Let no man despise thy youth.* What he says applies not just to Timothy but to the others as well. As far as they are concerned, he does not want Timothy's age to prevent their giving him the reverence he deserves, as long as he conducts himself in other respects as a minister of Christ. At the same time he admonishes Timothy himself to make up what he lacks in age by the earnestness of his ways, as if he had said, 'Take care to win for yourself, by the gravity of your bearing, so much respect that your youth which would otherwise tend to bring you into contempt may in no way lessen your authority.' Thus we learn that Timothy was still young, though he held an eminent place among so many pastors, and we see that it is vain to estimate a man's worth by the number of his years. He next tells them what true distinction consists of, not external ornaments like croziers, rings, cloaks or such children's toys, but soundness of doctrine and holiness of life. When he says *in word and manner of life*, this means in word and deed and in his whole life.

The virtues that are mentioned next are parts of godly behaviour, *love, spirit, faith,* and *purity.* By *spirit* I take him to mean fervent zeal for God, but I have no objection to its being interpreted in a more general way. *Purity* is not just the opposite of lust, but means complete purity of life. Thus we learn how foolish and ridiculous it is for people to complain that they receive no honour, when in fact there is nothing about them that is worth honouring, but they rather expose themselves to contempt by their ignorance, the example of their impure lives, their lightmindedness and other faults. The only way to win respect is by outstanding virtues which will protect us against contempt.

13. *Till I come.* He knows how diligent Timothy is, and yet he recommends to him a persevering reading of the Scriptures. For how can pastors teach others unless they themselves are able to learn, and if

so great a man is admonished to study to make progress day by day, how much more do we need such advice? Woe to the slothfulness of those who do not peruse the oracles of the Spirit day and night to learn from them how to discharge their office. His reference to his own coming adds weight to his admonition; for while Paul was hoping to come soon, he did not want Timothy to remain unemployed in the meantime, even for a short time. How much more care should we take to make plans to fill our whole life! In addition, in case leisurely reading should be thought enough, he shows that what he reads he must also use and tells him to attend to teaching and exhortation, as if he were advising him to learn in order to communicate what he has learnt to others. We should notice the order, how he mentions reading before teaching and exhortation, for Scripture is the source of all wisdom and pastors ought to draw from it all that they set before their flock.

14. *Neglect not the gift that is in thee.* He exhorts Timothy to use the grace with which he has been endowed for the upbuilding of the Church. God does not wish the talents He has bestowed on a man in order to bring forth increase to be lost or buried uselessly in the earth. To *neglect* a gift is from sloth and carelessness to fail to make use of it, so that through lack of use it becomes rusty and degenerates. Thus each of us should consider what ability he possesses, in order to make full use of it.

He says that grace *was given* him *through prophecy*. How was this? It was because, as we have already said, the Holy Ghost had by revelation designated Timothy for admission to the rank of pastor. Thus he had not been chosen in the usual way by the judgment of men, but had been first named by the Holy Spirit.

He also says that the gift was conferred *with the laying on of hands*, meaning that along with his ministry he was given the gifts necessary to perform it. It was the usual practice of the apostles to ordain ministers by the laying on of hands. I have already given a brief explanation of the origin and meaning of this ceremony and the rest can be found in the *Institute*. Those who think that in this passage *presbytery* is a collective term meaning the college of presbyters are in my view correct. Although, having considered the matter, I do agree that another explanation fits well—that it is the name of an office. By the ceremony of laying on of hands he indicates the act of ordination to the presbyterate, so that his meaning is that Timothy, having been called to the ministry by the voice of the prophets, and ordained to it by a solemn rite, was at the same time endued by the Holy Spirit with grace for the discharge of his office. From this we gather that the ceremony was not in vain, since God by His Spirit effected that consecration which men symbolized by the laying on of hands.

15. *Be diligent in these things.* The greater the difficulty in ministering faithfully to the Church, the more earnestly should a pastor apply all his powers to it, and not only for a short time but with unfailing perseverance. Paul reminds Timothy that there is no place in this work for indolence or slackness, for it requires the greatest carefulness and assiduity.

That thy progress may be manifest. His meaning is that he is to work in such a way that through him the Church may be more and more built up and edified, and that results worthy of his labour may appear. This is not the achievement of a single day, so that he should strive to make progress every day. Some take this to refer to Timothy's personal progress, but I think that it describes the effect of his ministry.

In all. The phrase may be masculine or neuter, so that two meanings are possible, either 'that all men may see the progress that springs from his labours' or 'that on every side and in every way the progress may appear'. I prefer the latter.

16. *Take heed to thyself.* A good pastor must be careful about two things: to be diligent in his teaching and to keep his own integrity. It is not enough that he should rule his life by all that is honourable and take care not to give a bad example, if he does not add to a sanctified life a continual diligence in teaching. And teaching will be of little worth if there is not a corresponding uprightness and holiness of life. Thus Paul has good reason to urge Timothy to give heed both to himself personally and to his teaching for the general advantage of the Church. Once again he commends constancy to him, that he may never grow weary, for many things happen which can divert us from the right course, if we do not firmly set ourselves to resist them.

In doing this. The zeal of pastors will be greatly increased when they are told that both their own salvation and that of their people depends upon their serious and earnest devotion to their office. And, since teaching which contains solid edification does not usually make much of a showy display, Paul advises him to be concerned with what is profitable, as if he had said, 'Let men who seek glory feed on their own ambition and congratulate themselves on their own cleverness, but you content yourself with being exclusively devoted to the salvation of yourself and your people.' This is advice that applies to the whole body of the Church, not to be weary of that simplicity which both quickens souls to life and preserves them in health. Nor should it seem strange that Paul ascribes to Timothy the work of saving the Church, for all that are won for God are saved and it is by the preaching of the Gospel that we are gathered to Christ. And just as the unfaithfulness or negligence of a pastor is fatal to the Church, so it is right for its salvation to be ascribed to his faithfulness and diligence. It is indeed true that it is God alone who saves and not even the smallest part of His glory can rightly be transferred to men. But God's glory is in no way diminished by His using the labour of men in bestowing salvation. Thus our salvation is the gift of God, since it comes from Him alone and is effected only by His power, so that He alone is its Author. But that does not exclude the ministry of men, nor does it deny that that ministry may be the means of salvation, for it is on that ministry that, as Paul says elsewhere, the welfare of the Church depends (Eph. 4.11). This ministry is itself entirely God's work, for it is He who makes men good pastors and leads them by His Spirit and blesses their work so that it may not be in vain. If a good pastor is in this way the salvation of those who hear him, let bad and careless men know that their ruin will be ascribed to those who are set over them. For just as the salvation of his flock is a pastor's crown, so all that perish will be required at the hand of careless pastors.

A pastor is said to *save himself* when he serves his calling by fulfilling faithfully the office entrusted to him, not only because he thus avoids the dreadful judgment the Lord threatens through Ezekiel (33.8), 'His blood will I require at thine hand', but because it is customary to speak of believers winning their salvation when they persevere in the course of their salvation. I have spoken of this mode of expression in my commentary on the second chapter of Philippians (2.12).

CHAPTER FIVE

Rebuke not an elder, but exhort him as a father; the younger men as brethren: the elder women as mothers; the younger as sisters in all purity. Honour widows that are widows indeed. But if any widow hath children or grandchildren, let them learn first to shew piety towards their own family, and to requite their parents: for this is good and acceptable in the sight of God. (1-4)

1. *Rebuke not an elder harshly.* He now recommends to Timothy gentleness and moderation in correcting faults. Correction is a medicine that always has some bitterness to it and is therefore disagreeable. Besides, since Timothy was a young man, severity in him would have been intolerable, had it not been modified somewhat. Thus he enjoins him to reprove older people as he would his own parents and in fact he uses an even milder word—*exhort* them. We cannot but think of our father and mother with respect, and towards them mildness is bound to take the place of harsh vehemence. Yet we should notice that he does not mean that Timothy should spare old people or indulge them, so that they could sin with impunity and without correction. He only means that some respect should be paid to their age, that they may more patiently submit to admonition.

Moreover he wishes moderation to be shown even towards younger people, though not to the same degree. For the vinegar must always be mixed with oil, but with this difference, that respect should be shown to older people whereas equals should be treated with brotherly gentleness. Thus he teaches pastors to consider not only what their office requires, but also with special care what the age of different individuals requires, for the same treatment does not suit all men. Let us therefore bear in mind that if actors on the stage observe decorum, it should not be neglected by pastors in their high station.

2. The pharse *with all purity* refers to younger women, for at their age any suggestion of suspicion is to be dreaded. Yet Paul does not forbid Timothy to act wantonly or immodestly towards young men, for there was no need of such a prohibition, but only tells him to take care not to give ill disposed persons any excuse for criticism. To that end he requires a chaste gravity in all their dealings and conversation with one another, so that he may converse the more freely with young people without any unfavourable reports.

3. *Honour widows.* The word honour in this passage does not mean

deference but rather the special care which bishops took of widows in the ancient Church. Widows were taken under the Church's protection to be supported out of the common funds. It is as if he had said, 'In choosing widows to take under the care of yourself and your deacons you ought to consider who *are widows indeed*.' We shall later explain more fully what this means, but here we should note why Paul does not admit widows unless they are quite alone and without children, for it was in these circumstances that they dedicated themselves to the Church, so as to withdraw from all private family concerns and be rid of every encumbrance. Thus Paul is right to forbid the reception of mothers of families, who are already bound by a different kind of duty. In calling them 'widows indeed' he alludes to the Greek word, which is derived from χηροῦσθαι, a verb meaning to be deprived or destitute.

4. *If any widow*. This passage is explained in different ways. The ambiguity arises from the fact that the second clause can refer both to the widows and to their children. It is true that the verb *learn* is plural and the word widow is singular, but it may still be the subject of the verb, as a change of number is quite usual when the subject refers not to an individual but to a class. Those who think that it refers to widows explain it thus, 'Let them learn by the dutiful government of their family to repay to their children the good upbringing they themselves received from their elders.' So Chrysostom and some others. Some however think that it gives a simpler sense to take children and grandchildren as the subject and, in their view, he wants them to learn that their widowed mother or grandmother is the person towards whom they should show their dutiful care. For there is nothing more natural than ἀντιπελαργία, the return to a parent of filial affection, and it should not be excluded from the Church. Thus before the Church has to carry the burden, let the children do their duty. These are the views of other commentators, but I would ask my readers to consider if this interpretation of my own would not fit the context better: Let them learn to behave in a godly manner at home, as if to say, It would be a good preparation, to train themselves for the worship of God by performing godly duties at home towards their own people. Since Paul saw that the very rights of nature were being violated in the name of religion, to correct this fault he gave instructions that widows should be trained for the worship of God by a domestic apprenticeship. Almost all commentators take the verb εὐσεβεῖν in an active sense, because it is followed by an accusative, but that is not a final argument, since it is quite usual for Greek to omit a preposition as being understood. And it suits the context to explain the meaning as being that, by cultivating human piety they should train themselves in the worship

of God, lest a foolish and trifling devotionalism should suppress their natural human feelings. Once again let widows learn to repay what they owe their elders by the way they rear their own offspring.

This is good and acceptable. It is universally agreed to that to fail in gratitude to one's parents is to be unnatural, for natural affections require it. And not only is it a universal and natural conviction that affection to parents is the second degree of godliness, but the very storks teach us gratitude by their example. This is the etymology of the word ἀντιπελαργία. But not satisfied with this, Paul declares that God has commanded it, as if he had said, 'There is no reason for anyone to think that this has its origin only in human conviction, for God has so ordained it.'

> *Now she that is a widow indeed and desolate hath her hope set on God, and continueth in supplications and prayers night and day. But she that giveth herself to pleasure is dead while she liveth. These things also command, that they may be without reproach. But if any provideth not for his own, and specially his own household, he hath denied the faith, and is worse than an unbeliever.* (5-8)

5. *Now she that is a widow indeed and desolate.* Here he makes his meaning more explicit than before by explaining that real widows are those who are solitary and without children. Such, he says, *have their hope set on God.* Not that all of them do this or that they alone do it, for we see many widows, childless and with no relations, who are haughty and shameless and quite ungodly both in heart and life, and, on the other hand, there is nothing to prevent people who have many children from having their hope in God, like Job and Jacob and David. Were it not for this hope, then to have many children would be a curse, whereas in various places Scripture counts it among God's greatest blessings.

But when Paul says here that widows hope in God, he says it in the same sense as in I Cor. 7.32 where he says that the unmarried study only to please God, meaning that their affections, unlike those of married people, are undivided. He means that they have nothing to distract them from a singleminded devotion to God, for they have nothing in the world on which they can rely. By saying this he commends them, for when human resources and every other refuge fails them, it is the duty of the Church to stretch forth her hand to help them. Thus the plight of a childless and desolate widow implores a pastor's aid.

She continueth in supplications. This is his second reason for commending widows, that they devote themselves continually to prayer. Thus it follows that they should be helped and supported at the Church's expense. But by these two qualifications he is also distinguishing between the worthy and the unworthy, for these words are almost equivalent to an injunction to receive only those who expect no help from men but depend upon God only, and who have given up other concerns and occupations in order to devote themselves to prayer. Others are not qualified or useful for the Church. Furthermore, this assiduity in prayer demands freedom from other concerns and those who are busy regulating the affairs of a family have less freedom and leisure. We are all indeed commanded to pray without ceasing, but we must consider the demands that are made upon every man by his situation in life, before we demand of him retirement and freedom from other concerns for the sake of prayer.

What Paul praises in widows, Luke claims for Anna, the daughter of Phanuel (Luke 2.36), but the same would not be possible for everyone, since their way of life is different. There will be stupid women, caricatures rather than imitators of Anna, who will rush from altar to altar or do nothing but sigh or mutter till the middle of the day. They will make this an excuse to free themselves from all their domestic duties and if, on returning home, they do not find everything arranged to their liking, they will disturb the whole family by their foolish cries and will sometimes go as far as blows. Let us therefore remember that there are good reasons why leisure for prayer by day and night is the special privilege of widows and the childless, for they are free from the things that very properly hinder those who rule a family from doing the same.

This passage gives no countenance to monks or nuns, who for the sake of an easy living, sell their murmurings or wails. Such were once the Euchites or Psallians, and the monks and priests of Rome are no different, except that the Euchites thought that by continual prayer they could make themselves godly and holy, whereas the monks imagine that with less assiduity they can sanctify others as well. Paul has nothing of this in mind, he only meant to point out how much more leisure for prayer widows with nothing else to distract them have.

6. *But she that giveth herself to pleasure.* Having described the true widows, Paul now contrasts them with others who are not to be accepted. The Greek participle he uses, σπαταλῶσα, means one who indulges herself and leads an easy and luxurious life. Thus in my view Paul is criticizing those who abuse their widowhood in this way, so that they lead a life of pleasant idleness, loosed from the marriage yoke and free from every annoyance. For we see many whose care is only for their own freedom and convenience and who behave with too much levity. Paul says of such a woman that she *is dead while she liveth.* Some commentators think this refers to her unbelief, but I do not

agree. To me a more suitable meaning is that a woman is said to be dead when she is useless and good for nothing. For what purpose is there in living, except that our deeds should bear fruit? Or, alternatively, we might put the emphasis on the word *liveth*. Those who want an easy life are for ever quoting the proverb, 'Life is not to live but to live well.' Thus the meaning would be, 'If they think themselves happy in doing what they like, and that the only life worth living is made up of leisure and pleasure, then I for my part say they are dead.' Some may think this interpretation too ingenious, and so I only wanted to mention it in passing without committing myself to it. What is certain here is that, in calling useless women dead, Paul is condemning idleness.

7. *These things also command.* He means that he is not only telling Timothy what he ought to do, but the women themselves should be diligently admonished against giving way to faults of that kind. It is the duty of a pastor not only to set himself against the wicked and selfish practices of those who behave improperly, but also by his teaching and continual admonitions to guard against all such dangers, as much as in him lies. Prudence and consistency demanded that widows should not be received unless they were worthy, but it was right to give a reason for the refusal, and it was even necessary to forewarn the Church in case unworthy women should be brought forward or should present themselves. Also Paul commends this kind of instruction because of its usefulness, as if he had said that it is by no means to be despised for being common, since it is directed towards a good and perfect life. Now there is no lesson in God's school that should be more carefully learnt than the study of a holy and perfect life. In short, moral instruction is far more important than ingenious speculations, which are of no obvious or practical use, as the text says, 'All scripture is profitable that the man of God may be perfect etc.' II Tim. 3.16.

8. *But if any provideth not for his own.* Erasmus translates it, as though it were feminine in gender, 'If any woman provideth not...', but I think that it is more likely to be a general statement. Even when Paul is dealing with some quite particular topic, it is his custom to base his argument on general principles and to draw from particular conclusions a universally applicable doctrine. And this statement has more point when it is applied both to men and to women. He says that those who do not care for their own people, and especially for their own household, have *denied the faith;* and rightly so, for there is no reverence towards God in a man who can thus lay aside all feelings of humanity. Faith which makes us the sons of God could never let us degrade ourselves below the brute beasts. Such inhumanity is open contempt of God and a denial of the faith. Not content with this, Paul goes further

and says that he who neglects his own *is worse than an unbeliever*. That is true for two reasons. The further a man progresses in the knowledge of God, the less excuse he has. Thus those who shut their eyes against the clear light of God are worse than unbelievers. Secondly, this is a kind of obligation that nature itself teaches, for they are στοργαὶ φυσικαί, natural affections. And if under the guidance of nature unbelievers are inclined to love their own, what shall we think of those who are moved by no such feeling? Do they not go beyond even the ungodly in their brutality? If someone objects that there are many cruel and brutal parents among unbelievers, the explanation is easy, for Paul is speaking here only of those parents who, under the guidance of nature, do care for their offspring. If anyone degenerates from this, he should be counted quite unnatural. It is asked why the apostle should prefer the claims of a man's household to those of his own children. The answer is that when he speaks of 'his own' and 'especially his own household', he uses both expressions to include children and grandchildren. For although children may have been given away in adoption, have passed into another family by marriage, or in some other way have left the parents' house, yet the claims of nature are never altogether abrogated, and the obligation of the elders to govern the younger as those God has entrusted to them, or at least to care for them as much as they can, is never entirely removed. Towards children still at home the obligation is greater; their parents must take care of them, both because they are of their own blood, and because they are part of the household over whom they are set.

> *Let none be enrolled as a widow under threescore years old, having been the wife of one man, well reported of for good works; if she hath brought up children, if she hath used hospitality to strangers, if she hath washed the saints' feet, if she hath relieved the afflicted, if she hath diligently followed every good work. But younger widows refuse: for when they have waxed wanton against Christ, they desire to marry; having condemnation because they have rejected their first faith. And withal they learn also to be idle, going about from house to house; and not only idle, but tattlers and busybodies also, speaking things which they ought not.*
> (9-13)

9. *Let none be enrolled.* He lays down once again what widows should be received into the Church's care and is even more explicit and detailed than before. First he says that they must be sixty years old, for since they were being supported at the public expense, it was but right that they should have reached old age. And another and even stronger reason was that it was intolerable that they should dedicate themselves to the service of the Church if there still remained any like-

lihood of their being remarried. They were received on condition that the Church should help them in their destitution and that they on their side should be employed in ministering to the poor, as far as their health allowed. Thus there was a mutual obligation between them and the Church. It was not right that those who were still strong and in the full vigour of life should be a burden to others, and with them there was good reason to fear that they would change their minds and want to marry again. For these two reasons he does not want women under sixty to be received. The danger of a woman's desiring to remarry was sufficiently remote if she was over sixty, especially if all her life she had been married to only one husband. The fact that a woman has reached that age and has been content with one husband may be taken as a sort of pledge of her continence and chastity. Not that he disapproves of second marriages or attaches any kind of stigma to those who have contracted them; he rather encourages the younger widows to marry again, but he wanted to be very careful in avoiding the imposition of an enforced chastity on women who needed husbands. He returns to this subject later.

10. *Well reported of for good works.* The qualifications that follow are designed to ensure that widows are both honourable and hardworking. For there is no doubt that the communities of widows were honourable and highly deserving, so that Paul wants admitted to them only those women who have excellent reports of the whole of their past life. The communities were not intended for leisure or lazy inactivity but to help the poor and sick until the women were worn out and could honourably rest in retirement. Thus to have them prepared to perform such an office, he wants them to have had long experience of the duties that belong to it, such as labour and diligence in bringing up children, hospitality, helping the poor and other charitable works.

If it is asked whether all barren women are to be rejected because they have never borne children, the answer is that what Paul is condemning here is not childlessness, but the pleasure-loving irresponsibility of mothers who refuse to endure the labour of rearing their children, and thus prove that they will be quite heedless of duties to strangers. At the same time he makes to godly matrons who have not spared themselves the offer that as an honourable reward they will in their old age be received into the bosom of the Church.

By *washing of feet* he means by synecdoche all the services usually rendered to the saints, for at that time it was the custom to wash a brother's feet. A duty of this kind could seem to be mean and almost servile, and he mentions it as a characteristic of women who are diligent without being dainty or fastidious. The thing mentioned next has to do with liberality, and he puts it in more general terms by saying,

I TIMOTHY 5 [v. 10-11

if she hath diligently followed every good work, for here he is speaking of acts of kindness.

11. *Younger widows refuse*. He does not mean that they should be excommunicated from the Church or be brought into any kind of disgrace, but only that they should be excluded from this honourable order of widows that he has been discussing. If God's Spirit, speaking through Paul, has laid it down that no woman of less than sixty is worthy of that order, because under that age the unmarried state is dangerous, what effrontery it was at a later period to impose a rule of perpetual celibacy on young women in all the vigour of their youth. Paul, I repeat, does not allow abstention from marriage till they are in the weakness of old age and beyond the danger of incontinence. Later they reduced the age at which virgins might take the veil to forty, and later again to thirty, till at last they began to accept all freely without any age qualification. They urge that continence is much easier for virgins, who have never had a husband, than for widows. But they will not succeed in avoiding the danger against which Paul is here guarding and telling us to guard. It is rash and indeed cruel to set a trap for girls who are still young and would be better married.

For when they have waxed wanton against Christ. By women who wanton against Christ he means those who forget the state of life to which they have been called and indulge in unbecoming frivolity. They ought to have restrained themselves with modesty as becomes respectable matrons. Thus a more luxurious and less disciplined way of life is equivalent to wantonness against the Christ to whom they had pledged themselves to be faithful. As Paul had seen many examples of this, as a remedy against it, he lays down that no woman should be accepted whose age would ever lead her to desire marriage.

For how many monstrous evils is the forced celibacy of nuns responsible under the Papacy? What barriers does it not deliberately break through? Thus, though at first sight it might have seemed acceptable, yet they should have learned from so much terrible experience and have complied with Paul's advice. But in fact they are so far from doing this that every day they provoke God's wrath more and more by their obstinacy. And I am not speaking of nuns only, for they compel both priests and monks also to observe the same perpetual celibacy. Yet shameful lusts rage among them so that scarcely one in ten keeps himself chaste. In monasteries ordinary fornication is the least of evils. If they would incline their minds to hear God speaking through Paul, they would at once have recourse to this remedy he prescribes, but so overweening is their pride that they subject to furious persecution all who remind them of it. Some take the phrase 'against

Christ' with the word 'marry', but although it makes little difference to the meaning, the first mentioned rendering is preferable.

12. *Having condemnation.* Some take this to mean, 'deserving reproof', but I take it to indicate something more severe, that Paul is terrifying them by a condemnation to eternal death. It is as if he were reproving them by saying that that excellent order which would have united them to Christ was the very cause of their condemnation instead. And the reason is added—that they entirely reject the Christian faith into which they were baptised. I know that some interpret this differently, to mean that by marrying they betray the pledge they gave to the Church, since they would have promised to live unmarried all their lives. But this is a poor explanation, and why in that case should he speak of their first faith? Thus Paul takes them to task with great vehemence and emphasizes the seriousness of their offence, in that not only have they brought shame upon Christ and the Church by departing from the way of life they undertook, but they have broken their first faith by wicked revolt. It usually does happen that, when a person once transgresses the bounds of modesty, she goes on to become involved in every kind of shameless disgrace. He blamed them for their frivolity that was so disgraceful in the eyes of the godly and for their lustfulness that was liable to reproof. This led them to rush headlong into more and more disgrace till at last they rejected Christianity. This amplification is extremely appropriate, for what could be more absurd than the fact that their very desire to do people good should be the occasion of their own denial of Christ.

The attempt of the Papists to find in this passage support for a vow of perpetual celibacy is absurd. Granting that it was the custom to obtain from the widows an undertaking in explicit terms, this will not help their case. For we must consider the purpose behind this undertaking. The reason why widows promised to remain unmarried was not in order to live a holier life than they could if married, but because they could not be devoted at the same time both to their husbands and to the Church. But under the Papacy they pledge themselves to celibacy as though it were a virtue acceptable to God for its own sake. Secondly, the widows renounced their freedom to marry at an age when they were no longer marriageable. For they had to be at least sixty, and by being content with a single marriage, must have given evidence of their chastity. But now vows of celibacy are made among the Papists before that age and even when the ardour of youth is at its greatest. Now we disapprove of this tyrannous rule of celibacy for two main reasons. First, because they pretend that by it they win merit before God, and, secondly, because by their rash vows they plunge souls into ruin. Neither defect can be found in the ancient institution described in this passage. They did not take a direct vow of continence, as though the married state were less pleasing to God, but only because the office for which they were chosen required it, nor did they renounce their freedom to marry till it would have been absurd and untimely to marry, however free they might have been. In short these widows were as different from the nuns as the prophetess Anna from Claudia, the Vestal Virgin.

13. *And withal they learn also to be idle.* There is nothing more becoming to a woman than keeping a house; so that among the ancients a tortoise was the symbol of a good and honourable mother of a family. But there are many women who suffer from the opposite vice. Nothing pleases them better than to be free to run from one place to another, especially when they are free from domestic concerns and have nothing to do at home. Also these widows had easier access to many people, because of the respect due to the public status they held. This opportunity, granted to them by the kindness of the Church, they abused for idleness and then, as usually happens, idleness led to curiosity which is the mother of talkativeness. Horace's maxim is very true, 'Shun an inquisitive man, for he always talks too much.' 'No trust is to be placed in inquisitive people', says Plutarch, 'for as soon as they have heard anything, they are never at rest till they have blurted it out.' This is specially true of women who are by nature inclined to be talkative and cannot keep a secret. Thus Paul has good reason to link together idleness, curiosity and talkativeness.

> *I desire therefore that the younger widows marry, bear children, rule the household, give none occasion to the adversary for reviling: for already some are turned aside after Satan. If any woman that believeth hath widows, let her relieve them and let not the church be burdened; that it may relieve them that are widows indeed.* (14-16)

14. *I desire therefore that the younger widows marry.* The supercilious laugh at this instruction of Paul's. 'As if', they say, 'there were any need to encourage any further a desire that is already far too strong: for who does not know that nearly all widows have a spontaneous desire to marry.' Fanatics would estimate this teaching about marriage as quite unbecoming for an apostle of Christ's. But when all is considered, men of sound judgment will agree that what Paul teaches here is completely salutary and necessary. On the one hand, widowhood provides many with a greater opportunity for licentiousness and, on the other, there are always coming forward hypocritical deceivers who think that sanctification consists of celibacy, as if it were angelical perfection, and who either totally condemn marriage or pour scorn upon it as if it savoured of pollution of the flesh. There are few, both

among men and among women, who consider their calling. How rarely do you find a man who willingly undertakes the burden of governing a wife, for it is a business that involves countless vexations! How reluctantly does a woman, on her side, submit to the yoke. Thus, when Paul orders younger women to marry, he is not inviting them to nuptial delights, and when he tells them to bear children, he is not encouraging them to indulge in lust, but rather, in view of the weakness of their sex and the temptations of their age, he advises them to contract a chaste marriage and by so doing to submit to the burdens that matrimony imposes. He does this specially to avoid any appearance of making their rejection from the order of widows imply something disgraceful, for his meaning is that their lives will be as acceptable to God, if they care for their household, as if they had remained widows. For God has no regard for the superstitious notions of men, but values more than anything else the obedience with which we accept our calling, rather than letting ourselves be carried away by our own inclinations. Being consoled in this way, widows have no reason to complain of injury or take it amiss that they are excluded from one kind of honour. For they are told that they are no less pleasing to God in the married state, because they are obeying His call. When he speaks of *bearing children*, he sums up in one phrase all the annoyances comprised in rearing offspring, and, in the same way, under *ruling the household* he includes all the duties of housewifery.

Give none occasion to the adversary. A husband is a protection to his wife, so that widowhood is exposed to many sinister suspicions. There can be no purpose in needlessly arming the enemies of the Gospel with means for attack. But it is very difficult for a widow still in the flower of her age to act with such caution that wicked men will be able to find no pretext for slandering her, so that if they really desire to do something edifying in order to shut the mouth of evil speakers, they should choose a state of life less liable to suspicion. Here I take it that the reference is to the common adversaries of the Gospel rather than to the private enemies of any woman, for Paul speaks generally.

15. *For already some are turned aside.* There is nothing so holy but that it is impossible for some ill to come of it because of human wickedness. Nevertheless essential things must remain fixed, whatever the result and even if the heavens should fall. But there are others about which we are free to choose, and in the light of experience it is sometimes prudent to discontinue something that used to be quite acceptable, as in the present case. It was not at all necessary that women who were still young should be admitted into the order of widows, experience had shown that it was a dangerous and harmful practice, so that Paul is right to want to guard against it in future so that nothing

similar should occur. And if the defection of some women was enough to persuade Paul to lay down a general rule to remedy the situation, how many good reasons would the Papists have today for abolishing their impure practice of celibacy, if they had any concern for what is edifying. But they choose rather to strangle countless millions of souls in the cruel bonds of an ungodly and devilish rule rather than loose a single knot: this shows what a difference there is between their savage cruelty and Paul's holy zeal.

After Satan. The expression should be noted, for no man can turn aside from Christ even by a hair's breadth without following Satan, for he is the lord of all who do not belong to Christ. Thus we are warned how fatal it is to turn aside from the right way, for it makes us Satan's slaves instead of God's children and brings us out from under Christ's government to be placed under Satan's sway.

16. *If any woman that believeth.* Since individuals are usually glad to cast their burdens on the whole Church, he expressly orders them to guard against this. He speaks of believers who ought to care for widows connected with them, for in the case of widows who renounced their relationships with unbelievers, it was right that they should be maintained by the Church. And if it is wrong for men to spare themselves and let the Church be burdened by expense, we can infer from this how much worse is the sacrilege of those who by fraud or robbery profane what was once dedicated to the Church.

> Let the elders that rule well be counted worthy of double honour, especially those who labour in the word and in teaching. For the scripture saith, Thou shalt not muzzle the ox when he treadeth out the corn. And the labourer is worthy of his hire. Against an elder receive not an accusation, except at the mouth of two or three witnesses. Them that sin reprove in the sight of all, that the rest also may be in fear. I charge thee in the sight of God, and Christ Jesus, and the elect angels, that thou observe these things without prejudice, doing nothing by partiality. (17-21)

17. *Let the elders that rule well.* To maintain the good order of the Church it is highly necessary that the presbyters should not be neglected but that due regard should be paid to them. For what could be more unkind than to have no care for those who have the care of the whole Church. Here πρεσβύτερος describes not an age but an office. I have no objection to Chrysostom's interpretation of *double honour* as meaning support and reverence, and anyone who wishes may follow him. But to me it seems more likely that there is a comparison here between presbyters and widows. Paul has formerly commanded that widows should be held in honour: but presbyters are more worthy of honour than they, and, in comparison with them, should be shown double

honour. But in order to make it clear that he does not commend shams he adds *who rule well*, that is who discharge their office faithfully and diligently. For although a person should obtain a position a hundred times over, and should boast of the title, unless he also fulfills the duties of the office, he has no right to ask to be maintained at the Church's expense. His meaning is, in short, that the honour is due not to the title, but to the work performed by those appointed to the office.

But he gives priority to those *who labour in the word and in teaching*, that is, those who are diligent in teaching the Word. For these two expressions mean the same thing, the preaching of the Word. But to prevent any misunderstanding that by the Word he means a purposeless, and as they call it, speculative study of it, he adds teaching. From this passage it may be inferred that there are two kinds of presbyters, since they were not all ordained to teach. The plain meaning of the words is that there were some who ruled well and honourably, but who did not hold a teaching office. The people elected earnest and well-tried men, who, along with the pastors in a common council and with the authority of the Church, would administer discipline and act as censors for the correction of morals. Ambrose complains that this custom has fallen into desuetude through the carelessness, or rather, the pride of the teachers who wanted undivided power for themselves. To return to Paul, he orders that a livelihood should be provided especially for the pastors who are engaged in teaching. For the ingratitude of the world is such that it is not very concerned about supporting ministers of the Word, and Satan uses this as a means of depriving the Church of teaching, by frightening many by a dread of poverty and want, so that they are unwilling to bear this burden.

18. *Thou shalt not muzzle the ox*. This is a 'political' precept, a general commendation of equity, as we have already said in dealing with Corinthians. For, if we are forbidden from being unkind to brute beasts, how much more kindness is required of us towards our fellow-men. His meaning is that they must not make a wrong use of the labours other men undertake on their behalf. At the present day the practice of treading out the corn is unknown in many parts of France, where flails are used for threshing. Only in Provence do they know what is meant by treading out the corn. But this has nothing to do with the meaning of the passage, for the same thing can be said about the ox that pulls the plough.

He does not quote *The labourer is worthy of his hire*, as a passage of Scripture but as a proverbial saying which common sense dictates to all. In the same way when Christ said the same thing to His apostles, He was expressing something which common consent acknowledged to be true. Thus it follows that those who allow cattle—to say nothing of men—whom they make to sweat for their own interests, to go hungry are cruel and forgetful of all the claims of equity. How much more intolerable is the ingratitude of those who refuse a livelihood to their pastors, who do for them something that it is quite impossible worthily to repay.

19. *Against an elder receive not an accusation.* Having given instructions about stipends for pastors, he now tells Timothy not to let them be exposed to slanderous attacks or burdened with unsubstantiated and unsupported accusations. It may seem absurd that he should state a law that applies to all men, as if it applied specially or exclusively to presbyters. For God requires in all cases that they should be established 'by the mouth of two or three witnesses' (Deut. 17.6, Matt. 18.16). Why then does the apostle evoke this law for the protection of presbyters alone, as if it were a privilege peculiar to them, to have their innocence protected against false accusations? I reply that it is necessary to guard against the malice of men in this way. For none are more exposed to slanders and insults than godly teachers. This comes not only from the difficulty of their duties, which are so great that sometimes they sink under them, or stagger or halt or take a false step, so that wicked men find many occasions of finding fault with them; but added to that, even when they do all their duties correctly and commit not even the smallest error, they never avoid a thousand criticisms. It is indeed a trick of Satan to estrange men from their ministers so as gradually to bring their teaching into contempt. In this way not only is wrong done to innocent people whose reputation is undeservedly injured, but the authority of God's holy teaching is diminished. And it is this that, as I have said, Satan is chiefly concerned to achieve, for not only does Plato's saying apply here that 'the multitudes are malicious and envy those above them', but the more sincerely any pastor strives to further Christ's kingdom, the more he is loaded with spite, the more fierce do the attacks upon him become. And not only so, but as soon as any charge is made against ministers of the Word, it is believed as surely and firmly as if it had been already proved. This happens not only because a higher standard of integrity is required from them, but because Satan makes most people, in fact nearly everyone, over credulous so that without investigation, they eagerly condemn their pastors whose good name they ought to be defending. Thus Paul has good reason for preventing such a great injustice and he says that presbyters are not to be given over to the malice of evil men till they have been convicted by legal testimony. And indeed it is no wonder that they have so many enemies, since it is their duty to reprove the faults of all men, to oppose all wicked desires and to restrain by their severity all whom they see to be going astray. What therefore

would be the result if we were to pay heed indiscriminately to all the slanders that are spread abroad about them?

20. *Them that sin reprove in the sight of all.* Whenever some measure is taken for the protection of good men, bad men twist it to keep themselves from condemnation. Thus Paul here modifies what he has just said about unjust accusations, so that none may be able on this pretext to escape the punishment due to his sin. And certainly we can see with how many different privileges the Papacy protects its clergy, so that even if they live the most scandalous lives, they are yet immune from every accusation. Certainly, if all the safeguards Gratian piled up are observed (*Caus.* ii, q. 4 & q. 7), there will be no danger of their ever being forced to give an account of their lives. Where will they find the seventy-two witnesses required to condemn a bishop under the disgraceful decree of Sylvester? Furthermore, since all laymen are forbidden to bring any accusation, and the inferior clergy forbidden to give trouble to their superiors, what is to prevent them laughing with impunity at all judgments made against them? It is therefore right to observe Paul's moderate instructions most carefully, so that insolent tongues shall be restrained from defaming presbyters with trumped up accusations and yet that every one of them who behaves badly shall be severely corrected. For I take this injunction to apply to presbyters, that those who live dissolute lives should be publicly reproved. Why so? In order that the others, seeing that not even those who are superior in rank and worth are spared, may take warning from such an example and fear the more. For just as presbyters show the way to others by the example of an honourable life, so, if they go wrong, it is right that severe discipline should be exercised against them as an example to all. For why should greater forbearance be shown to men whose faults do more serious harm than those of other men? Let it be understood that Paul speaks here of crimes or heinous sins which give rise to public scandal, for if any presbyter commits a fault not in that category, it is clearly preferable that he should be admonished privately rather than openly accused.

21. *I charge thee in the sight of God.* Paul brought in this solemn appeal, because this was a matter not only of the most serious importance but also of the most extreme difficulty. There is nothing harder than to pronounce judgment with complete impartiality, so as to avoid showing undue favour, or giving rise to suspicions, or being influenced by unfavourable reports, or being excessively strict and in every case to consider nothing but the matter in hand. Only by closing our eyes to personal considerations can we reach an equitable judgment. Let us remember that in this warning to Timothy all pastors are included, and by it Timothy is being shielded against all wicked desires which

often give trouble even to the best of men. He thus sets Timothy in God's presence that he may know that he should exercise his office with as much conscientious care, as if he were doing it in the presence of God and His angels. Having mentioned God, he adds Christ also, for it is to Him that the Father has made over all His own authority to pass judgment, and it is before His judgment seat that we shall all one day appear. He adds to Christ the angels, not that they are judges, but as future witnesses of carelessness or rashness or self-seeking or bad faith. They are present as spectators, for they have been given charge to care for the Church. And indeed the man who is not shaken out of his carelessness and laziness by the thought that the government of the Church is conducted under the eye of God and His angels must be worse than stupid, and have a heart harder than stone. And when this solemn appeal is added, our fear and anxiety must be redoubled. He calls the angels *elect* not only to distinguish them from reprobate angels, but on account of their excellence, that their testimony may awaken deeper reverence.

Without prejudice. Πρόκριμα means quite literally prejudice—a judgment made beforehand. But its meaning is rather the excessive haste we show in rashly pronouncing a judgment on a matter we have not well considered, or our immoderate partiality in deferring to people more than we should, or in preferring some because we think them better than others. In the decisions of a judge this is always wrong. Thus what Paul is condemning here is either lack of serious care, or respect of persons. What follows has more or less the same purpose, that there must be no turning aside to one side or the other. It is impossible to over-emphasize the difficulty of those who exercise the office of judge in keeping themselves from being influenced by the attacks that are made upon their partiality from so many different quarters. Some manuscripts read πρόσκλησιν but the other reading is better.

> *Lay hands hastily on no man, neither be partaker of other men's sins; keep thyself pure. Be no longer a drinker of water, but use a little wine for thy stomach's sake and thine often infirmities. Some men's sins are evident, going before unto judgment; and in some men also they follow after. In like manner also there are good works that are evident; and such as are otherwise cannot be hid. (22-25)*

22. *Lay hands hastily on no man.* There can be no doubt that he wished to guard Timothy from ill-will and to avoid the many complaints which are continually arising against the godly servants of Christ, when they refuse to comply with the self-seeking requests that are continually being made to them. Some accuse them of being stern,

others of being spiteful, some even protest that they are cruel if they do not immediately accept those who recommend themselves to them by boasting of their own good qualities—and we have more than enough experience of all these in our own day. Paul advises Timothy not to depart from a judicious caution and not to let himself be carried away by undue enthusiasm; not that Timothy needed such an exhortation, but Paul wanted by his authority to restrain others who might have given Timothy trouble.

The laying on of hands means ordination. He uses the sign for the thing signified and forbids him to admit too easily any who have not been fully examined. There are those who out of a desire for novelty would seek to ordain some person who is hardly known at all, just because he has given one or two not unsatisfactory performances. It is the duty of a prudent and earnest bishop to resist this impetuous desire, as Paul tells Timothy to do here.

Neither be partaker. He means that the bishop who assents to an illicit act of ordination brings on himself the same guilt as its impetuous instigators. Some explain it thus, 'if he admits those who are unworthy, any faults they may later commit will involve him in blame, or at least in part of it'. I think the following a simpler explanation, 'Though others rush at this rashly, do not associate yourself with them, lest you share their guilt.' For it often happens that even when our own judgment is sound, we allow ourselves to be carried away by the folly and stupidity of others.

Keep thyself pure. I understand this still to refer to the same subject, as if he had said, 'If others do anything wrong, see that you are not involved in its contagion by giving it your assent and approbation. If you cannot stop them from polluting themselves, you should hold aloof from their counsels, so that you may keep yourself pure.' If anyone prefers a more general explanation, he is welcome to his opinion, but my own interpretation in my view suits the context better.

23. *Be no longer a drinker of water.* Because this statement interrupts the train of thought, some suspect that Paul did not write it. But we have noticed that Paul is not always careful about the order or arrangement of what he says, and it is not at all unusual for him to mix up statements on different subjects without any order. Also it is possible that what was originally a note in the margin found its way in at this point by a transcriber's error. But there is no need to take much trouble over this question, if we bear in mind what I have just said about Paul's habit of sometimes mixing different subjects.

What he says amounts to this, that Timothy should form the habit of drinking a little wine for his health's sake. He does not forbid him to use water at all but tells him only not to make it his customary drink.

That is what the verb ὑδροποτεῖν means. But why does he not simply advise him to drink wine? He seems by speaking of 'a little' wine to be guarding against intemperance, and yet surely there was no fear of that in a man like Timothy. My explanation is that it was put this way to obviate the slanders of wicked men who would otherwise have been quick to pour scorn on his advice, either for this reason or some other like it, 'What sort of philosophy is this which encourages a man to drink wine? Is this the way we rise to heaven?' To meet jeers of this kind, Paul says that he is providing only for a case of necessity, and at the same time he recommends moderation. It is clear that Timothy was so frugal and indeed austere in his way of life, that he did not even take proper care of his health. It is certain that his motive for doing this was neither ambition nor superstition. From this we infer that he was not only far from indulging in delicacies and luxury, but to make himself more ready for the Lord's work, he even refrained from some of his ordinary food. He abstained therefore not from natural inclination but in his zeal for continence. How few there are today who need to be forbidden water, how many rather that need to be restricted to drinking wine soberly! It is also evident how needful it is for us, even when we want to act aright, to ask from the Lord the Spirit of wisdom who will teach us moderation. Timothy indeed had the right intentions, but, since he was rebuked by the Spirit of God, we are taught that his excessive austerity was a fault. At the same time a general rule is enunciated, that, while we should be temperate in eating and drinking, every one of us should take care of his health, not for the sake of prolonging life, but so that, as long as we live, we may be useful and profitable to God and our neighbours.

And if excessive abstinence is blameworthy when it brings on or promotes disease, how much more should superstition be avoided! What judgment shall we pass on the obstinacy of the Carthusians who would rather have died than tasted a morsel of flesh in extreme necessity? And if those who live frugally and soberly are commanded not to injure their health by excessive austerity, no light punishment awaits intemperate people who waste their strength in gluttony. Such people do not need merely to be admonished, but like brute beasts to be held back from their fodder.

24. *Some men's sins are evident.* Nothing is more distressing to faithful ministers of the Church than to fail to see any way of correcting evils, to be compelled to bear with hypocrites whose wickedness they know, to be unable to exclude from the Church many who are harmful pests, or even to stop them from spreading their poison by secret arts. And so Paul sustains Timothy with this consolation, that some day, when it pleases God, they shall be publicly exposed. In this way he

confirms him in patience, for he ought calmly to wait for the right time which God in His wisdom has appointed. There is another kind of base conduct which sorely distresses good and holy pastors, that, when they have conscientiously discharged their duties, they are provoked by many unfair criticisms, they are burdened by much ill-will, they see actions that deserve praise being blamed instead. Paul deals with this too, by telling Timothy that there are some good works which will come to light only at a later time. Thus, if the praise due to them is, so to speak, buried deep in the earth because of men's ingratitude, that also should be borne with equanimity till the time of revelation comes.

But he does more than provide a remedy for these ills. We often fail in choosing ministers, for unworthy men steal in by craft, and the right men are unknown to us; or, though we ourselves judge rightly, we cannot bring others to accept our judgment, so that the best men are rejected in spite of all our efforts, and evil men either insinuate or force themselves forward. In these circumstances the state of the Church and our own situation inevitably give rise to great anxiety. Paul makes a strenuous effort to remove, or at least to alleviate, this cause of offence. His meaning may be summed up as follows, 'Things that cannot immediately be set to rights must be endured; we must suffer and sigh till the time is ripe for a remedy, and we must not apply force to diseases, till they either mature or are exposed. On the other hand, when virtue does not attain its due reward, we must await the full time of revelation, bear with the world's stupidity and wait quietly in the darkness till the day dawns.' Having thus briefly explained his general meaning, I turn to the words themselves.

When he says *Some men's sins are evident before* he means that they are discovered early and come to men's knowledge, as it were, before the time. He says the same thing in a different way when he adds that they run or hasten to their judgment. We see many people who rush on precipitately and of set purpose bring condemnation upon themselves, although the whole world desires to save them. Whenever this happens let us remember that the reprobate are urged on to their own ruin by the secret instigation of God's providence.

And in some they follow after. Erasmus' rendering, 'Some they follow after', I do not accept. Although it would seem to suit the Greek construction better, the sense requires us to understand the preposition ἐν, for the change of case does not destroy the contrast. He has said that the sins of some hasten fast to their judgment, and now he adds the converse that the sins of others are noticed more slowly. But instead of the genitive 'of some', he uses the dative 'in some'. His meaning however is that, although some men's sins are concealed longer than we would wish and come late to light, yet they will not stay hidden for ever, they will have their time. If Erasmus' rendering is preferred, the meaning must remain the same, that, although God's vengeance does not hasten, it follows slowly behind.

25. *In like manner also there are good works.* He means that sometimes godliness and other virtues win men's praise quickly and opportunely, so that good men are held in honour. But if that does not happen, the Lord will not allow innocence and uprightness to be oppressed for ever. They are often obscured by clouds of slanderous accusations, but at last the promise will be fulfilled (Dan. 2.3, Matt. 13.43). God will make them shine forth like the dawn. But we need a calm spirit to endure, for we are men and we must always observe the limitations of our knowledge and not overstep them, for that would be to usurp the prerogative of God.

CHAPTER SIX

Let as many as are servants under the yoke count their own masters worthy of all honour, that the name of God and the doctrine be not blasphemed. And they that have believing masters, let them not despise them because they are brethren; but let them serve them rather because they that partake of the benefit are believing and beloved. (1-2)

It appears that in the early days of the Gospel slaves were full of expectation, as if the signal for their emancipation had been given, for in many passages Paul has to restrain that desire. And certainly slavery was such a hard condition that it is no wonder it was exceedingly hated. Now it usually happens that men grasp firmly at anything that has the slightest appearance of being to the advantage of the flesh. Thus when told that we are all brothers, they at once drew the conclusion that it was unreasonable for them to be the slaves of brethren. But even if none of this ever occurred to them, wretched men always stand in need of consolation to soothe the bitterness of their afflictions. Besides it was a hard thing to persuade them to bend their necks willingly and cheerfully to so harsh a yoke. Such is the aim of Paul's teaching here.

1. *As many as are servants.* Because of the false persuasion of his own excellence that every man entertains, there is no one who cheerfully submits to having others rule over him. Those who cannot avoid the necessity do unwillingly obey those who are over them, but inwardly they fret and rage, because they think they suffer injury. The apostle with a single word puts an end to all disputes of this kind by requiring a voluntary submission from all those who are under the yoke. He means that they should not ask whether they deserve that lot or a better one; it should be enough that they are bound to that condition.

When he enjoins them to *count worthy of honour the masters* whom they serve, he requires from them not only faithfulness and diligence in performing their duties, but that they should regard with sincere respect their masters as people placed in a higher rank than themselves. No man renders what is due to a prince or a master, unless he has regard to the eminence to which God has raised them, and thus honours them as one subject to them. For though they are often unworthy, the very authority which God bestows upon them always entitles them to honour. Besides, no man willingly renders service and obedience to his master, unless he believes that he ought to do so. Thus submission begins with this honour of which Paul wishes rulers to be accounted worthy.

That the name of God. We are always more ingenious than we should be when it comes to seeking our own advantage. Thus slaves who have unbelieving masters are always ready with the objection that it is wrong that those who serve the devil should rule over the sons of God. But Paul uses the same argument to reach the opposite conclusion, that they should obey unbelieving masters in order that the name of God and of the Gospel should not be evil spoken of; as though the God whom we worship were inciting us to rebellion; as though the Gospel were making obstinate and disobedient those whose duty it was to be subject to others.

2. *And they that have believing masters.* The name of brother might appear to establish equality and abolish domination. But Paul argues that on the contrary slaves should submit themselves the more willingly to masters, because they acknowledge them to be God's children, and are bound to them by ties of brotherly love and share with them in the same grace. It is no small honour that God has made us equal to the lords of this earth in the thing that matters most, for we share with them the same adoption. This should be a powerful inducement to bear servitude with patience. Besides servitude is more endurable under mild masters who love us and whom we love. For the bond of faith reconciles those of very different rank and status.

> *These things teach and exhort. If any man teacheth a different doctrine, and consenteth not to sound words, even the words of our Lord Jesus Christ, and to the doctrine which is according to godliness; he is puffed up, knowing nothing, but doting about questionings and disputes of words, whereof cometh envy, strife, railings, evil surmisings, wranglings of men corrupted in mind and bereft of the truth, supposing that godliness is a way of gain. (2–5)*

2. *These things teach and exhort.* He means that these are things he ought to teach with persistent emphasis, and desires that exhortation should accompany the teaching. It is as if he had said that this kind of teaching should be repeated daily and that men need not only to be taught but also roused and urged on by frequent exhortations.

3. *If any man teacheth a different doctrine.* The word in the Greek is a compound verb and may also be rendered 'to teach other things'. But there is no doubt about his meaning; he is condemning all who do not accept this kind of teaching, even if they do not openly and avowedly oppose sound doctrine. It is possible not to profess any ungodly or manifest error and yet to corrupt the doctrine of godliness by silly boastful babbling. For when there is no progress or edification from any teaching, it has already departed from the institution of Christ.

But although Paul is not speaking of the avowed originators of ungodly doctrines, but rather about empty and irreligious teachers, who out of self-seeking or avarice deform the simple and genuine doctrine of godliness, yet we see how sharply and vehemently he attacks them. And it is no wonder; for it is almost impossible to overstate the amount of harm done by hypocritical preaching, whose only aim is ostentation and vain display. But it becomes clearer from what follows whom exactly he is blaming here. For the next clause—*and consenteth not to sound words*—is intended as an explanation for men of that kind, carried away by foolish curiosity, usually despise anything profitable and solid, and indulge in foolish antics, like unruly horses. And what is that but to reject *the sound words of Christ*? They are called sound because their effect is to confer soundness upon us, or because they are fitted to promote soundness.

Doctrine which is according to godliness means the same. For it will be consistent with godliness only if it establishes us in the fear and worship of God, if it builds up our faith, if it trains us in patience and humility and all the duties of love. Thus anyone who does not try to teach profitably, does not teach rightly; whatever display it may make, teaching is not sound unless it tends to the profit of its hearers. Paul charges these profitless teachers first with foolish and empty pride. Secondly, since the best punishment for self-seekers is to condemn all the things they delight in as ignorance, he says that they *know nothing*, though they are puffed up with many subtle arguments. They have nothing solid but only empty wind. At the same time he warns all godly men not to let themselves be carried away by that kind of vain display but to remain rather steadfast in the simplicity of the Gospel.

4. *Doting about questionings.* Here is an indirect comparison between the soundness of Christ's teaching and this 'doting'. For when these subtle questioners have wearied themselves with their long-winded talk, what result have they to show for all their efforts except that their disease grows worse continually? Not only do they spend themselves for nothing, but their foolish curiosity brings about this doting. Thus it follows that they are far from profiting rightly from their teaching, as Christ's disciples should.

Paul has good reason to mention together *questionings and disputes of words*, for by the first term he does not mean the kind of question that either springs from a moderate and sober desire to learn, or contributes to a clear explanation of useful points, but rather the kind of question that today is dealt with in the schools of the Sorbonne, to make a display of intellectual ability. There one question leads to another, for there is no end to them, when everybody indulges his vanity in seeking to know more than he ought, and these give rise to infinite quarrels. As in hot weather thick clouds cannot be dispersed without thunder, so these thorny questions are bound to break out into disputes. He gives the name λογομαχία to contentious disputes concerned with words rather than with anything real, which are, as is commonly said, without substance or foundation. If anyone investigates carefully the kind of questions that are of burning concern to sophists, he will find that they do not arise from anything real, but are concocted out of nothing. In short, Paul's purpose was to condemn all questions which would involve us in sharp disputes over matters of no consequence.

Whereof cometh envy. He shows from its results how much we should try to avoid an ambitious curiosity; for ambition is the mother of envy. And wherever envy is in control, there also come rage, brawlings, contentions and the other evils Paul enumerates here.

He adds that by such things men are *corrupted in mind and bereft of the truth.* It is quite clear that here he is censuring the sophists who have no concern for edification and turn God's Word into trivialities and a source of ingenious discussions. If his only point was that by this the doctrine of salvation was made of no effect, that in itself would be an intolerable profanation, but his reproof is far heavier and graver, for he shows the pernicious evils and harmful plagues that result from this. From this passage we should learn to detest sophistry as a thing inconceivably harmful to the Church of God.

5. *Godliness is a way of gain.* The meaning is that godliness is equivalent to gain or is a way of making gain, because for these men all Christianity is to be measured by the gains it brings. It is as if the oracles of the Holy Spirit had been given for no other purpose than to serve their avarice; they do business with them as though they were goods up for sale. Paul forbids the servants of Christ to have any dealings with such men. He does not only forbid Timothy from imitating them, but tells him to avoid them as harmful pests. Although they do not openly oppose the Gospel, but make a profession of it, yet their company is infectious. Besides if the crowd sees us to be familiar with these men, there is a danger that they will use our friendship to insinuate themselves into its favour. We should therefore take great pains to make everyone understand that we are quite different from them, and have nothing at all in common with them.

But godliness with contentment is great gain: for we brought nothing into the world, for neither can we carry anything out; but having food and covering we shall be therewith content. But they that desire to be rich fall into a temptation and a snare and many foolish and hurtful lusts, such as drown men in destruction and perdition. For the love of money is a root of all kinds of evil: which some reaching after have been led astray from the faith, and have pierced themselves through with many sorrows. (6-10)

6. *Godliness with contentment is great gain.* In an elegant manner and with an ironical turn he quickly throws back at his opponents the same words with the opposite meaning, as if he had said, 'They act wrongly and wickedly in making merchandise of Christ's teaching, as if godliness were gain, and yet understood rightly it is true that godliness is a great and most abundant gain.' He calls it so, because it brings us full and perfect blessedness. Those who are bent on acquiring money and who make godliness contribute to their gain are therefore guilty of sacrilege. But godliness is itself a sufficiently great gain to us, because through it we become not only the heirs of the world but are enabled to enjoy Christ and all His riches.

With contentment. This may refer either to an inner disposition or to a sufficiency of wealth. If it is understood as a disposition, the meaning will be that the godly who desire nothing but are content with their poverty have obtained a great gain. But if it is taken to mean a sufficiency of possessions—an interpretation just as acceptable to me—it will be a promise like that of Ps. 34.10, 'The lions do lack and suffer hunger; but they that seek the Lord shall not want any good thing.' The Lord is always present with His people and, according as their necessity requires it, He bestows on each His portion from His own fulness. Thus true blessedness consists in godliness and this sufficiency is as good as an increase of gain.

7. *For we brought nothing into the world.* He adds this in order to define the limit of what is sufficient for us. Our covetousness is an insatiable abyss, unless it be restrained and the best way to hold it in check is that we should desire nothing more than the necessity of this life demands; for the reason why we do not accept the limit is that our anxiety stretches over a thousand lifetimes, which we vainly imagine to ourselves. Nothing is more common and nothing more generally agreed than this statement of Paul's, but as soon as we have all agreed with it—we see this happening every day—every man foresees that his wants will swallow up vast fortunes, as if he had a stomach large enough to contain half the earth. This is what Ps. 49.13 says, 'Although the folly of the fathers appears in hoping to dwell here forever; yet their posterity approve of their way.' To ensure that a sufficiency will satisfy us, let us learn to control our desires so that we may want no more than is necessary to support our life. When he names food and covering he excludes luxury and overflowing abundance. For nature is content with a little and all that goes beyond natural usage is super-

fluous. Not that a more liberal use of possessions should be condemned as bad in itself, but a desire for it is always sinful.

9. *They that desire to be rich.* Having exhorted Timothy to contentment and to despise riches, he now warns him how dangerous a desire for them can be and especially in ministers of the Church, who are his special concern here. It is not riches that are the cause of the evils Paul mentions here, but a desire for them, even if the person is poor. And here he is describing not only what generally happens but what is almost always bound to happen. For all who have as their aim this ambition to be rich, give themselves over into captivity to the devil. What the heathen poet says is most true, 'He who wishes to be rich also wishes to be rich quickly.' Thus it follows that all who violently desire to be rich are carried away by their impetuosity. This is the source of these foolish, or rather, mad impulses that later plunge them into ruin. This evil is universal, but it shows up more conspicuously in pastors of the Church, for they are so maddened by greed that they will stop at nothing, however foolish, as soon as the glitter of silver or gold dazzles their eyes.

10. *For the love of money.* There is no need to be too careful in comparing other vices with this. It is true that ambition and pride often bring forth worse fruits, and yet ambition does not spring from covetousness. The same is true of sexual lusts. But it was not Paul's intention to include under covetousness every kind of vice we can name. What then does he mean? Simply that innumerable evils do spring from it, just as we often use the same form of expression when we say that discord or gluttony or drunkenness or any other vice of that kind produce every kind of evil. And it is especially true of the base greed for gain, that it produces all sorts of evils every day: countless frauds, falsehoods, perjury, cheating, robbery, cruelty, judicial corruption, quarrels, hatred, poisonings, murders, and nearly every other kind of crime. Statements of this kind occur again and again in heathen writers and those who applaud hyperboles in Horace or Ovid have no right to complain of Paul's extravagant language. Daily experience proves that he has simply, alas, described the facts as they are. But let us remember that the crimes that spring from avarice may also arise, and often do, from ambition or envy or other evil dispositions.

Which some reaching after. The Greek word ὀρεγόμενοι is not used properly here, in saying that they reach after the love of money, but there is no difficulty about the meaning, which is that from avarice there can come the greatest evil of all—apostasy from the faith. Those who suffer from this plague gradually degenerate till they completely renounce the faith. Hence those *sorrows* which he mentions, for I take him to mean the dire torments of conscience which usually befall men past all hope; though God has also other methods for trying covetous men and making them their own tormentors.

But thou, o man of God, flee these things; and follow after righteousness, godliness, faith, love, patience, meekness. Fight the good fight of faith, lay hold on the life eternal, whereunto thou wast called, and didst confess the good confession in the sight of many witnesses. I charge thee in the sight of God, who quickeneth all things, and of Christ Jesus, who before Pontius Pilate witnessed the good confession; that thou keep the commandment, without spot, without reproach, until the appearing of our Lord Jesus Christ: which in his own times he shall show, who is the blessed and only Potentate, the King of kings and Lord of lords; who only hath immortality dwelling in light unapproachable; whom no man hath seen, nor can see: to whom be honour and power eternal. Amen. (11-16)

11. *But thou, o man of God, flee these things.* By calling Timothy a man of God he adds weight to his exhortation. If it is thought right to restrict the application of his call to *follow after righteousness, goodness, faith and patience* to what he has just been saying, then this will be his remedy for correcting greed for money. He tells Timothy that the desires he ought to follow are spiritual. But it can apply more broadly to the wider context, that Timothy, by keeping himself free of all vanity, should avoid that vain curiosity, περιεργίαν, which he condemned a little before. He who is fully occupied with necessary concerns will easily keep free of things that are superfluous. He mentions certain sorts of virtue, under which we may take it that others are also included. Everyone who devotes himself to the pursuit of righteousness, who aims at godliness, faith and love and follows patience and meekness, cannot but abhor avarice and its fruits.

12. *Fight the good fight.* In the next epistle he says that no man who is a soldier becomes involved in matters alien to his calling. Thus here, to restrain Timothy from excessive concern with earthly cares, he exhorts him to fight. Carelessness and self-indulgence spring from the desire of men to serve Christ without trouble, as if it were a pastime, whereas Christ calls all His servants to warfare. To encourage him to fight this fight bravely he calls it good, that is blessed, and therefore not in any way to be avoided. For if earthly soldiers do not hesitate to fight when the outcome is uncertain and they are in danger of death, how much more bravely ought we to fight under the guidance and banner of Christ, where we can be certain beforehand of victory, more especially since a reward awaits us, far beyond the rewards usually given by commanders to their men, a glorious immortality and heavenly blessedness. It would be unworthy, if with such a hope before us we should faint or grow weary. And this is what he goes on to say.

Lay hold on the life eternal. It is as if he had said, 'God calls thee to life eternal, therefore despise the world and strive to obtain it.' By telling them to lay hold upon it, he forbids them to give up or grow weary in mid course as if he had said, 'Nothing has been achieved until we have obtained the future life to which God invites us.' Thus in Phil. 3.12 he declares that he still strives to make progress because he has not yet attained.

But since men would fight rashly and to no purpose if they did not have God to direct their course, to stimulate them into activity, he mentions also their *calling*. Nothing can fill us with courage more than the knowledge that we have been called by God. For from that we may infer that our labour, which is under God's direction and in which He stretches out His hand to us, will not be in vain. Thus it would be a very serious accusation against us to have rejected God's call. It should however be the strongest encouragement to us to be told, 'God hath called thee to eternal life. Beware of being distracted by anything else or of falling short in any way, before thou hast obtained it.'

And didst confess the good confession. By mentioning Timothy's former life Paul incites him still more to persevere. It is more shameful to fail after having made a good beginning than never to have begun at all. He addresses this powerful argument to Timothy, who, up till now, had acted valiantly and won praise, that his end should correspond to his beginning. By confession I take him to mean not something spoken in words but rather something actually performed and that, not on a single occasion but throughout his whole ministry. Thus the meaning is, 'You have many witnesses of your clear confession both in Ephesus and in other countries, who have seen you living out faithfully and seriously your profession of the Gospel and, having thus given such a good example, you cannot now show yourself to be anything but a good soldier of Christ without incurring the greatest shame and disgrace.' By this we are taught the general lesson that the more we excel, the less excusable it is if we then fail, and the more we are bound to carry on in the right course.

13. *I charge thee.* By the vehemence of this solemn appeal Paul shows how difficult and rare an achievement it is to persevere rightly in the ministry of the Gospel right to the end. Although he is exhorting others through Timothy, he here addresses him personally as well.

The things he says about Christ and God are relevant to the present subject. When he ascribes to God the *quickening of all things*, he wishes to meet the offence of the Cross, which offers nothing but the appearance of death. His meaning is therefore that we should shut our eyes when ungodly men show us the threat of death, or rather we should fix our gaze on God alone who restores the dead to life. The whole point is that, turning away from the world, we should learn to look only to God.

What he immediately adds concerning *Christ* provides a remarkable confirmation of this. For we are reminded that we are not sitting at Plato's feet to learn philosophy and to hear him carrying on useless disputations in the shade, but the teaching we profess has been ratified by the death of the Son of God. For Christ made His *confession before Pilate* not in many words but in reality, that is by His voluntary submission to death. For although Christ chose to keep silent before Pilate rather than speak in His own defence, since He had come there already devoted to a certain condemnation, yet in His very silence there was a defence of His teaching no less magnificent than if He had pleaded His case with a loud voice. For He ratified it with His own blood and with the sacrifice of His death better than with any words. He calls this a *good* confession. Socrates also died and yet his death was not a satisfying confirmation of the doctrine he held. But when we are told that the blood of God was shed, this is an authentic seal to His teaching that takes all our doubt away. Thus, whenever our hearts waver, let us remember immediately to look to the death of Christ for strength. What cowardice it would be to desert such a leader who goes before us to show us the way.

14. *That thou keep the commandment.* By the word commandment here he means all that he has said up to now about Timothy's office, the sum of which was that he should show himself a minister faithful to Christ and the Church. For there is no need to extend the meaning to include the whole Law. It is much simpler to take it in relation to the duties of the office that has been laid upon him. For we are made ministers of the Church only on condition that God lays down all that He wishes us to do. Thus to keep the commandment means to discharge in good faith the duty laid upon him. I certainly take it as referring entirely to Timothy's ministry.

The case and inflection of the two adjectives that follow would allow them to refer either to the commandment or to Timothy, but the translation I have given, which refers them to Timothy, is much the more suitable. Paul tells Timothy he must take great care over the sanctity of his life and the purity of his ways, if he wishes to discharge his office aright.

Until the appearing of our Lord Jesus Christ. It is impossible to overemphasize the necessity at that time for all godly men to have their minds fixed entirely upon the day of Christ, since innumerable offences were taking place all over the world. They were being attacked on every side, everyone hated them and cursed them, they were exposed to general mockery and every day they were opposed by fresh afflictions: and meanwhile no fruit of all their many toils and troubles could be seen. What remained except in thought to fly away to that blessed day of our redemption? But the same reasons hold equally today with us. Satan shows us so many things that, apart from this hope, would a thousand times draw us away from the right course. I say nothing of fire and sword and exiles and all the furious attacks of our enemies, I say nothing of slanders and other such vexations. How many things there are within that are far worse! Ambitious men openly attack us, Epicureans and Lucianists mock at us, impudent men insult us, hypocrites rage against us, those who are wise after the flesh do us harm, indirectly, and we are harassed in many different ways on every side. It is in short a great miracle that, weighed down by the burden of such a heavy and dangerous office, any one of us should persevere. The only remedy for all these difficulties is to look forward to Christ's appearing and always to put our trust in it.

Because we are sometimes hasty in our wishes and come near to prescribing a day and an hour to God, in case He should delay in executing what He has promised, Paul takes an early opportunity to restrain overhasty expectations of Christ's advent. That is the force of the words, *which in His own times He will show*. Men wait for something with greater patience when they know that the right time for it has not yet arrived. The only way in which we can patiently bear with the order of nature is to let ourselves be restrained by the thought that we should be acting inopportunely, if we allowed our desires to struggle against it. We know that a time for Christ's appearing has been appointed and we ought patiently to wait for it.

15. *The blessed and only Potentate*. These titles of honour are used to exalt God's kingly power so that we may not be dazzled by the brilliancy of the princes of this world. Such instruction was specially needed at that time when the greatness and power of all the kingdoms were tending to obscure the majesty and glory of God. For all the men of power were not only deadly enemies of God's kingdom, but were arrogantly attacking God and trampling His holy name under their feet. And the more proudly they poured scorn on true religion, the more successful they thought themselves. In such a situation who would not have reached the conclusion that God was miserably defeated and oppressed? We see in Cicero's *Pro Flacco* what heights of insolence he reaches against the Jews because of their afflicted state. When good men see the ungodly thus puffed up with prosperity, they are sometimes cast down; thus to turn their eyes from that passing splendour, Paul ascribes to God alone blessing, principality and kingly power. In calling Him the only Prince, he is not overthrowing civil government, as though there should be no magistrates or kings in the

world; he means that it is God alone who rules in His own right and by His own power. This follows from the next phrase which is added by way of explanation.

King of kings and Lord of lords. He means that the powers of this world are subject to His supreme dominion, depend upon Him, and stand or fall at His will. God's authority is beyond all comparison, because all the rest are nothing before His glory and whereas they fade and quickly perish, His authority will endure for ever.

16. *Who only hath immortality.* Paul is concerned here to show that there is no happiness, no worth or excellence, no life apart from God. He now says that God alone is immortal, that we may know that we and all His creatures do not live of ourselves, but only borrow life from Him. From this it follows that when we look up to God as the source of immortality, we should hail this present life as of no worth. But the objection may be raised that immortality belongs to the soul of men and to angels and thus cannot be said to belong to God alone. My answer is that Paul is not denying that God confers immortality on whatever of His creatures He chooses, but it is still true that only He possesses it. It is as if he had said that God is not only immortal in His own right and by His own nature, but has immortality in His power, so that it does not belong to creatures, except in so far as He imparts to them strength and power. For if you take away God's strength which is instilled in the human soul, it will immediately fade away and the same may be said of the angels. Thus, strictly speaking, immortality does not have its seat in the souls either of men or angels, but is imparted from another source—the secret inspiration of God, as Acts 17.28 has it, 'In him we live and move and have our being.' If anyone desires a fuller and more detailed discussion of these points, he should read the twelfth book of Augustine's *City of God*.

Dwelling in light. He means two things, that God is hidden from us, and yet the cause of His obscurity does not lie in Him, as though He were shrouded in darkness, but in us who cannot approach His light because of the weakness of our perception or rather the dullness of our minds. We must take Him to mean that God's light is *unapproachable* to anyone who tries to approach it in his own strength. For if God in His grace had not opened a way of access to us, the prophet would not say, 'Those who draw near to Him are enlightened' (Ps. 34.5). Yet it is true that while we are circumscribed by this mortal flesh, we shall never penetrate into the heart of God's deepest secrets so completely that nothing is hidden from us. For we know in part and we see through a glass darkly (I Cor. 13.9-12). Thus by faith we do enter into God's light, but only in part, so that it is still rightly said to be a light unapproachable to man.

Whom no man hath seen. This is added to explain the same point more clearly, that men may learn to look in faith to Him whose face they cannot see with their eyes, or even with the understanding of their minds. For I take this to refer not only to our bodily eyes, but also to the mind's faculty of discernment. We must always consider what the apostle's purpose is. It is hard for us to overlook and disregard all those things of which we have present vision, in order to strive after God, whom we never see. For always the thought comes into our minds, 'How do you know there is any God when you only hear of Him but do not see Him?' The apostle forearms us against this danger by saying that this is not a question for our senses, since it exceeds our capacity. We do not see Him because our sight is not keen enough to reach to such a height. Augustine enters into a long discussion of this statement because it seems to contradict I John 3.2, 'Then we shall see Him as He is, for we shall be like Him.' This is a question he discusses in many passages, but I think his best answer to it is to be found in his letter to the widow Pauline. As far as the meaning of the present passage is concerned, the answer is simple, that we cannot see God in our present nature, as he says elsewhere, 'Flesh and blood cannot inherit the kingdom of God' (I Cor. 15.50). For we must be renewed and made like God before it can be given to us to see Him. Thus to keep our curiosity within limits, let us always remember that in seeking an answer to this question, the way we live is of more importance than the way we speak. And let us also remember the wise caution Augustine gives us, to be on our guard, lest, while we are disputing about how God can be seen, we lose that peace and holiness without which no man can ever see Him at all.

> *Charge them that are rich in this present world, that they be not highminded, nor have their hope set on the uncertainty of riches, but on God, who giveth us richly all things to enjoy; that they do good, that they be rich in good works, that they be ready to distribute, willing to communicate; laying up in store for themselves a good foundation against the time to come, that they may lay hold on the life which is life indeed. O Timothy, guard that which is committed unto thee, turning away from the profane babblings and oppositions of the knowledge which is falsely so called; which some professing have erred concerning the faith. Grace be with you.* (17-21)
>
> *The first epistle to Timothy was sent from Laodicea which is the capital of Pacatian Phrygia.*

17. *Charge them that are rich.* Since many of the Christians were poor and down-trodden, it is probable that, as usually happens, they were despised by the rich and that might especially be the case in Ephesus,

which was an opulent city; for in such places pride is apt to be even worse. But let us learn from this what a dangerous thing material affluence is. Paul has good reason to address such a severe warning especially to the rich; it is to remedy the faults which almost always accompany riches, just as our shadow accompanies our body, and this happens through the depravity of our minds which make of the gifts of God occasions for sin. He mentions specifically two things of which rich men ought to beware, pride and false security, the first springing from the second. It looks as if *nor have their hope etc.* was added so that Paul might draw attention to the source of their pride. The only reason why rich men grow insolent and take great delight in despising others is that they imagine that they themselves are specially and supremely blessed. The vain confidence comes first and the haughtiness follows.

When Paul wishes to correct these faults, he first speaks slightingly of riches, for the phrase *in this world* is intended to lower them in our esteem. For all that belongs to this world shares its nature, so that it is fleeting and quickly passes away. He shows the falseness and emptiness of the confidence that is placed in riches by reminding us that our possession of them is so transitory that it is like a thing unknown. For when we think we have them, in a moment they slip out of our hands. How foolish it is to place our hope in them!

But in the living God. The man who grasps this will find it easy not to trust in riches any more. For it is God alone who supplies all things for the necessary purposes of our life and we transfer His prerogative to riches, when we put our confidence in them. Notice the implied contrast in his saying that God gives abundantly to all. The meaning is that, even if we have a full and overflowing abundance of all things, yet we have nothing except by the kindness of God alone. It is His generosity only that provides us with all that we need. It follows that it is a great mistake to rely on riches and not to depend completely on God's kindness, in which there is for us a sufficiency of food and of everything else. Thus we conclude that we are forbidden to trust in riches, not only because they belong only to this mortal life but because they are nothing but smoke. We are nourished not by bread alone but by God's kindness.

By saying *richly*, εἰς ἀπόλαυσιν, he is describing God's great liberality to us, to all men and to brute beasts; His kindness extends far and wide beyond our necessity.

18. *That they do good.* He adds another remedy to those already mentioned to correct a depraved attachment to riches and lays down what is the right use of our possessions. A man's opportunities to do good to others increase with the abundance of his riches, and because

we are always more reluctant than we should be to give to the poor, he uses many words in commending this virtue. Also he adds an incitement in the promise of a reward. By giving and sharing generously they will obtain for themselves treasure in heaven which is better than any they can have on earth.

By the word *foundation* he means something that has a firm and lasting duration, for spiritual riches which we lay up for ourselves in heaven are not exposed to the ravages of worm, thief or fire but remain permanently safe from all danger. Nothing on earth, by contrast, has a solid foundation, for all things change.

The inference drawn by the Papists from this passage, that we can by good works merit eternal life, is extremely foolish. It is true that everything spent on the poor is acceptable to God, but since even the most perfect of us scarcely fulfil the hundredth part of their full duty, our liberality does not deserve to be taken into account before God; in fact if God should call us to a full reckoning, there would be nobody not plunged into confusion, so far are we from giving all that is due. But after God has reconciled us to Himself by free grace, He accepts our services such as they are, and bestows on them a reward they do not deserve. Thus our reward does not depend upon considerations of merit, but on God's gracious acceptance, and is so far from being opposed to the righteousness of faith that it may be viewed as an appendix to it.

20. *O Timothy.* There are three different interpretations of the phrase, *that which is committed unto thee.* My view is that it simply means the grace bestowed on Timothy for the discharge of his office. It is called a thing committed for the same reason as it is called elsewhere a talent, for God's gifts are bestowed on condition that we shall one day have to give an account of them, if our negligence has prevented their being used for their intended purpose. He admonishes him to preserve carefully what has been given to him, or rather what has been committed to him in trust, not to let it be corrupted or adulterated and not to deprive himself of it by his own fault. It often happens that our ingratitude or our abuse of God's gifts result in their withdrawal; thus Paul exhorts Timothy to strive to keep in a good conscience and for proper use the thing committed to him.

Turning away from the profane babblings. The purpose of this admonition is that he should be devoted to solid teaching, and this can happen only if he turns away from all ostentation, for where a desire to please predominates, there is no longer any concern for edification. Thus when speaking about the thing committed, it was very much to the point that he should go straight on to add this caution to avoid empty talkativeness. The rendering of κενοφωνίας as 'vanities of voices' is one

I do not object to, except in so far as it involves an ambiguity which has led to a wrong interpretation; 'voices' is often taken to mean words, such as fate or fortune, whereas, in my view, he is rather censuring the high-sounding talk and the bombastic verbosity of those who are not content with the simplicity of the Gospel but turn it into profane philosophy. Thus the κενοφωνίαι do not consist of specific single words, but of that swollen bombastic talk which is continually and disgustingly pouring forth from ambitious men who seek applause for themselves more than progress for the Church. And by this word Paul describes it most aptly, for along with a sound of something high and lofty, there is really nothing underneath, but only empty jingle which he also calls profane, since the power of the Spirit is quenched as soon as the doctors blow their trumpets and start to display their eloquence.

In spite of such a clear and distinct prohibition by the Holy Spirit, this plague does continually break out, and has done from the very beginning, but has so increased in the Papacy that the trademark of the theology which there predominates is a living imitation of the profane and empty eloquence of which Paul here speaks. I say nothing of the innumerable errors, follies and blasphemies with which their books and endless disputations abound. But even though they taught nothing contrary to godliness, because their whole teaching is nothing but big bombastic words, since it is completely inconsistent with the majesty of Scripture, with the power of the Spirit, with the earnestness of the prophets and the sincerity of the apostles, it is therefore an absolute profanation of genuine theology. What, I ask, do they teach about faith or repentance, or calling on God or human incapacity, the help of the Holy Spirit or the free remission of sins, or about the work of Christ, that can have any value in building up men solidly in godliness? But we shall have to speak more of this in expounding the second epistle. Certainly anyone endowed with moderate intelligence and impartiality will agree that all the high-sounding terms of popish theology and all the authoritative definitions of doctrine that make such a noise in their schools are nothing but profane κενοφωνίαι—and no better term for describing them can be found. It is most just that those who turn aside from the purity of scripture should be punished for their arrogance by ending in profanation. The teachers of the Church cannot therefore be too careful in avoiding corruptions of that kind and in defending young men from them.

The Vulgate adopted the reading καινοφωνίας instead of κενοφωνίας and translated it 'novelties', and it seems from the commentaries of the fathers that this reading, which is found even now in some Greek codices, was once widely accepted, but the former reading which I have followed is far more appropriate.

And oppositions. This is also very exact and elegant. So tendentious are the subtleties on which men seeking glory pride themselves, that they overwhelm the true doctrine of the Gospel which is simple and unpretentious. Thus by 'oppositions to true knowledge' the apostle means exhibitions of pomp which court and win the world's applause. For ambition is always contentious and leads to disputes, so that those who wish to show off are always ready to draw the sword on any subject. But Paul's chief point is that the vain teaching of the sophists, rising aloft into airy speculations and subtleties, not only obscures the simplicity of true doctrine by its complications, but also oppresses it and makes it contemptible, for the world is usually carried away by outward show.

Paul does not want Timothy to attempt something of the same kind by way of emulation, but because things that seem to be subtle or adapted to ostentation are more interesting and impressive to human curiosity, Paul maintains that so-called knowledge which exalts itself over the simple and humble doctrine of godliness is not knowledge at all. This should be carefully noted so that we may learn to ridicule boldly and pour scorn on all that feigned knowledge which fills the world with admiration and amazement, but in which there is no solid edification. The only thing which on Paul's authority truly deserves to be called knowledge is that which instructs us in the confidence and fear of God, that is, in godliness.

21. *Which some professing.* He shows from its results also how harmful a thing this is, and how much we should avoid it. God's way of punishing the arrogance of those who for the sake of winning a reputation, corrupt and deform the doctrine of godliness, is to allow them to lose the soundness of their understanding, so that they become involved in many absurd errors. We see that this is what has happened under Popery. For when they begin to turn the mysteries of our religion into profane philosophy, countless monsters of false belief follow.

Faith. In this as in former passages faith means the sum of religion and sound doctrine. Warned by such examples, if we are horrified at the thought of defection from the faith, let us adhere to the pure word of God and detest sophistry and all subtleties which are hateful corruptions of godliness.

THEME OF PAUL'S SECOND EPISTLE TO TIMOTHY

It cannot be inferred with any certainty from Luke's account at what time the first epistle was written. But I have no doubt that after that time Paul had personal contact with Timothy, and it may well be, if the general view is accepted, that he employed him as his companion and assistant in many places. However, it is easy to conclude that he was still at Ephesus when this letter was written to him, for, towards the end, Paul sends greetings to Priscilla and Aquila and Onesiphorus. This last belonged to Ephesus, and Luke tells us that the other two remained there when Paul sailed for Judaea.

The chief purpose of this letter is to confirm Timothy both in the faith of the Gospel and in his pure and constant preaching of it. But the circumstances of the time add especial weight to these exhortations. Paul had before his eyes the death he was ready to suffer as a testimony to the Gospel. Thus all that we read here about the kingdom of Christ, the hope of life eternal, the Christian warfare, confidence in confessing Christ, and the certainty of doctrine should be seen as written not merely in ink but in Paul's lifeblood; for he asserts nothing for which he is not ready to offer the pledge of his death. Thus the epistle may be regarded as a solemn and urgent ratification of Paul's doctrine.

It is important to remember what we have already pointed out in relation to the first epistle, that the apostle wrote not merely for the sake of one man, but was laying down to one man teaching of general application, which he could afterwards pass on to others.

First, having praised Timothy for the faith in which he had been reared from childhood, he exhorts him to persevere faithfully both in the doctrine he has been teaching and in the office entrusted to him, and, at the same time, in case Timothy should be discouraged by the news of his imprisonment or by the defection of others, he glories in his apostleship and in the reward that awaits him. He also praises Onesiphorus, so as to encourage others by his example. And since those who wish to serve Christ have a hard task, he uses metaphors from farming and warfare. Farmers do not hesitate to spend much labour in cultivating the soil before any fruit appears; soldiers set themselves free from all other cares and concerns to devote themselves entirely to arms and their general's commands.

Next, he gives a brief summary of his Gospel and commands

THEME OF PAUL'S SECOND EPISTLE TO TIMOTHY

Timothy to hand it on to others and to take care to transmit it to posterity. He mentions again his own imprisonment and bursts out into holy enthusiasm to animate others by his courage. He calls us all to contemplate with him the crown that awaits us in heaven. He also commands him to abstain from contentious disputations and vain questionings, commending to him a zeal for edification; and to show more clearly what a dreadful evil this is, he declares that it has ruined some, and mentions two by name, Hymenaeus and Philetus, who fell into the monstrous absurdity of denying the faith of the resurrection and suffered a fearful punishment because of their presumption. But since lapses of that kind usually cause serious scandal, especially when they involve distinguished men of high reputation, he teaches that godly men should not be disturbed by them, since not all who profess Christ's name are true Christians, and since the Church must be subject to this kind of affliction if it is to exist in this world among evil and ungodly men. But in case this should unduly disturb timid minds, he wisely softens it by saying that the Lord will preserve to the end His own people whom He has chosen for Himself.

Next he returns to exhorting Timothy, so that he may persevere faithfully in the discharge of his ministry. To make him the more faithful, he foretells what dangerous times await the good and godly and what destructive men will soon arise against them. But against all this he fortifies him with the hope of a happy and successful outcome. More especially, he recommends to him to engage constantly in sound teaching, pointing out the proper use of the Scripture, that he may know that by it he will be fully equipped for the solid edification of the Church.

Next he reminds him that his own death is now near, but he does so as a conqueror hastening to a glorious triumph, which is a clear proof of his amazing confidence. Lastly, having asked Timothy to come to him as soon as possible, he points out the need arising from his present position. That is the main subject of the letter's concluding section.

CHAPTER ONE

Paul, an apostle of Jesus Christ by the will of God, according to the promise of the life which is in Christ Jesus, to Timothy, my beloved child: Grace, mercy, peace, from God the Father and Christ Jesus our Lord. (1-2)

1. *Paul, an apostle.* The opening words show clearly that Paul had in view not Timothy alone, but others through him. With Timothy there would have been no need for such a lofty assertion of his apostleship, and this ornamental language would have served no purpose with somebody already completely convinced of the validity of his claims. What he is doing here is laying claim to the public authority that belonged to him before all men, and he does it the more carefully because, with his death approaching, he wishes to gain approval for the whole course of his ministry, and to set the seal on his doctrine which he had spent so much labour in teaching, that it might be held sacred by posterity, and to leave a true representation of it in Timothy.

First, as is his custom, he describes himself as an *apostle of Christ*. It follows that he is not speaking as a private person who is to be listened to without much attention, being a mortal man liable to error, but as one who represents the person of Christ. But since the dignity of his office is too high for any man, unless he receives it by the special gift and election of God, he immediately magnifies his calling by saying that he was appointed to it *by the will of God*. Since God is the source and guarantee of his apostleship, it is beyond all dispute.

According to the promise. To make his calling the more certain, he connects it with the promises of eternal life, as if he had said, 'As from the beginning God has promised eternal life in Christ, so now He has made me the minister appointed to publish that promise.' This also shows the purpose of his apostleship, that he should lead men to Christ, that they may find life in Him. He speaks with great precision when he adds that the promise of life had already been given to the fathers long ago; and yet he also says that this life is in Christ, that we may know that the faith of those who lived under the Law must have looked to Christ, and the life contained in the promises was to some extent held in suspense, till it was exhibited in Christ.

2. *My beloved child.* By this phrase he not only declares his love for Timothy but secures for him a place of authority, for he wants him to be acknowledged as one who may rightly be called his own son. The

reason for calling him this is that Paul had begotten him in Christ. For although this honour belongs to God alone, it is transferred to those faithful ministers whose Work He uses to regenerate us.

Grace, mercy. The word mercy, which he has inserted here, is not usually found in his ordinary salutations and I think that he introduced it when he was expressing his feelings with more than ordinary intensity. Moreover he seems to have inverted the order. Yet it is not unfitting that mercy should be put after grace, to make clearer the nature and source of that grace, as if he had said that God loves us because He is merciful. Mercy may also be explained as meaning God's daily blessings which are so many testimonies of His mercy. For whenever He helps us, frees us from ills, pardons our sins, bears with our weaknesses, He does so because He has mercy upon us.

> *I thank God, whom I serve from my forefathers in a pure conscience, how unceasing is my remembrance of thee in my supplications night and day; longing to see thee, remembering thy tears, that I may be filled with joy; having been reminded of the unfeigned faith that is in thee; which dwelt first in thy grandmother Lois, and thy mother Eunice; and, I am persuaded, in, thee, also.* (3-5)

3. *I thank God.* The usual interpretation is that Paul gives thanks to God and then goes straight on to give as the reason for his thanksgiving the fact that he is unceasingly mindful of Timothy. But my readers should consider whether the following does not give an equally good, or even better sense, 'as often as I remember you in my prayers, as I do continually, I give thanks for you' for the particle ὡς often has that meaning. Indeed it is hard to draw from the other translation any meaning at all. According to my interpretation, prayer will be a sign of concern, and thanksgiving a sign of joy; for he never thinks of Timothy without remembering the outstanding excellencies with which he has been endowed. From this his thanksgiving springs; for to remember the gifts of God is always delightful and pleasant to godly men. Both are proofs of real goodwill. He calls his *remembrance* of Timothy ἀδιάλειπτον because he never forgets him when he prays.

Whom I serve from my forefathers. He says this in opposition to those well-known slanderous accusations brought against him by Jews everywhere, that he had forsaken the religion of his people and become an apostate from the Law of Moses. He declares that on the contrary he worships the God of whom he had been taught by his fathers, the God of Abraham who revealed Himself to the Jews, who gave His Law by the hand of Moses, and not some newfangled god newly invented by himself.

But here it may be asked whether Paul is on a sufficiently solid foundation in glorying in following the religion handed down from his fathers. For this could be a plausible pretext for all sorts of superstitions, and it would be a crime if anyone departed by a hairsbreadth from the customs of his ancestors, of whatever kind they might be. The answer is easy; Paul is not laying down a fixed rule by which everybody who follows the religion he received from his fathers should be thought to be worshipping God aright, and anyone who departs from their customs is open to blame. We must always take into account the fact that Paul was not descended from idolaters, but from the children of Abraham, who worshipped the true God. We know how in John 4.22 Christ disapproves of all the fictitious cults of the Gentiles and declares that the Jews alone observe the right method of worshipping God. Thus Paul here is not relying merely on the authority of his forefathers, nor is he referring to all his ancestors indiscriminately, but is simply rejecting the false opinion which charged him with having turned from the God of Israel and fashioned for himself a strange god.

In a pure conscience. It is certain that Paul's conscience had not always been pure, for he confesses that he was deceived by hypocrisy in giving way to sinful desires (Rom. 7.8). The excuse Chrysostom makes for him, that as a Pharisee he opposed the Gospel not from malice but from ignorance, is not satisfactory; for a pure conscience is no common claim to make and cannot be separated from sincere and earnest reverence for God. Thus I limit his reference to the present time, taking his meaning to be that he worships the same God as his ancestors, but now he does it with a pure and heart-felt affection, since he has been enlightened by the Gospel.

This statement has the same purpose as the many protestations he makes in Acts, 'I serve the God of our fathers, believing all things which are according to the law and the prophets' (Acts 24.14); again, 'And now I stand here to be judged for the hope of the promise made of God unto our fathers, unto which promise our twelve tribes hope to attain' (Acts 26.6-7), and again, 'Because of the hope of Israel I am bound with this chain' (Acts 28.20).

In my supplications night and day. This makes it clear how great his faithfulness in prayer was; and yet what he affirms of himself is only what he commends to all his followers. We should be moved and inspired to imitate such examples, in order at least to make such an essential practice more frequent among us. If anyone takes daily and nightly prayers to mean prayers Paul was in the habit of offering at stated hours, there is nothing absurd in that view, but I take the meaning to be simpler, that for him there was no time when he was not engaged in prayer.

5. *Having been reminded.* He commends both Timothy's faith and that of his grandmother and mother, more to encourage him than to praise him. For when anyone has made a good and brave beginning, his progress should give him courage to advance further, and examples from his own family circle are stronger enticements to him to press on. Thus he sets before him his grandmother, Lois, and his mother, Eunice, by whom he was reared in his infancy in such a way that he could suck in godliness along with his mother's milk. By this godly nurture Timothy is admonished not to fall away from his past and his forebears. There is some doubt as to whether these women were converted to Christ and this was the beginning of the faith Paul here applauds, or whether the faith attributed to them is outside Christianity. The latter seems to be much more likely. For although many superstitions and corruptions abounded everywhere at that time, the Lord always had His own people, whom He did not allow to be corrupted with the majority, but whom He sanctified for Himself, so that there might always be among the Jews some pledge of the grace he had promised Abraham. Thus there is no absurdity in saying that they lived and died in faith in the Mediator, although Christ had not yet been revealed to them. But I make no positive assertion and it would be rash to do so.

And, I am persuaded, in thee also. This clause confirms me in my last conjecture, for here, in my view, he is not speaking of Timothy's present faith. It would detract from his confident commendation of Timothy's faith if he were now to say only that he thought it equal to his mother's and grandmother's. I take the meaning to be that Timothy, from his boyhood, when he had not yet obtained a knowledge of the Gospel, was so imbued with reverence and faith in God, that it was a living seed which later increased and grew.

> *For the which cause I put thee in remembrance that thou stir up the gift of God, which is in thee through the laying on of my hands. For God gave us not a spirit of fearfulness; but of power and love and soberness. Be not ashamed, therefore, of the testimony of our Lord, nor of me his prisoner: but suffer hardship with the gospel according to the power of God; who saved us, and called us with a holy calling, not according to our works, but according to his own purpose and grace, which was given us in Christ Jesus before times eternal, but hath now been manifested by the appearing of our Saviour Jesus Christ, who abolished death, and brought light and immortality to light through the gospel. Whereunto I was appointed a herald and an apostle and a teacher to the Gentiles. For the which cause I suffer also these things: yet I am not ashamed; for I know him whom I have believed, and I am persuaded that he is able to guard that which I have committed unto him against that day.* (6-12)

6. *For the which cause I put thee in remembrance.* He means that the more abundant the share of grace Timothy has received, the more intent he should be in his desire to make daily progress. We should notice how the words *for this cause* connect this passage with what goes before. For this exhortation is highly necessary, for it often happens, and it is indeed most natural, that excellence of gifts produces carelessness and sloth, and this is the way in which Satan labours continually to extinguish all that is of God in us.

Which is in thee through the laying on of my hands. There is no doubt that Timothy was invited to be a minister by the common votes of the Church and was not chosen by the private selection of Paul acting alone, but it is quite understandable that Paul should ascribe the election to himself personally, since he was its chief instigator. But here he is dealing with his ordination rather than his election, that is with the solemn rite of institution. Besides it is not altogether clear whether in ordaining a man as a minister, the custom was for all to lay their hands on his head, or for one man alone to do it in their name and as their representative. I am more inclined to suppose that it was one man only who laid on hands. As far as the ceremony is concerned, the apostles borrowed it from the ancient custom of their people, or, rather, they retained it, since it was still in use. This is a part of that decent and orderly procedure, which Paul commends elsewhere (I Cor. 14.40). There still remains doubt whether this present reference to laying on hands is in relation to ordination, for at that time the graces of the Spirit to which he refers in Rom. 12 and, I Cor. 13, were conferred by laying on of hands on many people who were not being instituted as pastors. My view is that it can be inferred from the first epistle that Paul is dealing with the pastor's office here, for this passage agrees with what he says there, 'Neglect not the gift that is in thee which was given thee ... by the laying on of the hands of the presbytery' (I Tim. 4.14).

That point settled, the question arises whether grace is conferred through the outward sign. My answer is that all ministers ordained were commended to God by the prayers of the whole Church and in this way grace was obtained for them from God. It was not given in virtue of the outward sign, although that sign was not employed in vain or uselessly, but was a faithful token of the grace they received from God's own hand. This inaugural ceremony was not a profane act, invented only to obtain authority in the eyes of men, but was a legitimate act of consecration before God, something that could be done only by the power of the Holy Spirit. Here Paul uses the sign to stand for the whole transaction, for he means that Timothy was endued with grace when he was offered to God as a minister. There is a synecdoche here, whereby the part is made to stand for the whole.

But there is still another question that arises here. If it was only at his ordination that Timothy obtained the grace needed to discharge his office as a minister, what is to be made of the election of a man not yet fit or qualified, but still lacking God's gift? I answer that its being given to him then did not exclude his having had it before. It is certain that he excelled both in doctrine and in other gifts before Paul appointed him to the ministry. But there is no inconsistency in holding that when God purposed to use him in His work and called him to it, He then fitted and enriched him even more with new gifts or gave him a double portion of those He had given before. Thus it does not follow that Timothy had no gift before his ordination, but rather that it shone forth more brightly when the teaching office was laid upon him.

7. *For God gave us not a spirit of fearfulness.* This confirms his previous statement by which he continues to urge Timothy to give evidence of the power of the gifts he has received. He appeals to the fact that God governs His ministers by the *spirit of power* which is the opposite of the *spirit of fearfulness.* It follows from this that they should not relapse into laziness but should rouse themselves in great assurance and eager activity and display in visible results the Spirit's power. There is a passage in Rom. 8.15 which, at first sight, is very like this one, but the context shows that the meaning is different. There he is dealing with the confidence in their adoption possessed by all believers, but here his concern is specially with ministers, and he exhorts them in the person of Timothy to rouse themselves to active deeds of valour: for the Lord does not wish them to perform their office coldly and without vigour, but to press on powerfully relying on the efficacy of the Spirit.

Of power and love and soberness. From this we learn that none of us possesses in himself the loftiness of spirit and unshaken confidence needed in the exercise of our ministry; we must be endued with new power from on high. The hindrances are so many and so great that no human courage can be adequate to overcome them. Thus it is God who equips us with the Spirit of power. For those who otherwise show great strength immediately fall when they are not sustained by the power of the Spirit of God.

Secondly, we infer that those who are timid and weak like slaves so that, when need arises, they do not dare take any action for the defence of the truth, are not governed by the Spirit who rules over the servants of Christ. Thus it follows that very few of those who are called ministers of Christ today give any sign of being genuine. For how often is there to be found among them one who relies on the power of the Spirit and confidently sets at nought all the powers in high places that range themselves against Christ? Do not most, nearly all, care more for their own interests and their own leisure? Do they not sink down dumb as soon as any trouble breaks out? The result is that in their ministry there appears none of the majesty of God. The word *spirit* is here used figuratively, as in many other passages.

But why after power does he add love and soberness? In my view, it is to distinguish the power of the Spirit from the intemperate zeal of fanatics who rush on in reckless haste and boast that they have the Spirit of God. He explicitly states, therefore, that the powerful energy of the Spirit is tempered by love and soberness, that is, by a calm concern for edification. Paul is not denying that the same Spirit was given to prophets and teachers before the publication of the Gospel, but he means that these two graces should be especially evident and powerful under the reign of Christ.

8. *Be not ashamed therefore.* He said this because it was thought to be a disgraceful thing to confess the Gospel, so that he tells Timothy not to let ambition or fear of infamy hinder him in his confident preaching. He states this as an inference from what he has just been saying. The man who is armed with God's power will not be upset by the world's clamour, but will count it an honour that ungodly men cover him with disgrace. The Gospel is here well named, *the testimony of our Lord*, for although He has no need of our help, yet He lays on us the duty of giving testimony to Him and thus of maintaining His glory. This is a great and special honour bestowed by Him on us all, so that there is no Christian who should not consider himself a witness to Christ, but especially bestowed on pastors and teachers, as Christ said to His apostles, 'Ye shall be witnesses unto me' (Acts 1.8). For the more the world shows its hatred for the teaching of the Gospel, the greater courage should pastors show in their labours to confess it openly.

By adding *nor of me* he admonishes Timothy not to refuse to be his companion in a common cause. When we begin to withdraw from the company of those who are suffering persecution, our aim must be to make the Gospel free from all persecution. Although there was no lack of wicked men who were mocking Timothy by saying, 'Do you not see what has happened to your master? Do you not know that the same reward awaits you as well? Why are you pressing upon us a doctrine that you see the whole world hissing at?'—still, he must have been cheered by this exhortation. Paul says to him, 'You have no need to be ashamed of me, for I have nothing to be ashamed of, for *I am the prisoner of Christ*, I am in chains not for any crime or evil deed, but for His name.' He tells Timothy how to do what he asks, by preparing himself to suffer the afflictions that are connected with the Gospel, for to shrink from the cross or to try to avoid it always means to be ashamed of the Gospel. Thus Paul has two good reasons for encouraging him to be bold in his confession, and for speaking about bearing the cross, that he may not do it in vain.

He adds *according to the power of God*, for we would immediately succumb, if He did not support us. The phrase has in it both admonition and consolation. The admonition is to turn our eyes away from our present weakness and, in reliance on God's help, to venture and strive for things beyond our own strength; the comfort is that if we suffer anything on account of the Gospel, God will come and deliver us and in His power we shall conquer.

9. *Who saved us*. From the greatness of the blessing he shows how much we owe to God, for the salvation He has bestowed upon us easily swallows up all the ills we have to bear in this world. The word 'saved', although its meaning can be general, here in this context refers only to eternal salvation. His meaning is that they had received through Christ not a passing or transitory deliverance but eternal salvation, so that they are extremely lacking in gratitude if they spare their fleeting life or reputation rather than acknowledge Him as their Redeemer.

He makes our *calling* the sure seal of our salvation. For as man's salvation was completed in Christ's death, so God makes us share in it through the Gospel. To magnify this calling further he says it is *holy*. This should be carefully noted, for just as we must look exclusively to Christ for salvation, so He would have died in vain and for nothing if He did not call us to share in this grace. So even after salvation is procured for us by His death, the second blessing still remains to be given, that He should insert us into His Body and communicate His benefits to us that we may enjoy them.

Not according to our works. He now draws attention to the source both of our calling and of our whole salvation. We did not possess works that might have enabled us to take the initiative out of God's hand, so that our salvation depends entirely on His gracious purpose and election. In the two words 'purpose' and 'grace' there is a hypallage so that the second word should be treated as an adjective—'according to His gracious purpose'. Although Paul usually uses the word 'purpose' to mean God's secret decree which depends on Himself alone, he chose here to add 'grace' to make his point more explicit and completely to exclude all reference to works. The antithesis in this verse is itself enough to make it quite clear that there is no place for works where God's grace reigns, especially since we are reminded of God's election by which He anticipated His choice of us before we were born. The same subject is dealt with more fully in connexion with Ephesians 1 and I only touch upon it now, having discussed it at greater length there.

Which was given us. He argues from the order of the time that salvation was given to us by free grace, since we had done nothing beforehand to deserve it. For if God chose us before the foundation of the world, He could not have paid any regard to works for there were none and we ourselves did not yet exist. The sophistical evasion that God was influenced by the works that He foresaw does not require a long answer. What kind of works would these have been, if God had rejected us, since election is itself the source and origin of all good things. This giving of grace which he mentions is certainly meant to refer to the predestination by which we are adopted as God's children. I wanted to remind my readers of this, for often God is said to give us this grace only at the time when it begins to work effectively in us. But here Paul is dealing with what God determined with Himself from the beginning, so that then He gave it to people who were not yet born quite apart from any consideration of merit, and He kept it stored away among His treasures till the time came when He could make it clear by the result that He determines nothing in vain.

Here as in Titus 1 he calls the endless series of years from the foundation of the world *times eternal*. The ingenious discussion over this matter which Augustine raises in many passages is alien to Paul's mind; his meaning is quite simply 'before the times began to take their course from all past ages'. It should further be noticed how he makes Christ the sole foundation of salvation, for apart from Him no man is either adopted or saved, as Ephesians 1 also says.

10. *But hath now been manifested.* Note how appropriately he connects the faith we have from the Gospel with God's secret election and assigns to each its own place. God has called us through the Gospel, not because He has suddenly taken thought for our salvation but because He had so determined from all eternity. Christ has appeared for that salvation now, not because the power to save has but recently been conferred upon Him, but because this grace was laid up for us in Him before the creation of the world. The knowledge of these things has been revealed to us by faith. In this way the apostle wisely connects the Gospel with God's most ancient promises, so that its supposed novelty might not bring it into contempt.

But the question arises whether all this was hidden from the fathers who lived under the Law, for if it was revealed only at Christ's advent, it follows that before that it was concealed. My answer is that Paul is speaking of the full manifestation of the very thing on which the fathers also built their faith, so that this takes nothing away from them. The reason why Abel, Noah, Abraham, Moses, David and all the godly obtained the same salvation as we do was that they also placed their faith in Christ's appearing. When he says that grace was revealed to us by the appearing of Christ, he does not exclude the fathers from participation in it, for the same faith gives them a part with us in this appearing. Christ was yesterday the same as He is today (Heb. 13.8) but He did not manifest Himself by His death and resurrection before the time fixed by the Father. To this time our faith and that of the fathers look together, for in it is the only pledge and completion of our salvation.

Who abolished death. In ascribing the manifestation of life to the Gospel he does not mean that it has its origin in the Word without reference to Christ's death and resurrection, for the Word depends for its power on the matter it contains; he means rather that the only way in which the fruits of this grace can come to men is through the Gospel, as is said in II Cor. 5.19: 'God was in Christ reconciling the word to himself and hath committed to us the word of reconciliation.' It is a remarkable and memorable commendation of the Gospel, that it should be called the means by which life appears.

To *'life'* he adds *immortality*, as if he had said 'true and immortal life', unless you prefer to take life to mean regeneration on which there follows a blessed immortality which is still the object of hope. For our life does not consist of what we have in common with the brute beasts, but rather of our participation in the image of God. But since the true nature and value of that life does not appear in this world, to explain it he has properly added immortality, which is the revelation of that life which now lies concealed.

11. *Whereunto I was appointed.* He has good reason to commend the Gospel thus highly along with his own apostleship. Satan labours above all else to banish from our minds by every possible means faith in sound doctrine, and since it is not always easy to do this by an open attack upon our faith, he comes against us secretly and by indirect methods, and in order to destroy faith in their teaching, he brings into suspicion the calling of godly teachers. Thus Paul, having the prospect of death in front of him and knowing well the old well-tried snares of Satan, determined to assert both the teaching of the Gospel in general and the genuineness of his own calling. Both were necessary, for although we may be given long discourses about the dignity of the Gospel, they will do us no good unless we grasp what the Gospel is. Many will give their assent to the general principle of the certain authority of the Gospel and yet will have no sure idea of what they are committed to follow. That is why Paul wishes to be explicitly acknowledged as a faithful and legitimate minister of the life-giving teaching of which he has just reminded them; that is why he describes himself by several titles which all mean the same. He calls himself a *herald* whose duty it is to make public the decrees of princes and magistrates, the name of *apostle*

belongs to him as his very own, and because there is a special relationship between a *teacher* and his pupils, he describes himself by this third title, that those who learn from him may know that they have a master appointed by God.

And to whom does he say that he was appointed? *To the Gentiles*—for the heart of the controversy was about them, since the Jews denied that the promises of life applied to any but the sons of Abraham after the flesh. In order therefore that the salvation of the Gentiles may not be called in question, he declares that it was to them he was specially sent by God.

12. *For the which cause I suffer also these things.* It is well known that the rage of the Jews was kindled against Paul for this reason more than any other, that he gave the Gentiles a common share in the Gospel. But *for the which cause* refers to the whole of the preceding passage and should not be restricted to the last phrase about the Gentiles. He now brings forward two arguments to prevent his imprisonment from in any way detracting from his authority. First he shows that the cause of his imprisonment, far from being disgraceful was rather honourable to him, since he has been imprisoned not for any kind of bad behaviour but because he obeyed God's call. It is an unbelievable comfort to us when we can meet the unjust judgments of men with a good conscience. Second he argues that there is nothing shameful in his imprisonment from his hope of a happy outcome. The man who is armed with this defence can overcome the greatest trials, whatever they may be. And when he says that he is *not ashamed*, he is by his example encouraging others to show the same courage.

For I know whom I have believed. This is the only refuge to which all believers should resort when the world condemns them as lost and hopeless, that they should think it enough to have God's approval, for what would happen if they relied on men? From this we should infer what a great difference there is between faith and mere human opinion. Faith does not depend on human authority, nor is it a hesitant and doubtful trust in God; it must be joined with knowledge or else it will not be strong enough against the endless attacks Satan makes upon it. The man who like Paul has this knowledge will know by experience that our faith is rightly called the victory that overcomes the world, and that Christ had good reason to say that 'the gates of hell shall not prevail' (Matt. 16.18). That man will be able to rest quietly amidst every storm and tempest because he has a sure conviction that God, who cannot lie or deceive, has spoken and what He has promised He will certainly perform. On the other hand the man who has not this truth firmly fixed in his mind will always waver this way and that like a reed in the wind. This passage deserves close attention, for it explains most excellently the power of faith by teaching us that in the most desperate plight we should glorify God by not doubting that He will be true and faithful and that we should accept the Word with the same assurance as if God Himself had appeared to us from heaven. The man who lacks this conviction understands nothing. We should always remember that Paul is not philosophizing in the dark, but, with the reality itself before his eyes, is solemnly declaring the great value of a confident assurance of eternal life.

I am persuaded that he is able. Although the force and greatness of our dangers often throw us into despair or at least tempt our minds to distrust, we have to be armed with the defence of knowing that there is adequate protection for us in God's power. So Christ, in bidding us be confident, uses this argument, 'The Father who gave you to me is greater than all' (John 10.29). By this he means that we are in no danger since the Lord who has received us into His protection is abundantly able to resist them all. Not even Satan dares to suggest directly the thought that God is unable to fulfil what He has promised, for our minds would shrink from so great a blasphemy, but by preoccupying our eyes and minds with other things he takes away from us all sense of God's power. A mind must therefore be thoroughly purged if it is not only to experience that power, but retain the experience amid temptations of every kind.

Whenever Paul speaks of God's power we must understand by it his actual or effectual (ἐνεργουμένην) power, as he himself calls it elsewhere (Col. 1.29). Faith always connects God's power with His word, which it does not think of as something remote and distant but rather something inward which it has in its possession. Thus it is said of Abraham in Rom. 4.20, 'He did not hesitate nor dispute but gave God the glory, being certainly persuaded that what he had promised He was also able to fulfil.'

Note how he describes eternal life as *that which I have committed unto him*; from this we learn that our salvation is in God's hand, just as a depository holds in his hands the property we entrust to him for safe keeping. If our salvation depended upon ourselves, it would be continually exposed to very many dangers; but being committed to such a guardian it is out of all danger.

> *Hold the pattern of sound words which thou hast heard from me, in faith and love which is in Christ Jesus. That good thing which was committed unto thee guard through the Holy Ghost which dwelleth in us. This thou knowest, that all that are in Asia are turned away from me; of whom are Phygelus and Hermogenes. The Lord grant mercy unto the house of Onesiphorus: for he oft refreshed me, and was not ashamed of my chain;*

but, when he was in Rome, he sought me diligently, and found me (the Lord grant unto him to find mercy of the Lord in that day); and in how many things he ministered at Ephesus, thou knowest very well. (13-18)

13. *Hold the pattern.* Some take this to mean, 'Let your doctrine be an example which others can imitate', but I do not accept this. Equally far from Paul's meaning is Chrysostom's interpretation, that Timothy should have at hand the image of virtues, engraven on his heart by Paul's teaching. My own view is that the apostle is telling Timothy to hold fast the doctrine he has learnt, not only in its substance but in the very form of its expression. For ὑποτύπωσις, the word used here, means a vivid picture, as if the object concerned were actually before our eyes. Paul knows how prone men are to rebel and fall away from true doctrine and for this reason he carefully warns Timothy not to depart from the form of teaching which he had received, and to regulate his method of teaching by the rule laid down for him—not that we should be unduly scrupulous over words, but it is exceedingly harmful to corrupt doctrine even in the smallest degree. From this we may understand the value of the theology of the Papists, for it has degenerated so far from the pattern Paul here commends that it is more like the riddles of diviners and soothsayers than teaching based on God's Word. What trace of Paul, I ask, is there in all the books of the schoolmen? This licentious corrupting of doctrine shows how wise Paul was to tell Timothy to keep its original form.

Sound words are contrasted here not only with teachings that are manifestly godless, but with fruitless questionings which lead not to health but only to sickness.

In faith and love. I know that often the particle ἐν can mean 'with', following Hebrew usage, but here it seems to me to have a different meaning. Paul has added this as a mark of sound doctrine to tell us what it contains and how it may be summed up, and he includes all this, as is his custom, under faith and love. Both of these he places *in Christ* as their foundation, since the knowledge of Christ consists chiefly of these two parts, for although *which is* is in the singular and agrees with the word love, it must be understood as applying to faith as well. Those who translate 'With faith and love' take it to mean that Timothy is to add to sound doctrine the affections of godliness and love. I agree that nobody can persevere in sound doctrine without being endued with true faith and unfeigned love. But in my view the first explanation fits better, that Paul uses these two words to explain more fully what 'sound words' are and what they deal with. He declares that the whole of his doctrine consists of faith and love, which have their source and beginning in the knowledge of Christ.

14. *That good thing which was committed unto thee guard.* This exhortation has a wider scope than the last, for he tells Timothy to think of what God has given him, and to expend upon it the care and diligence that its high value deserves. When a thing is of little value we do not usually require such a strict reckoning as when its value is very high. By 'that which was committed' I take him to mean both the dignity of his ministry and all the other gifts bestowed upon Timothy. Some restrict its meaning to his ministry alone, but I think that it refers mainly to his qualifications for that ministry, that is all the gifts of the Spirit in which he excelled. He uses the word 'committed' for another reason also—to remind Timothy of the account of his ministry he must one day render, for we must faithfully administer all that God has entrusted to us.

That good thing, τὸ καλόν in Greek, means something of high or outstanding value. Erasmus has rendered it well as 'that excellent thing' and I have followed his version. But how is it to be guarded? We must take care lest by our indolence what God has conferred upon us should be lost or taken away because of our ingratitude or abuse of it. There are many who reject God's grace and many more who, after they have received it, deprive themselves of it. But since the power to guard it is not in us, he adds *through the Holy Ghost*, as if to say, 'I do not ask from you more than you can give, for the Holy Spirit will supply what is lacking in yourself.' From this it follows that we must not judge of man's ability by God's commands, for as He gives commands in words, so He writes His words on our hearts and by giving us strength sees to it that He does not command in vain. What follows about the *dwelling of the Spirit within us* means that He is present as a help to believers, provided they do not reject what is offered to them.

15. *This thou knowest.* These defections he mentions might have unsettled many minds and given rise to various suspicions, for we usually put the worst possible construction on such things. Paul meets scandals of this kind with heroic courage, that all good men may learn to abominate the treachery of those who have deserted the servant of Christ at a time when all alone and at the peril of his life he was upholding the common cause; and that they may not waver when they know that Paul is not left without the help of God. He names two of the deserters—probably the best known—in order to put a stop to these slanderous attacks. For it usually happens that deserters from the Christian warfare seek to excuse their own disgraceful conduct by inventing whatever accusations they can against faithful and upright ministers of the Gospel.

Phygelus and Hermogenes, knowing that their cowardice would rightly be held in infamy by believers and that they stood condemned of base treachery, would not have hesitated to load Paul with false accusations and shamelessly to damage his innocence. Thus Paul, to give the lie to their falsehoods, singles them out for the mention they deserve. In our day also there are many who, either because they are not admitted to the ministry here in Geneva, or because they have been expelled from their office because of their wickedness, or because we will not support them in idleness, or because they have committed theft or fornication and have been forced to flee, forthwith wander through France and beyond and try to establish their own innocence by directing against us all the accusations they can. And some brethren are foolish enough to accuse us of cruelty if any of us paints such men in their true colours. It would be desirable that all these men should have their foreheads branded so that they may be recognised at first sight.

16. *The Lord grant mercy.* From this prayer we may infer that good offices done to the saints are not done in vain, even if they themselves cannot repay them. For when he prays to God to reward them, it is equivalent to a promise. At the same time Paul shows his own gratitude by transferring to God the duty of recompense, since he himself cannot pay the debt. What if he had had ample means of recompense? Then indeed he would have given evidence that he was not ungrateful. We should note further that although it is Onesiphorus alone who is praised for his beneficence, yet for his sake Paul prays for a blessing for his whole family. From this we may infer that God's blessing rests not only on a righteous man himself but on his whole house. God's love for His people is so great that it spreads itself over all who are connected with them. When he says that Onesiphorus *was not ashamed of my chain*, that is proof not only of his liberality but of his zeal, since he willingly exposed himself to danger and to the reproach of men in order to help Paul.

18. *The Lord grant unto him to find mercy.* Some take the meaning to be, 'May God grant him to find mercy before the judgment seat of Christ'; and that is indeed somewhat more tolerable than to explain Genesis 19.24 'The Lord rained fire from the Lord' as meaning that the Father rained from the Son. It may be that the strength of Paul's emotions made him, as he often does, repeat himself superfluously.

This prayer shows how much richer is the reward that awaits those who do good to the saints without hope of earthly recompense than if they received it at once from human hands. And note what he prays for—that Onesiphorus may find mercy. For the man who is merciful to his neighbours will find the same mercy shown to him by God and we are more than foolish if this promise does not greatly encourage and stimulate us to show kindness. It follows also from this that God does not reward us according to our merits, but His best and most outstanding reward is when He pardons us and shows Himself to be not a severe judge but a kind and indulgent Father.

CHAPTER TWO

Thou therefore, my child, be strengthened in the grace that is in Christ Jesus. And the things which thou hast heard from me among many witnesses, the same commit thou to faithful men, who shall be able to teach others also. Suffer hardship with me, as a good soldier of Christ Jesus. No soldier on service entangleth himself in the affairs of this life; that he may please him who enrolled him as a soldier. And if also a man contend in the games, he is not crowned, except he have contended lawfully. The husbandman must labour before he partake of the fruits. Consider what I say; for the Lord shall give thee understanding in all things. (1-7)

1. *Thou therefore be strong.* As before he told him to guard the thing committed to him by the Spirit, so now he enjoins him to be strengthened in grace. By this expression he means that he should be roused from laziness and inactivity, for the flesh is so sluggish that even those endowed with excellent gifts grow slack in mid course if they are not frequently aroused. But someone asks 'What is the point in exhorting a man to be strong in grace, unless our free will has some part to play in co-operation with grace?' I reply that what God requires from us in His Word, He also supplies by His Spirit, so that we are strengthened in the grace that He provides. And yet exhortations are not superfluous, because God's Spirit teaches us inwardly and sees to it that they do not sound in our ears fruitlessly and in vain. Thus the man who sees that this present exhortation can be fruitful only by the secret power of the Spirit will never use this passage in support of free will.

He adds *that is in Christ Jesus* for two reasons; to show that grace comes from Christ alone and from no other, and that no Christian will be left without it. For since the one Christ is common to all, it follows that all share in His grace, and thus the grace is said to be 'In Christ' because all who are Christ's should have it. The affectionate address that he uses in calling Timothy *my child* tends to win grace, that his teaching may the better penetrate to the heart.

2. *And the things which thou hast heard from me.* He shows once again how anxious he is to spread sound doctrine to posterity. Not only does he exhort Timothy as before to preserve its form and features, but also to hand it down to godly teachers, that being widely spread it may take root in many hearts. He foresaw that it could easily perish unless it were quickly scattered abroad by many ministers. And indeed we see

what Satan accomplished a little after the death of the apostles, for, as though there had been no preaching for many centuries, he raised up innumerable madnesses which in their monstrous absurdity outdid the superstitions of all the Gentiles. It is no wonder that Paul, wishing to guard against such a great evil, zealously desires his doctrine to be committed to all godly ministers who are qualified to hand it on. It is as if he had said, 'See to it that after my death reliable witness to my teaching remains. And this will happen only if, besides teaching yourselves what you have learnt from me, you have it published more widely by others. Thus, whenever you find men fit for this work, commit this treasure to their trust.'

He calls them *faithful men*, not because they have faith, for that is something all Christians share, but because they possess an outstandingly large measure of faith. It is right to render the word as 'faithful', since there are but few concerned to perpetuate and conserve the remembrance of the doctrine entrusted to them. Many are motivated by different kinds of ambitions, some by greed, some by malice and some are held back by their fear of danger, so that here special faithfulness is required.

Among many witnesses. He does not mean that he produced witnesses in a formal and legal way in the case of Timothy; but, since controversy might arise as to whether Timothy's teaching was derived from Paul or was of his own invention, he banishes all doubt by pointing out that he had not spoken secretly in a corner, but that many were alive who could testify that everything Timothy was teaching they had themselves heard from Paul. Timothy's teaching would thus be beyond suspicion, since he had many fellow disciples who could bear testimony to it. From this we learn how much trouble a servant of Christ should take to preserve and guard the purity of his teaching not only in his own lifetime but for as long as his care and labour can extend it.

3. *Suffer hardship.* Strong necessity has made him add this second exhortation. Those who offer Christ their service must be ready to bear hardships so that without patient endurance of evils there will never be perseverance. That is why he adds *as befits a good soldier of Christ*, meaning that all who serve Christ are soldiers whose warfare consists less in inflicting evil on others than in patiently bearing it in themselves. It is of the greatest importance that we should consider these things. We see many people every day abjectly laying down their arms, who once made a great show of valour. Why so? Because they cannot become used to the cross. They are so soft that they shrink from warfare and their only notion of fighting is to struggle fiercely with their adversaries. They cannot bear to learn what it means to possess their souls in patience.

4. *No soldier on service.* He develops his military metaphor further.

Strictly speaking, he was using this metaphor when he called Timothy a soldier of Christ, but ne now goes on to compare secular warfare with spiritual and Christian warfare, as follows, 'The rule of military discipline is that as soon as a soldier has enrolled under a commander he leaves his home and all his affairs and thinks only of the war; so also we, in order to be devoted completely to Christ, have to be free from all the entanglements of this world.' By *the affairs of this life* he means the care of governing his family and his ordinary occupations, just as farmers leave their fields and merchants their shops and trade till they have completed their period of service. Applying the comparison to the present subject, we see its meaning is that everyone who wishes to fight under Christ's command must relinquish all the trifles and diversions of the world and devote all his energies to the fight. We must, in short, remember the old proverb, *Hoc age*—Do what lies to your hand—which means that in performing our sacred duties we should be so entirely concentrated upon them that nothing else will occupy our care and attention.

The common reading 'No man that fights for God . . .' completely corrupts Paul's meaning. Here Paul is addressing the pastors of the Church in the person of Timothy. His statement is of universal application but it is specially suited to ministers of the Word. First, let them see the things that hinder them in their work and let them free themselves from them and so follow Christ. Next, let other men also see, each in his own station, what keeps them from Christ, that our heavenly commander may have as much authority over us as any mortal man claims over the soldiers of the world who have pledged themselves to his service.

5. *And if also a man contend in the games.* He goes on to deal with perseverance in case anybody should think that he has done enough if he has been engaged in one or two conflicst. Now he takes his metaphor from athletes, none of whom gains the prize till he has been victorious right to the end of the race. Thus also in I Cor. 9.24 he says, 'All run in a race but one receiveth the prize. Even so run that ye may attain.' If a man grows weary at the beginning of the struggle and at once withdraws from the field to rest, he will be condemned for indolence instead of being crowned. Since Christ wishes us to strive all our days, the man who fails half-way to victory loses his honour, even though he may have begun bravely. *To contend lawfully* means to carry on the struggle in such a way and for as long as the law requires, that none may leave off before the appointed time.

6. *The husbandman must labour.* I am aware that others render this verse differently and I agree that they give a word-for-word translation of Paul's Greek. But if the context is examined carefully, my view will

be preferred. Besides, the use of 'labouring' for 'to labour' is a well-known Greek idiom. Greek writers often use the participle instead of the infinitive.

The meaning is therefore that husbandmen do not gather the fruit until they have worked hard in cultivating the earth by sowing and other work. But if husbandmen do not shrink from toil to obtain fruit after a time, and if they wait patiently for the harvest, how much more absurd it is for us to refuse the labours Christ enjoins upon us when we have the promise of such a great reward.

7. *Consider what I say.* He does not add this because his comparisons are obscure but so that Timothy may ponder for himself how much more excellent is warfare under Christ's command and how much richer His reward. For even if we ponder it ceaselessly we hardly grasp it at the end.

The prayer that follows is added by way of correction. Since our minds do not easily rise to the contemplation of the incorruptible crown of a future life, Paul appeals to God to give Timothy understanding. From this we may gather that unless the Lord opens our eyes, we are taught in vain, just as His commandments are given in vain unless He Himself supplies the power to fulfil them. For who could have taught better than Paul, and yet, that his teaching may be profitable, he prays that God may inform his pupil's mind.

Remember Jesus Christ, risen from the dead, of the seed of David, according to my gospel: wherein I suffer hardship unto bonds, as a malefactor; but the word of God is not bound. Therefore I endure all things for the elect's sake, that they also may obtain the salvation which is in Christ Jesus with eternal glory. Faithful is the saying; for if we died with him, we shall also live with him; if we endure, we shall also reign with him: if we shall deny him, he also will deny us: if we are faithless, he abideth faithful; for he cannot deny himself. (8-13)

8. *Remember Jesus* He now mentions expressly a part of his teaching which he wished to go down to posterity entire and uncorrupted. It is likely that this is the point about which he was most anxious, and that will become clear in what follows, when he comes to speak of the error of Hymenaeus and Philetus. They were denying the resurrection by holding falsely that it was already past, and here Paul bears testimony to his own faith concerning it. How needful this admonition of Paul's was the ancient historians show; for Satan began to exert all his strength to destroy this article of our faith. There are two parts of it, that Christ was born of the seed of David and that He rose from the dead. Immediately after the time of the apostles came Marcion who sought to destroy belief in the reality of Christ's human nature; after him there

follow the Manichaeans, and, even in our day the same plague is spreading. As far as the resurrection is concerned, how many have tried in so many different ways to overthrow our hope of it. This affirmation of Paul's is therefore as if he had said, 'Let no man corrupt my Gospel or falsify it with slanders. Thus have I taught and thus have I preached, that Christ who was man born of the seed of David rose from the dead.'

He speaks of *my gospel* not because he claims to be its author but rather its minister. In the resurrection of Christ we all have a sure pledge of our own. For he who confesses that Christ has risen, affirms also that we shall rise, for Christ has risen not for Himself but for us. The Head must not be separated from His members. Besides, in Christ's resurrection there is contained the completion of our redemption and salvation. For he adds that it is resurrection *from the dead*. Christ who was dead rose again. Why? For what purpose? Here we have to think of it in relation to ourselves and consider the effect and fruit of His death and His rising. For we must always remember this principle, that Scripture does not usually speak of these things as cold facts and mere matters of history, but makes indirect reference to their fruit.

Of the seed of David. This phrase not only asserts the reality of Christ's human nature but also claims for Him the honour and name of Messiah. Some heretics deny that Christ was true man, some imagine that He descended from heaven, some that He had no more than the appearance of a man. Paul declares that on the contrary He was of the seed of David and in this way undoubtedly asserts that He was true man, born of our humanity as the Son of Mary. This testimony is so clearly expressed that the attempts of heretics to evade it only proved their own shamelessness. Jews and other enemies of Christ deny that He is the One who was for long promised, but Paul says that He is David's Son and has His origin in that family from which the Messiah must come forth.

9. *Wherein I suffer hardship.* Here he anticipates an objection, for in the eyes of the ignorant his imprisonment detracted from the credibility of his Gospel. He acknowledges that to all outward appearances he is in prison like any criminal, but adds that this has not prevented the Gospel from having free course. Rather what he suffers is to the advantage of the elect, for it tends to confirm them. Such is the unshaken courage of Christ's martyrs, when they are so exalted by the knowledge of the good cause which they serve, that they can despise not only bodily pains and tortures but every kind of disgrace. Moreover, all godly men should take courage when they see ministers of the Gospel attacked and insulted by adversaries, so that they do not for that reason reverence their teaching less, but rather may give God the glory when they see how by His power the Gospel can break through

all the hindrances the world puts in its way. If we were not excessively devoted to the flesh, this by itself would be enough to console us in the midst of persecutions, the knowledge that even if we are oppressed by the cruelty of the ungodly, nevertheless the Gospel is extended and spreads far and wide. All that they may attempt, far from obscuring or extinguishing the light of the Gospel, can only make it shine more clearly. Let us therefore endure gladly, or at least with a quiet mind, having our body and our good name put in prison, provided that God's truth breaks through and spreads itself far and wide.

10. *Therefore I endure all things.* He shows by its results that his imprisonment, far from being a cause of reproach, is in fact highly profitable to the elect. When he says that he *endures for the elect's sake*, he shows how for him the upbuilding of the Church counts for far more than his own safety. For he is ready not only to die, but even to be thought a criminal to promote the welfare of the Church. In this passage the teaching is the same as in Col. 1.24 where he says that he fills up what is lacking in the sufferings of Christ, for His Body's sake, which is the Church. The Papists rashly interpret this to mean that Paul's death was in satisfaction for our sins, but this passage refutes that completely. As if Paul would claim more for his death than that it would confirm the godly in faith, for there immediately follows by way of explanation that the salvation of believers is founded in Christ alone. A fuller discussion of his meaning will be found under the passage I have quoted.

With eternal glory. This is the end of the salvation we obtain in Christ. Our salvation is to live to God and this begins with our regeneration and is completed by our full liberation from the miseries of this mortal life, when God takes us and gathers us into His Kingdom. To this salvation there is added a participation in heavenly, that is divine, glory and so to magnify the grace of Christ, he calls our salvation eternal glory.

11. *Faithful is the saying.* He uses this as a preface to what follows, for there is nothing so alien to the wisdom of the flesh as to believe that we must die in order to live and that death is the entrance into life. We gather from other passages that it is Paul's custom to use this preface before anything specially important or hard to believe. The meaning is that the only way we can share Christ's life and glory is by sharing first His death and humiliation; as he says in Romans 8.29 all the elect were 'predestined that they might be conformed to His image'. This is said both to exhort and to comfort believers. Who could fail to be stirred by this exhortation, that we ought not to be borne down by our afflictions, since we shall have such a happy deliverance from them. The same thought abates and sweetens all the bitterness of the cross,

since neither pains nor torments nor reproaches nor death should dismay us, seeing that we share them with Christ, and especially since all these things are the forerunners of our triumph. Thus by his own example Paul puts heart into all believers to bear with a light heart the afflictions in which already they have a foretaste of future glory. But if this is too much for us to believe by ourselves and the cross so overpowers us and fills our gaze that we cannot discern Christ, let us remember to use this shield, 'Faithful is the saying.' Where Christ is present, there is also life and blessedness. We must hold firmly to this fellowship we have with Christ so that we do not die by ourselves but with Him that we may be the companions of His glory. By *death* here he means the outward mortification of which he speaks in II Cor. 4.10.

12. *If we shall deny him.* He adds this solemn warning to shake off sloth. His threat is directed to those who from terror of persecution give up their confession of Christ's name, and he warns them that they will have no part with Him. How unworthy it is that we should think more of the fleeting life of this world than of the holy name of the Son of God. And why should He number among His people those who treacherously deny Him? Here weakness is no excuse, for if men did not willingly deceive themselves with empty flatteries, they would be equipped with the Spirit of fortitude and would resist faithfully. When men basely deny Christ, the cause is not only weakness but infidelity. It is because they are blinded by the allurements of the world that they cannot see the life of God's Kingdom. But this teaching requires meditation more than explanation. Christ's words are plain, 'Whosoever denies me, I shall also deny him' (Matt. 10.33). It remains for everyone to consider in his own heart that this is no childish threat but a solemn pronouncement by our Judge, which will be found true at the appointed hour.

His next statement, *he abideth faithful*, seems at first sight incredible but the meaning is as follows, 'Our faithlessness cannot in any way detract from the Son of God and His Glory. Being all sufficient in Himself He has no need of our confession.' It is as if he had said, 'Let all who will desert Christ, for they deprive Him of nothing; when they perish, He remains unchanged.' He now goes on to explain that Christ is not like us and does not deviate from His own truth. Thus it is clear that all who deny Christ are disowned by Him. In this way Paul takes from ungodly apostates the comforting thoughts by which they seek to soothe themselves. Because they change their colours according to their circumstances, they imagine that Christ too is double-faced and variable, but Paul says that this is impossible. At the same time we must firmly hold to what I have mentioned in connexion with an earlier passage, that our faith is founded on the perpetual and unchangeable truth of Christ so that no human unfaithfulness or apostasy should be able to shake it.

Of these things put them in remembrance, charging them in the sight of the Lord, that they strive not about words, to no profit, to the subverting of them that hear. Give diligence to present thyself approved unto God, a workman that needeth not to be ashamed, dividing aright the word of truth. But shun profane babblings: for they will proceed further in ungodliness, and their word will eat as doth a gangrene: of whom is Hymenaeus and Philetus; men who concerning the truth have erred, saying that the resurrection is past already, and overthrow the faith of some. (14-18)

14. *Of these things put them in remembrance.* 'These things' is emphatic; he means that the summary of the Gospel he has just given along with its added exhortations is so important that a good minister should never grow weary of dealing with them. They are things that deserve constant treatment and men cannot be reminded of them too often. 'These are things', he says, 'which I want you not just to declare once but to take pains to impress frequently on men's minds.' The sole aim of a good teacher must be edification and he should give it his whole attention. On the negative side he enjoins him not only to avoid profitless questions himself but to prevent others from being led away by them. Λογομαχεῖν means to be earnestly engaged in contentious disputations and it usually springs from a desire to be clever.

Charging them in the sight of the Lord means to put them in terror and from the severity of his words we can gather what a dangerous thing quarrelsome speculation is to the Church—that is knowledge that disregards godliness and cares only for self-display. All the so-called speculative theology of the Papists belongs to this category.

To no profit. He condemns λογομαχία on two scores, because it is fruitless and because it does great harm by disturbing men who are weak in the faith. In my translation I have followed Erasmus' rendering because it agrees with Paul's meaning, but I want my readers to note that Paul's words should be taken as meaning 'that which is useful for nothing'. The Greek reads εἰς οὐδὲν χρήσιμον and I take χρήσιμον as a nominative rather than an accusative, for that way the style flows better, as if he had said, 'What use is it when no good comes from it but much evil? For the faith of many is subverted.' Let us notice first that teaching is rightly condemned on the sole ground that it does no good. God's purpose is not to pander to our inquisitiveness but to give us profitable instruction. Away with all speculations that produce no edification! But the second reason is much worse, when questions are raised that are not only fruitless but tend *to the subverting of them that hear.* I wish that this could be taken to heart by those who are always looking for wordy battles, searching out a quarrel in every question and quibbling over single words or syllables. But they are carried away by ambition, which, as I know by experience with some of them, is sometimes an almost fatal disease. What the apostle says about the subversion of those that hear is completely proved by daily observation. It is natural that amidst disputes we lose our grasp of the truth and Satan makes ill use of quarrels as a pretext to upset or destroy their faith.

15. *Give diligence to present thyself.* The source of all doctrinal disputes is that clever men wish to show off their abilities before the world, and Paul here lays down the best and most fitting remedy for this by telling Timothy to keep his eyes fixed on God. It is as if he had said, 'Some men seek popular applause, but let it be your aim to approve yourself and your ministry to God.' There is indeed nothing more likely to check a foolish desire for display than to remember that it is God we have to deal with.

Erasmus translates ἀνεπαίσχυντον as 'that needeth not to blush or to be ashamed' and I have no fault to find. But I prefer to take it actively, 'that doth not blush, or is not ashamed', both because that is the more customary Greek usage, and because it seems to fit the present passage better. There is an implied contrast; those who disturb the Church with their contentions are so fierce against each other because they are ashamed of being worsted, and they think it disgraceful to admit that there is anything they do not know. Paul on the other hand calls them back to God's judgment and tells them first not to be lazy disputers but *workmen.* By this word he indirectly rebukes the foolishness of those who wrack themseves in doing nothing. Let us therefore be workmen who build up the Church, and let us set about God's work in such a way that some fruit may appear; then there will be no cause to be ashamed. For even if we cannot compete with talkative braggarts in disputing, it will be sufficient if we excel them in our zeal for edification, our industry and courage, the efficacy of our teaching. In short, he charges Timothy to work with diligence that he may not be ashamed before God; whereas the only kind of shame ambitious men dread is to lose their reputation for acuteness or abstruse knowledge

Dividing aright. This is a fine metaphor which accurately explains the main purpose of teaching. For since we should be satisfied only with God's Word, what purpose is there in having daily sermons and even in the office of pastor itself? Does not everybody have a chance to read the Scriptures for himself? But Paul assigns to teachers the duty of carving or dividing the Word, like a father dividing the bread into small pieces to feed his children. He advises Timothy to 'divide aright' lest, like men without skill, he succeeds only in cutting the surface and leaves the inmost pith and marrow untouched. But I take what is said here to have general application and to refer to a judicious dispensing of the Word which is adapted to the profit of those that hear it. Some mutilate it, some dismember it, some distort it, some break it in pieces, some, as I have said, keep to the outside and never come to the heart of the matter. With all these faults he contrasts a right dividing, that is, a manner of exposition adapted to edify. This is the rule by which we should judge every interpretation of Scripture.

16. *Shun profane babblings.* I have already dealt with these words in my commentary on the last chapter of I Timothy and I refer my readers to it. To deter Timothy from this profane and noisy garrulity he tells him that it is like a labyrinth or rather a deep whirlpool, from which there is no escape and into which men plunge deeper and deeper.

17. *And their word will eat as doth a gangrene.* Benedictus Textor, the physician, has drawn my attention to the fact that Erasmus has translated this passage badly, for he has confused two different diseases and made them one, speaking of cancer instead of gangrene. But Galen in many passages and especially in the definitions in his book *On Unnatural Swellings* distinguishes the one from the other. Paul Aegineta, following Galen, defines cancer in his sixth book as 'an irregular swelling, with fearful rims, of hideous appearance, bluish red in colour and unaccompanied by pain'. Later he differentiates two types of cancer, as do other physicians; some cancers are concealed and have no ulcers while others, where there is a preponderance of the black bile from which they originate, do ulcerate. But as for gangrene. Galen in the work already cited and also in his second book to Glauco, Aetius in his fourteenth book and the same Aegineta in his fourth book lay down that it comes from great inflammations which may attack any member, deprive the affected part of heat and vital energy so that it begins to die. If the part is completely dead the Greek authorities call the disease σφάκελος, the Latins *sideratio* and the common people St Anthony's fire. Cornelius Celcus distinguishes the two by holding that cancer is the genus and gangrene the species, but his error is clearly refuted in many passages by physicians of proved authority. He may also have been led astray by the similarity of the Latin words *cancer* and *gangraena*, but a similar mistake is not possible with the Greek words. Καρκίνον corresponds to the Latin *cancer* and means both a crab and the disease, while the grammarians think that gangrene is derived ἀπὸ τοῦ γραίνειν which means to consume. We must therefore abide by the term **gangrene**, which is the word Paul uses and which agrees with what he says about eating or consuming.

We have now dealt with the etymology, but all the medical authorities agree that the nature of the disease is such that unless counteracted as quickly as possible it will spread to adjoining parts and penetrate right into the bones, and not cease to consume until it has destroyed the man. Since therefore gangrene is quickly followed by mortification (νέκρωσις or *sideratio*) which soon infects the rest of the members till it ends in the complete destruction of the body, Paul aptly compares false doctrines with this deadly contagion. For if once they are allowed in they spread till they completely destroy the Church. Since the contagion is so destructive we must attack it early and not wait till it has gathered strength by progress, for then there will be no time to give assistance. The dreadful extinction of the Gospel among the Papists came about because, through the ignorance or sloth of the pastors, corruptions prevailed for a long time without hindrance and gradually destroyed the purity of doctrine.

Of whom are Hymenaeus and Philetus. He singles out these pests so that all may be on their guard against them, for if we allow people who are contriving the ruin of the whole Church to remain concealed, we only give them an opportunity to do harm. We ought indeed to conceal the faults of our brethren, but only of those whose contagion is not widely spread. Where many are in danger, not to expose the hidden evil in good time is cruel dissimulation. Can it be right that, in order to spare one, a hundred or a thousand should perish through my silence? Paul intended this information not just for Timothy, but desired to bear witness to all nations and ages of the ungodliness of these two men in order to shut the door against their depraved and deadly teaching. Having said that they have departed from the truth, he gives an example of their errors: they were giving out *that the resurrection is past already*. This means that they invented some sort of allegorical resurrection, as has been attempted in our day by some impure curs. By this trick Satan overthrows the fundamental article of our faith concerning the resurrection of the flesh. Since this is an old obsolete dream which is so severely condemned by Paul, it ought to disturb us the less; but when we are told that from the very beginning of the Gospel *the faith of some has been overthrown*, such an example should arouse us to diligent carefulness that we may quickly ward off such plagues from ourselves and from others. Such is the propensity of men to vanity that there is no absurdity so monstrous that the ears of some will not be open to hear it.

Howbeit the firm foundation of God standeth, having this seal, The Lord knoweth them that are his: and, Let every one that nameth the name of the Lord depart from unrighteousness. Now in a great house there are not only vessels of gold and of silver, but also of wood and of earth; and some unto honour, and some unto dishonour. If a man therefore purge

v. 19] II TIMOTHY 2

himself from these, he shall be a vessel unto honour, sanctified, meet for the Lord's use, prepared unto every good work. (19-21)

Howbeit the firm foundation of God standeth. We know only too well how much scandal is produced by the defections of those who once professed the same faith as we ourselves, and this is especially so in the case of men who are well known and of outstanding reputation. If some ordinary man apostatizes, we are not so much moved. But those whom men held in high repute, so that they seemed to be pillars of the Church, cannot fall without involving others in their ruin, at least, if their faith has no other support. This is Paul's concern here, and he says that this is no reason for godly men to lose heart even if they see falling those whom they thought most firm in the faith. To console them he points out that men's fickleness or unfaithfulness cannot prevent God from preserving His Church to the end. First he reminds us of God's election which he calls figuratively a foundation, meaning by this word its firm and enduring constancy. All this tends to prove the certainty of our salvation, provided that we belong to God's elect. It is as if he had said, 'God's elect do not depend upon changing events, but rest upon a solid and immovable foundation, for their salvation is in God's hand. Just as "every plant which the Heavenly Father hath not planted must be rooted up" (Matt. 15.13) so the root which His hand has fixed cannot be injured by winds or storms.' Let us remember first therefore that in spite of this great weakness of the flesh the elect are nevertheless not in danger, for they do not stand in their own strength but are founded on God. And if the foundations men lay are so firm, how much more so will that which is laid by God Himself! I know that some take this to refer to doctrine, 'Let no man judge the truth of the teaching by the faithlessness of those who profess it', but it is easily inferred from the context that Paul is speaking of the Church of God or of the elect.

Having this seal. The word *signaculum* has caused misunderstanding, for some have taken it to mean a mark or impression, so I have used the word *sigillum*, a seal, which is less ambiguous. For Paul's meaning clearly is that the salvation of the elect is in God's secret keeping, like a signet ring, for the Scripture declares that they are 'written in the book of life' (Ps. 69.28, Phil. 4.3). Both the word seal and the clause that follows remind us that we are not to judge according to our own opinion whether the number of the elect is great or small. For what God has sealed He intends to be as it were a closed book to us: also, if it belongs to God *to know who are His*, it is not surprising that often a great number of them are unknown to us and that we should make mistakes as to who they are. We should note why he speaks of a seal;

it is to remind us when we are faced with such defections that, as John says (I John 2.19), 'those who went out from us were not of us'. In this there is the twofold advantage that our own faith will not be shaken and, if unexpected things happen, we shall not be dismayed, as we often are. Secondly, being sure that in spite of this the Church will be safe, we shall more patiently allow the reprobate to depart to their own fate for which they were destined, for the number with which God is satisfied remains untouched. Thus, whenever any sudden change takes place contrary to our expectation and hope, let us at once remember that the Lord knows who are His own.

Let every one depart from unrighteousness. He has met the scandal caused by defection by saying that it should not produce excessive alarm among believers, and now he goes on to use such hypocrites as an example to teach us not to mock God by a like feigned profession of Christianity. It is as if he had said, 'Since God punishes hypocrites by exposing their wickedness in this way, let us learn to fear Him with a sincere conscience lest a like fate befall us.' Thus any man who calls on God's name, that is, professes to belong to God's people and wishes to be numbered among them, must put far from him all ungodliness. For here *to call on the name of Christ* means to boast in His title and to glory in belonging to His flock, just as in Isaiah 4.1 to invoke the name of a man over a woman means that the woman is to be reckoned his lawful wife, and in Genesis 48.16 to invoke the name of Jacob on all his posterity means that the family name is being preserved in uninterrupted succession, because it is descended from him.

20. *In a great house.* He now moves on and introduces a comparison to show that when we see fall away shamefully men who for a time made a distinguished show of piety and zeal, far from being disturbed by it, we should accept it as a seemly and suitable arrangement of God's providence. Who will find fault with a large house with an abundance of every kind of equipment, if it has not only vessels suited for display but also others that are mean and shameful? The diversity can even be ornamental, if the sideboard and table glitter with gold and silver, while the kitchen is furnished with vessels of wood and earthenware. Why should we be surprised if God, who is such a rich and abundant Father to His family, has different kinds of men as different kinds of furniture in His great house? Commentators do not agree as to whether the great house means the Church alone or the whole world. The context tends to suggest that we should take it to mean the Church, for Paul is not talking about strangers but about God's own family. But what he says is of general application and elsewhere Paul extends it to refer to the whole world, as in Romans 9.21 where he includes all the reprobate under the same terms used here. Thus there is no reason to

argue if someone takes this to refer to the world, but there is no doubt that Paul's object is to show that we should not think it strange to find bad men mixed with good, and this happens chiefly in the Church.

21. *If a man therefore purge himself from these.* If the reprobate are vessels of dishonour, the dishonour is confined to themselves; they do not disfigure the house or bring any shame on the head of the family, who destines each vessel in his varied furnishings to the use for which it is suited. But let us learn, from their example, to suit ourselves to honourable and higher uses. For in the reprobate we see as in a mirror a reflection of how detestable a man's state is, if he refuses to serve God from the heart. Such examples give good reasons to exhort men to devote themselves to a holy and blameless life.

Many misinterpret this passage to bring within the power of man's will and works things that Paul elsewhere declares to be the prerogatives of God's mercy (Rom. 9.16). But this is quite frivolous. Paul is not dealing here with the ground of man's election, as he does in Romans 9; he only means that we are different from the ungodly whom we see to have been born for destruction. Thus it is foolish to try to draw from these words inferences as to whether or not it is man's power to include himself in the number of God's children and to bring about his own adoption. This is not the subject here. Let this short warning be enough against those who bid a man bring about his own predestination, as though Paul were telling men to do what has been done before they were born, or rather before the foundation of the world.

Others infer from this passage that free will is sufficient to prepare a man to be fit and qualified to obey God, and they seem at first sight to be less foolish than those of whom we have been speaking, but in fact they have no solid case either. The apostle is enjoining that those who desire to consecrate themselves to God should purge themselves from the pollution of the ungodly, and in many places God commands the same. We find here nothing different from what we have seen in many Pauline passages, and especially in II Corinthians (6.17), 'Be ye clean who bear the vessels of the Lord.'[1] It is beyond all controversy that we are called to sanctification, but the question about a Christian's duty and vocation is different from the question about his ability or power to fulfil it. We do not deny that believers are required to purify themselves: but the Lord elsewhere declares this to be His own work, when He promises through Ezekiel (36.25) that He will send clean waters that we may be cleansed. Thus we should beseech the Lord to cleanse us instead of vainly exercising our strength to do it without His help.

[1] cf. Isaiah 52.11.

A vessel sanctified unto honour means one set apart for honourable and illustrious uses. A thing that is *useful* to the head of the family is something that is fitted to agreeable uses. Later he explains the metaphor by adding that we must be *prepared unto every good work*. Away with the mad cries of the fanatics who say, 'I will serve God's glory as Pharaoh did; what difference does it make as long as God is glorified?' Here God declares openly how He desires to be served, by a good and holy life.

But flee youthful lusts and follow after righteousness, faith, love, peace with them that call on the Lord out of a pure heart. But foolish and uninstructive questionings refuse, knowing that they engender strifes. And the Lord's servant must not strive but be gentle towards all, apt to teach, forbearing. In meekness correcting them that oppose themselves, if peradventure God may give them repentance unto the knowledge of the truth, that they may recover themselves out of the spare of the devil, by whom they have been taken captive to do his will. (22-26)

22. *Flee youthful lusts*. This follows from what he has just said about foolish questions and from his rebuke of Hymenaeus and Philetus whose self-seeking and empty curiosity had led them astray from right faith. He now therefore goes on to exhort Timothy to shun such a dangerous plague. And to this end he advises him to avoid *youthful lusts*, meaning by that not sexual sins or other disgraceful desires or any of those licentious courses in which young men often indulge, but rather those impetuous feelings and impulses to which the excessive warmth of youth makes young men prone. In controversy young men become heated much more quickly than those of mature age, they are more easily angered, they make more mistakes from lack of experience and rush at things with greater boldness and rashness. Thus Paul has good reason to tell a young man to guard himself carefully against the faults of his age which would otherwise easily involve him in useless disputes.

Follow righteousness. He recommends qualities of the opposite kind to keep his mind from being carried away by any youthful excess. It is as if he had said, 'These are the things to which you ought to give your whole attention and on which you should spend all your care.' First he mentions *righteousness*, that is, a right way of living, and then he adds *faith* and *love* of which it consists. *Peace* is very relevant to his present concern, for those who delight in the questionings he forbids are bound to be contentious and quarrelsome.

Here 'to call upon God' stands by synecdoche for worship in general, or it is possible to take it as meaning 'to make a profession of faith'. But since calling upon God is the chief part of divine worship, it often stands for the whole of religion or the worship of God. But when he bids him seek peace *with them that call on the Lord* it is not clear whether he is holding out all believers as an example to Timothy and saying that he ought to pursue peace as all true worshippers of God pursue it, or whether he is enjoining Timothy to cultivate peaceful relations with them. The latter interpretation seems the more suitable.

23. *Foolish and uninstructive questionings refuse.* He calls them foolish because they are uninstructive, that is, they lead to no increase of godliness, however good an opportunity for cleverness they may offer. We are really wise only when we are wise to some good purpose and this is something we should note carefully. For we see what foolish admiration the world accords to futile trifles and how eagerly it seeks them. In order that a desire to please may not lead us to seek men's favour by such a display, let us always remember this statement of Paul, that questions the world considers of great importance are nevertheless foolish because they are unprofitable.

Next he explains the evil they usually produce and says that they give occasion for quarrelling and conflicts—a fact we experience every day. And yet most men, although they have so many examples to warn them, derive no profit from them.

24. *And the Lord's servant must not strive.* Paul's train of thought is as follows, 'The servant of God must stand aloof from contentions; but foolish questions are contentious; therefore everyone who wishes to be reckoned a servant of God must shun them.' And if superfluous questions are to be avoided on this one ground that it is unseemly for God's servant to fight, how shameless it is for people to have the effrontery to seek applause by starting endless controversies. Look at the theology of the Papists, what is there in it but the art of contending and disputing? Thus the more proficient in it a man is, the more unfit he will be for serving Christ.

In bidding Christ's servant be *gentle* he requires the virtue which is the opposite of the disease of contentiousness. What immediately follows refers to the same point, that he should be διδακτικός, apt to teach. He will not be able to teach without moderation and some equability of temper. For what limit will a teacher observe if he is warmed for the fight? The more qualified a man is for teaching, the more he shuns disputes and controversies.

The hastiness of some men often produces either irritation or weariness, and so he adds *forbearance*, explaining at the same time why it is necessary—because a godly teacher ought to try to bring back the obstinate and rebellious to the right path, and that can be done only by restrained gentleness.

25. *If peradventure God may give them repentance.* The phrase 'if sometime' or 'if peradventure' emphasizes what a difficult undertaking this

is, to the point of being almost impossible and hopeless. Paul's meaning is that gentleness should be shown even to those who least deserve it, and even if at first there is no apparent hope of progress, still the challenge must be accepted. For the same reason he reminds us that *God will grant it*. Since the conversion of a man is in God's hands, who knows whether those who today seem unteachable may be suddenly changed by God's power into different men? Thus when we remember that repentance is God's gift and work, we shall hope the more earnestly and, encouraged by this assurance, will give more labour and care to the instruction of rebels. We should consider it our duty to sow and to water and, while we do that, we should expect God to give the increase. Thus our endeavours and labours are by themselves useless, and yet by God's favour they are not fruitless. We can also infer from this what repentance means for those who were for a time disobedient to God. Paul says that it begins with *knowledge of the truth*, meaning that man's mind is blinded for as long as he stubbornly holds out against God and His doctrine. Illumination is followed by liberation from servitude to the devil. Unbelievers are so intoxicated by Satan that in their stupor they are unaware of their misery. But, when God makes the light of His truth shine upon us, He wakens us out of that deadly sleep, breaks through the snares in which we were imprisoned, and having removed all the obstacles forms us in His obedience.

26. *By whom they have been taken captive*. It is indeed a dreadful condition when the devil has such power over us that he drags us as captive slaves here and there at his pleasure. And yet this is the condition of all those whose overweening pride breaks their bond of obedience to God, and we see every day in the reprobate open evidence of this tyrannical domination of Satan; for they would not rush with such fury and brutal violence into every kind of base and disgraceful crime if they were not driven to it by Satan's secret power. That is what we saw in connexion with Ephesians 2.2, that Satan exercises his power in unbelievers. Such examples warn us to take care to keep ourselves under the yoke of Christ and to yield ourselves to the governance of His Spirit. And yet the fact that that they are in this kind of captivity does not give the ungodly any excuse for claiming that they do not sin, because they act at Satan's instigation; for although the irresistible impulses to evil that carry them away result from Satan's domination over them, they do nothing under compulsion, but with their whole heart are inclined to go where Satan drives them. The result is that their captivity is voluntary.

CHAPTER THREE

But know this, that in the last days grievous times shall come. For men shall be lovers of self, lovers of money, boastful, haughty, railers, disobedient to parents, unthankful, unholy, without natural affection, implacable, slanderers, without self control, fierce, no lovers of good, traitors, headstrong, puffed up, lovers of pleasure rather than lovers of God; having a form of godliness, but having denied the power thereof: from these also turn away. For of these are they that creep into houses, and take captive silly women laden with sins, led away by divers lusts, ever learning, and never able to come to the knowledge of the truth. (1-7)

1. *But know this.* By this forewarning he intended to increase Timothy's diligence still more. When things go as we wish, we become more careless; but necessity makes us more alert. Thus Paul warns him that the Church will be subject to grievous diseases which will require in its pastors uncommon faithfulness, diligence, carefulness, wisdom and unwearied constancy. It is as though he were warning Timothy to prepare himself for the arduous and deeply anxious struggles that awaited him. From this we should learn not to yield or be terrified in face of any difficulties but rather rouse our hearts to resist. Under *the last days* he includes the universal condition of the Christian Church. He is not comparing his own age with ours, but rather teaching what the future condition of Christ's Kingdom will be. Many imagined that there would be a blessed peace immune from every trouble, but his meaning is that even under the Gospel there will not be such a state of perfection that all vices will be banished and every kind of virtue flourish; therefore the pastors of the Christian Church will have to deal with the ungodly and the wicked just as much as the prophets and godly priests of old. It follows that this is no time for idle repose.

2. *For men shall be.* We should note what the hardness or danger of this time is in Paul's view to be, not war, famine or diseases, nor any of the other calamities or ills that befall the body, but the wicked and depraved ways of men. To good men who fear God there is nothing more distressing than to see such moral corruption. As they value God's glory above all things, so they suffer grievous anguish when it is attacked or despised.

Secondly, we should note the people of whom he speaks. He does not attack or accuse external enemies who are openly opposed to the name of Christ, but people who belong to the family and wish to be reckoned among the members of the Church. For God wishes to try His Church to the point of letting her carry such pests in her own bosom, though she shudders at the thought of nurturing them. Thus if today there are mixed with us many whom we justly abhor, let us learn to groan patiently under that burden, since we are told that this is the lot of the Christian Church.

It is surprising how men who have the great sins that Paul here mentions should be able to keep up an appearance of godliness, as he says they do. But daily experience should keep us from being too surprised, for such is the amazing audacity and wickedness of hypocrites that they are completely shameless in excusing even their grossest faults, having once learnt to shelter themselves falsely under God's name. In ancient times countless vices abounded in the life of the Pharisees, and yet they enjoyed a reputation for outstanding holiness, as though they were free from every stain. And today also, although the impurity of the Roman clergy is so great that it stinks in the nostrils of the whole world, for all their wickedness they do not cease to make proud claims to all the rights and titles of saints. Thus Paul's statement that hypocrites, though chargeable with the grossest faults, nevertheless deceive by wearing a mask of godliness, should not seem strange with these examples of it before our eyes. And the world deserves to be deceived by these wicked scoundrels, since it either despises or cannot bear real holiness. Also Paul here enumerates vices of a kind that are not immediately visible and which can accompany a pretended holiness. For what hypocrite is not proud, or a lover of self, or a despiser of others, or harsh and cruel, or fraudulent? But all these are hidden from men's eyes. There is no need to go through this list item by item for it needs no detailed explanation. But readers should note that $\phi\iota\lambda\alpha\upsilon\tau\iota\alpha$, which comes first, can be regarded as the source from which all the others that follow spring. For the man who loves himself claims superiority in everything, despises all others, is cruel, indulges in covetousness, treachery, anger, disobedience against his parents, neglect of good and all such things. As it was Paul's purpose to brand false prophets with such marks, that they might be seen and known by all, so it is our duty to open our eyes and see those who are thus pointed out.

5. *From these also turn away.* This exhortation makes it quite clear that Paul is not speaking of distant posterity, or prophesying what would happen after many centuries, but is pointing out present evils and thus applying to his own time what he has just said about the last days. For how could Timothy turn away from those who would not

appear for many centuries? Thus right from the beginning of the Gospel that Church began to suffer from such corruptions.

6. *Of these are they.* You would think that here Paul was drawing a true to life picture of the monastic orders. But without mentioning monks by name, the marks by which Paul distinguishes false and pretended teachers are sufficiently clear, insinuating themselves into families, being snares for silly women, given to mean flattery, imposing upon people by various superstitions. We should note carefully these marks if we want to distinguish between useless drones and good ministers of Christ. Those who are such are here pointed out so clearly that they cannot succeed in excusing themselves. *To creep into families* means to enter stealthily or by methods of cunning.

Also he speaks here of women rather than men, for they are more liable to be taken in by such imposters. He says that they *are led captive*, because false prophets of this kind gain influence over them by various methods, partly by prying curiously into their affairs and partly by flattering them. He immediately adds that such women are *laden with sins*, for if they were not fettered by a bad conscience they would not let themselves be led away at the will of others in every way. *Lusts* I take to mean in general foolish and frivolous desires by which women who do not sincerely seek after God, but who wish to be thought religious and holy, are led away. There is no limit to the disguises they can assume, when once they depart from a good conscience. Chrysostom prefers to take it to mean impure and obscene desires, but in view of the context I prefer my own explanation. For it immediately follows that they are *always learning* but never learn to be really wise. This fluctuation between various desires comes about when they have nothing solid in themselves and are tossed about in different directions. They learn, because they are curious and have restless minds, but in such a way that they never reach any certainty or truth. This is an absurd way of learning and quite different from real knowledge. And yet such people think themselves outstanding in wisdom, but what they really know is nothing, as long as they do not hold the truth which is the foundation of all knowledge.

> *And like as Jannes and Jambres withstood Moses, so do these also withstand the truth; men corrupted in mind, reprobate concerning the faith. But they shall proceed no further; for their folly shall be evident unto all men, as theirs also came to be. But thou didst follow my teaching, conduct, purpose, faith, longsuffering, love patience, persecutions, sufferings; what things befell me at Antioch, at Iconium, at Lystra; what persecutions I endured: and out of them all the Lord delivered me. Yea, and all that would live godly in Christ Jesus shall suffer persecution.* (8-12)

8. *As Jannes and Jambres.* This comparison confirms what I have already said about the last days. For he means that what is happening to us under the Gospel is the same as the Church has experienced almost from its first beginning, and certainly from the promulgation of the Law. The Psalmist speaks in the same terms of the conflicts of the Church, 'Many a time have they afflicted me from my youth up, let Israel now say. The ungodly ploughed upon my back, they made long their furrows' (Ps. 129.1, 3). Paul reminds us that it is not surprising that enemies should rise up against Christ and resist His Gospel, seeing that Moses had those who contended against him in the same way. These examples from ancient antiquity should be a great consolation to us. It is generally agreed that the two men here named were magicians put forward by Pharaoh, but it is not clear from what source Paul learnt their names, although it is probable that many facts relating to the events of the exodus were handed down and God never let the memory of them perish. It is also possible that in Paul's time there were extant commentaries on the prophets which gave a fuller account of matters which Moses only touches briefly. We may guess that two are named because, God having raised up for His people two leaders, Moses and Aaron, Pharaoh decided to oppose them with the same number of magicians.

9. *But they shall proceed no further.* He encourages Timothy for the conflict by offering a confident assurance of victory. For although false teachers will trouble him, Paul promises that in a short time they will be shamefully confounded. But this promise is not borne out by the event and a little later the apostle seems to contradict himself by saying that they will get worse. There is no force in Chrysostom's solution, that although they themselves will get worse every day, they will do no harm to others, for Paul expressly adds that they err and cause others to err. And this is confirmed by experience. A better explanation is that Paul was viewing them from different aspects. His statement that they will make no progress is not general, but means only that the Lord will expose their madness to many who at first were deceived by their enchantments.

Thus when he says that *their folly shall be evident unto all men*, this is a figure of speech in which the whole stands for the part. Those who are most successful at deception do at first make great boastings and win loud applause, so that it seems there is nothing beyond their power; but their deceptions quickly come to nothing, for the Lord opens the eyes of many so that they begin to see what was for a time hidden from them. Yet the folly of false prophets is never so completely uncovered as to be made known to all. Also, no sooner is one error driven out than new ones immediately spring up to take its place. Both pieces of advice are therefore required. In order that godly pastors may not be brought to despair, as though they were carrying on a battle against errors to no effect, they are to be told about the good success that the Lord will give to His own teaching. And yet to keep them from thinking that their work is done when they have fought in one or two battles, they are to be reminded that there will always be fresh calls to fight. We shall deal with this second point later. In the present context it is enough for us to see that he holds out to Timothy the sure hope of a successful outcome, to encourage him to fight. And he confirms this by the example he has already quoted. Just as God's truth prevailed against the magicians' tricks, so he promises that the teaching of the Gospel will be victorious against every kind of newfangled false imaginings of men.

10. *But thou didst follow my teaching.* This is another argument to urge Timothy on. He is no ignorant raw recruit going forth into the arena, for Paul himself has already formed him by a long course of his own teaching. He refers not only to doctrine; for the other things he mentions are also of great importance. In this verse he paints for us a lively picture of a good teacher, as one who shapes his pupils not only by his words but, so to speak, opens his own heart to them so that they may know that all his teaching is sincere. That is what is meant by the word *purpose.* He adds other practical proofs of an earnest and unfeigned sincerity, *faith, love, longsuffering, patience.* Such fundamental lessons had been imparted to Timothy in Paul's schools. But he does not merely remind him of what he has taught him, but bears testimony to Timothy's past life in order to encourage him to persevere. He praises him as one who has imitated his own virtues, as if he had said, 'You have been long accustomed to follow my instructions; continue therefore as you have begun.' His intention is that Timothy should constantly have before him the example of his own faith, love and patience and so he reminds him especially of his persecutions which were best known to him.

11. *And out of them all the Lord delivered me.* The fact that afflictions always have a happy end is a consolation that much mitigates their bitterness. If anyone objects that the happy end he claims is not always obvious, I agree that this is true as far as outward appearances (*sensus carnis*) are concerned, for Paul himself had not yet been set free. But by delivering us often, God testifies that He is with us and will always be so. From our present experience of His help our confidence should extend into the future. It is as if he had said, 'You know from experience that God has never failed me, so that there is no reason for you to hesitate to follow my example.'

12. *Yea and all who would live godly.* The recollection of his own

persecutions makes him add that all that has happened to him will also come to all godly men. He says this partly that believers may be ready to accept this situation, and partly that good men may not regard him with suspicion because of the persecutions he endures at the hands of the ungodly, for it sometimes happens that adverse fortunes give rise to adverse criticisms. If anyone is in disfavour with men, people immediately declare that he is hated by God. By this general statement Paul declares that he is among God's children, and at the same time warns his brethren to make ready to endure persecutions. For if this rule holds for 'all who would live godly in Christ', it follows that those who wish to avoid persecutions must renounce Christ. It is in vain to try to detach Christ from His cross, and it is only natural that the world should hate Christ even in His members. And since cruelty goes with hatred, persecutions come. We should reckon with the fact that if we are Christians we shall be liable to many tribulations and struggles of different kinds.

But the question will be asked, whether all then must be martyrs. It is clear that there have been many godly men who have never undergone banishment or prison or sudden flight or any other kind of persecution. I answer that Satan has more than one way of persecuting Christ's servants. But it is absolutely necessary that all of them should endure the hostility of the world in some form in order that their faith may be exercised and their constancy proved. Satan, who is Christ's perpetual foe, never allows anyone a whole lifetime without disturbance, and there will always be wicked men to be thorns in our sides. In fact, as soon as a believer shows signs of zeal for God, the rage of all the ungodly is kindled, and though they may not have a drawn sword, they spue out their venom either by criticizing or slandering or making an upheaval in some other way. Thus, although all are not faced with the same attacks and not involved in the same battles, they have a common warfare to wage and will never be wholly at peace and exempt from persecutions.

> *But evil men and impostors shall wax worse and worse, deceiving and being deceived. But abide thou in the things which thou hast learned and hast been assured of, knowing of whom thou hast learned them; and that from a babe thou hast known the sacred writings which are able to make thee wise unto salvation through faith which is in Christ Jesus. Every scripture inspired of God is also profitable for teaching, for reproof, for correction, for instruction which is in righteousness: that the man of God may be complete, furnished completely unto every good work.* (13-17)

13. *But evil men.* It is the most bitter persecution of all when we see

evil men with their sacrilegious boldness and their blasphemies and errors gathering strength. Paul says elsewhere that Ishmael persecuted Isaac not by the sword but with mockery (Gal. 4.29). Thus we may infer that in the last verse Paul was not describing only one kind of persecution, but was speaking generally of all the distresses that God's children have to endure when they contend for their Father's glory. I have already spoken of how evil men will grow worse and worse; he is foretelling that they will be obstinate in their resistance and successful in doing harm and corrupting others. One worthless man will always be more effectual in destroying than ten faithful teachers in building up, even though they labour with all their might. Tares are never lacking for Satan to injure the pure corn, and even when we think false prophets have been driven out, others immediately spring up from elsewhere. They have this power to do harm, not because falsehood is by its own nature stronger than truth or because the wiles of the devil have greater power than God's Spirit, but because men are naturally inclined to vanity and errors and embrace more readily things that agree with this natural disposition, and also because they are blinded by God's just act of vengeance against them and are thus led captive slaves at Satan's pleasure. The chief reason why the plague of godless doctrines is so successful is that men's ingratitude deserves that it should be so. It is of great importance that godly teachers should be reminded of this, that they may prepare themselves for continual warfare and not be discouraged by delay, or yield to the pride and insolence of their adversaries.

14. *Abide thou.* Although ungodliness is increasing and making progress, he tells Timothy nevertheless to stand firm. Certainly this is the real test of our faith, that with unwearying zeal we should resist all the devil's devices, refusing to alter course with every wind that blows, and thus remain fixed on God's truth as on a sure anchor.

Knowing of whom thou hast learnt. His intention here is to commend the certainty of his teaching, for we should not persevere in things in which we have been wrongly instructed. If we wish to be Christ's disciples we must unlearn all that we have learnt apart from Him. For example, our own pure instruction in the faith began when we rejected and forgot all that we had been taught under Papistry. The apostle is not telling Timothy to retain indiscriminately all the teaching handed on to him, but only what he knows to be true; his meaning is that we must make a selection. His claim that what he teaches is to be received as divine revelation is not made on his own behalf as a private individual. Rather he boldly asserts his apostolic authority to Timothy, knowing that his faithfulness was well known and his calling proved as far as he was concerned. Being surely persuaded that he had been taught by Christ's apostle, Timothy could gather from that that the teaching had its source not in a man but in Christ. This passage teaches us that we should exercise the same care both to avoid false assurance in matters that are uncertain, that is, all the things that men teach, and hold the truth of God with unshaken firmness. We also learn that we must add to our faith discernment that can distinguish the Word of God from the word of man so that we do not accept at random whatever is offered to us. There is nothing more alien to faith than an easy credulity that bids us accept everything indiscriminately no matter what its nature or source may be, for the chief foundation of faith is to know that it has its origin and authority in God. By adding that Timothy had been *entrusted with*[1] his teaching, he adds force to his exhortation. To commit a thing in trust to someone is more than simply to hand it over. Timothy had not been instructed as one of the common people, but in order that he might faithfully hand over to others what he had received.

15. *And that from a babe.* The fact that he had been accustomed from his boyhood to read the Scriptures was also a powerful urge to fidelity, for this long established habit can make a man much better prepared to meet any kind of deception. It was a wise care that in ancient times was taken to make sure that those who were intended for the ministry of the Word should from their boyhood be instructed in the solid doctrine of godliness, and should drink deep of the sacred writings, so that when they came to fulfil their office they should not be untried apprentices. Thus if anyone has aquired from his youth a knowledge of the Scriptures he should count it a special blessing of God.

Which are able to make thee wise. It is a very high commendation of Holy Scripture to say that the wisdom which suffices for salvation cannot be found elsewhere, and the next verse explains his meaning more fully. But at the same time he tells us what we ought to look for in the Scripture itself, for false prophets also make use of it to find a pretext for their teaching. In order that it may be profitable to salvation to us, we have to learn to make right use of it. What if somebody is interested only in curious speculations? What if he adheres only to the letter of the Law and does not seek Christ? What if he perverts the natural meaning with interpretations alien to it? He has good reason to recall us to the faith of Christ, which is the centre and sum of Scripture. For what immediately follows also depends on faith.

16. *All scripture*—or 'the whole of Scripture', although it makes no difference to the meaning. He now explains more fully his brief commendation. First he commends the Scripture because of its authority, and then because of the profit that comes from it. To assert

[1] R.V. 'assured of'.

its authority he teaches that it is *inspired of God*, for, if that is so, it is beyond all question that men should receive it with reverence. This is the principle that distinguishes our religion from all others, that we know that God has spoken to us and are fully convinced that the prophets did not speak of themselves, but as organs of the Holy Spirit uttered only that which they had been commissioned from heaven to declare. All those who wish to profit from the Scriptures must first accept this as a settled principle, that the Law and the prophets are not teachings handed on at the pleasure of men or produced by men's minds as their source, but are dictated by the Holy Spirit. If anyone object and ask how this can be known, my reply is that it is by the revelation of the same Spirit both to learners and teachers that God is made known as its Author. Moses and the prophets did not utter rashly and at random what we have received from them, but, speaking by God's impulse, they boldly and fearlessly testified the truth that it was the mouth of the Lord that spoke through them. The same Spirit who made Moses and the prophets so sure of their vocation now also bears witness to our hearts that He has made use of them as ministers by whom to teach us. Thus it is not surprising that many should doubt the authority of Scripture. For although the majesty of God is displayed in it, only those who have been enlightened by the Holy Spirit have eyes to see what should have been obvious to all, but is in fact visible only to the elect. This is the meaning of the first clause, that we owe to the Scripture the same reverence as we owe to God, since it has its only source in Him and has nothing of human origin mixed with it.

And is profitable. There now follows the second part of his commendation, that Scripture contains the perfect rule of a good and happy life. In saying this he means that Scripture is corrupted by sinful abuse when this profitable purpose is not sought in it. He is indirectly rebuking those triflers who were feeding the people with empty speculations as with wind. For the same reason we may today condemn all who abandon concern for edification and agitate over ingenious but profitless questions. Whenever ingenious trifles of that kind are introduced, they should be warded off with this phrase as with a shield, 'Scripture is profitable.' It follows from this that it is wrong to use it unprofitably. In giving us the Scriptures, the Lord did not intend either to gratify our curiosity or satisfy our desire for ostentation or provide us with a chance for mythical invention and foolish talk; He intended rather to do us good. Thus the right use of Scripture must always lead to what is profitable.

For teaching. Here he enumerates one by one the many and varied uses of Scripture. First of all he mentions teaching, since it takes precedence over all the others. But since doctrine is by itself often cold and lifeless, he adds *reproof* and *correction*. It would take too long to set out here what we learn from the Scriptures, and he has already in the previous verse given a brief summary of it in the word 'faith'. This is indeed the chief part of our knowledge—faith in Christ. Next follows instruction on the regulation of our lives, to which are added the incitements of exhortations and reproofs. Thus the man who makes a right use of the Scripture lacks nothing either for salvation or for living well. The only difference between 'reproof' and 'correction' is that the second is the result of the first. To acknowledge our iniquity and have a conviction of God's judgment upon it is the beginning of repentance. *Instruction in righteousness* means instruction in a godly and holy life.

17. *That the man of God may be complete.* Here complete means perfect, a man in whom there is nothing at all defective, for he asserts without qualification that the Scripture is sufficient to achieve perfection. Thus any man who is not satisfied with the Scripture seeks to know more than he ought, and more than it is good for him to know.

But here a question arises. In speaking of the Scripture Paul means what we call the Old Testament; how can he say that it can make a man perfect? If that is so, what was added later through the apostles would seem to be superfluous. My answer is that as far as the substance of the Scripture is concerned, nothing has been added. The writings of the apostles contain nothing but a simple and natural explanation of the Law and the prophets along with a clear description of the things expressed in them. Paul was therefore right to celebrate the praises of the Scripture in this way, and since today its teaching is fuller and clearer by the addition of the Gospel, we must confidently hope that the usefulness of which Paul speaks will become much more evident to us, if we are willing to make the trial and receive it.

CHAPTER FOUR

I charge thee therefore in the sight of God, and of Jesus Christ, who shall judge the quick and the dead, and by his appearing and his kingdom; preach the word; be instant in season, out of season; reprove, rebuke, exhort, with all longsuffering and teaching. For the time will come when they will not endure the sound doctrine; but, having itching ears, will heap to themselves teachers after their own lusts; and will turn away their ears from the truth, and turn aside unto fables. (1-4)

1. *I charge thee therefore.* We should carefully note how appropriately he connects the Scripture with preaching by the use of the word 'therefore'. This also refutes certain fanatics who in their arrogance boast that they have no further need of teachers, since the reading of Scripture is quite sufficient. But when Paul speaks of the usefulness of Scripture, he concludes not only that everyone should read it, but that teachers ought to administer it, which is the duty laid upon them. Thus since all wisdom is contained in the Scriptures, and neither we nor our teachers should seek it from any other source, he who ignores the help of the living voice and is content with silent Scripture will find how wrong it is to disregard a way of learning enjoined by *God* and *Christ*. Let us remember that the fact that the reading of the Scripture is recommended to all does not annul the ministry of pastors, so that believers should learn to profit both by reading and by hearing, since God has not ordained either in vain.

Here as in a matter of great importance Paul adds a solemn charge, bringing before Timothy God as avenger and Christ as judge, if he should cease to exercise his office as teacher. As God gave a pledge of how much care He has for the salvation of His Church by not sparing His only begotten Son, so He will not allow to go unpunished the negligence of pastors through which the souls He has redeemed at such cost perish or become the prey of Satan. He makes special mention of the judgment of Christ because He will require of us, who are His representatives, a stricter account of our failures in His ministry.

Who shall judge the quick and the dead—that is, those whom He finds still alive at His coming and also those who have already died. Thus none shall escape His judgment.

Christ's appearance and kingdom. The two words mean the same, for although He now rules in heaven and in earth, till now His kingdom has not been made clearly manifest; rather it lies in the shadow of the cross and is violently opposed by His enemies. His kingdom will be truly established when He has vanquished His enemies and brought to nought every opposing power, and so openly displays His majesty.

2. *Be instant in season.* By these words he commends not merely perseverance but even aggressiveness in overcoming all hindrances and difficulties; for being by nature timid and slothful we easily give way before the very smallest hindrances and sometimes we even welcome them as excuses for our laziness. We should consider how many ways Satan has ready to hinder us in our course, and how slow to follow and how soon wearied are those who are called. Thus the Gospel will not for long hold its own, if pastors do not ruthlessly press its claims. Now this ruthless persistence (*importunitas*) refers both to pastor and people, to the pastor that he may not exercise his office of teaching merely at his own chosen times and to suit his own convenience, but sparing himself no labour or trouble may drive himself on. For the people constant assiduity means to stir up those who are asleep, to stop those who are rushing headlong in the wrong way, and to put right the things that concern the vain world.

He tells Timothy to be instant in *reproving, rebuking, exhorting,* thus indicating that we need many incentives to keep us on the right course. If we were as teachable as we should be, Christ's ministers could guide us merely by pointing out the right way. But, as things are, sane advice and merely moderate exhortations are not enough to shake off our unresponsiveness, unless there is added to them the greater vehemence of reproofs and chidings.

With all longsuffering. This is a most needful qualification. Reproofs either fail to have any effect because they are too violent or because they disappear into thin air, not being founded in sound *teaching*. Exhortations and accusations can be no more than aids to teaching and without it have little force. We see examples of this in people who possess much zeal and great asperity but are not equipped with solid teaching. They wear themselves out, they shout at the top of their voices and make a great noise, but all to no avail because they are building without a foundation. I am speaking of those who are in other ways good men, but have insufficient learning and too much emotional fervour, for those who marshal all their energy to oppose sound doctrine are far more dangerous and do not deserve to be mentioned here. In short Paul means that reproof should be founded on teaching, that it may not deservedly be despised as useless.

He says next that zeal should be tempered with longsuffering gentleness. Nothing is more difficult once we begin to grow warm than to set a limit to our fervour. But if we are carried away by our impatience, then we strive in vain. For besides making us ridiculous, our harshness annoys people. Besides, severe and harsh men are usually unable to endure the obstinacy of those with whom they have to deal, and cannot submit to the many annoyances and indignities which we have to swallow, if we wish to be useful. Thus severity must be seasoned with gentleness that it may be known to spring from a peaceful heart.

3. *For the time will come.* From the depravity of men he shows how careful pastors ought to be. For the Gospel would soon be extinguished and would pass from men's memories, if godly men did not strive with all earnestness to preserve it. His meaning is that we must make full use of our opportunities while some reverence for Christ still remains, as if he had said that when a storm is seen to be coming we must not take our time at our work but hurry with all diligence, because soon there will not be the same opportunity.

When he says that *they will not endure sound doctrine*, he means not only that they will dislike or despise it, but that they will actually hate it; he calls it sound because of its effect in instructing us in godliness. In the next verse he calls it *truth*, meaning that sound doctrine is a pure and natural handling of God's Word, and he contrasts it with *fables*, useless imaginings by which the straightforwardness of the Gospel is corrupted. From this we may learn, first, that the more determined men become to despise the teaching of Christ, the more zealous should godly ministers be to assert it and the more strenuous their efforts to preserve it entire, and more than that, by their diligence to ward off Satan's attacks. And if ever this was needed, in our own time the ingratitude of men makes it more necessary than ever. For those who at first eagerly accept the Gospel and show no ordinary enthusiasm for it, a little later develop a distaste for it which at last becomes positive hatred. Ohters reject it violently, or hear it with contempt or make a mockery of it from the very beginning. Still others cannot bear its yoke and kick against it, and out of hatred for holy discipline are entirely estranged from Christ, or even changed from being His friends into being His open enemies. Yet, far from giving up in discouragement, we should fight even against such monstrous ingratitude and in fact strain every nerve in the struggle far more than if Christ's offer was being universally and willingly accepted.

Secondly, since we have been warned of such contempt and even rejection of the Word of God, we should not be amazed as if this were some new spectacle when we see what is here foretold by the Spirit being fulfilled. And since we are by nature prone to vanity, it is not anything new or uncommon that we should be more willing to listen to fables than to the truth. In addition, since the Gospel is unimposing and humble in its outward appearance, its teaching fails to satisfy either our curiosity or our pride. There are very few endowed with a taste for spiritual things so that they relish newness of life and all that belongs to it.

Paul is here foretelling one special great outbreak of godlessness in one particular age in the future and telling Timothy to be ready to meet it.

Will heap to themselves teachers. We should note the word 'heap' by which he means that their madness will be so great that they will not be content with a few imposters but will want a great crowd. As there is always an insatiable desire for vain and harmful things, the world seeks on every side and without limit all the means of its own destruction it can devise and imagine, and the devil always has available as many teachers of this kind as the world requires. There has always been a plenteous harvest of wicked men, as there is today, and Satan has never any lack of helpers or of means for deceiving men.

The just reward of this great depravity which nearly always prevails among men is that God and His sound teaching are either rejected or despised and falsehood is gladly embraced. The fact that false teachers so often abound and sometimes come forth in swarms should be ascribed to God's righteous judgment. We deserve to be overwhelmed by this kind of rubbish, since God's truth finds no place in us, or, if admitted, is immediately driven from possession, and we are so devoted to myths and fables that even a multitude of deceivers is not too much for us. What a rubbishy crowd of monks there are in the Papistry, and yet if one godly pastor has to be maintained instead of ten monks and as many priests, complaints are immediately raised about the expense. The way of the world is such that by heaping up with all its enthusiasm countless deceivers, it desires to stamp out all that is of God. Many errors have no other cause but the free desire of men to be deceived rather than rightly instructed. That is why Paul adds the expression, *having itching ears*, when he wishes to assign a cause to so much evil. This elegant metaphor means that the world will have ears so delicate and so continually eager for something new, that it will heap up for itself many different teachers and will continually be carried away by fresh fabrications. The sole remedy for this vice is that believers should be taught to adhere closely to the pure teaching of the Gospel.

> *But be thou sober in all things, suffer hardship, do the work of an evangelist, fulfil thy ministry. For I am already being offered, and the time of my departure is come. I have fought the good fight, I have finished the course, I have kept the faith: henceforth there is laid up for me the crown of righteousness, which the Lord, the righteous judge shall give to me at that day: and not only to me, but also to all them that have loved his appearing.* (5-8)

5. *But be thou sober.* He carries on with his exhortation to make sure that the more grievous the troubles become, the more conscientiously will Timothy labour to cure them, and the more pressing the dangers, the more intently will he keep watch. And since struggles come to the ministers of Christ from the very moment when they begin to discharge their office faithfully, he also reminds him to be firm and immovable in enduring adversity.

To *do the work of an evangelist* is to do that which belongs to an evangelist. It is not clear whether this word has a general meaning and denotes all ministers of the Gospel, or whether it describes some special office. I am more inclined to the second view, since it is clear from Ephesians 4.11 that there was an intermediate order of ministry between the apostles and the pastors (*ordinem inter Apostolos et Pastores medium*), so that evangelists were assistants second to the apostles. It is most likely that Timothy, whom Paul had associated with himself as his closest colleague in all his concerns, was above ordinary pastors in the rank and dignity of his office (*gradu et officii dignitate*), and was not merely one of their number. To make an honourable mention here of the office would both encourage him and commend his authority to others, and Paul has both these aims in view.

If with the Vulgate we read 'fulfil' in the last clause the meaning will be, 'the only way you can fully discharge the ministry entrusted to you is by doing what I have commanded: see to it then that you do not fail in mid course.' But since the verb πληροφορεῖν very often means 'to render certain' or 'to prove', I prefer this interpretation which suits the context very well, that Timothy, by keeping watch and patiently bearing afflictions and being instant in teaching, is successfully proving the reality of his ministry, since all such indications acknowledge him to be a faithful minister of Christ.

6. *For I am already being offered.* He now gives the reason for the solemnity of the charge he has given. It is as if he had said, 'As long as I was alive I could stretch out my hand to help you; you have never been without my constant exhortations, my advice has greatly assisted you and my example has been a great source of strength. Now the time is coming when you will have to teach and encourage yourself and begin to swim without support. Take care that nothing in you may be seen to be changed by my death.'

We should note the expressions he uses to describe his death. By the word *departure* he indicates that when we die we do not altogether perish; it is only a departing of the soul from the body. Thus we infer that death is only a passing of the soul from the body and this definition contains a testimony to the immortality of the soul.

Offering or sacrifice was a term specially suited to Paul's death, since he was dying for maintaining the truth of Christ. For although all godly men are sacrifices acceptable to God both in the obedience of their lives and in their deaths, martyrs are sacrificed in a more pre-eminent way by shedding their blood for Christ's name. In addition the word σπένδεσθαι which Paul uses here does not mean any kind of sacrifice but specifically one used to ratify a covenant. Thus his meaning in this passage is the same as in Philippians 2.17 where he explains himself more fully, 'Yea and if I am offered upon the sacrifice of your faith, I rejoice.' His meaning is that the faith of the Philippians will be ratified only by his death, as the same way as covenants were ratified in ancient times by slain animal sacrifices; not that the certainty of our faith is strictly speaking founded on the constancy of the martyrs, but it does tend greatly to confirm us. Here Paul celebrates his death by commending it as the ratification of his teaching, that it might encourage believers to persevere rather than grow weary, as often happens.

The time of my departure. This expression should also be noted because by it he most fittingly removes our excessive dread of death by pointing to its nature and its effect. The only reason that men should be so greatly disturbed at the merest mention of death is that they think that in death they completely perish. By calling it a 'departure' he declares that man does not perish, but his soul is only parted from his body. It is for the same reason that he fearlessly declares that *the time is come*, for he could not do that unless he despised death. It is part of man's nature to dread and shrink from death and he can never completely free himself from it; but faith must overcome that fear and refuse to let it keep us from leaving the world obediently, whenever God calls us.

7. *I have fought the good fight.* Since it is usual to judge a thing by its result, Paul's fight could be condemned, since it had an unhappy end. Thus he boasts that, whatever the world may think, it has been a good fight. This is a proof of his outstanding faith, for not only did all men think Paul extremely wretched, but his death too was going to be shameful. Thus who would not say that he had struggled without success? But he himself does not depend upon men's twisted judgments, but in his great courage he rises above every calamity, so that nothing can interfere with his happiness and glory. Thus he declares that the fight he has fought has been good and honourable and even rejoices in the prospect of death because it is the goal he has been striving to attain. We know that runners have achieved what they wish for when they reach the goal. His meaning is that death is the goal of Christ's athletes, since it marks the end of their labours, and also that we should never rest content with this life, since it is of no advantage

to have run vigourously from the starting point to mid-course, if we do not in the end reach the goal.

What follows about having *kept the faith* may have two meanings, either that he was a faithful soldier to his Captain right to the end, or that he had continued faithfully in the right doctrine. Either sense suits well; indeed the only way he could prove his fidelity to the Lord was by a constant profession of the pure doctrine of the Gospel. I have no doubt that here his allusion is to the soldier's solemn vow of loyalty, as if he had said that he had always been a good and faithful soldier to his Captain.

8. *Henceforth*. As he has gloried in his good fight, the course finished and the faith kept, so now he claims that his labours have not been in vain. It is possible to make a strenuous effort and yet not to attain the due reward. But Paul says that his reward is sure. He gains this certainty from turning his eyes to the day of resurrection, and we should do likewise. If we look around we see nothing but death, so that we should not concentrate on the appearances of the world, but should have before our minds the coming of Christ. The result will be that nothing can lessen our happiness.

Because he speaks of *the crown of righteousness* and *the righteous judge* and uses the verb *give* or *render*, the Papists try to use this passage to bolster up the merit of works in opposition to God's grace, but their reasoning is absurd. Justification by free grace conferred upon us through faith is not at variance with the rewarding of works; the two are rather completely consistent—man is freely justified by Christ's grace and yet God will render to him the reward of his works. For as soon as God has received us into His favour, He also regards our works with favour and deigns to give them a reward which is not due to them. Here the Papists make two mistakes, first in inferring from this passage that we put God in our debt by doing good works of our own free will, and also in imagining that God is bound to us, as if our salvation had any other source but His own free grace. But it does not follow that because God justly gives us what He does give us, He therefore owes us something. For He is just even in His undeserved acts of grace. And He renders the reward He has promised not because we first take the initiative with any obedience of our own, but because with the same generosity that He shows us at the beginning, He adds to His first gifts others that are bestowed later. Thus it is vain and perverse for the Papists to try to prove from this passage that good works have their origin in the power of free will, since there is no absurdity in holding that God crowns with a reward His own gifts in us. It is equally vain and foolish for them to try to use this passage to destroy the righteousness of faith, since there is no inconsistency between the kindness of God by which He freely accepts a man not imputing his sins and His rewarding of good works, where with the same generosity He gives what He has promised.

And not to me only. In order that all other believers may fight with the same courage, he invites them to share his crown. For his unbroken faithfulness could not serve as an example to us, if we did not have the same hope of a crown before us. He mentions an outstanding characteristic of believers when he calls them *all them that have loved his appearing.* For wherever faith is strong it does not let our hearts fall asleep in this world but raises them up to hope in the final resurrection. His meaning is that all who are so devoted to this world and love this passing life so much that they do not care about Christ's coming and do not feel any desire for it, deprive themselves of immortal glory. Alas for our stupidity which so dominates us that we never think seriously of Christ's coming, when we should be giving it our whole attention. He also excludes from the number of believers those who are afraid and in terror at the thought of Christ's coming, for it cannot be loved unless it is regarded as pleasant and joyful.

> *Do thy diligence to come shortly unto me: for Demas forsook me, having loved this present world, and went to Thessalonika; Crescens to Galatia, Titus to Dalmatia. Only Luke is with me. Take Mark and bring him with thee: for he is useful to me for ministering. But Tychicus I sent to Ephesus. The cloke that I left at Troas with Carpus, bring when thou comest, and the books especially the parchments.* (9-13)

9. *Do thy diligence.* Since he knew that the time of his death was at hand, I do not doubt that there were many matters concerning the good of the Church which he wished to discuss personally with Timothy. Therefore he does not hesitate to ask him to come from over the sea. Certainly there must have been very good reasons to justify bringing him away from the church over which he was set on such a long journey. We can gather from this how very important meetings between such men are, for what Timothy would learn in a short time would be of such great profit to all the churches for a long time, that the loss of six months or even a whole year would be trivial in comparison. And yet from what follows it appears that Paul summoned Timothy for personal reasons of his own also, since he was being bereft of faithful supporters—not that he was rating his own personal needs higher than the good of the Church, for the Gospel itself was involved in which all believers have a common interest. Since he had to defend it from prison, he needed the others to work with him in its defence.

10. *Having loved this present world.* It was indeed disgraceful for such

a man to love the world better than Christ. But we are not to suppose that he completely denied Christ and gave himself over again to ungodliness or the allurements of the world, but only that he cared more for his own convenience and safety than for the life of Paul. He could not stay with Paul without involving himself in many troubles and vexations and a real risk to his life; he was exposed to many reproaches, he was laid open to many insults, he was forced to give up caring for his own concerns, and in these circumstances he was overcome by his dislike for the cross and decided to look to his own interests. Nor can it be doubted that the world gave him a favourable opportunity to help him on his way. We may conjecture that this man was one of the most outstanding of Paul's companions from the fact that Paul names him with only a few others in Colossians 4.14 and also in Philemon 24 where he also numbers him among his assistants. Thus it is not surprising that he should censure him here so sharply for caring more for himself than for Christ.

The others he goes on to mention had gone away from him with good reasons and with his own consent. It is clear from this that he did not look after his own interest to the extent of depriving the churches of their pastors, but only to get from them some relief. Doubtless he would always take good care to summon or keep with him those whose absence would not harm other churches. For this reason he had sent Titus to Dalmatia, and others elsewhere at the time when he was sending for Timothy. Not only so, but to keep the church at Ephesus from being destitute or forlorn during Timothy's absence, he sent Tychicus there and he mentions this to Timothy to assure him that there will be someone to take his place while he is away.

13. *The cloak which I left at Troas, bring.* Commentators are not agreed about the meaning of the word φαιλόνης; some think it is a chest or box for books, others that it is a kind of traveller's cloak with special protection against cold and rain. Whatever meaning is preferred the question may be asked why Paul should ask for either a cloak or a chest to be be brought to him from so far, as if there were no craftsmen or cloth or wood in Rome. If we say it is a chest filled with books or manuscripts or letters, we shall have our answer, for such things could not be replaced at any price. But since many will not accept this conjecture, I willingly translate it cloak, and it is not absurd that Paul should want it brought so far, since from long use it would be more comfortable for him and he would want to avoid expense. Still, to tell the truth, I am more attracted to the first interpretation, since he immediately goes on to mention *books and parchments.* It is obvious from this that although the apostle was already preparing for death, he had not given up reading. Where are those who think that they have

progressed so far that they need do no more, and which of them dare compare himself with Paul? Still more does this passage refute the madness of the fanatics who despise books and condemn all reading and boast only of their ἐνθυσιασμούς, their private inspirations by God. But we should note that this passage commends continual reading to all godly men as a thing from which they can profit.

Here someone will ask what Paul meant by asking for a cloak if he thought he was going to die immediately. This difficulty is another reason why I think that he means a chest, but there may have been some other use for a cloak at that time, unknown to us today. It is a matter over which I am not very concerned.

> *Alexander the coppersmith did me much evil: the Lord will render to him according to his works: of whom be thou ware also; for he greatly withstood our words. At my first defence no one took my part, but all forsook me: may it not be laid to their account. But the Lord stood by me and strengthened me that through me the proclamation might be confirmed (the message might be fully proclaimed R.V.) and that all the Gentiles might hear: and I was delivered out of the mouth of the lion. The Lord will deliver me from every evil work, and will save me unto his heavenly kingdom: to whom be the glory for ever and ever. Amen. Salute Prisca and Aquila, and the house of Onesiphorus. Erastus abode at Corinth: but Trophimus I left at Miletus sick. Do thy diligence to come before winter. Eubulus saluteth thee and Pudens, and Linus and Claudia, and all the brethren. The Lord be with thy spirit. Grace be with you.* (14-22)

14. *Alexander.* This man was a dreadful example of apostasy. He had professed some zeal in furthering Christ's kingdom, but afterwards he carried on open warfare against it. This is the most dangerous and envenomed kind of enemy. But from the beginning the Lord determined that His Church should not be exempt from this kind of evil lest our courage should fail when we are tried in the same way. We should note what the many evils are which Paul complains that Alexander had brought upon him—namely that he opposed his teaching. Alexander was a tradesman, not educated in the schools to be a great disputer; but enemies at home have always been well placed to do harm. And the wickedness that such men propagate is always believed by the world, so that sometimes ill disposed and shameless ignorance creates more difficulty and trouble than great cleverness and learning. Besides, when the Lord brings His servants into battle with riffraff of this kind, He purposely conceals them from the world's view that they may not delight in pompous displays of cleverness.

We may gather from Paul's words that he had suffered nothing worse than opposition to his sound teaching. If Alexander had attacked his person or committed an assault upon him, he would have endured that with greater equanimity, but when the truth of God is assailed his dedicated heart burns with indignation, because this saying must apply to all Christ's members, 'The zeal of thy house hath eaten me up' (Ps. 69.9). This explains why he breaks out into such a very stern imprecation, asking that the Lord may repay him. A little later when he is lamenting that all men deserted him, he does not call down God's vengeance upon them but rather intercedes for their pardon. Since he is so gentle and merciful to all others, why is he so severe and inexorable to this one man? He desires God to forgive the others, because they had fallen through fear and weakness, for we ought to have compassion on our brethren's weakness. But Alexander had risen up against God with malice and sacrilegious audacity and was openly attacking the truth he had once confessed, and such wickedness deserves no mercy.

But we are not to think that in this prayer for vengeance Paul was carried away by excessive anger. It was from the Spirit of God and out of a well directed zeal that he came to pray for eternal perdition for Alexander and mercy for the others. It is by the Spirit's guidance that Paul here pronounces a heavenly judgment, so that we may infer how dear to God is His own truth and how severely He visits vengeance on those who oppose it. Especially it should be noted what a dreadful crime it is to fight with malice against true religion. But in case anyone should mistakenly follow the apostle's example and rashly pronounce imprecations of this kind, there are three things here that must be noted. First, we are not to avenge injuries done to ourselves lest self-love and a concern for our own private interest should carry us away, as they usually do. Secondly, when we are asserting God's glory we should not confuse it with our own private passions, for they always disturb good order. Third, we should not pass judgment on everyone without discrimination but only upon wicked men who prove themselves so by their ungodliness, so that our wishes may agree with God's own judgment; otherwise there is reason to fear that we shall receive the same reply that Christ gave to his disciples who were thundering indiscriminate denunciations against all who did not comply with their own wishes, 'Ye know not what manner of spirit ye are of' (Luke 9.55). They seemed to be taking Elijah for their authority, for he had prayed to God in the same way (II Kings 1.10), but since they were of a very different spirit from Elijah, their imitation of him was absurd. Thus it is necessary that the Lord should make His judgment plain before we burst out into such imprecations, so that our zeal may be guided and restrained by His Spirit. And whenever we remember Paul's violent reaction against this one man, we should also bear in mind his wonderful gentleness towards those who basely deserted him, in order that by his example we may learn compassion for the weakness of our brethren.

I should like to ask those who imagine that Peter presided over the Roman Church where he was at this time. In their view, he was not yet dead, for they tell us that his death was exactly a year after Paul's, and they make his pontificate last seven years. Here Paul mentions his first defence and his second appearance before the court could not be quite so soon. If Peter is not to lose the title of Pope, must he be pronounced guilty of faithlessly deserting Paul with the rest? Certainly when the whole matter is duly examined, our conclusion will be that all that is believed about Peter's papacy is a foolish tale.

17. *But the Lord stood by me.* He adds this to remove the scandal which he saw could arise from so many having basely deserted him and his cause. Though the Roman Church failed in its duty, he says that the Gospel suffered no loss because of it, since he himself alone, depending on heavenly power, was able to bear the whole burden, and far from being discouraged by the fear that possessed everyone else, he only saw more clearly that God's grace stands in no need of any support from any other source. He is not boasting of his own fortitude but giving thanks to the Lord that when he was brought to his extremity, he did not give way or lose heart at such a dangerous trial. He acknowledges that God's hand has supported him, and it is enough for him that the inward grace of the Spirit was like a shield to him to defend him against the attacks made upon him. He adds the reason, *that the proclamation might be confirmed.* By proclamation he means the office of publishing the Gospel among the Gentiles that had been entrusted especially to him. The preaching of others, being confined to the Jews, was not so like a heraldic proclamation. He has good reason to use this word in many passages. For it was no ordinary confirmation of his ministry, that at the very time when the whole world was furiously raging against him and all human help was deserting him, he yet remained unshaken. Thus he proved in practice that his apostleship was from Christ. He now adds the manner of the confirmation, *that all the Gentiles might hear* that the Lord had so wonderfully helped him: for from this they could infer that both Paul's calling and their own were from the Lord.

I was delivered out of the mouth of the lion. Many think that the lion means Nero. I am inclined to think that he uses the expression for danger in general, as if he had said 'out of a blazing fire' or 'from the jaws of death'. He means htat he escaped only by God's marvellous help, since the danger was so great that otherwise it would at once have swallowed him up.

He declares that he is hoping for the same help in the future, not to avoid death, but to avoid being overcome by Satan, or deviating from the right course. What we should chiefly desire is not the safety of our body, but that we should rise superior over every trial, that we may be ready to die a hundred times over rather than think of soiling ourselves by one evil work. I am well aware that some take the expression *evil work* in a passive sense meaning the violent attacks of the ungodly, as if Paul had said 'The Lord will not allow the ungodly to do me any harm. But the other meaning is far more suitable, that He will keep him pure and free from every wicked deed, for he immediately adds *unto his heavenly kingdom*, by which he means that the only true salvation is when either by life or by death the Lord leads us into His kingdom.

This is a notable passage for maintaining against the Papists the uninterrupted communication of God's grace. Having acknowledged that salvation has its beginning in God, they ascribe its continuation to man's free will, so that perseverance is not a heavenly gift but a human virtue. But Paul, in ascribing to God the work of leading us into His kingdom, openly asserts that we are ruled by God's hand during the whole course of our life, until with all our warfare completed we obtain the victory. And we have a memorable example of this in Demas, whom he has just mentioned, for from being a noble athlete of Christ, he became a base deserter. What follows we have already dealt with elsewhere and there is no need of additional explanations.

The Epistle of Paul to
TITUS

JOHN CALVIN
SENDS GREETINGS TO
WILLIAM FAREL AND PETER VIRET
TWO EMINENT SERVANTS OF CHRIST AND
HIS OWN DEARLY BELOVED COLLEAGUES AND BRETHREN

To publish this commentary of mine with your names inscribed upon it is only a small gift, but I trust that you will not find it unacceptable, since it was the subject of the Epistle with which it deals that led me to dedicate it to you. The task of putting the finishing touches to the building that Paul had begun but had left uncompleted was undertaken by Titus, and I stand in almost the same relationship to you. For when with great labour and much risk you had set your hands to raise up this church at Geneva, I arrived later first of all as your assistant, and then afterwards I was left behind as your successor, to strive to the best of my ability to carry on the work that you had begun so successfully and so well. To this day my colleagues and I are engaged on this work, and although we have not been as successful as we might have wished, we are doing it heartily and faithfully, according to our small ability.

To return to you: since I bear the same relationship to you as Paul made Titus bear to him, this similarity seemed to be a good reason for choosing you in preference to all others as the men to whom I should dedicate this work. It will at least be a testimony to this present age and perhaps also to posterity of the holy bond of friendship that unites us. I think there has never been in ordinary life a circle of friends so heartily bound to each other as we have been in our ministry. With both of you I discharged here the office of pastor, and so far from there being any appearance of rivalry, I always seemed to be of one mind with you. Later we were separated and you, Farel, were called to the church of Neuchâtel which you had rescued from the papal tyranny and brought to Christ, and you, Viret, stand in the same relationship to the church of Lausanne.

But while each of us keeps to his own post, our union brings together God's children in Christ's fold and unites them in His body, and at the same time it scatters not only our external enemies who carry on open war against us, but those nearer internal enemies who attack us from within. This also I count among the benefits of our union, that unclean dogs whose bites cannot succeed in tearing and rending the Church only stir it up to no effect by their barking. We cannot hold their influence in too great scorn, since we have good reason to glory

DEDICATION

before God and have the clearest evidence to show to men that our alliance and friendship have been entirely consecrated to Christ's name, have hitherto been profitable to His Church, and have no other aim than that all men should be at one with us in Him. Farewell most excellent and honourable brethren. May the Lord Jesus continue to bless your godly labours.

Geneva, 29th November, 1549

THEME OF PAUL'S EPISTLE TO TITUS

PAUL had only laid the foundations of the church in Crete when he had to hurry on elsewhere, since he was not the pastor of one island only but the apostle of the Gentiles. He therefore commissioned Titus as an evangelist to carry on his work. It is clear from this epistle that immediately after Paul's departure Satan made great efforts not only to overthrow the government of the church, but also to corrupt its doctrine.

There were some who out of selfish ambition wished to be raised to the rank of pastors and when Titus would not comply with their wicked desires, they spoke ill of him to many. There were also some Jews who tried to use the Law of Moses as their pretext for introducing a great number of trifling regulations and observances, and they were being heard eagerly and with great favour. Paul's intention in writing was therefore to arm Titus with his authority to help him to bear such a great burden. There is no doubt that some boldly scorned him as only one of the company of ordinary pastors. It is also possible that complaints were being circulated that he was taking upon himself more than he had a right to, since he refused to accept pastors until they had won his approval.

Thus we may infer that this is not so much a private letter to Titus as a public epistle to the Cretans. It is not probable that Titus should be blamed for being too ready to elevate unworthy persons, to the office of bishop (*ad episcopatum*), or that he should have to have laid down for him what kind of doctrine he should teach the people, as though he were an ignorant novice; but since he was not receiving the honour due to him, Paul clothes him with his own personal authority both for ordaining ministers and in the whole government of the church. Because there were many who foolishly desired another form of doctrine than that they had received from him, Paul repudiates all others and grants his sole approval to the teaching of Titus, encouraging him to continue as he has begun.

First he teaches what kind of people should be chosen as ministers. Among other qualifications he requires that a minister should be instructed in sound doctrine by which to resist adversaries. Here he takes opportunity to censure the ways of the Cretans and especially rebukes the Jews who made holiness consist in drawing distinctions between foods and other outward ceremonies. To refute their follies he contrasts with them the genuine practices of godliness and Christian living, and to impress it upon them more closely, he describes the duties that belong to different vocations. He tells Titus to inculcate these carefully and continually, and at the same time he tells the others not to grow weary of hearing them, and shows that this is the purpose of the redemption and salvation obtained through Christ. If any contentious person oppose him or refuse to submit, he bids him set that man aside. We now see that Paul's sole object is to support the cause of Titus and to stretch out a helping hand to assist him in carrying through the Lord's work.

CHAPTER ONE

Paul, a servant of God, and an apostle of Jesus Christ, according to the faith of God's elect, and the knowledge of the truth which is according to godliness, in hope of eternal life, which God, who cannot lie, promised before times eternal; but in his own seasons manifested his word in the preaching wherewith I was intrusted according to the commandment of God our Saviour; to Titus, my true child after a common faith: grace and peace from God the Father and Christ Jesus our Saviour. (1-4)

1. *A servant of God.* This long and detailed commendation of his apostleship shows that Paul had in mind the whole Church rather than Titus alone. For Titus had no question to raise against his apostleship; and it is Paul's custom to proclaim the praises of his calling when he wishes to assert and maintain his authority. Thus according to what he knows of the disposition of those to whom he is writing, he deals either extensively or sparingly in these ornaments. Since his purpose here is to bring to order those who were engaged in insolent rebellion, he extols his apostleship in lofty terms. He writes this letter not for Titus to read it alone in his room, but for it to be published openly.

First he calls himself a servant of God and then adds the particular designation of his ministry, that he is *an apostle of Christ*. Thus he descends from the genus to the species. We should remember that, as I have said alsewhere, the word 'servant' does not just mean ordinary subjection, so that all believers could be called God's servants, but means a minister to whom some definite office has been assigned. In this sense the prophets of old were marked off by this title, and Christ Himself is the chief of the prophets. 'Behold my servant, him have I chosen' (Isaiah 42.1). Thus David in view of his kingly dignity calls himself a 'servant of God'. Perhaps Paul has also his eye on the Jews in calling himself God's servant, for they were in the habit of lessening his authority by bringing the Law against him. He wishes to be considered an apostle of Christ so that he may glory in being also in this special way a servant of God. He thus shows that these two titles are not only consistent with each other but joined by an indissoluble tie.

According to the faith of God's elect. If anyone has doubts about his apostleship, he gives very strong reason to believe in it by connecting it with the salvation of God's elect, as if he had said, 'there is a mutual relationship between my apostleship and the faith of God's elect, so that nobody can reject it without being a reprobate and a stranger from the true faith'. By the elect he means not only those who were alive at that time, but all that had been from the beginning of the world. He means that he teaches no doctrine that does not agree with the faith of Abraham and all the Fathers. Thus if anyone today wishes to be considered Paul's successor, he must prove that he is a minister of the same doctrine. But these words contain an implied contrast, to make it clear that the unbelief and obstinacy of many in no way detract from the Gospel. For at that time as today, the weak in faith were greatly scandalized because the greater part of those who claimed to belong to the Church rejected the pure doctrine of Christ. For this reason Paul shows that even if all indiscriminately boast of the name of God, very many of that crowd are nevertheless reprobates. As he says elsewhere (Romans 9.7) 'Not all who trace their descent from Abraham according to the flesh are the rightful children of Abraham.'

And the knowledge of the truth. I consider that here the copulative 'and' has the effect of explaining what has gone before and so is equivalent to 'namely' or 'that is'. For he is explaining the nature of the faith he has already mentioned, although this is not a full definition of it but a description suited to the present context. In order to support his claim that his apostleship is free from all imposture and error, he declares that his message contains nothing but well-known and ascertained truth, which can instruct men in the pure worship of God. But since each word has its own importance, it will be very useful for us to examine them one by one.

First, when he calls faith 'knowledge' he is not merely distinguishing it from opinion but from that unformed or implicit faith contrived by the Papists. For by implicit faith they mean something devoid of all light of understanding. By saying that it is of the essence of faith to know the truth, he plainly shows that there is certainly no faith without knowledge.

By the word 'truth' he explains still more clearly the certainty which the nature of faith requires: for faith is not satisfied with probabilities but holds to what is true. Moreover he is not speaking here of any kind of truth, but that which is contrasted with the vanity of human understanding. For as God has revealed Himself to us through that truth, it alone is worthy of the name 'the truth'—a name given to it in many parts of the Scripture. John 16.13 'The Spirit shall guide you into all the truth', John 17.17 'Thy word is truth', Galatians 3.1 'Who hath bewitched you that you obey not the truth?', Colossians 1.5 'Hear the word of the truth, the Gospel of the Son of God', I Timothy 2.4 'He willeth that all men should come to the knowledge of the truth', and I Timothy 3.15 'The Church is the pillar and ground of the truth.' In short, the truth is that pure and right knowledge of God which frees us from every error and falsehood. We should value it the more dearly as nothing is more wretched than to wander through our whole life like lost sheep.

The phrase that follows *which is according to godliness* qualifies in a special way the truth of which he has been speaking, and at the same time commends his teaching from its fruit and end, since its only aim is to further the right worship of God and to guard pure religion among men. In this way he defends his teaching from all suspicion of vain curiosity, as he did before Felix (Acts 24.10) and again before Agrippa (26.1). Since all superfluous questionings which do not tend to edification should rightly be suspect and even detested by godly men, the only legitimate commendation of doctrine is that it instructs us in the reverence and fear of God. Thus we are taught that the man who has made most progress in godliness is the best disciple of Christ, and the only man who should be counted a real theologian is he who can build up men's consciences in the fear of God.

In hope of eternal life. This addition undoubtedly indicates the cause, for that is the meaning of the Greek preposition ἐπί. So we may translate it 'On account of the hope' or 'in the hope'. Meditation on the life of heaven is the beginning both of true religion and of desire for godliness. In the same way in Colossians 1.5, when he is praising the faith and love of the Colossians, he makes them depend upon 'the hope laid up in heaven'. Sadducees and those who confine our hope to this world, whatever they may claim, can only produce contempt for God, while they reduce men to the level of animals. Thus it should always be the aim of a good teacher to turn men away from the world that they may look up into heaven. I readily agree that God's glory ought to be more to us than our own salvation, but we are not now concerned with the question as to which of these comes first in order of precedence. All I say is that men never truly seek God till they have confidence to approach him, and so they never apply their minds to godliness till they have been instructed in the hope of a life in heaven.

2. *Which God promised.* Augustine reads here 'before eternal times' and gets into difficulties about the eternity of time, till at last he explains eternal as meaning time that goes beyond all antiquity. In meaning, he and Jerome and other commentators agree that before the foundation of the world God determined to give the salvation which He has now manifested through the Gospel. Thus Paul, on his view would here be using the word 'promised' inaccurately to mean 'decreed', since before the creation of men there was none to whom He could make any promise. For this reason, although I do not reject this interpretation, when I examine the whole matter in greater detail, I am compelled to accept a different rendering—that eternal life was promised to men

many long ages ago, and not only to those who were alive at that time but for our own age also. It was not for Abraham's benefit alone that God said 'In thy seed shall all nations be blessed' (Gen. 22.18) but He has in view all who lived after him. There is no difficulty in the fact that in II Timothy 1.9 he says that salvation was given to men 'before times eternal' in a different sense. For the meaning of the word is the same in both passages. For since the Greek word αἰών means the uninterrupted succession of time from the beginning to the end of the world, in the Timothy passage Paul is saying that salvation was given or ordained to God's elect before the passage of time began. But in this passage where he speaks of a promise he does not include all ages so as to lead us back beyond the creation of the world, but says simply that many ages have passed since salvation was first promised. If anyone wants to take 'times eternal' as a concise mode of expression for the ages themselves, he may do so. But since salvation was given by God's eternal election before it was promised, in Timothy the act of giving salvation is put before all ages, and thus we have there to understand the word 'all'. But here his meaning is simply that the promise is more ancient than a long succession of ages, because it began immediately from the foundation of the world. In this sense he shows in Romans 1.2 that the Gospel which was proclaimed only when Christ had risen from the dead was promised in the Scriptures through the prophets, for there is a great difference between the grace shown in the present era and the promise given of old to the fathers.

Who cannot lie. The adjective ἀψευδής is added not merely to glorify God but more to confirm our faith. Whenever the subject of our salvation is dealt with, we should remember that it is founded on the Word of Him who cannot deceive or lie. Indeed the only foundation of all religion is the unchangeable truth of God.

3. *But He manifested His word.* There was already some revelation of it when God of old spoke through the prophets: but since at His advent Christ openly manifested what they had dimly predicted, and because it was only then that Gentiles were received into the covenant, Paul says that what had before been shown in part has now in this sense been made manifest.

In His own seasons means the same as 'the fulness of time' in Galatians 4.4. He reminds us that the time that the Lord chose to do this must have been the most opportune time, and he mentions this to meet the temerity of those who dare to ask why it was not sooner or why it is today rather than tomorrow. To restrain this immoderate curiosity, he teaches that the times are in God's hands and at His disposal so that we must believe that everything is done in due order and at the right time.

His Word. Either we are to supply the preposition 'by' (which is quite usual in Greek); or, if we do not want to add anything to complete the sentence, we are to understand Paul as calling Christ the Word. I would myself be content with this explanation, if it were not a little forced. John does speak in this way at the beginning of his epistle, I John 1.1, 'That which we have heard, that which we have seen with our eyes, that which our hands handle concerning the Word of life and the life was manifested'. But I prefer the simpler meaning that God has manifested life through His Word, or has manifested the Word of life through the preaching of the Gospel. *The preaching* of which he speaks is the published Gospel and certainly the chief thing we hear in it is that Christ is given to us, and in Him there is life.

Moreover, since all men are not without distinction suited to such a great office, and since no man should thrust himself into it, he asserts his calling according to his custom. Here we should learn—as we have so often noted before—that this honour is not due to any man until he has given proof that God has ordained him. For even the ministers of Satan proudly boast that they are called of God, but there is no truth in their words. But when Paul mentions his calling it is something well known and well attested. Further, we learn from this passage why men were made apostles—in order to publish the Gospel; as he says elsewhere (I Cor. 9.16) 'Woe is unto me if I preach not the Gospel: for I have a stewardship intrusted to me.' Thus those who behave as dummies in the midst of idleness and luxury are too impudent by far in claiming to be their successors.

God our Saviour. He gives the same title both to the Father and to Christ, since each of them is indeed our Saviour, but in a different way. The Father is Saviour because He has redeemed us by the Son's death that He might make us heirs of eternal life: but the Son is our Saviour because He shed His blood as the pledge and price of our salvation. Thus the Son brought us salvation from the Father, and the Father bestowed it through the Son.

4. *To Titus, my true child after a common faith.* From this it is clear in what sense a minister of the Word is said to Geget spiritually those whom he brings into obedience to Christ, namely, in such a way that he himself is also begotten. Paul calls himself the father of Titus in respect of his faith, but immediately adds that this faith is common to both of them, so that both of them share the same Father in heaven. Thus God in no way takes from His own prerogative in allowing those by whose ministry He regenerates whom He will to be called spiritual fathers along with Himself: for by themselves they do nothing, but only through the efficacy of the Spirit. An explanation of the rest of this

v. 4–5] TITUS 1

verse will be found in the commentaries on the earlier epistles and especially on 1 Timothy.

For this cause left I thee in Crete, that thou shouldest set in order the things that were wanting, and appoint elders in every city, as I gave thee charge; if any man is blameless, the husband of one wife, having children that believe, who are not accused of riot or unruly. (5-6)

5. *For this cause*. This beginning proves clearly that he is not so much advising Titus for his own sake as commending him to others so that none may hinder him. Paul declares that he has appointed him to take his own place and for that reason all should recognize him and receive him with reverence as his representative. The apostles had no fixed place assigned to them but were charged with spreading the Gospel throughout the whole world, and so when they left one city or district to go to another, it was their custom to choose suitable men as their deputies to complete the work they had begun. Thus Paul says that he laid the foundation of the Church in Corinth, but there were other workmen who had to build on his foundation and thus carry the building further. This applies to all pastors since churches will always stand in need of increase and progress till the end of the world. But over and above the ordinary pastoral office Titus was charged with the task of organizing the church. Pastors are normally set over churches that are already constituted and brought to some order, but Titus had the additional burden of organizing churches whose affairs were not yet rightly ordered and of giving them a fixed method of government and discipline. When the foundation was laid, Paul departed and it then became Titus' duty to raise the building above the ground so that its structure would be well proportioned.

This is what he calls *setting in order the things that are still wanting*. The building of a church is not so easy a task that it can all at once be perfectly completed. It is uncertain how long Paul was in Crete, but he had spent some time there and had faithfully directed his labours towards the establishment of Christ's kingdom. He had in abundance the greatest skill to be found among men, he was quite untiring in his labours, and yet he confesses that he has left the work rough and incomplete. From this we see the difficulty and we today know by experience that it is not the work of one or two years to restore a fallen church to a tolerable state. Those who have made diligent progress for many years must still be concerned to correct many things.

Further, we should note well Paul's modesty in freely allowing someone else to complete what he has begun. And even though Titus is greatly his inferior, he does not refuse to have him as ἐπανορθωτής, 'Corrector', to put the finishing touches to his own work. This should be the disposition of godly teachers, not that each should selfishly strive to have everything done as he wants it, but they should help each other and when any one of them has worked with greater success, the others should congratulate rather then envy him.

And yet the things that Paul wanted set to rights were not things he had left undone through ignorance, forgetfulness or carelessness, but things he could not complete for lack of time. In a word, he calls on Titus to set right things he would have dealt with himself, had he stayed in Crete longer, not by varying or changing anything, but by adding what was lacking, since the difficulty of the task did not allow everything to be done at once in one day.

And appoint elders in every city. In the spiritual upbuilding of the Church, it is in priority second only to doctrine that pastors should be appointed to care for governing the Church. Thus Paul mentions it here before anything else. It should be carefully noted that churches cannot safely remain without the ministry of pastors, so that, wherever there is a considerable body of people, a pastor should be appointed over them. In saying that each town should have a pastor he does not mean that none should have more than one, but only that no town should be without pastors.

Elders or presbyters (*seniores*) were not, as is well known, so called because of their age, for sometimes men still young—like Timothy— were chosen for this office. In all languages it has always been the practice for governors to be called, for honour's sake, elders. Although we may infer from I Timothy that there were two kinds of elders, here the context makes it quite clear that teachers (*doctores*) are to be understood, that is, those ordained to teach, for almost immediately he will refer to the same people as bishops.

But he may seem to give Titus too much authority when he tells him to appoint ministers for all the churches. This would be almost royal power and would deprive individual churches of their right to elect and the college of pastors of their right to judge, and that would be to profane the whole administration of the Church. The answer is easy; he is not giving Titus permission to do everything arbitrarily by himself and impose whatever bishops he likes on churches, but is only ordering him to preside as moderator at elections, as is necessary. This mode of expression is very common. By it a consul, regent or dictator is said to have created consuls when in fact he held a public assembly to elect them. In the same way Luke says of Paul and Barnabas in Acts 14.23 that they ordained elders in every church, not that they alone appointed in a dictatorial way pastors untried and unknown in the local churches, but because they ordained suitable men who had been elected or asked for by the people. From this passage we do indeed learn that there was not such an equality among the ministers of the Church as to prevent one from having authority and judgment over others (*unus aliquis auctoritate et consilio praeesset*). But this has nothing to do with the profane custom of collations, as it holds sway under the Papacy. The method of the Apostle was very different.

6. *If any man is blameless.* To keep any from being angry with Titus for being too rigorous or severe in rejecting some, Paul takes the whole blame upon himself. He declares that he has given explicit instructions that none should be admitted who has not the qualifications he describes. Thus, as he has a little before declared that it was he who authorized Titus to preside as moderator at the appointment of pastors, that others might concede him this right, so now he describes the injunction he has given in order that Titus may not be exposed to false accusations of strictness by wicked or ill disposed and ignorant men.

Since this passage paints us a picture of a lawful bishop, we should note it carefully. But as I have already explained nearly everything here in the commentary on I Timothy, it will be enough to touch upon it lightly here.

By ἀνέγκλητον, blameless, he does not mean someone who is free from every fault, for no such man could ever be found, but one marred by no disgrace that could diminish his authority—he should be a man of unblemished reputation.

We have already explained in relation to I Timothy why he says he is to be *the husband of one wife*. Polygamy was so common among the Jews that the depraved custom had almost turned into a law. If anyone had married two wives before he became a Christian it would have been inhuman to compel him to put away the second. Thus the apostles were prepared to tolerate a thing that was otherwise wrong, since they could not correct it. Besides, those who had already implicated themselves in more than a single marriage, even if they had been ready to give proof of repentance by keeping only one wife, had already demonstrated their incontinence, and that could have been a stain on their reputation. It is as if Paul were telling them to elect those who had lived chastely in marriage, satisfied with one wife, and was excluding those whose lust had been shown in their having many wives. At the same time, a man who becomes a widower by his wife's death and marries again should be considered the husband of one wife. Paul tells them to elect men who *are* husbands of one wife, not men who *have been* so.

Having believing children. Since prudence and earnestness are required in a pastor, it is desirable that his family should share these qualities. For how can a man rule the Church if he cannot control his own house? Besides, not only must the bishop himself be free from reproach, but his whole household must reflect a chaste and honourable discipline. Thus he lays down to Timothy in great detail the qualities that a bishop's wife should possess. But here his first requirement is that the children should be believers, that it may be obvious that they have been nurtured in the sound teaching of godliness and in the fear of the Lord. Second, they must not be over-abounding in luxury, so that here also their training in temperance and frugality may be recognized. Thirdly, they must not be *unruly* for he who cannot obtain any reverence or submission from his children could scarcely restrain his people by the bridle of his discipline.

> *For the bishop must be blameless, as God's steward; not selfwilled, not soon angry, no brawler over wine, no striker, not greedy of filthy lucre; but given to hospitality, devoted to kindness* (R.V. *a lover of good*), *soberminded, just, holy, temperate; holding to the faithful word which is according to the teaching, that he may be able both to exhort in the sound doctrine and to convict the gainsayers.* (7-9)

7. *For the bishop must be blameless.* He again repeats that those who aspire to episcopal office must be of untarnished reputation and he confirms this by saying that since the Church is God's house, every man who governs there is, as it were, God's steward. Now a man who accepted a perverse steward with an evil reputation would be ill spoken of among men: thus it is far more unworthy and intolerable for men of that kind to be made rulers over God's family. The Latin word *dispensator*—bailiff or manager, which Erasmus has here retained from the Vulgate does not express Paul's meaning. For in order that greater care may be shown in elections, he gives to the episcopate the honourable title of stewardship, that is, it is a government of God's house, as he says to Timothy (I Tim. 3.15) 'that thou mayest know how you ought to behave yourself in God's house, which is the Church of the living God, the pillar and ground of the truth'.

Also this passage plainly shows that there is no difference between a presbyter and a bishop, for he now freely applies the second title to those he has formally called presbyters, and in discussing this subject he uses both names indiscriminately with the same meaning, as Jerome has also noted in his commentary on this passage and also in his letter to Evagrius. It is clear from this how much deference has been paid to human opinions, since the language used by the Holy Spirit has been set aside and the usage introduced by the will of men has prevailed. For my own part I find no fault with the custom which has prevailed from the very earliest days of the Church whereby each assembly of bishops has one man as moderator. But to take the title of the office which God has given to all and to transfer it to one man and deprive the rest of it is both unjust and absurd. Besides to pervert the language of the Holy Spirit so as to make the very words have a different meaning from the one He has chosen smacks of excessive and unholy temerity.

Not selfwilled. He has good reason to condemn this fault in a bishop, since it is his duty not only to deal kindly with those who approach him of their own freewill, but also to entice those who hold back, that he may lead all together to Christ. But αὐθάδεια τῆς ἐρημίας ἐστὶ ξύνοικος, as Plato says in a letter to Dion, that is, selfwill by which a man is too much concerned with himself is closely allied to solitude. For fellowship and friendship cannot be cherished when everyone pleases himself and refuses to yield or accommodate himself to others. And indeed every αὐθάδης when opportunity offers, immediately becomes a schismatic. From this it is clear what a harmful plague this is, when it tears the Church to pieces with quarrels. With this fault he contrasts, first, teachableness and then kindness and modesty towards all. For a bishop will never teach unless he is prepared first to learn. Augustine praises highly a saying of Cyprian, 'Let him be as patient to learn as he is skilful to teach.' Besides, bishops often need counsel and warnings; if they refuse to be advised, if they reject sound counsels, they will rush blindly on with great injury to the Church. The remedy for these evils is that they should not be wise in their own conceits.

I have preferred to translate φιλάγαθον 'devoted to kindness', rather than with Erasmus 'a lover of good things'. For Paul seems to be connecting this virtue with hospitality and contrasting them both with greed and meanness.

He calls him *just* meaning that he does no man any wrong; holiness refers to his relationship to God and even Plato makes this distinction between these two words.

9. *Holding to the faithful word.* This is the first endowment of a bishop who is chosen specially in order to teach, for the Church cannot be governed except by the Word. By 'faithful' word he means teaching that is pure and which has come from the mouth of God. He wishes a bishop to hold it fast so that he is not only well instructed in it, but constant in asserting it. For there are fickle people who easily allow themselves to be carried away by different kinds of teaching, while others are brought to the point of deserting their defence of the truth by the depression of fear or the influence of something that happens to them. So Paul lays it down that only those who have firmly embraced God's truth must be chosen—so firmly, that they will never allow it to be wrested from them or themselves to be shaken loose from it. There is indeed nothing more dangerous than this fickleness of which I have spoken whereby a pastor does not steadfastly maintain the doctrine of which he should be the unshaken

protagonist. In short, there is required in a pastor not only learning but such zeal for pure doctrine that he will never depart from it.

But what is meant by *which is according to the teaching*? His meaning is that it should be useful in building up the Church. Paul does not usually give the title of 'teaching' to anything known or learnt unless it produces some advancement in godliness. Rather he condemns as vanity all unprofitable speculations, however ingenious they may be. Thus Romans 12.7, 'He that teacheth let him do it in doctrine'—that is, let him study to do good to his hearers. In other words, if the first duty of a pastor is to be instructed in the knowledge of sound doctrine, and the second to hold fast his confession with unwavering courage, the third is that he should adapt the method of his teaching to edification and not, out of ambition, fly about among the subtleties of frivolous curiosity, but rather seek only the solid advantage of the Church.

That he may be able. A pastor needs two voices, one for gathering the sheep and the other for driving away wolves and thieves. The Scripture supplies him with the means for doing both, and he who has been rightly instructed in it will be able both to rule those who are teachable and to refute the enemies of the truth. Paul notes this double use of the Scripture when he says that he should be able *both to exhort and to convict the gainsayers*. From this we may learn both what is the real knowledge a bishop should have and what use he ought to make of it. A bishop is really wise when he holds the right faith, and he makes the right use of his knowledge when he applies it to building up the people. It is a notable tribute to the Word of God when he says that it is adequate not only for governing the teachable but for breaking the stubborn opposition of its enemies. The power of God's truth is such that it easily prevails against all falsehoods. Let the popish bishops go now and boast of their succession from the apostles, for the majority of them are so unskilled in all doctrine that they think that their ignorance is no small part of their worth.

> *For there are many unruly men, vain talkers and deceivers, specially they of the circumcision, whose mouths must be stopped; men who overthrow whole houses, teaching things which they ought not, for filthy lucre's sake. One of themselves, a prophet of their own said, Cretans are always liars, evil beasts, idle gluttons. This testimony is true.* (10-13a)

10. *For there are many unruly men.* Having laid down the general rule which is to be observed everywhere, in order to make Titus more intent to adhere to it, he explains to him the urgent necessity which should stir him to action above all else. He warns him that he has to

deal with many obstinate and wild people, that many are swollen with vanity and idle talk and many are deceivers, so that leaders ought to be chosen who are qualified and well equipped to oppose them. For if the children of this world increase their solicitude and watchfulness in the face of danger, it would be disgraceful for us to sleep in false security, as if all was at peace, when Satan is mustering all his forces against us. *Unruly men*—the Vulgate renders this word by 'disobedient' and Erasmus by 'unmanageable'. He means those who cannot endure to be subjected to discipline and throw off the yoke of obedience. By *vain talkers* he means not the authors of false doctrines, but those addicted to ambitious self-display who care for nothing but unprofitable subtlties. Ματαιολογία is the opposite of useful and solid teaching, so that it includes all trifling and frivolous speculations which have nothing in them but empty bombast, because they contribute nothing to godliness and the fear of God. Such is the whole scholastic theology as it is found today in Popery. He also calls the same people *deceivers*. It is possible to take this as referring to a different class of evildoers, but my view is that he has the same people in mind, for the teachers of such trifles attract and almost cast a spell over men's minds so that they no longer accept sane teaching.

He says that such people are to be found chiefly among the Jews, because it was of great importance that such plagues should be universally recognized. We should not listen to those who plead that the reputation of a few individuals should be spared in a matter that involves great danger to the whole Church. And the Jewish nation was all the more dangerous, since it claimed superiority over all others by reason of its sacred descent. That is why Paul reproves the Jews more sharply—to deprive them of their opportunity of doing harm.

11. *Whose mouths must be stopped.* A good pastor should always be on the watch not by his silence to allow wicked and harmful doctrines to creep in, and not to give wicked men an unhindered opportunity to spread them. But the question arises, How is it possible for a bishop to compel obstinate and self-willed men to be silent? For such people even when they are worsted in argument still do not hold their peace but often, the more openly they are refuted and vanquished, the more insolent they become. Their malice is strengthened and inflamed and they become completely shameless. My answer is that when they have been smitten by the sword of God's Word and put to confusion by the power of the truth, the Church can command them to be silent; and if they persist, they can at least be excluded from the fellowship of believers, that every opportunity for doing harm may be taken from them. By 'shutting their mouths' Paul simply means to refute their vain talk even if they do not stop making a noise, for a man convicted

by God's Word, however much he may chatter, has nothing left he can say.

Who overthrow whole houses. If the faith of one single man is in danger of being overthrown, if there is at stake the ruin of a single soul redeemed by Christ's blood, the pastor should immediately gird himself to resist; how much less can he endure to see whole houses overthrown!

He tells us how they are overthrown by saying *teaching things that they ought not.* From this we may gather how dangerous it is to depart even by a hairsbreadth from sound doctrine. For he does not say that the teachings by which the faith of many was overthrown were openly godless; we may take him to mean all kinds of corruptions by which men are turned aside from the desire for edification. Because of the great weakness of the flesh we are exceedingly prone to fall, and the result is that Satan through his ministers quickly and easily destroys what godly teachers have built up with great and persistent toil.

Next he indicates the source of the evil—*for filthy lucre's sake*, and thus warns us what a great plague that is in teachers. As soon as they give themselves up to the pursuit of gain, they are bound to start courting popularity and favour, and this quickly results in the adulteration of pure doctrine.

12. *A prophet of their own.* I have no doubt that this refers to Epimenides who was a Cretan. For when Paul says that he was 'one of themselves' and 'a prophet of their own' he undoubtedly means that he was of Cretan birth. It is not clear why he should call this man a prophet. Some think that it is because the book from which Paul here quotes is called περὶ χρησμῶν, *On Oracles*; others think that Paul is speaking ironically and saying that they have indeed found a prophet worthy of a people who refused to listen to God's servants. But since poets are sometimes called prophets in Greek, just as they are called *vates*, seers, in Latin, I take it to mean simply a teacher. They were so called because poets were always reckoned to be 'divine and moved by divine inspiration' (θεῖον καὶ ἐνθουσιαστικόν). Thus Adimatus in the second book of Plato's *Republic*, having called poets 'sons of the gods', adds that they were also their prophets. Thus Paul seems here simply to be conforming to the usual practice. It is of no importance to know on what occasion Epimenides calls his fellow-countrymen liars, although it is in fact in connexion with their boast that they have the tomb of Jupiter: but, since the poet takes it from an old and well-known report, the apostle quotes it as a proverbial saying. If you wish to have a translation of the Greek in question, it may be rendered thus, 'A Cretan is a lying, lazy glutton, and always he will prove an evil brute.'

From this passage we may gather that it is superstitious to refuse to make any use of secular authors. For since all truth is of God, if any ungodly man has said anything true, we should not reject it, for it also has come from God. Besides, since all things are from God, what could be wrong with employing to His glory everything that can be rightly used in that way? But on this subject the reader is referred to Basil's essay πρὸς τοὺς νέους, in which he instructs young people as to what help they should receive from heathen authors.

13. *This testimony is true.* However worthless the witness, Paul accepts the truth that he has spoken, for there is no doubt that the Cretans of whom he speaks so severely were very wicked men. The apostle, who is accustomed elsewhere to deal so mildly with those who deserved the utmost severity, would not have spoken so harshly of the Cretans without the best of reasons. For what worse reproaches can be imagined than to make these shameful charges that they are lazy, given over to gluttony, completely untrustworthy and wicked brutes. Nor are these vices charged against a few individuals, but the whole nation is condemned. Wonderful indeed is God's purpose in calling such a wicked people infamous for its vices, to be among the first to share in His Gospel, and equally marvellous is His kindness in bestowing the grace of heaven on those who were not worthy even to live in this world. Thus in that corrupt country, as though at the heart of hell, the Church of Christ held its position and went on expanding, even though it was infected with the contagion of the evil habits that prevailed there. For here Paul is reproving not only outsiders, but expressly singling out those who had professed Christ's name. Seeing that these hateful vices have already taken root and are spreading on every side, he does not spare the reputation of the whole people, that he may cure those among them for whom there was hope of healing.

> *For which cause reprove them sharply, that they may be sound in the faith, not giving heed to Jewish fables, and commandments of men who turn away from the truth. To the pure all things are pure: but to them that are defiled and unbelieving nothing is pure; but both their mind and their conscience are defiled. They profess that they know God; but by their works they deny him, being abominable and disobedient, and unto every good work reprobate.* (13b-16)

13. *For which cause reprove them.* One of the most important parts of the tact and wisdom needed by a bishop is the ability to adapt the manner of his teaching to the character and habits of his people. He will not deal with the stubborn and insubordinate in the same way as with the meek and teachable. To the latter we should show a mildness suited to their teachableness, but the stubborness of the former must be corrected with severity, for, as they say, it takes a hard wedge to re-

move a hard knot. He has already given the reason why Titus is to be sharp and unbending in rebuking the Cretans—they are wicked brutes.

That they may be sound in the faith. It is not clear whether he is here contrasting this 'soundness' with the diseases he has already mentioned, or simply telling them to remain in sound faith, but I prefer the second view. Since they are already full of faults and may easily become more and more depraved, he wants them to be kept more strictly and exactly within the limits of sound faith.

Next he points out that sound faith is faith uncorrupted by any fables. And in guarding against the danger, he explains the remedy, not to listen to fables, for God wishes us to be so absorbed in His Word that there will be no chance for empty trifles to force their way in. When once God's truth has gained entry, all that is against it will be so unattractive that it will not be able to lay hold on our minds. If therefore we desire to keep the faith entire, we should learn carefully to restrain our senses, that they may not surrender to strange inventions. For as soon as a man begins to listen to fables, he will lose the purity of his faith.

14. *To Jewish fables.* He calls all frivolous fictions fables, or, as we should say, trifles. For what he immediately adds about the *commandments of men* has the same meaning. And he calls enemies of the truth those who were not satisfied with the pure teaching of Christ but mixed up their own inanities with it, for all that springs from human invention should be reckoned as fabulous. He attributes this fault chiefly to the Jews, who under pretence of obedience to divine law were introducing superstitious rites. The Gentiles understood that for their whole life they had been completely deceived and they more easily learnt to renounce their former way of life, but the Jews who had been reared in true religion stubbornly defended the ceremonies to which they had been accustomed, and could not be persuaded that the Law had been abrogated. Thus they were disturbing all the churches, for as soon as the Gospel was planted in any place, they began assiduously to corrupt its purity by mixing their own leaven with it. Thus Paul does not only forbid them in general terms to decline from sound doctrine, but singles out the pressing evil that needed to be met, so that they may be on their guard against it.

15. *To the pure all things are pure.* He touches on one type of this fabulous teaching; for the distinctions between foods and the purifications and washings that Moses had prescribed for his own time were still being insisted upon as necessities, and almost the whole of sanctity was made to consist of these observances. We have explained elsewhere how dangerous to the Church this could be. First, the snare of bondage was laid for men's consciences and second, ignorant people

who were in bondage to this superstition had a veil drawn over their eyes, so that they could not make progress in pure knowledge of Christ. If any Gentile refused to submit to this unaccustomed yoke, the Jews vehemently struggled for it, as though it were the chief article of religion. Thus Paul has good reason to set himself against such corrupters of the Gospel. In this passage he does not only refute their error, but wittily ridicules their vanity in labouring anxiously to no profit about abstaining from certain kinds of food and things of that nature.

In the first clause of the verse he asserts our Christian freedom, declaring that nothing is unclean to believers, and at the same time he indirectly attacks the false apostles to whom that inner purity which alone has value with God was of no importance. In this way he rebukes their ignorance in not understanding that Christians are pure quite apart from legal ceremonies. Thus he chastises their hypocrisy in neglecting uprightness of heart and occupying themselves with vain practices. Since the subject now in hand is not bodily health but peace of conscience, his point is that the distinction between foods which held under the Law has now been abrogated. For the same reason it is clear that those who impose religious scruples on men's consciences in this matter do wrong, for this is not teaching intended only for one single age, but an eternal pronouncement of the Holy Spirit, which cannot rightly be set aside by any new law. Thus this passage may be fittingly and suitably quoted against the tyrannical law of the Pope which prohibits the eating of flesh at certain times. I am quite familiar with the worthless explanations they produce to defend it. They say that they do not forbid flesh, because they hold it to be unclean—for, they declare, all foods are in themselves clean and pure—but abstention from flesh is enjoined for a different reason, that the lusts of the flesh may be restrained. As if the Lord had in former times forbidden men to eat the flesh of the swine, because He judged swine to be unclean. Even the fathers under the Law reckoned everything that God had created to be in itself pure and clean; but they held them unclean because God's commandment had forbidden their use. Thus the apostle calls all things clean only in the sense that the use of all things is free as regards conscience. Thus if some law binds consciences to any necessity of abstention, it wickedly deprives believers of the freedom granted them by God.

But to them that are defiled. This is the second clause in which he pours scorn on the useless and foolish precautions of such teachers. He says that they achieve nothing by guarding against uncleanness in certain foods, because they are incapable of touching anything that is clean. Why so? Because they themselves are defiled, and when they touch things that were in themselves pure, they make them polluted.

To the defiled he adds *unbelievers*, not as another distinct class, but as an explanatory addition to bring out his meaning. Since in God's sight there is no purity apart from faith, it follows that unbelievers are all unclean. Thus they will not obtain the cleanness they desire by any laws or regulations, for being themselves impure, nothing in the world can be pure to them.

Both their mind and their conscience are defiled. He indicates the source from which all the uncleanness that is spread through all man's life springs. For if the heart be not well purified, although works shine bright and have a sweet savour before men, yet they will call forth God's disgust by their foul smell and filthiness. For 'the Lord looketh on the heart' (I Sam. 16.7) and 'His eyes are on the truth' (Jer. 5.3). So it happens that things that men count excellent are an abomination in His eyes.

By the *mind* he means the understanding, while *conscience* refers rather to the disposition of the heart. Here there are two things to be noted: a man is judged before God by the sincere disposition of his heart and not by external works, and second, the stain of unbelief is so great that it pollutes not only the man but everything that he touches as well. For this subject the reader is referred to Haggai, chapter 2. In the same way Paul teaches elsewhere that all things are sanctified to us by the Word, because men use nothing purely, till they receive it in faith from God's hand.

16. *They profess that they know God.* He treats them here as they deserve as hypocrites who insist upon minute observances, but fearlessly despise the chief part of the Christian life. The result is that they give proof of their vanity by showing their contempt for God in open crimes. And this is what Paul means, that those who make a parade of abstaining from one kind of food, indulge in bold wantonness, as though they had completely shaken off the yoke; that their ways are impure and full of wickedness and not a trace of virtue is to be seen in their whole life. By calling them βδελυκτούς, abominable, he seems to be alluding to the pretended sanctity to which they gave their whole attention. Paul declares that they gain nothing, since they do not cease to be profane and detestable. He has good reason to accuse them of being *disobedient*, for none are so proud as hypocrites, who exhaust themselves so much over ceremonies in order to be able with impunity to set at nought the chief requirements of the Law. We may conveniently give the word ἀδοκίμους, reprobate, an active meaning, as though he had said that those who wish to be thought such wise teachers in trifles are destitute of judgment and understanding in regard to good works.

CHAPTER TWO

But speak thou the things that befit the sound doctrine: that aged men be temperate, grave, soberminded, sound in faith, in love, in patience: that aged women likewise be reverent in demeanour, not slanderers, nor enslaved to much wine, teachers of that which is good; that they may train the younger women, to love their husbands and their children, to be soberminded, chaste, workers at home, kind, being in subjection to their own husbands, that the word of God be not blasphemed. (1-5)

1. *But speak thou.* He points out how fables may be driven away, that Titus should devote himself to edification. For he calls *sound doctrine* teaching which can build men up in godliness, for all trifles vanish away before solid teaching. By ordering him to speak things that befit sound doctrine, he means that Titus must continually be employed in teaching them. It would not be enough to make mention of them once or twice only. Paul does not speak of the preaching of a single day, for as long as Titus holds the office of pastor he wants him to be occupied with this preaching.

Doctrine is called sound because of its effect, just as, on the contrary, he says that foolish men waste their energies on questions that are of no profit. Sound therefore means wholesome, that which actually feeds souls. Thus by a single word which is as good as a solemn edict he banishes from the Church all speculations that serve to promote ostentation rather than to advance godliness, as he has already done in both epistles to Timothy.

He distinguishes two parts of sound doctrine. The first is that by which God's grace in Christ is commended to us, so that we know where to look for salvation; the second that by which our life is trained to the fear of God and to innocence. But although the first, having to do with the faith, is by far the more important and so is to be impressed upon us with far greater zeal, Paul in this letter to Titus was not careful about observing the proper order. He is dealing with a man of experience, and he would insult him if he were to spell out the faith to him word by word, as he would do for apprentices and beginners. It is true that in the person of Titus he is instructing the whole Cretan church, but he observes the rules of decorum so as not to seem to lack confidence in Titus' wisdom. Also he dwells longer on his exhortations, because men who were devoted to useless questionings needed chiefly to be recalled to a concern for a holy and upright life. There is nothing more likely to restrain the wandering curiosity of men that to be reminded of the duties in which they should be occupied.

2. *That aged men be temperate.* He begins with particular duties, in order to adapt his words better to the needs of his readers, not only in order to suit their capacity but to press home his point to every individual. General teaching is less effective, but when he reminds every man of his own calling by mentioning a few examples, everyone is made aware that the Lord has given him a clear enough command as to the duty he ought to be fulfilling. We must not look for any fixed scheme here, for Paul's purpose was only to indicate briefly the subjects with which godly teachers ought to deal, not to enter into a full discussion of them.

First he mentions *aged men*. He desires them to be temperate, because excessive drinking is a fault all too common in old age. *Gravity* which he mentions next comes from well regulated habits, for there is nothing more disgraceful than for an old man to indulge in youthful lusts and by his incontinence increase the shamelessness of the young. In the life of an old man there should be σεμνότης, a becoming gravity which will constrain the young to respect. From that there will immediately follow the *sobermindedness* which he mentions next.

Sound in faith. I do not know if there is here an indirect reference to the various diseases of old age, with which he is contrasting soundness of soul. It seems to me to be so, although I do not press the point. He has good reason to sum up Christian perfection under these three heads—*faith, love, patience.* By faith we worship God, for neither prayer nor any other godly exercise is of any avail without it. Love includes all the second table of the commandments and next comes patience, as a seasoning for the other two. For faith without it would not last long and many things happen every day—unworthy conduct or bad temper—which anger us so much that we would be quite disinclined for, and indeed incapable of the duties of love, if the same patience did not support us.

3. *That aged women likewise.* We very often see women advanced in years either continue to dress themselves with the lightness of youth, or have something superstitious among their apparel and it is rare for them to achieve the golden mean. Paul wished to guard against both faults, prescribing a middle course suited both to decorum and religion, or, to put it more simply, to show by their very dress that they are holy and godly.

He goes on to correct two other faults to which they are often addicted, when he forbids them to be *slanderers* and *enslaved to much wine.* Talkativeness is a disease among women and old age usually makes it worse. In addition to this, women are never satisfied with their talking till they have become prattlers and scandal-mongers attacking everybody's reputation. The result is that old women by their slanderous garrulity, as by a lighted torch, often set many homes on fire. Many are also given to drinking and with all modesty and gravity forgotten they display a quite indecent wantonness.

To make them more attentive to their duties, he points out that it is not enough for their own lives to be decent, unless they also train *the young women* by their instruction in an honourable and modest way of life. He therefore tells them that they are by their example to make those who are younger soberminded, since otherwise the ardour of their youth might carry them away.

To love their husbands. I do not agree with those who think that this is a review of the instructions that elderly women should give to young women. Careful attention to the context shows clearly that Paul is continuing with his list of the duties of women which apply to the older women as well. Besides, the construction would be inappropriate σωφρονίζωσι, σώφρονας εἶναι. However in reminding older women of their duties, he at the same time offers to the younger an example they should follow, and so teaches both at once. Briefly put, he wants women to be restrained from licentious love affairs by conjugal love and affection for their children, to regulate their households soberly and with moderation; he tells them not to wander about in public places, but to be chaste and modest and subject to their husbands. For women who excel in other virtues sometimes make that an excuse for arrogance and disobedience to their husbands.

When he adds *that the word of God be not blasphemed*, this is taken to refer to women married to unbelieving husbands who might judge the Gospel by the bad behaviour of their wives, and this seems to be confirmed by Peter's words in I Peter 3.1. But what if he does not speak only of husbands? It is more probable that he requires this strictness of life so that their faults may not bring the Gospel into general disrepute. For the rest of the verse reference may be made to the commentary on I Tim. 5.

The younger men likewise exhort to be soberminded; in all things shewing thyself an ensample of good works; in thy doctrine shewing uncorruptness, gravity, sound speech that cannot be condemned; that he that is of the contrary part may be ashamed, having no evil thing to say of us. Exhort servants to be in subjection to their own masters, and to be well-pleasing to them in all things; not gainsaying; not purloining, but shewing all good fidelity; that they may adorn the doctrine of God our Saviour in all things. (6-10)

6. *The younger men likewise.* His only injunction about the young

men is that they should be instructed to be temperate, for temperance, as Plato teaches, sets right the whole mind of man. It is as if he had said, 'Let them be well regulated and obedient to reason.'

7. *In all things shewing thyself.* Doctrine will have little authority unless its power and majesty shine in the life of a bishop as in a mirror. Thus he tells the teacher to be a pattern which his pupils can follow.

What follows is ambiguous because of the obscurity of the original. First he writes *in doctrine* and immediately adds the words *uncorruptness and gravity* in the accusative case. Ignoring other interpretations, I shall simply offer the one that seems to me most probable. First, I connect the words 'of good works in thy doctrine', for having enjoined Titus to inculcate zeal for good works in his teaching he wants the good works that correspond to this teaching to be seen in his own life. The preposition 'in' indicates the suitability of the good works to the teaching. In what follows there is no obscurity, for he tells him to be upright and grave, in order that his way of life may reflect his teaching.

Sound speech refers in my view to ordinary life and private conversation, for it would be absurd to take it to mean public instruction, since his concern here is that Titus should in his words and deeds live a life that agrees with his preaching. Thus he tells him that his words must be pure and free from all corruption.

That cannot be condemned may apply either to Titus himself or to his speaking. I prefer the former, so that the other nouns in the accusative may depend upon it, as good Greek syntax allows. The meaning would then be, 'that you may prove yourself unblamable in gravity, integrity and sound speech.'

8. *That he that is of the contrary part.* Although a Christian man should have other ends in view, he ought not to neglect to stop the mouths of the ungodly, as we are often admonished not to give them any opportunity for slandering us. Everything bad they can seize hold of in our life is twisted maliciously against Christ and His teaching. The result is that by our fault God's sacred name is exposed to insult. Thus the more closely we see ourselves being watched by our enemies, the more intent we should be to avoid their slanders, so that their ill-will strengthens us in the desire to do well.

9. *Exhort servants.* It has already been said that Paul here is merely touching on certain subjects by way of example and does not deal with them fully, as he would in an exhaustive discussion. Thus when he tells servants to be *well-pleasing to their masters in all things*, this desire to please must be limited to things that are right, as we may gather from similar passages in which this exception is explicitly stated, that they should do only what is in accordance with God's will.

It may be observed that the apostle insists chiefly that those who are under the power of others should be obedient and submissive, and he has good cause to do so. For there is nothing more contrary to man's natural disposition than submission and there was a danger that they might make the Gospel a pretext for rebelliousness, holding that it was unfitting for them to submit to the dominion of ungodly men. Pastors must show the greatest care and attention in subduing and checking this rebelliousness. He censures two faults common among servants, a petulant answering back and a propensity to steal. The classical comedies are full of instances of the excessive talkativeness of servants who mock their masters and there was good reason why in ancient times 'slave' and 'thief' became interchangeable terms. Wisdom requires us to fit our instructions to the way of life of individuals in this way.

By *fidelity* he means faithfulness towards their masters; thus *to shew all fidelity* means to act faithfully without fraud or harm in transacting their masters' affairs.

10. *That they may adorn the doctrine.* This exhortation should spur us on greatly when we are told that by honourable behaviour we adorn the doctrine of God which is the reflection of His glory. And we see that this usually happens, just as on the other hand our wicked life brings us into disgrace, for it is usually judged by our works. But we should also observe this, that God deigns to receive an adornment from slaves, whose condition was so low and mean that they were scarcely reckoned as men. For he does not mean domestic servants, as we have them today, but bond-slaves, who were bought with money and held in possession like cattle or horses. If the life of men like that is an ornament to the Christian name, those who are in an honourable station should much more see to it that they do not stain it by their baseness.

> *For the grace of God hath appeared, bringing salvation to all men, instructing us, to the intent that, denying ungodliness and worldly lusts, we should live soberly and righteously and godly in this present world; looking for the blessed hope and appearing of the glory of our great God and Saviour Jesus Christ; who gave himself for us, that he might redeem us from all iniquity, and purify unto himself a people for his own possession, zealous of good works. These things speak and exhort and reprove with all authority. Let no man despise thee.* (11-15)

11. *For the grace of God hath appeared.* He bases his argument on the purpose of God in redemption, which he shows to be zeal to live a godly and upright life. It follows from this that it is the duty of a good teacher to exhort men to a holy life rather than occupy their minds with empty speculations. As Zacharias says in his song (Luke

1.74-75), 'He hath redeemed us that we should serve him in holiness and righteousness all our days.' In the same vein Paul says 'The grace of God hath appeared . . . instructing us'; he means that God's grace, should itself instruct us to order our lives aright. Some are quick to turn the preaching of God's mercy into an excuse for licentiousness, while carelessness keeps others from thinking about the renewal of their life. But the revelation of God's grace necessarily brings with it exhortations to a godly life.

Bringing salvation to all men. He expressly declares that salvation comes to all men, having especially in mind the slaves of whom he has just been speaking. He does not mean individuals, but rather all classes of men with their diverse ways of life, and he lays great emphasis on the fact that God's grace has condescended even to slaves. Since God does not despise even the lowest and most degraded class of men, it would be extremely foolish that we should be slow and negligent to embrace His goodness.

12. *Denying ungodliness.* He now lays down the rule by which we may order our lives well, and tells us that we ought to begin by renouncing our former way of life, two features of which he mentions— *ungodliness and worldly lusts*. Under ungodliness I include not only the superstitions in which they had erred, but the irreligious neglect of God that prevails among men until they have been enlightened into the knowledge of the truth. For although they make some profession of religion, they never fear and reverence God sincerely from the heart, but rather have slumbering consciences, so that nothing is further from their thoughts than their duty to serve God. By worldly lusts he means all the affections of the flesh, since our only regard is for the world till the Lord has drawn us to Himself. Meditation on the heavenly life begins after our regeneration; before that our desires are directed to the world and cling to it.

Soberly and righteously and godly. He has already mentioned these three as giving a comprehensive summary of Christian living, and now he makes the same point again. Godliness is religion in relation to God, whereas righteousness is exercised towards men. The man endowed with both lacks no part of perfect virtue, for in God's Law there is complete perfection to which nothing else can ever be added. But as the exercises of godliness depend on the first table of the Law, so temperance, which he also mentions in this passage, has no other aim than to keep the Law, and, as I said before about patience, is added like a kind of seasoning to the other two. There is no inconsistency in mentioning sometimes patience and sometimes temperance as the completion of a holy life; they are not distinct qualities since σωφροσύνη includes patience within itself.

He adds *in this present world*, since God has appointed our present life for the proving of our faith. Although the fruit of good deeds does not yet appear, yet the hope should be enough to urge us on to do well, and this is what he goes on to say.

13. *Looking for the blessed hope.* He finds a basis for his exhortation in the hope of future immortality, and certainly if that hope is deeply settled in our minds, it cannot but lead us to devote ourselves wholly to God. On the other hand, those who do not cease to live to the world and the flesh have never really known the importance of the promise of eternal life. For the Lord in calling us into heaven removes us from the earth.

Hope here stands for the things hoped for; otherwise it would be a wrong way of speaking; he gives the name hope to the blessed life that is laid up for us in heaven. At the same time he declares when we shall enjoy it and what we ought to look to, when we desire and meditate upon our salvation.

I take the *glory of God* to mean not only the glory which He shall have in Himself, but also the glory which He will then diffuse everywhere so that all His elect shall be given a share in it. He calls God *great*, because His greatness, which men who are blinded by the dazzle of the vain world now reduce and sometimes, as much as in them lies, annihilate, will show itself fully on the last day. The lustre of the world, as long as it shines brightly in our eyes, so blinds them that the glory of God lies hidden, as it were, in darkness. But by His advent Christ will disperse all the world's empty show, so that nothing will any longer obscure the brightness of His glory or take from its greatness. It is indeed true that the Lord demonstrates His majesty every day by His works, but because blindness keeps men from seeing it, it may still be said to be hidden in obscurity. Paul wants believers to meditate now by faith on the glory that will be revealed on the last day, that God may be magnified, even although the world either despises Him or at least does not esteem Him according to His true excellence.

It is not clear whether we should take the next words in close connexion—'the glory of Christ, the great God and Saviour'—or separately of the Father and the Son—'the glory of the great God and of our Saviour, Jesus Christ'. The Arians seized on this latter interpretation and tried to prove from it that the Son is less than the Father, holding that Paul calls the Father 'the great God' in order to distinguish Him from the Son. In order to refute this false allegation, orthodox Church teachers have strongly maintained that both titles are applied to Christ. But there is a shorter and surer refutation of the Arians, for after Paul has spoken of the revelation of the glory of the great God, he immediately adds Christ to show that the revelation is in His person. It is as if he had said that when Christ appears, the greatness of God's glory shall be revealed to us.

From this we learn, first, that our greatest incentive to increased activity and willingness in doing good should be the hope of a future resurrection; second, that believers should always have their eyes fixed upon it, lest they grow weary in following the right course, for, unless we entirely depend upon it, we shall continually be carried away into the world's vanities. But in case the thought of the advent of the Lord in judgment should fill us with terror, Christ is presented to us as the Saviour who will also be our future Judge.

14. *Who gave Himself for us.* This is another source of exhortation, based on the purpose or effect of Christ's death. Christ offered Himself for us that He might redeem us from slavery to sin and purchase us for Himself as His possession. His grace necessarily brings with it newness of life, for those who go on serving sin make void the blessing of redemption. But now we are rescued from the bondage of sin that we may serve God's righteousness.

From this he immediately passes to the second point about *a people for his own possession, zealous of good works,* by which he means that the fruit of redemption is lost to us, if we are still held fast in the net of the world's sinful desires. To express more clearly the fact that we have been consecrated to good works by the death of Christ, he uses the word purify, for it would be unworthy for us to let ourselves be polluted by the very stains that by His death God's Son has purged from us.

15. *These things speak.* This last sentence is equivalent to an injunction to Titus to dwell continually on this edifying teaching and never to grow weary of it, for it cannot be too much insisted upon. He also tells him to add to teaching the incitements of exhortation and reproof, for men are not sufficiently reminded of their duty, unless they are also vehemently urged to do it. The man who understands all that Paul has been saying and who has it always on his lips will have good reason not only to teach but to correct.

With all authority. I do not agree with Erasmus who renders ἐπιταγήν diligence in giving orders. Chrysostom's view is more probable, for he takes it to mean severity against the more atrocious sins, but I do not think that even he has explained Paul's meaning aright. His point is that Titus should claim for himself authority and respect in teaching these things. For men given up to curiosity and anger about trifles dislike commands to live a godly and holy life as being common and vulgar. In order that Titus may meet this dislike, he is told to add the weight of his authority to his teaching.

It is in my view with the same intention that he immediately adds

Let no man despise thee. Some think that he is admonishing Timothy to win men's attention and respect by the integrity of his life, and it is quite true that holy and blameless conduct gives authority to teaching; but Paul's aim is different, for here he is addressing the people rather than Titus. Because many at that time had ears so delicate that they held the simplicity of the Gospel in scorn, because they had such an itch for novelty that there was hardly any room left for edification, he beats down their pride and strictly charges them to stop despising sound and profitable teaching in any way. This confirms what I said at the outset; this letter was written to the men of Crete rather than to one single individual.

CHAPTER THREE

Put them in mind to be in subjection to rulers, to authorities, to be obedient, to be ready unto every good work, to speak evil of no man, not to be contentious, to be gentle, shewing all meekness toward all men. For we also were aforetime foolish, disobedient, deceived, serving divers lusts and pleasures, living in malice and envy, hateful, hating one another. (1-3)

1. *Put them in mind.* It is evident from many passages that the apostles had great difficulty in keeping the common people in subjection to the authority of magistrates and princes. By nature we all desire imperious power, so that no one is willing to submit himself to another. Besides, seeing that at that time practically all the worldly powers were opposed to Christ, they thought them unworthy of any honour. The Jews especially, being an indomitable people, were for ever rebelling and raging. Thus, having mentioned particular duties, Paul now wishes to give a general admonition that they should calmly respect the order of civil government, obey the laws and submit to the magistrates. For the subjection to princes and obedience to magistrates he requires extends also to edicts and laws and other civil duties.

What he immediately adds about being *ready for every good work* may be applied to the same subject, as if he had said, 'All who do not refuse to live a good and honest life will willingly yield obedience to magistrates,' for, since they have been appointed for the preservation of human life, he who desires their removal or shakes off their yoke is the enemy of equity and justice and so devoid of all humanity. If anyone prefers to interpret this phrase without reference to the immediate context, I have no objection. There is no doubt that in this sentence he is commending to us kindness towards our neighbours in our whole life.

2. *To speak evil of no man.* He now lays down the way in which they can promote peace and friendship with all. For we know that there is nothing more congenial to human nature than for every man to think less of others than of himself, so that many are proud of God's gifts to them and despise their bethren, and despising soon leads to insult. Thus he tells Christians not to glory over others or to reproach them, however superior to others they may be. Not that he wishes them to condone the faults of ungodly men; he is condemning only the propensity to slander.

When he tells them *not to be contentious* he is in fact telling them how to avoid quarrels and altercations. The Vulgate has translated it well by 'not quarrelsome', for there are other ways of fighting than with sword or fist. It is evident from what follows that this is what he means, for the remedy which he prescribes for this evil is to be kind and gentle to all. Kindness is contrasted with the utmost rigour of the law, and gentleness with bitterness. If we wish to avoid every kind of quarrel and fight, we must learn first to deal gently with many things and to ignore many more. For those who are immoderately severe and ill-tempered carry with them a fire that kindles quarrels. He adds *towards all men* to show that we should bear even with the lowest and the meanest of men. Believers held ungodly men as worth nothing and so undeserving of any forbearance and Paul wants to correct such severity, for its only source is pride.

3. *For we also were aforetime foolish.* Nothing is more likely to subdue our pride and moderate our severity than to be shown that the charges we make against others may fall back on our own heads. A man who is forced to seek pardon for himself finds it easy to forgive others and the only reason why we are so unwilling to forgive our brethren is our ignorance of our own faults. Those who have a zeal for God are indeed severe with sinners, but because they begin with themselves, their severity is always mixed with compassion. Thus, in order that believers may not severely and inhumanly mock at others who are still held in ignorance and blindness, Paul reminds them what kind of men they themselves have been; as if he had said, 'If those on whom God has not yet bestowed the light of faith are to be treated so harshly, there was at one time equally good reason to harry you without mercy. You would not then have wanted anyone to be so unkind to you, therefore now show the same moderation towards others.' There are two implications of Paul's words here that need to be noted. The first is that those who have now been enlightened by the Lord should be kept humble by the recollection of their own former ignorance, and so should not exalt themselves proudly over others, nor treat them more harshly and severely than they thought they themselves should be treated when they were in a like condition. The second is that what has happened to themselves should prompt them to think that those who are outside the Church today may tomorrow be engrafted into it, and with their faults corrected may come to share in the gifts of God which at present they lack. In believers we can clearly see both things happening, for they were once darkness, but afterwards began to be light in the Lord. The thought of their former condition should incline them to συμπάθεια, fellow-feeling and God's present grace to them is proof that others also can be brought to salvation. So we see that we

ought to humble ourselves before God, that we may be gentle towards our brethren. Pride is always cruel and a despiser of all men. In another passage (Galatians 6.1) where he exhorts us to gentleness he bids each one of us remember his own weakness; here he goes further since he wants us to recall those faults from which we have already been delivered, so that we may not pursue too keenly those that still dwell in others.

Further, from Paul's description here of human nature before it is reformed by Christ's Spirit, we can see how wretched we are apart from Christ. First he calls unbelievers *foolish*, for all man's wisdom is vanity as long as he does not know God; then he calls them *disobedient*, for only faith is true obedience to God and unbelief is always stubborn and rebellious, although it is possible here to translate ἀπειθεῖς by 'unbelieving' so as to describe the kind of foolishness. Thirdly he says that unbelievers are *deceived*, for Christ alone is the Way and Light of the world, so that those who are estranged from God must wander astray in their whole lives.

Up to this point he has been describing the nature of unbelief, but now he adds the results that spring from it, namely *divers lusts and pleasures, living in malice and envy* and such like. It is true that individuals do not suffer in equal measure from all these faults; but since all are enslaved to wicked desires, although they are different in different men, Paul covers in a general way all the fruits unbelief can bring forth in different people. This matter is explained towards the end of Romans 1.

Since Paul distinguishes the sons of God from unbelievers by these marks, if we wish to be reckoned believers, we must have a heart purged from all envy and free from all malice, and we must both love in return. It is unreasonable that we should be dominated by the desires he here describes as 'divers' because, in my view, the desires that agitate a carnal man are like dashing waves which beat against each other, toss the man this way and that so that he changes and varies almost every moment. All who abandon themselves to carnal desires share this restlessness, for there is no stability except in the fear of God.

> *But when the kindness of God our Saviour, and his love toward man, appeared, not by works done in righteousness, which we did ourselves, but according to his mercy he saved us, through the washing of regeneration and renewing of the Holy Ghost, which he poured out upon us richly, through Jesus Christ our Saviour, that, being justified by his grace, we might be made heirs according to the hope of eternal life.* (4-7)

In this sentence either the principal clause is that God saved us by His mercy, or it is incomplete. In that case it will be better to undertand that men were changed for the better and made new because God had mercy upon them; as if he had said, 'You began to be different from others when God regenerated you by His Spirit'. But since Paul's words as they stand give a full meaning, there is really no need to make any addition. He includes himself along with the others that his exhortation may be more efficacious.

4. *But after kindness and love appeared.* First it may be asked whether God's kindness began to be known in the world only at the time when Christ was manifested in the flesh, for it is certain that from the first the fathers knew and experienced God's kindness, mercy and favour towards them, so that this was not the first manifestation of His kindness and fatherly love towards us. The answer is simple, that the fathers under the Law tasted God's goodness only by looking towards Christ on whose advent all their faith depended. Thus God's kindness may be said to have appeared when He showed this sure pledge of it and gave actual proof that He had not so often promised salvation to men in vain. 'God so loved the world that he gave his only begotten Son' (John 3.16) or as Paul says elsewhere 'God commendeth his own love towards us, in that, while we were yet sinners he sent his own Son' etc. (Romans 5.8). It is usual in the Scriptures to say that the world was reconciled to God by Christ's death, although we know that He was a kind Father in all ages. But because we can find no reason for God's love toward us and no ground for our salvation except in Christ, there is good reason for saying that God the Father has shown His kindness to us in Him.

But there is a different reason for it in this passage where Paul is not speaking as usual of that manifestation of Christ when He came as man into the world, but of His manifestation in the Gospel, when He offers and reveals Himself in a special way to the elect. At Christ's first coming Paul was not renewed, for, although Christ was raised in glory and salvation in His name had shone upon many not only in Judaea but in neighbouring lands, Paul, blinded by unbelief, was still labouring to extinguish this grace by every means in his power. His meaning is therefore that God's grace appeared to himself and to others when they were enlightened in the knowledge of the Gospel. No other application of this passage would be suitable, for he is not speaking indiscriminately of the men of his own time, but is specially addressing those who have been separated off from the rest, as if he had said that once they were like unbelievers who were still plunged in darkness, but now they are different from them, not by their own merit but by God's grace. In 1 Corinthians 4.7 he uses the same argument to beat down all fleshly arrogance, 'For who maketh thee to differ?' or who is it that makes you more honoured than others?

Kindness and love. He is right to mention first the kindness that prompts God to love us. He will never find in us anything worthy of His love, but He loves us because He is kind and merciful. Besides, although He gives witness of His kindness and love to all men, we know it only by faith when in Christ He declares Himself our Father. Paul enjoyed innumerable gifts of God before he was called to the faith of Christ, and these could have given him a taste of God's fatherly kindness, and he had been from infancy educated in the teaching of the Law; and yet he was in darkness so that he had no sense of God's kindness till the Spirit enlightened his mind and Christ came forth as witness and pledge of God the Father's grace, from which without Him we are all strangers. Thus he means that God's loving kindness (*humanitas*) is revealed only by the light of faith.

5. *Not by works.* We should remember that here Paul is addressing believers and is describing the way in which they have entered God's kingdom. He declares that they have not by their works in any way deserved to share in salvation, or that they should be reconciled to God through faith, but they obtained this blessing solely by the mercy of God. We may gather from his words that we bring nothing to God, but He goes before us in the initiative of His pure grace without any regard for works. For when he says 'not by the works *that we have done*' he means that till we are regenerated by God we can do nothing but sin. This negative statement depends upon his previous affirmation that those not yet reformed in Christ are foolish and disobedient, led away by divers lusts, and what good work could proceed from such a mass of corruption?

It is madness therefore to imagine that a man may approach God by what are called his own 'preparations'. All their life men go further and further from Him, till by His own hand He brings them back from wandering into His way. In short Paul ascribes the fact that we rather than others have been chosen to participate in Christ entirely to God's mercy, since there were in us no works of righteousness. This argument would not be valid unless it were agreed that everything we attempt before we believe is unrighteous and hateful to God. But some foolish men use the fact that the verb here is in the past tense as an excuse to argue that God has regard to a man's future merits when He calls him. They argue that Paul's denial that God is moved by our merits in bestowing grace upon us applies only to the past. Thus if it is only righteousness before His call that is excluded, future righteousness may be taken into account. But this argument assumes a principle that Paul everywhere rejects, when he says that election by free grace is the foundation of good works. If we owe it entirely to the grace of God that we are fit to live well, what future works of ours is God to look upon? If before God calls us iniquity holds such sway over us that it will not cease to advance till it reaches its height, how can God be induced to call us out of a regard for our future righteousness? Away with such trifling! Paul mentioned past works with the sole object of excluding all merit. His meaning may be expressed thus, 'If we boast of any merit, what kind of works did we do?' The maxim holds good that men will not be better in the future than they have been in the past, unless God corrects them by His calling.

He saved us. He speaks of faith and teaches that we have already received salvation. Thus although, since we are entangled in sin, we bear about a body of death, yet we are certain of our salvation, provided that we are engrafted into Christ by faith. So John 5.24, 'He that believeth on the Son of God hath passed out of death into life.' Yet a little later, by introducing the word faith, he will show that we have not yet entered into full possession of what Christ has procured for us by His death. Thus it follows that from God's side our salvation is complete, but our full enjoyment of it is deferred till the end of our warfare. The apostle is making the same point in Romans 8.24 when he says that we are 'saved by hope'.

Through the washing of regeneration. I have no doubt that there is at least an allusion here to baptism and, I have no objection to the explanation of the whole passage in terms of baptism; not that salvation is obtained in the external symbol of water, but because baptism seals to us the salvation obtained by Christ. Paul is dealing with the manifestation of God's grace which, we have said, consists of faith. Since therefore baptism is part of this revelation, in so far as it is designed to confirm faith, Paul is right to mention it here. Besides, since baptism is our entrance into the Church and the symbol of our engrafting into Christ, it is appropriate for Paul to introduce it here, when he wishes to show how God's grace has appeared to us. The train of thought of the passage is this: 'God saves us by His mercy and He has given us a symbol and pledge of this salvation in baptism, by admitting us into His Church and engrafting us into the Body of His Son.'

The apostles usually base an argument on the sacraments when they wish to prove what is signified in them, because it should be accepted as a fixed principle among godly men, that God does not play games with us with empty figures but inwardly accomplishes by His own power the thing He shows us by the outward sign. Thus baptism is fittingly and truly said to be 'the washing of regeneration'. The power and use of the sacraments are rightly understood, when we connect sign and thing signified in such a way that the sign is not made vain and unefficacious, and when we do not for the sake of exalting the sign take from the Holy Spirit what belongs to Him. Although ungodly men are neither washed nor renewed by baptism, yet it retains its efficacy as far as God is concerned, for although they reject God's grace, it is still offered to them. But here Paul is addressing believers in whom baptism is always efficacious and is therefore rightly spoken of in connexion with its reality and effect. By this way of speaking we are reminded that if we do not wish to make holy baptism null and void, we must prove its power by newness of life

And renewing of the Holy Ghost. Although he mentions the sign to exhibit God's grace clearly to us, yet to prevent us from fixing our whole attention upon it, he soon reminds us of the Spirit, that we know that we are not washed by water but by His power, as Ezekiel says, 'And I will sprinkle clean water upon you, even my Spirit' (Ezek. 36.25, 27). Paul's words here agree so completely with the prophet's that they are in fact saying the same thing. This was why I said at the beginning that, although Paul is dealing specifically with the Holy Spirit, he also alludes to baptism. It is God's Spirit who regenerates us and makes us new creatures, but since His grace is invisible and hidden, a visible symbol of it is given to us in baptism. Some take the word 'renewing' to be in the accusative, and I do not disapprove, but in my view the other reading fits better.

6. *Which he poured out upon us.* In the Greek the relative 'which' agrees with both 'washing' and 'Spirit', both nouns being neuter, but it makes very little difference to the meaning. The metaphor will be more elegant if the relative is taken with 'washing'. Nor is it inconsistent with this that all indiscriminately are baptized, for when he speaks of the washing poured out upon us, he refers less to the sign than to the thing signified, in which the reality of the sign consists.

When he says *richly* he means that the more each of us excels in the greater gifts, the more he stands in debt to God's mercy which alone enriches us, for in ourselves we are completely poor and destitute of all good things. If anyone objects that not all God's sons share such great richness, for some have but a sparse share in God's mercy, the answer is that no man's share is so small that he may not justly be called rich, for the smallest drop of the Spirit is, so to speak, like an everflowing fountain that never runs dry. We may rightly speak of rich abundance, since however small the share we have been given, it is never exhausted.

Through Jesus Christ. It is He alone in whom we are adopted; thus it is through Him that we are made to share in the Spirit who is the earnest and witness of our adoption. By this phrase Paul teaches that the Spirit of regeneration is given only to those who are members of Christ.

7. *That being justified by his grace.* If we understand regeneration in the strict and normal sense, it might be thought that the apostle makes

'justified' mean the same as 'regenerated' and this is sometimes its meaning, but only rarely. But here there is no need for us to depart from its proper and more natural meaning. Paul's purpose is to ascribe to God's grace all that we have and are, that we may not exalt ourselves in pride over others. Here therefore he is commending God's mercy and attributing our salvation entirely to it. Since he had been speaking of the faults of unbelievers, he was bound to mention the grace of regeneration which is the medicine for curing them. But this does not stop him from returning immediately to his praise of mercy, and he combines both blessings together when he says that our sins have been freely pardoned and we have been renewed unto obedience to God. It is certainly quite clear that Paul maintains that justification is the free gift of God, and the only question is what he means by 'being justified'. The context seems to demand that it should have a wider meaning than the imputation of righteousness, but this use of the word is, as I have said, very rare with Paul, and there is nothing to prevent its being restricted to the forgiveness of sins.

When he says *by His grace* this can be taken both of Christ and of the Father, and we should not contend for either interpretation, because it always remains true that we have received righteousness by the grace of God through Christ.

Heirs according to the hope of eternal life. This clause is added by way of explanation. He has said that we have been saved by God's mercy, but our salvation is still hidden, and he says now that we are heirs of life, not because we have attained to its present possession, but because hope brings us full and complete assurance of it. The meaning may be summed up as follows, 'When we were dead we were restored to life through the grace of Christ, when God the Father bestowed upon us His Spirit, by whose power we are purified and renewed; and this is our salvation. But because we are still in the world, we do not yet enjoy eternal life, but obtain it only by hoping.'

> *Faithful is the saying, and concerning these things I will that thou affirm confidently, to the end that they which have believed God may be careful to maintain good works. These things are good and profitable unto men: but shun foolish questionings, and genealogies, and strifes, and fightings about the law; for they are unprofitable and vain.* (8-9)

8. *Faithful is the saying.* This is the way he speaks when he wishes to make a solemn assertion, as we have seen in both the epistles to Timothy. Thus he immediately adds *these things I will that thou affirm.* Διαβεβαιοῦσθαι has a passive inflection but an active meaning; it means to affirm something strongly. Titus is here told to disregard everything else and teach the things that are certain and without doubt, to press them and

dwell upon them, while others are talking idly of things of little importance. From this we conclude that a bishop should not be rash in asserting anything, but only those things which he has ascertained to be true. 'These', he says, 'affirm, because they are true and deserve to be believed.' We are thus reminded that it is also the duty of a bishop to assert and maintain strongly and boldly things that are surely established and that build up godliness.

Excel in good works.[1] He includes all the instructions he has given about the duties that belong to each individual and the care to live a good and godly life; contrasting the fear of God and well-regulated conduct with idle speculations. He wishes the people to be instructed in such a way that those who have believed in God may make good works their chief concern.

The verb προΐστασθαι is used in different senses in Greek, so that this passage admits of various interpretations. Chrysostom explains it as meaning that they should be concerned to help their neighbours by giving alms. Προΐστασθαι does sometimes mean to give help, but in this case the construction would suggest that it is the good works that are to be helped, and that is difficult. The word 'promote' would suit better, *avancer* in French. Or we might say, 'Let them strive as those that have the pre-eminence', for that is one meaning of the word. Or perhaps some will prefer, 'let them take care to give good works the chief place', and it would be perfectly fitting for Paul to enjoin that these things should prevail in the lives of believers, since others usually disregard them. But although the expression is ambiguous, Paul's intention is quite clearly to point out that the purpose of Christian teaching is that believers should exercise themselves in good works. He wishes them to give them their careful attention and care, and when he says φροντίζωσι he seems to be making an elegant allusion to the empty contemplations of those who indulge in philosophical speculations without any advantage or application to life.

Yet he is not so concerned with the good works as to forget, while he is gathering the fruit, that the root of them is faith. He takes account of both parts and gives to faith its rightful priority. It is those who believe in God who are told to be careful for good works, and by this he means that faith must come first, so that the good works will follow.

These things are good. I take this to refer to the teaching rather than to the works, in this sense, 'It is excellent and to their profit that men should be so instructed'; thus the things that he has just told Titus to affirm with zeal are the same as those which are here called good and useful to men. Τὰ καλά can be translated either 'good' or 'beautiful' or 'honourable', although in my view 'excellent' is the best rendering.

[1] R.V. *maintain good works.*

He indicates that everything else that is taught is worthless, because fruitless and useless, while, on the contrary, that which leads to salvation is worthy of praise.

9. *But shun foolish questionings.* There is no need to discuss the meaning of this passage at length. He contrasts questionings with sound and certain teaching, for although you have to seek in order to find, yet there is a limit to seeking in order that you may grasp what it is profitable to know and may adhere firmly to the truth once it is known. Those who inquire curiously into everything and are never at rest may truly be called 'questionarians' (*questionarii*). In short the things held in highest esteem by the schools of the Sorbonne are here condemned by Paul. For the whole theology of the Papists is nothing but a labyrinth of questions (*quaestiones*). He calls them *foolish*, not because at first sight they seem to be so—often they deceive us by an empty show of wisdom—but because they contribute nothing to godliness.

When he adds *genealogies* he mentions one class of foolish questions by way of example, for men forget to gather fruit from the sacred histories and seize on the lineage of races and trifles of that kind, and weary themselves with them to no end. We have spoken of this folly in commenting on the beginning of I Timothy.

He rightly adds *strifes,* because in questionings the ruling motive is ambition, and the inevitable result is that they at once break out into contention and quarrels, for everyone wishes to be the conqueror. This is accompanied by a rashness in affirming things which are uncertain, and this of necessity provokes conflicts.

Fightings about the law. This is the scornful description he gives of the debates initiated by the Jews with the Law as their pretext. Not that the Law itself gives rise to them, but because these men, pretending to defend the Law, were disturbing the peace of the Church with their absurd controversies about the observance of ceremonies, the choice of foods and such things.

For they are unprofitable. In teaching we are always to have regard to usefulness so that all that is not conducive to godliness may be excluded. There is no doubt that the sophists in their ranting about things of no worth boasted of them as highly worthy and useful to know, but Paul does not admit any usefulness except in building up faith and a holy life.

A man that is heretical, after a first and second admonition refuse; knowing that such a one is perverted and sinneth, being self-condemned. When I shall send Artemas unto thee, or Tychicus, give diligence to come unto me to Nicopolis: for there I have determined to winter. Set forward

Zenas the lawyer and Apollos on their journey diligently, that nothing be wanting unto them. And let our people also learn to maintain good works for necessary uses, that they may be not unfruitful. All that are with me salute thee. Salute them that love us in faith. Grace be with you all. (10-15)

10. *A man that is heretical.* He had good reason to add this, for there will be no end of quarrels and altercations, if we wish to conquer obstinate men in argument, for they will never lack words, and they will derive fresh courage from their wickedness so that they will never grow weary of fighting. Thus, having laid down for Titus what form of doctrine he ought to teach, he now tells him not to waste much time in debating with heretics, because one battle will always lead to another, and one dispute give rise to a second. This is the cunning of Satan, that by the wicked talkativeness of such men he entangles good and faithful pastors so as to distract them from their concern with teaching. Thus we should beware not to let ourselves become involved in quarrelsome arguments, because then we shall never be free to devote our labour to the Lord's flock, and argumentative people will never cease to trouble us.

In telling him to avoid such people, it is as if he had said that he must not spend much effort in satisfying them, for there is nothing better than denying to them the chance to fight they desire. This warning is highly necessary, for even those who would be glad to take no part in verbal battles are sometimes drawn into controversy, because they think that it would be shameful cowardice to yield. Besides there is no nature so peaceable that it is not liable to be provoked by the fierce taunts of enemies, because it seems intolerable that they should attack the truth without any reply, as they do. And there is no lack of men who are either fractious or too hot tempered who are eager for the fray. But Paul does not wish Christ's servants to be too much or too long employed in disputing with heretics.

We must now see what it is he means by the word *heretic.* There is a familiar and well-known distinction between an heretic and a schismatic which in my view Paul here disregards. For by heretics he does not only mean those who embrace and defend known error or some pernicious doctrine, but in general those who do not assent to the sound teaching which he has just laid down. Thus he includes under this name all ambitious, unruly, contentious people who are led astray by sinful passions and disturb the peace of the Church; in short anyone who by his shameless pride breaks the unity of the Church is called a heretic by Paul.

But we have to exercise moderation in not immediately making a heretic of everyone who does not agree with our opinions, for there are some matters on which Christians may disagree among themselves without being divided into sects. Paul himself makes this point elsewhere when he bids them wait in unbroken harmony for the revelation of God (Phil. 3.15). But if anyone comes to the point of obstinacy at which from selfish motives he separates from the body, or draws away some of the flock, or hinders the advance of sound doctrine, we must strenuously resist him. Heresy or sectarianism is completely opposed to the unity of the Church. Since this is precious to God and should be very highly regarded by us, we should hold heresy in the greatest abhorrence. Thus the name of sect or heresy, although held in honour by philosophers and statesmen, is rightly considered infamous among Christians. We now understand what Paul means when he tells us to refuse and avoid heretics.

But we should at the same time pay attention to what immediately follows—*after a first and second admonition*, for we have no right to decide that a man is a heretic or to reject him, unless we have first tried to bring him back to a sound mind. Further, he does not mean any kind of admonition, or one given by a private individual, but an admonition by a minister with the public authority of the Church. His words amount to saying that heretics should be rebuked with solemn and severe censure.

Those who infer from this passage that the originators of pernicious doctrines are to be restrained by excommunication alone, and no further measures of greater rigour are to be taken against them do not argue conclusively. There is a difference between the duty of a bishop and that of a magistrate. In writing to Titus Paul does not deal with what belongs to the office of magistrate but solely with a bishop's duties. Still, moderation is always best, so that instead of being restrained by force and violence, they may be corrected by the discipline of the Church, if they can indeed be cured.

11. *Knowing that such a one is ruined*.[1] He calls a man 'ruined' when there is no hope of repentance for him, because, if further efforts could restore any man, we should certainly not withhold them. The metaphor is taken from a building which is not merely destroyed in some part, but completely demolished so that there is no chance of its being repaired.

He points out next the sign of this ruin, an evil conscience, when he says that those who do not yield to admonitions are *self-condemned*. Since they obstinately reject the truth, it is certain that their sin is voluntary and deliberate and therefore it would be vain to admonish them.

[1] R.V. *perverted*.

At the same time we gather from Paul's words that we must not rashly and without deliberation pronounce anyone a heretic, for he says *knowing* that he is ruined. Let the bishop beware of yielding to his own passionate temper and treating with excessive hardship as a heretic someone he does not yet know to be such.

13. *Zenas the lawyer.* It is uncertain whether he means a man skilled in the civil law or in the Law of Moses, but since we can infer from Paul's words that he was a poor man needing outside help, the probability is that he belonged to the same order as Apollos, that is an interpreter of the Law of God among the Jews. Such people were more often in want than those who conducted legal cases in court. I said that Zenas' poverty can be inferred from Paul's words, because the expression *set him forward* here means to supply him with provisions for his journey, as is clear from the context. In order that the Cretans on whom he lays this burden may not complain of being loaded with the expense, he reminds them that they must not be unfruitful and must therefore be urged to zeal in good works. But we have already discussed this way of speaking. Whether therefore he tells them to excel in good works, or to assign them the highest rank, he means that it is good for them to have a chance offered for exercising liberality, that they may not be unfruitful on the pretext that there is no opportunity or necessity that requires it.

What follows has already been explained in the other epistles.

The Epistle of Paul to
PHILEMON

PAUL'S EPISTLE TO PHILEMON

Paul, a prisoner of Christ Jesus, and Timothy, our brother, to Philemon, our beloved and fellow-worker, and to Apphia our sister, and to Archippus our fellow-soldier, and to the church in thy house; grace to you and peace from God our Father and the Lord Jesus Christ. I thank my God always, making mention of thee in my prayers, hearing of thy love, and of the faith which thou hast towards the Lord Jesus, and toward all the saints; that the fellowship of thy faith may become effectual, in the knowledge of every good thing, which is in you, unto Christ. For I had much joy and comfort in thy love, because the hearts of the saints have been refreshed through thee, brother. (1-7)

The sublime quality of Paul's spirit, although seen better in his more important writings, is also apparent in this epistle, in which by his treatment of it he raises up a theme in itself low and mean to God in his usual way. He is sending back a runaway slave and thief to his master and asking that he should be forgiven. In pleading his cause he discusses Christian forbearance with such weight that he seems to be thinking about the interests of the whole Church rather than the private affairs of a single man. On behalf of a man of the lowest condition he condescends to such modesty and humility that hardly anywhere else do we have such a living picture of the meekness of his character.

1. *A prisoner of Christ Jesus.* In the same sense in which he elsewhere calls himself an apostle or minister of Christ, he now calls himself His prisoner, because the chains with which he was bound for the sake of the Gospel were the ornaments or badges of the commission he exercised on Christ's behalf. He mentions them here, not because he needs to strengthen his authority, or because he was afraid of being despised—there is no doubt that Philemon held him in too great esteem for there to be any need for him to state his claims—but because he was about to plead the cause of a runaway slave, the chief part of which was a plea for forgiveness.

To Philemon. It is probable that this Philemon held the rank of pastor, for Paul calls him his *fellow-worker* and that is not a title he usually bestows on a private individual. He also addresses *Archippus*, who also seems to have been a minister of the Church, at least if he is the same person who is mentioned towards the end of Collosians, and that is not at all improbable, for he addresses him as a *fellow-soldier*, a designation which applies specially to ministers. For although all Christians share in this warfare, teachers are, so to speak, Christ's standard-bearers and ought to be ready to fight harder than the others; and Satan usually presses them more sorely. It is possible that Archippus was Paul's colleague and shared in some of the struggles in which he was involved, for this is the word which Paul uses whenever he mentions persecutions.

He bestows the highest praise on Philemon's family when he calls them *the church in thy house*, and it is no small praise of the head of the house that he has so regulated his family that it is like the Church and that he fulfils the office of pastor in his own home. And we should not forget that this man had a wife who was like himself, because Paul has good reason to commend her also.

4. *I thank my God always*. It should be noted that he prays for the very same people for whom he gives thanks. Even the most perfect men who deserve the highest praise need to be prayed for, as long as they live in the world, that God would grant them not only to persevere to the end but also to make progress day by day.

The praise which he bestows on Philemon includes briefly the whole perfection of a Christian man. It consists of two parts, faith towards Christ and love to his neighbours, for all the duties of our life relate to either of these. Faith is said to be *towards* Christ, because it looks specially to Him. It is through Him alone that God the Father can be known, and in Him alone can be found all the blessings that faith seeks. But he does not limit love to the saints in such a way as to deny that it should be shown to others. The teaching of love is that we should not despise our own flesh, but should treat with honour the image of God inscribed in our human nature, and it thus includes the whole human race. But since those who belong to the household of faith are necessarily bound to us by a closer tie, and since God commends them specially to us, they rightly have first claim on our love.

The arrangement of this passage is somewhat confused, but there is no lack of clarity in its meaning, except for some doubt as to whether the adverb *always* belongs to the first or the second clause. The meaning can be indicated in this way; whenever the apostle prayed for Philemon, he included thanksgiving for him in the prayer, because his godliness gave such cause for rejoicing, for we often pray for those in whom we can find nothing but what calls for grief and tears. Yet it is usually considered better to take 'always' with the second clause—that Paul gives thanks for Philemon and always mentions him in his prayers. The first sense seems better to me, but the reader is free to choose.

In the rest of the verse there is an inversion of the natural order, because after he has spoken of love and faith, he adds *towards Christ and the saints*, whereas the meaning would rather require that Christ should be mentioned immediately after faith, since it is to Him that our faith looks.

6. *That the fellowship of thy faith.* This clause is rather obscure, but I shall try to elucidate it in such a way that my readers may grasp Paul's meaning. First we should see that the apostle is not continuing with his praise of Philemon, but is explaining what it is he asks for him when he makes mention of him in his prayers. What then did he ask? That his faith, exercising itself in good works, might prove itself genuine and not unprofitable. He calls it the 'fellowship of thy faith' because faith does not remain inactive and hidden within but shows itself to men by its actual results. For although faith has its residence hidden in the heart, it communicates itself to men through good works. It is as if he had said 'that by communicating itself your faith may prove its efficacy in every good thing'.

The knowledge of every good thing means experience. He wishes that his faith should prove itself efficacious by its effects, and this happens when the people among whom we live know our godly and holy life. Thus he speaks of *every good thing which is in you*, for every good thing in us reveals our faith.

The phrase εἰς Χριστόν can be rendered *unto Christ*, but I would, if I could, prefer to take it as meaning ἐν Χριστῷ. For the gifts of God are given to us only in so far as we are members of Christ, but since *in you* comes immediately before, I am afraid that the harshness of the expression would make it unacceptable. Thus I have not ventured to make any change in the words, but I wanted to mention it to my readers, so that they might consider it and then choose which they prefer.

7. *I had much joy.* Although the Greek prefers the rendering 'grace', I think we should translate it as joy. For there is little difference between χάριν and χαράν, and it would be easy to change a single letter by mistake. Besides this is not the only passage in Paul in which χάριν means joy, at least if we follow Chrysostom on this matter. What connexion is there between grace and comfort? At any rate, his meaning plainly is that he finds great joy and comfort in the fact that Philemon has brought relief to the necessities of the godly. It is love beyond the ordinary which can find such joy in good done to others. Besides the apostle is not only expressing his personal joy, but says that many have rejoiced because of Philemon's kindness and benevolence in bringing aid to the godly.

Because the hearts of the saints have been refreshed. To refresh the heart is an expression used by Paul meaning to give relief from afflictions or to aid the wretched, so that with composed minds and free from all trouble and grief they may find repose. For by the heart he means the feelings and ἀνάπαυσις means tranquility. Thus those who make this passage refer to the stomach and its nourishment, on the ground that in Greek the word literally means bowels, are quite mistaken.

> *Wherefore, though I have all boldness in Christ to enjoin thee that which is befitting, yet for love's sake I rather beseech, being such a one as Paul the aged and now a prisoner also of Christ Jesus: I beseech thee for my child, whom I have begotten in my bonds, Onesimus, who was aforetime unprofitable to thee, but now is profitable to thee and to me: whom I have sent back to thee in his own person, that is, my very heart: whom I would fain have kept with me, that in thy behalf he might minister unto me in the bonds of the gospel: but without thy mind I would do nothing; that thy goodness should not be as of necessity, but of free will. (8-14)*

8. *All boldness in Christ*, that is, though I have authority to command thee, thy love makes me prefer to ask instead. He claims the right to command on two grounds, both because he is an *elder*[1] and *a prisoner of Jesus Christ*. He says that because of Philemon's love he prefers to put it to him as a request, because we exercise authority and issue commands when we wish to extort from people things that they are unwilling to give. But since those who are ready and willing to do their duty listen more willingly to a calm explanation of what is required than to an exercise of authority, Paul has good reason to entreat when he is dealing with an obedient man. By his example he teaches pastors to try to lead their pupils gently rather than drive them on, for when he condescends to entreat and gives up his right to command, he has far greater power to obtain what he wishes. Moreover he claims nothing for himself but only in Christ, that is, on account of the office which Christ has conferred upon him; for he does not mean to suggest that those whom Christ has made apostles lack authority.

By adding τὸ ἀνῆκον, *that which is befitting*, he means that teachers have not power to demand whatever they like; their authority is confined within the limits of what is befitting and otherwise consistent with a man's duty. Thus, as I have just said, pastors are reminded that, whenever this method is likely to be successful, the hearts of their people should be won over by the greatest friendliness, but in such a way that those who are led so gently may know that they are being required to do less than they ought.

Here the word *elder* refers not to age but to office. He does not call himself an apostle here because he is dealing with a colleague in the ministry of the Word, and so addresses him in a familiar way.

10. *I beseech thee for my child*. Since less importance is usually attached to requests that are not supported by persuasive explanations, Paul

---
[1] R.V. *the aged*.

shows that he is performing a necessary duty in interceding for Onesimus. Thus it is of importance to note the depths of his condescension in calling one who is a slave, runaway and thief his own son. When he says that Onesimus was *begotten* by him, he means not that it was done by his own power, but only through his instrumentality; for it is not the work of any man to reshape and renew a human soul in the image of God, and it is with this act of spiritual regeneration that he is now dealing. But since a soul is made regenerate by faith, and since faith comes from hearing (Rom. 10.17), he who ministers doctrine plays the part of a father. Moreover, since the Word of God proclaimed by man is the seed of eternal life, it is not surprising that he from whose mouth we receive that seed should be called our father. At the same time we must not forget that although a man's ministry is efficacious in the regeneration of a soul, it is, strictly speaking, God who regenerates by the power of His Spirit. This manner of speaking does not in any way imply any opposition between God and man, but shows only how God acts through men. His saying that he has begotten Onesimus *in his bonds* adds weight to his commendation.

12. *That is, my very heart.* He could say nothing more likely to assuage Philemon's wrath. For if he had refused to forgive Onesimus, he would have been treating cruelly Paul's own heart. Paul's kindness is marvellous in not hesitating to take to his heart a common slave, who was also a thief and a fugitive, in order to protect him from his master's anger. And if the conversion of a man to God were taken seriously enough, we also would take to ourselves in the same way those who show that they have sincerely and genuinely repented.

13. *Whom I would fain have kept with me.* This is another way of appeasing Philemon, that Paul should be sending back to him the slave of whose services he himself stood in the greatest need. For it would have been most ungenerous to reject such attention (*studium*) from Paul. He hints that to have Onesimus sent back to him would be a welcome gift, so that this should be done rather than that he should be ill treated at home. He now adds further considerations, firstly that Onesimus was taking his master's place in providing this service, secondly that out of humility he did not wish to take it upon himself to deprive Philemon of his rights, and thirdly, that Philemon will deserve greater commendation, if after having his slave voluntarily and willingly returned to him he sends him back. From this last point we should infer that when Christ's martyrs are labouring for the testimony of the Gospel, we should help them with every kind office we can. For if we believe what Paul says here, that exile, imprisonment, flogging, insults and violent seizing of property belong to the Gospel, whoever refuses to share in these things separates himself from Christ. Without doubt

the defence of the Gospel is a responsibility common to us all. Thus the man who undergoes persecution on its behalf ought not to be regarded as a private individual, but as one who publicly represents the whole Church. To care for the Gospel is a duty common to all believers so that they should not, as they often do, leave it to one man.

14. *That thy goodness should not be.* This is an instance of the general rule that only freely offered sacrifices are pleasing to God. Paul says the same thing about almsgiving in II Corinthians 9.7. Τὸ ἀγαθόν means an act of kindness, and necessity is the opposite of a voluntary action, for under constraint there is no opportunity to show free willingness to do what is required, and the fact that a duty is voluntarily performed is its only title to real praise. It is worth noting that although Paul acknowledges Onesimus' former guilt, he declares that he has changed, and in case Philemon should have any doubts that his slave returns to him with a new disposition and different conduct, Paul says that he has proved his repentance by personal experience.

> *For perhaps he was therefore parted from thee for a season, that thou shouldest have him for ever; no longer as a servant, but more than a servant, a brother beloved, specially to me, but how much rather to thee, both in the flesh and in the Lord. If then thou countest me a partner, receive him as myself. But if he hath wronged thee at all, or oweth thee aught, put that to mine account; I Paul write it with mine own hand, I will repay it; that I say not unto thee how that thou owest me even thine own self besides.* (15-19)

15. *For perhaps he was parted from thee.* If we are angry over offences committed by men, our anger should be soothed when we see that things done in malice have been made to serve a different end by the purpose of God. A happy outcome is a cure for evils which God's hand offers to us to cancel out offences. So Joseph (Genesis 45.5), when he considers how God's marvellous providence has brought it about that he who was sold as a slave was yet raised to a high position in which he could provide for his father and his brothers, forgets his brothers' treachery and cruelty and says that he has been sent on ahead for their sakes.

Thus Paul reminds Philemon that he should not be greatly offended by the flight of his slave, for it has brought about something good, over which there can be no cause for regret. For since he was at heart a runaway, even though Philemon had him in his household, Philemon did not really possess him. Being wicked and disloyal he could be of no use to his master. Paul says that he was a wanderer for a little that by changing his place he might himself be changed and come back a new man. He wisely softens everything by calling his escape a departure, and by adding that it was only *for a season*, and lastly he contrasts the durability of the usefulness with the brief duration of the loss.

He goes on to mention another good result of the escape—not only has Onesimus been corrected by it, so that he will become a useful slave, but he has become his master's brother. But in case Philemon should still be upset over an offence still so recent, and should be unwilling to accept Onesimus as his brother, Paul first acknowledges him as his own brother. From this he infers that Philemon stands in a far closer relationship to him, because, although Onesimus was the same to both Paul and Philemon in the Lord according to the Spirit, according to the flesh Onesimus belonged to Philemon's family. Here again we see Paul's remarkable humility in honouring a worthless slave with the name of brother, and even calling him his most dear brother. But it would be a sign of haughty pride if he should be ashamed to count as his brother those whom God numbers among His sons.

When he says *how much rather to thee*, he does not mean that Philemon had a higher rank according to the Spirit; his meaning is rather, 'Seeing that he is specially a brother to me, he should be even more so to you, for you and he are bound to each other by a twofold relationship.'

We must take it as understood that Paul does not, like many others, rashly and vainly recommend a man insufficiently well-known to him, or praise his faith before he has made full trial and proof of it, so that we have in Onesimus a remarkable example of repentance. It is well known what bad characters slaves had, so that scarcely one in a hundred was ever of any real use. We may conjecture from his flight that Onesimus was hardened in iniquity by long custom and habit. It is therefore a rare and wonderful excellence for him to lay aside the faults by which his nature was polluted, to such an extent that Paul can declare truly that he has now become another man. From this case we may also gather the profitable doctrine that God's elect are sometimes brought to salvation in unbelievable ways against all general expectation by devious means and through labyrinths. Onesimus lived in a godly and holy household and yet, banished from it by his own evil actions, he deliberately withdrew far from God and eternal life. But God by His hidden providence wonderfully directed his ruinous flight, so as to bring him into contact with Paul.

17. *If then thou countest me a partner.* Here he humbles himself still further by making over his own rights and dignity to the runaway, putting him in his own place, just as a little later he will offer to stand surety for him. It was of the greatest importance that his master should be kind and gentle to Onesimus, so that immediate severity might not drive him to despair. That is what Paul works so hard to achieve.

By his example we are reminded with what affection we should help a sinner who has given us proof of his repentance. For if it is our duty to intercede with others for the pardon of the penitent, how much more should we ourselves treat them with kindness and gentleness.

18. *But if he hath wronged thee.* From this we may infer that Onesimus had stolen something from his master, as was the habit of runaway slaves, but he softens the badness of the deed by adding *or oweth thee ought*. Not only was there a bond between them in civil law, but the slave had become his master's debtor by the wrong he had done him. Paul's kindness is therefore all the greater in being ready to give satisfaction even for a crime.

By saying *I say not unto thee how thou owest me even thine own self besides*, he intended to make it clear how sure he was that his request would be granted; as if he had said, 'You could refuse me nothing, even if I asked for yourself.' What follows about hospitality etc. has the same purpose, as we shall soon see.

The question remains how Paul can promise to pay money, when, apart from the help the churches gave him, he had not the means even to live sparingly and frugally. In his circumstances of need and poverty it does indeed seem a ridiculous promise, but it is easy to see that by speaking in this way Paul is asking Philemon not to ask anything back from his slave. For although there is no irony in what he says, he is making an indirect request to Philemon to blot out and cancel this account. His meaning is, 'I do not want you to raise this issue against your slave, unless you want to consider me your debtor instead of him'. For he immediately adds that Philemon belongs to him entirely, and he who claims the whole man as his property has no need to be anxious about paying him money.

> *Yea, brother, let me have joy of thee in the Lord: refresh my heart in Christ. Having confidence in thine obedience I write unto thee, knowing that thou wilt do even beyond what I say. But withal prepare me also a lodging: for I hope that through your prayers I shall be granted unto you. Epaphras, my fellow-prisoner in Christ Jesus, saluteth thee; and so do Mark, Aristarchus, Demas, Luke, my fellow-workers. The grace of our Lord Jesus Christ be with your spirit. Amen.* (20-25)

20. *Yea, brother.* He says this to make the appeal stronger, as if he had said, 'It will clearly be proved that you and I are not at variance, but that you are sincerely attached to me, and all that you have is at my disposal, if you pardon past offences and receive into your favour this man who is so close to me.'

He again repeats the word that he had used before—*refresh my heart*. From this we infer that the faith of the Gospel does not overthrow civil order or cancel the rights of masters over their slaves, for although Philemon was not one of the common people, but Paul's fellow-labourer in tending Christ's vineyard, yet his right as master over his slaves which the laws allowed is not taken from him; he is only told to receive him kindly by granting him his pardon; in fact Paul humbly asks that he should be given his former place back again. Further Paul's humble request reminds us how very far from true repentance are those who stubbornly excuse their faults and confess them without shame or sign of humility, in a way that suggests they have never really sinned at all. Certainly when Onesimus saw such an outstanding apostle of Christ pleading his cause so anxiously, he must undoubtedly have been humbled even more, in order to induce his master to show him clemency. Paul for the same reason excuses himself for having written so boldly, because he knew that Philemon would do more than he asked.

22. *Prepare me a lodging.* This confidence must have been a strong stimulus to Philemon; and he holds out to him also the hope and delight of his own arrival. Although we do not know whether Paul was released from prison, this statement has nothing absurd about it, even if his hope in God's temporal kindness was not fulfilled. His confidence in his release was only on condition that it should seem good to God, and he always kept an open mind till events should make God's will plain. We should notice that he says that whatever believers ask in their prayers is 'given' to them. From this we infer that even if our prayers are successful, they do not prevail because of their own merit, for what is granted to them is of free grace.

24. *Demas.* This is the same person who later deserted Paul, as he says with sorrow in II Timothy 4.10. And if one of Paul's assistants became weary and discouraged and was afterwards drawn away by the vanity of the world, let none of us rely too much on our own zeal lasting even one year, but remembering how much of the journey still lies ahead, let us ask God for steadfastness.

INDEX OF SCRIPTURE REFERENCES

GENESIS
2.24	224
3.16	218
3.22	218
11.14	150
14.13	150
17.7	93
19.24	303
22.18	354
45.5	398
48.16	317

EXODUS
14.31	109
16.18	114
34.33	52

LEVITICUS
26.12	91

NUMBERS
16.11	171

DEUTERONOMY
8.3	114
17.6	263
30.14	229
30.15	44

I SAMUEL
16.7	367
16.14	55

II SAMUEL
22.50	214

I KINGS
22.2	55
22.21-23	237
22.22	55

II KINGS
1.10	342

PSALMS
2.8-10	209
2.12	207
6	70
18.50	214
19.8	48, 53
19.9	233
34.5	280
34.10	274
44.23	60
49.13	274
50.15	14
51.4	233
67.5	214
69.9	342
69.28	316
78.49	55
94.19	8
96.5	54
104.14	240
109.8	195
115.17	70
116.10	61
117.1	214
119.105	53
129.1-3	325

PROVERBS
5.15	108
16.1	19
19.7	111

ECCLESIASTES
40.17	157
40.28	157

ISAIAH
1.15	214
2.17	130

INDEX OF SCRIPTURE REFERENCES

ISAIAH (cont.)
4.1	317
5.15	130
7.3	171
38.3	70
40.8	20
42.1	351
42.23	127
49.8	84
52.7	80
52.11	91, 318n
65.17	76

JEREMIAH
1.10	133
5.3	367
9.1	167
9.24	137
29.7	206
31.31	40, 42
31.32	45

EZEKIEL
33.8	249
34.4	26
36.25	318, 383
36.27	40, 338
37.27	91

DANIEL
12.3	269

HAGGAI
2	367

MATTHEW
5.24	20, 215
5.45	240
10.33	311
11.13	45
11.19	233
11.28	211
11.29	127
11.30	127
13.43	269
15.13	316
16.18	299

MATTHEW (cont.)
18.16	263
18.18	80, 131
23.9	187

LUKE
1.74-75	373
2.34	44
2.36	253
7.29	233
7.35	233
9.55	342
9.58	111
10.16	80, 133, 174
23.43	157

JOHN
1.14	234
1.17	42
3.16	78, 176, 380
3.29	140
3.33	22
4.22	291
4.24	48, 238
5.24	382
7.14	132
8.15	132
10.29	300
10.38	78
12.43	16, 81
14.7	55
15.16	195
16.13	352
17.17	352

ACTS
1.8	295
5.1	203
5.1-10	131
6.3	228
9.12	156
9.15	195
13.6	203
13.6-11	131
14.23	357
15.28	109
17.28	280
18.23	230
19.23	11

INDEX OF SCRIPTURE REFERENCES

ACTS (cont.)
19.33	203
22.17	156
24.10	353
24.14	291
26.1	353
26.6–7	291
28.20	291

ROMANS
1	379
1.2	354
1.3	234
1.5	131
1.16	176, 208
1.17	45
1.18	45
3.4	22
3.23	16, 81
4.17	13
4.20	300
5.5	245
5.8	380
5.10	176
6.6	59, 63
7.8	291
7.10	44
8	107
8.15	46, 49, 294
8.24	382
8.29	60, 310
8.34	211, 212
8.36	60
9.7	352
9.16	318
9.21	317
10.17	212, 232, 397
11.20	48
11.33	199
12	293
12.7	361
12.8	107
14.17–19	74
15	164
15.9	214
16.26	131

I CORINTHIANS
1.13	67
1.14	67

I CORINTHIANS (cont.)
1.31	137
4.4	138
4.7	380
4.15	188
5	203
7.32	252
7.35	223
8.5	54
9.16	355
9.24	307
11.31	102
12.3	237
12.28	203
13	293
13.9–12	280
13.12	50
14.40	293
15.50	281

II CORINTHIANS
1.2	214
3.5	223
4.10	311
5.19	298
6.17	318
9.7	398
10.17	15

GALATIANS
1.8	20, 142
3.1	352
3.10	45
4.4	84, 354
4.5	214
4.29	328
6.1	379

EPHESIANS
1	296, 297
1.4	78
1.13	22
2	234
2.2	321
3.18	233
4.11	249, 336
5	140

405

INDEX OF SCRIPTURE REFERENCES

PHILIPPIANS
2.8	171
2.12	249
2.17	337
3.12	277
3.15	388
4.1	136
4.3	316
4.12	86

COLOSSIANS
1.5	352, 353
1.24	8, 310
1.29	300
2.1-18	211
2.3	232
2.21	243
3.5	59
4.1	113
4.14	340

II THESSALONIANS
2.9	164

I TIMOTHY
2.4	352
3.15	352, 359
4.14	293
5	370
6	314

II TIMOTHY
1.9	354
2.24	226
3.16	254
4.10	401

TITUS
1	227, 228, 297
1.7	223
1.15	240

PHILEMON
24	340

HEBREWS
4	212
4.15	210
5	212
12.9	188
13.8	298
13.17	174

JAMES
5.12	19

I PETER
1.25	20
2.8	44
3.1	370
4.13	9

II PETER
3.3	236

I JOHN
1.1	355
2.19	317
3.2	281
4.1	170

INDEX OF NAMES

Ambrose, 17, 29, 54, 57, 148, 170
Apollonius, 239
Arius, 233, 374
Augustine, 54, 117, 148, 159, 205, 280, 281, 297, 353, 360

Basil, 364
Budaeus, 17, 120

Chrysostom, 12, 28, 29, 31, 51, 54, 57, 63, 67, 83, 86, 89, 96, 103, 115, 128, 139, 148, 159, 164, 170, 215, 221, 226, 227, 251, 261, 291, 325, 375, 385, 395
Cicero, 279
Cyprian, 360

Dionysius, 157

Epimenides, 363
Erasmus, 9, 11, 12, 26, 37, 49, 64, 100, 102, 120, 128, 140, 141, 158, 223, 224, 233, 254, 268, 269, 302, 312, 359, 362, 375
Eutyches, 233

Galen, 314
Gratian, 264

Hilary, 53

Livy, 189

Marcion, 233, 308
Montanus, 238, 239

Nestorius, 233

Origen, 43

Plato, 138, 205, 263, 360, 363
Plutarch, 259
Polybius, 120

Quintilian, 222

Servetus, 75
Suetonius, 189

GENERAL INDEX

Arianism, 54, 56
Asceticism, 243f, 366
Assurance, 173, 352f
Atonement, 78f

Baptism, 382f
Bishop v. Ministry
  office of, 223, 359
  marriage of, 223f, 358f
  teaching office, 225f

Celibacy, 238f, 223f, 258f
Christ
  advent of, 278f
  confession of, 278
  contrasted with Moses, 40f
  cross of v. cross
  death of, 59, 74f, 171, 278, 355, 375
  divinity of, 171, 233, 374
  faithfulness of, 21, 311f
  as fulfiller, 21f
  gentleness of, 127
  grace of, 176, 375
  human nature of, 172, 210, 233, 308, 309
  intercession of, 210f
  as image of God, 55f
  kingdom of, 76
  knowledge of, 34f
  life in, 75f
  love of, 74
  as Messiah, 309
  in Old Testament, 299f
  person of, 233f
  priesthood of, 211
  propitiation of, 77f
  poverty and riches of, 109
  power of, 161f
  reconciliation in, 77f
  resurrection of, 60, 171, 309
  righteousness of, 81
  as sin offering, 81
  as '*vita legis*', 48f

Church, 33, 91, 106f, 140, 203, 231, 236f, 311, 317f, 322
Conscience, 202f
Conversion, 76, 321, 399
Cross, 63, 74f, 171, 311

Deacons *v* Ministry, 228 f
Death
  result of law, 43
  as mortification, 59f
  preparedness for, 68f
  shrinking from, 68f
Discipline, 29, 341, 362, 364, 388
Disputes, 190, 272f, 312f, 320, 386
Doctrine, 188f, 301, 368f

Edification of Church, 174f, 190, 312, 368
Elders, 357, 396
  teaching and ruling, 216f
Election, 296f, 316, 354
Excommunication, 30, 170, 203f, 362, 388
Expiation, 80, 212

Fables, 189f
Faith, 23, 26, 380
  as 'absence from the Lord', 69
  and assurance, 173, 299f
  as Christ's work, 39
  contrasted with sight, 69f
  in resurrection, 61
False apostles, 36, 38, 51, 76, 126f, 135f
Fasting, 241f, 366
Fear of God, 72, 94, 101
Flesh, 93, 128, 159f
Foods, 241f, 366
Forgiveness, 78f, 195, 198
Free Will, 193, 305, 238, 344

Gangrene, 314f

GENERAL INDEX

God
  in Christ, 78
  comfort of, 8, 96
  faithfulness of, 19f
  grace of, 197f, 373
  invisibility of, 281
  love of, 177, 379f
  mercy of, 79, 188
  power of, 122, 161f, 300
  promises of, 21, 93, 289, 353f
  providence of, 133f, 213, 399
  in reconciliation, 77f
  revealed in Christ, 58, 210
  righteousness of, 81
  as Saviour, 187, 209, 355
  unity of, 209f
  wrath of, 78
Godliness, 273f, 353
Gospel
  not ashamed of, 295f
  confirms law, 194
  contrasted with law, 40f
  means of life, 298
  means of reconciliation, 79f, 380f

Heresy, 387f

Idolatry, 89f, 93f
Immortality, 280, 298
Intercession of saints, 211f

Jesus Christ *v* Christ
Jews, 46f, 151
Judgment
  final, 71
  after flesh, 74f
  of God, 81, 102, 338
Justification, 100, 338, 380f, 384

Law
  contrasted with Gospel, 40f, 289
  function of, 192f
  fulfillment of, 191
  occasion of death, 45
  transience of, 45
Liberality, 107, 112, 122

Love
  to brethren, 118f
  of Christ, 74
  as end of law, 191
  compared with faith, 191, 301, 394
  of God, 177, 379f
Magistrates, 205f
Manichaeanism, 54, 238, 309
Marriage, 223f, 358f
Mediator
  Christ as, 78, 210f
Ministry, 34, 56
  afflictions of, 96f
  authority of, 80, 132f
  duties of, 264f, 306f, 332f
  essential, 231f
  as earthen vessels, 58f
  of reconciliation, 77f
  reputation of, 117, 227
  rewards of, 165
  qualifications of, 221f, 246f
  required qualities of, 85f, 322f, 385f
  sincerity of, 85
  teaching office, 225, 231f
  in upbuilding Church, 174f
Miracles, 164
Money
  Paul's collection of, 106f, 118f
  love of, 275f
Monks, 135f, 241f
Mortification, 59f

Ordination, 247, 265, 293f, 357f

Papists
  on celibacy, 239
  deference to bishops, 141f
  on good works, 63
  on fasting, 239, 366f
  on implicit faith, 352
  impurity of, 323
  on intercession of saints, 211
  on sacraments, 79, 80
  on post-baptismal sin, 80
Paul
  apostleship of, 7, 38, 51, 85f, 127f, 187, 289, 298f, 351f
  authority of, 132, 195

GENERAL INDEX

Paul (*cont.*)
  as chief of sinners, 199
  clemency of, 29f, 98
  consistency of, 19, 20, 25, 26
  death of, 336f
  faithfulness of, 195
  'foolishness' of, 139f, 145
  glorying of, 15f, 96, 135f
  journeyings of, 32
  lack of eloquence of, 142f
  moderation of, 112
  modesty of, 116, 132, 356
  past of, 195
  payment of, 144
  on his revelations, 155f
  as servant, 56, 57, 351f
  severity of, 98
  sincerity of, 51f, 85
  his status as Jew, 150
  sufferings of, 10f, 96f, 150f, 154f, 309f, 326f
  thorn in flesh, 159f
  weakness of, 161f
Perseverance, 344
Pope, 133, 146, 149, 343
Possessions, 282f
Prayer, 13, 14, 125, 160f, 205f, 210f, 214f, 291
Preaching
  authority of, 80
  as dividing word, 313f
  essential to Church, 231f
  mother of faith, 173
  means of reconciliation, 79
  results of, 35f, 355
Predestination, 208f
Propitiation, 77f

Reconciliation, 77f
Redemption, 372f
Repentance, 30, 99f, 320, 400
Rewards, 71f, 338
Righteousness, 81

Sacraments, 79, 241f, 382
Salvation, 100, 198, 355
  not universal, 208f, 373
  not by works, 296, 380f
Sanctification, 93f, 220, 319f
  of foods, 241f

Scriptures, the Holy
  authority of, 329f
  inspiration of, 329
  reading of, 246f, 329
  testaments contrasted, 40f
  uses of, 330f
Sin
  post-baptismal, 80, 213
  borne by Christ, 81
  against the Holy Ghost, **196f**
  original, 213
Slaves, 270f, 371f, 393f, 401
Spirit, the Holy
  in baptism, 382f
  communion of, 177
  as giver of faith, 39
  as guard, 302
  contrasted with letter, 40f
  in ordination, 247
  of power, 294
  of prophecy, 235f
  as seal, 23
  sin against, 196f
Sorrow, 99

Testaments
  old and new contrasted, 40f
Time
  of acceptance, 84

Unbelievers
  blindness of, 64f, 197
  ignorance of, 321, 379
  relations of Christians with, **89f**
  shrink from death, 68

Veil
  on Moses face, 46f

Warfare
  of Christians, 129f, 261, 276, **306**, 337f
Widows, 250f
Wine, 266f
Women
  aged, 369f
  in church, 216f
  dress of, 216
  family duties of, 254f
  faults of, 324
  subordination of, 217f

www.ingramcontent.com/pod-product-compliance
Lightning Source LLC
Chambersburg PA
CBHW020636300426
44112CB00007B/135